G000144813

Bed &
Breakfasts,
Country
Inns,
and Other
Weekend
Pleasures

THE WEST COAST

Fodor's Travel Publications, Inc.
New York • London • Toronto

ISBN 0–679–02151–5

First Edition

Fodor's Bed & Breakfasts, Country Inns, and Other Weekend Pleasures: The West Coast

Editor: Paula Rackow
Contributors: Bob Blake, Andrew Collins, Tom Gauntt, Caroline Haberfeld, Tara Hamilton, Pamela P. Hegarty, Amanda Jacobs, Jeff Kuechle, Marty Olmstead, Christopher Pennington, Larry Peterson, Melissa Rivers, Craig Seligman, Julie Tomasz, Terry Trucco, Loralee Wenger, Todd Whitley, Maria Zacharias, Bobbi Zane
Art Director: Fabrizio La Rocca
Cartographer: David Lindroth
Illustrators: Alida Beck, Karl Tanner
Cover Photograph: Hans Neleman/Image Bank
Design: Rochelle Udell and Fabrizio La Rocca

Special Sales

Fodor's Travel Publications are available at special discounts for bulk purchases (100 copies or more) for sales promotions or premiums. Special editions, including personalized covers, excerpts of existing guides, and corporate imprints, can be created in large quantities for special needs. For more information write to Special Marketing, Fodor's Travel Publications, 201 East 50th St., New York, NY 10022. Inquiries from Canada should be sent to Random House of Canada, Ltd., Marketing Department, 1265 Aerowood Drive, Mississauga, Ontario L43 1B9. Inquiries from the United Kingdom should be sent to Fodor's Travel Publications, 20 Vauxhall Bridge Rd., London, England SW1V 2SA.

MANUFACTURED IN THE UNITED STATES OF AMERICA
10 9 8 7 6 5 4 3 2 1

Contributors

Tom Gauntt, *who wrote the chapters on the north Oregon coast, Columbia River Gorge and Mt. Hood, and central and eastern Oregon, lives in Portland, Oregon. He is associate editor of Portland's* The Business Journal *and has written for* Emmy, Ford Times, Advertising Age, *and* Omni.

Pamela P. Hegarty, *who lives in the San Francisco Bay Area, has written extensively on travel in northern California and is the author of* San Francisco and Beyond: 101 Affordable Excursions. *Her work has appeared in* Woman's Day, Good Housekeeping, *and other prominent publications. She wrote the San Francisco and Bay Area chapters.*

Jeff Kuechle *lives in Portland, Oregon, and wrote the chapters on Portland and the Oregon wine country. He is a frequent contributor to Fodor's publications, and his work has also appeared in* Advertising Age, Ford Times, *and* Emmy. *He recently completed his first novel,* Sholto the Slayer.

Marty Olmstead, *a travel writer and editor who lives in Sonoma, California, wrote the California wine country chapter. She is coauthor of* Hidden Florida, *and writes for numerous publications about California food, wine, travel, and history.*

Melissa Rivers, *who lives near Portland, Oregon, wrote the Willamette Valley, southern Oregon, and south Oregon coast chapters. She has contributed to many travel guides, including* The Wall Street Journal Guide to Business Travel: Pacific Rim, *and* Hidden Pacific Northwest.

Terry Trucco, *who wrote the chapter on Sacramento and Gold Country, grew up nearby in northern California. Currently living in New York City, she writes on a variety of subjects, including travel, design, and beauty, for the* New York Times, *the* Wall Street Journal, Travel & Leisure, *and other publications.*

Loralee Wenger, *who wrote seven of the eight Washington chapters, lives in Seattle. She has written for* Glamour *and* Parade, *and for the* Washington Post, San Francisco Examiner, *and other newspapers. She contributed to Fodor's* Pacific North Coast *and* USA *guides.*

Maria Zacharias *lives in Spokane and wrote the Spokane and environs chapter. Formerly with ABC News and Time-Life Books, she has a Spokane-based editing and consulting business.*

Bobbi Zane, *who wrote six California chapters, lives in southern California. The publisher of* Yellow Brick Road, *a monthly newsletter devoted to bed-and-breakfast travel in the western United States, and the annual* California B&B Directory, *she has written for the* Los Angeles Times.

Contents

Foreword

While every care has been taken to ensure the accuracy of the information in this guide, the passage of time will always bring change, and, consequently, the publisher cannot accept responsibility for errors that may occur.

All prices and listings are based on information available to us at press time. Details may change, however, and the prudent traveler will avoid inconvenience by calling ahead.

Fodor's wants to hear about your travel experiences, both pleasant and unpleasant. When an inn or B&B fails to live up to its billing, let us know and we will investigate the complaint and revise our entries where the facts warrant it.

Send your letters to the editors of Fodor's Travel Publications, 201 E. 50th Street, New York, NY 10022.

Introduction

Fodor's Bed & Breakfasts, Country Inns, and Other Weekend Pleasures *is a complete weekend planner that tells you not just where to stay but how to enjoy yourself when you get there. We describe the B&Bs and country inns, of course, but we also help you organize trips around them, with information on everything from parks to beaches to antiques stores—as well as nightlife and memorable places to dine. We also include names and addresses of B&B reservation services, should properties we recommend be full or should you be inspired to go in search of additional places on your own. Reviews are divided by state, and, within each state, by region.*

All inns are not created equal, and age in itself is no guarantee of good taste, quality, or charm. We therefore avoid the directory approach, preferring instead to discriminate—recommending the very best for travelers with different interests, budgets, and sensibilities.

It's a sad commentary on other B&B guides today that we feel obliged to tell you our reviewers visited every property in person, and that it is they, not the innkeepers, who wrote the reviews. No one paid a fee or promised to sell or promote the book, in order to be included in it. Fodor's has no stake in anything but the truth: A dark room with peeling wallpaper is not called quaint or atmospheric, it's called run-down; a gutted 18th-century barn with motel units at either end is called a gutted 18th-century barn with motel units at either end, not a historic inn.

Is there a difference between a B&B and a country inn? Not really, not any more; the public has blurred the

*distinction—hence our decision to include both in the title.
There was a time when the B&B experience meant an extra
room in someone's home, often with paper-thin walls and
a shared bathroom full of bobby pins and used cotton balls.
But no longer; Laura Ashley has come to town with her
matching prints, and some B&Bs are as elegant as the
country's most venerable inns. The only distinction that
seems to hold is that a B&B was built as a private home
and an inn was built for paying guests. Most B&Bs serve
breakfast, but not all, and some serve dinner, too; most
inns have full-service restaurants. B&Bs tend to be run by
their owners, creating a homey, family feeling (which can
be anathema to those who relish privacy), while inns are
often run by managers; but the reverse is true, too. B&Bs
can cost more than inns, or less. B&Bs tend to be smaller,
with fewer rooms, but not always. The truth is that many
B&Bs are called so only to circumvent local zoning laws.*

*What all places in this guide—B&Bs or country inns—offer
is the promise of a unique experience. Each is one of
a kind, and each exudes a sense of time and place. All are
destinations in themselves—not just places to put your
head at night, but an integral part of a weekend escape.*

*So trust us, the way you'd trust a knowledgeable, well-
traveled friend. And have a wonderful weekend!*

***

A word about the service material in this guide:

*A mailing address is often included that differs from the
actual address of the property. A double room is for two
people, regardless of the size or type of beds; if you're*

looking for twin beds or a king- or queen-size bed, be sure to ask.

Rates are for two in the high season, and include breakfast; ask about special packages and off-season discounts. Mandatory state taxes are extra. Most places leave tipping to the discretion of the visitor, but some add a service charge to the bill; if the issue concerns you, inquire when you make your reservation, not when you check out.

What we call a restaurant serves meals other than breakfast and is usually open to the general public. Inns listed as MAP (Modified American Plan) require guests to pay for two meals, usually breakfast and dinner. The requirement is usually enforced during the high season, but an inn may waive it if it is otherwise unable to fill all its rooms.

B&Bs don't have phones or TVs in rooms unless otherwise noted. Pools and bicycles are free; "bike rentals" are not. Properties are open year-round, unless otherwise noted.

Michael Spring
Editorial Director

California, Oregon, and Washington

PACIFIC
OCEAN

Vancouver
Victoria
Bellingham
Anacortes
Port Townsend
Seattle
Olympia
Tacoma
Astoria
Portland
Salem
Hood River
The Dalles
Eugene
Roseburg
Port Orford
Crater Lake
Ashland
Eureka
Redding
Fort Bragg
Mendocino
Santa Rosa
Napa
Sonoma
Sacramento
San Francisco
Oakland
Santa Cruz
Monterey
San Luis Obispo
Santa Barbara
Ventura
Los Angeles
San Diego
Palm Springs

Calgary
BRITISH COLUMBIA
CANADA
USA
WASHINGTON
Spokane
Coeur d'Alene
MONTANA
Walla Walla
IDAHO
Boise
OREGON
Bend
Tahoe City
Reno
Carson City
NEVADA
Salt Lake City
UTAH
Fresno
Las Vegas
CALIFORNIA
Flagstaff
ARIZONA
Phoenix
MEXICO

N

0   100 miles
0   150 km

Special Features at a Glance

Name of Property	Accessible for Disabled	Antiques	On the Water	Best Value	Car Not Necessary	Full Meal Service	Historic Building	
CALIFORNIA								
The Alamo Square Inn					✓		✓	
Anaheim Country Inn		✓					✓	
"An Elegant Victorian Mansion"		✓					✓	
Applewood: An Estate Inn							✓	
Archbishops Mansion		✓		✓	✓		✓	
Auberge du Soleil						✓		
Aunt Abigail's		✓					✓	
Babbling Brook Inn	✓	✓					✓	
Ballard Inn	✓							
Bath Street Inn								
Bayberry Inn								
Bear Flag Inn		✓					✓	
The Bed and Breakfast Inn					✓			
Bed and Breakfast Inn at La Jolla	✓	✓					✓	
Beltane Ranch		✓		✓			✓	
Blackthorne Inn								
Blue Lantern Inn	✓		✓					
The Blue Whale Inn			✓					
Britt House		✓					✓	
Brookside Farm						✓		
Busch and Heringlake Country Inn		✓				✓	✓	
Carter House		✓						
Casa Madrona Hotel		✓	✓	✓		✓	✓	
Casa Tropicana			✓			✓		

Romantic Hideaway	Luxurious	Pets Allowed	No Smoking Indoors	Good Place for Families	Beach Nearby	Cross-Country Ski Trails	Golf Within 5 Miles	Fitness Facilities	Near Wineries	Good Biking Terrain	Skiing	Tennis	Swimming on Premises	Conference Facilities	Hiking Nearby
✓			✓	✓			✓							✓	
			✓												
			✓												
✓	✓		✓										✓		✓
✓	✓						✓							✓	
✓	✓							✓	✓	✓		✓	✓	✓	
✓			✓		✓		✓			✓		✓		✓	
			✓		✓	✓	✓			✓					
	✓		✓							✓					✓
			✓		✓					✓					✓
✓		✓	✓		✓					✓					✓
✓			✓		✓		✓			✓		✓		✓	
✓			✓												
	✓		✓		✓		✓								
			✓			✓	✓		✓	✓		✓			✓
✓			✓		✓	✓				✓					✓
✓	✓		✓	✓	✓		✓	✓		✓				✓	✓
	✓		✓		✓					✓					
			✓												
✓			✓		✓										✓
	✓		✓			✓				✓	✓				✓
	✓		✓											✓	
✓	✓			✓			✓			✓				✓	✓
✓			✓		✓					✓					

Name of Property	Accessible for Disabled	Antiques	On the Water	Best Value	Car Not Necessary	Full Meal Service	Historic Building	
Chaney House		✓	✓				✓	
Channel Road Inn		✓					✓	
Christmas House		✓					✓	
Chateau Tivoli		✓			✓		✓	
Cliff Crest Bed and Breakfast Inn		✓						
Cooper House		✓					✓	
Cottage Inn at Lake Tahoe			✓					
Cowper Inn		✓		✓	✓			
Cross Roads Inn								
Culbert House Inn		✓					✓	
The Driver Mansion Inn		✓					✓	
Eiler's Inn								
Fallon Hotel	✓	✓		✓			✓	
The Feather Bed							✓	
The Foxes Bed and Breakfast Inn		✓					✓	
The Gaige House							✓	
Garden Street Inn	✓	✓						
Gatehouse Inn	✓	✓	✓				✓	
Gingerbread Mansion		✓						
Golden Gate Hotel		✓		✓	✓		✓	
Gosby House		✓						
Gramma's Inn	✓	✓		✓	✓		✓	
Green Gables Inn		✓						
Grey Whale Inn	✓						✓	
Happy Landing Inn					✓			

Romantic Hideaway	Luxurious	Pets Allowed	No Smoking Indoors	Good Place for Families	Beach Nearby	Cross-Country Ski Trails	Golf Within 5 Miles	Fitness Facilities	Near Wineries	Good Biking Terrain	Skiing	Tennis	Swimming on Premises	Conference Facilities	Hiking Nearby
			✓		✓	✓		✓		✓	✓		✓		✓
			✓	✓	✓					✓					✓
✓							✓								
✓	✓	✓	✓	✓			✓								
			✓			✓	✓			✓					
✓			✓	✓		✓				✓	✓	✓		✓	✓
			✓	✓	✓	✓				✓	✓				✓
✓			✓	✓			✓			✓				✓	
			✓			✓			✓	✓					✓
✓	✓		✓	✓						✓		✓			✓
✓	✓		✓		✓		✓			✓		✓		✓	
				✓			✓								
✓			✓	✓	✓		✓			✓		✓			✓
			✓			✓				✓					✓
✓	✓		✓							✓		✓			✓
									✓				✓		✓
			✓												
			✓		✓					✓					
	✓		✓		✓										
		✓	✓	✓											
							✓			✓				✓	
✓			✓	✓											
						✓				✓					
			✓	✓										✓	
			✓	✓	✓	✓	✓								

Name of Property	Accessible for Disabled	Antiques	On the Water	Best Value	Car Not Necessary	Full Meal Service	Historic Building	
Harbor House			✓			✓	✓	
The Headlands Inn	✓	✓						
The Heirloom	✓	✓		✓			✓	
The Hensley House		✓		✓	✓		✓	
Heritage Park Bed & Breakfast Inn	✓	✓					✓	
High Country Inn		✓						
Hope-Merrill House		✓					✓	
Ingleside Inn		✓				✓		
Inn at Depot Hill		✓					✓	
Inn on Mt. Ada					✓	✓	✓	
Inn San Francisco		✓			✓		✓	
Inn at Summer Hill	✓							
Inn at Union Square	✓	✓		✓	✓		✓	
The Jabberwock		✓			✓			
J. Patrick House	✓							
Joshua Grindle Inn		✓					✓	
Julian Hotel		✓					✓	
Kenwood Inn		✓						
La Mer		✓						
Little Inn on the Bay			✓					
Loma Vista Bed and Breakfast								
Madrona Manor		✓		✓		✓	✓	
Magnolia Hotel		✓					✓	
Mansion Hotel		✓		✓	✓	✓	✓	
Martine Inn	✓	✓	✓				✓	

Romantic Hideaway	Luxurious	Pets Allowed	No Smoking Indoors	Good Place for Families	Beach Nearby	Cross-Country Ski Trails	Golf Within 5 Miles	Fitness Facilities	Near Wineries	Good Biking Terrain	Skiing	Tennis	Swimming on Premises	Conference Facilities	Hiking Nearby
✓			✓		✓									✓	✓
			✓				✓								
✓			✓		✓					✓				✓	✓
✓			✓	✓										✓	
			✓												
			✓			✓		✓		✓			✓		✓
			✓						✓				✓		
✓	✓						✓			✓			✓	✓	✓
✓	✓		✓												
✓	✓		✓		✓					✓				✓	✓
✓		✓		✓											
	✓		✓		✓										
✓	✓		✓	✓											
			✓		✓		✓			✓				✓	
			✓							✓					
			✓												
			✓							✓					✓
✓	✓		✓			✓			✓	✓			✓		✓
			✓		✓										
			✓		✓					✓					
			✓			✓				✓					
		✓	✓	✓	✓					✓	✓			✓	✓
			✓						✓	✓			✓		
✓	✓	✓			✓									✓	
	✓				✓		✓			✓				✓	

Name of Property	Accessible for Disabled	Antiques	On the Water	Best Value	Car Not Necessary	Full Meal Service	Historic Building
The Mill Rose Inn		✓		✓			✓
Old Monterey Inn		✓					
Old Thyme Inn		✓		✓			✓
The Old Victorian Inn		✓		✓			✓
Old Yacht Club Inn		✓					
The Parsonage		✓					✓
Pelican Cove Inn	✓						
The Pelican Inn		✓		✓		✓	✓
Petite Auberge		✓		✓	✓		✓
Quail Mountain							
Rachel's Inn	✓						
Rockwood Lodge		✓					
Rose Victorian Inn	✓	✓					✓
Roundstone Farm		✓		✓			
St. Orres				✓		✓	
Salisbury House							✓
Scotia Inn						✓	
Sea View Inn							
Seven Gables Inn		✓	✓				✓
Simpson House Inn		✓					
Sonoma Hotel		✓			✓	✓	✓
Sorensen's						✓	✓
Spencer House		✓		✓	✓		✓
Strawberry Creek Inn	✓	✓					
Ten Inverness Way		✓		✓			

California

Romantic Hideaway	Luxurious	Pets Allowed	No Smoking Indoors	Good Place for Families	Beach Nearby	Cross-Country Ski Trails	Golf Within 5 Miles	Fitness Facilities	Near Wineries	Good Biking Terrain	Skiing	Tennis	Swimming on Premises	Conference Facilities	Hiking Nearby
✓	✓		✓		✓	✓	✓			✓				✓	✓
✓	✓		✓		✓		✓			✓				✓	
✓		✓	✓	✓	✓	✓	✓			✓					✓
✓	✓		✓				✓			✓				✓	
			✓		✓			✓		✓					✓
✓			✓		✓					✓					✓
					✓										
✓	✓				✓	✓	✓			✓				✓	✓
✓	✓				✓										
			✓						✓	✓					
✓	✓			✓	✓		✓								✓
✓	✓		✓		✓	✓				✓	✓				✓
✓			✓		✓		✓								
✓			✓		✓	✓				✓					✓
✓	✓				✓										✓
			✓												
														✓	
				✓		✓		✓		✓					
				✓		✓		✓		✓					
	✓		✓							✓					✓
							✓		✓	✓					✓
		✓		✓		✓				✓	✓			✓	✓
✓	✓		✓			✓	✓			✓					✓
✓			✓							✓					✓
✓			✓	✓	✓	✓				✓					✓

Name of Property	Accessible for Disabled	Antiques	On the Water	Best Value	Car Not Necessary	Full Meal Service	Historic Building	
Terrace Manor		✓					✓	
Thistle Dew Inn		✓			✓			
Timberhill Ranch						✓		
Union Hotel/Victorian Mansion		✓					✓	
Union Street Inn		✓			✓		✓	
Victorian Inn on the Park		✓		✓	✓		✓	
Villa Royale	✓	✓				✓		
Vintners Inn	✓	✓				✓		
Washington Square Inn		✓		✓	✓			
White Sulphur Springs		✓					✓	
White Swan Inn		✓		✓	✓		✓	
Wine & Roses Country Inn	✓	✓					✓	
Winters Creek Ranch		✓						
OREGON								
Arden Forest Inn	✓			✓				
Astoria Inn							✓	
Bayberry Inn Bed and Breakfast								
Beckley House		✓					✓	
Bed and Breakfast by the River	✓	✓	✓	✓				
Black Bart's Bed and Breakfast								
The Boarding House		✓	✓				✓	
Brey House	✓		✓	✓				
Chamberlin House		✓						
Channel House			✓					

Romantic Hideaway	Luxurious	Pets Allowed	No Smoking Indoors	Good Place for Families	Beach Nearby	Cross-Country Ski Trails	Golf Within 5 Miles	Fitness Facilities	Near Wineries	Good Biking Terrain	Skiing	Tennis	Swimming on Premises	Conference Facilities	Hiking Nearby
														✓	
			✓				✓		✓	✓					✓
✓	✓		✓			✓	✓					✓	✓	✓	✓
✓	✓														
✓				✓	✓										
✓	✓			✓		✓	✓			✓					✓
✓	✓						✓			✓			✓		✓
									✓	✓				✓	✓
✓	✓		✓	✓											
			✓	✓		✓	✓			✓	✓		✓		✓
✓	✓													✓	
✓	✓		✓	✓	✓		✓			✓		✓		✓	
			✓			✓				✓					✓
			✓	✓			✓		✓	✓					
			✓				✓			✓					
			✓				✓			✓	✓				✓
			✓				✓			✓			✓		✓
			✓	✓		✓									✓
			✓							✓					
				✓	✓		✓			✓					✓
				✓	✓		✓			✓					✓
			✓												✓
✓					✓					✓					✓

Name of Property	Accessible for Disabled	Antiques	On the Water	Best Value	Car Not Necessary	Full Meal Service	Historic Building	
Chanticleer Inn					✓			
Chetco River Inn			✓	✓		✓		
Chriswood Inn				✓				
The Clinkerbrick House		✓		✓	✓			
Cliff Harbor Bed and Breakfast	✓		✓		✓			
Cliff House		✓	✓				✓	
Columbia Gorge Hotel	✓	✓	✓			✓	✓	
Coos Bay Manor				✓			✓	
Country Willows Bed and Breakfast Inn			✓	✓				
The Dome Bed and Breakfast	✓							
Eastmoreland Bed and Breakfast		✓						
Elliott House		✓		✓			✓	
Farewell Bend Bed & Breakfast								
Flying M Ranch			✓			✓		
Franklin House		✓					✓	
Franklin St. Station		✓					✓	
Frenchglen Hotel				✓		✓	✓	
General Hooker's B&B		✓					✓	
The Georgian House		✓		✓				
Gilbert Inn		✓					✓	
Grandview Bed & Breakfast		✓		✓			✓	
Hackett House				✓				
Hanson Country Inn		✓		✓			✓	
Heather House Bed and Breakfast		✓		✓				
Heron Haus		✓			✓		✓	

Romantic Hideaway	Luxurious	Pets Allowed	No Smoking Indoors	Good Place for Families	Beach Nearby	Cross-Country Ski Trails	Golf Within 5 Miles	Fitness Facilities	Near Wineries	Good Biking Terrain	Skiing	Tennis	Swimming on Premises	Conference Facilities	Hiking Nearby
✓	✓		✓								✓			✓	
			✓	✓	✓	✓								✓	
			✓				✓			✓				✓	
			✓	✓	✓		✓			✓					
			✓	✓	✓		✓								
✓	✓		✓		✓		✓			✓					
✓	✓	✓					✓			✓				✓	✓
										✓					
✓			✓				✓						✓	✓	✓
			✓	✓					✓	✓					
	✓		✓				✓	✓		✓					
✓			✓							✓					✓
✓				✓				✓		✓	✓				✓
		✓		✓		✓				✓		✓	✓		
				✓	✓		✓			✓					
				✓			✓			✓					
			✓							✓					✓
✓			✓		✓	✓	✓	✓		✓					
			✓				✓			✓					
✓	✓		✓		✓		✓			✓				✓	✓
			✓	✓			✓			✓					
			✓	✓											✓
			✓				✓		✓					✓	✓
			✓		✓		✓			✓					
✓	✓		✓			✓				✓			✓		✓

Name of Property	Accessible for Disabled	Antiques	On the Water	Best Value	Car Not Necessary	Full Meal Service	Historic Building	
The Highlands				✓				
Home by the Sea			✓					
Hood River Hotel	✓	✓				✓	✓	
House of Hunter		✓		✓				
The House at Water's Edge	✓	✓	✓					
Hudson House		✓					✓	
Inn at Manzanita			✓					
Jacksonville Inn		✓				✓	✓	
The Johnson House	✓	✓	✓					
K.C.'s Mansion By-the-Sea		✓	✓	✓			✓	
Kelty Estate		✓		✓			✓	
Lara House		✓						
Lighthouse			✓					
The Lyon and the Lambe		✓		✓	✓			
MacMaster House		✓				✓	✓	
Main Street Bed & Breakfast				✓				
Mattey House				✓			✓	
McGillivray's Log Home Bed and Breakfast	✓	✓						
Mirror Pond House			✓					
Mt. Ashland Inn								
Mountain Shadows				✓				
Mumford Manor		✓				✓	✓	
Old Stage Inn	✓	✓						
Old Welches Inn	✓	✓	✓				✓	
Orchard View Inn	✓	✓		✓				

Romantic Hideaway	Luxurious	Pets Allowed	No Smoking Indoors	Good Place for Families	Beach Nearby	Cross-Country Ski Trails	Golf Within 5 Miles	Fitness Facilities	Near Wineries	Good Biking Terrain	Skiing	Tennis	Swimming on Premises	Conference Facilities	Hiking Nearby
			✓		✓										✓
			✓		✓					✓					✓
			✓											✓	✓
			✓				✓		✓						✓
			✓			✓	✓			✓	✓	✓			✓
			✓	✓						✓					✓
✓			✓			✓				✓				✓	✓
		✓	✓					✓					✓	✓	
			✓			✓	✓	✓		✓					
	✓		✓			✓									
			✓				✓	✓		✓					
			✓	✓				✓		✓	✓				✓
			✓	✓	✓		✓			✓					✓
		✓							✓	✓				✓	
✓			✓			✓	✓			✓					✓
			✓							✓					
✓	✓					✓	✓			✓					
			✓						✓	✓					
								✓		✓	✓				✓
			✓	✓			✓			✓	✓			✓	✓
✓			✓			✓	✓								✓
✓	✓		✓			✓	✓			✓					✓
✓	✓		✓											✓	
✓			✓			✓	✓			✓	✓				✓
			✓				✓			✓					

Name of Property	Accessible for Disabled	Antiques	On the Water	Best Value	Car Not Necessary	Full Meal Service	Historic Building	
Portland Guest House		✓		✓	✓			
Portland's White House		✓			✓		✓	
River Banks Inn				✓				
River's Reach Bed and Breakfast	✓							
RiverPlace Alexis Hotel	✓		✓		✓	✓		
Sandlake Country Inn		✓					✓	
Shaniko Hotel				✓		✓	✓	
Sheridan Country Inn	✓		✓	✓				
Sonka's Sheep Station Inn			✓			✓		
Stange Manor		✓					✓	
State Street Bed & Breakfast								
Steamboat Inn	✓		✓			✓		
Steiger Haus		✓		✓				
Sunshine Bed and Breakfast							✓	
Sylvia Beach Hotel	✓	✓	✓	✓		✓	✓	
Tu Tu Tun Lodge	✓		✓			✓		
Whiskey Creek Bed & Breakfast	✓	✓	✓	✓				
Williams House		✓	✓				✓	
Willowbrook Inn Bed and Breakfast								
The Winchester Country Inn						✓	✓	
Wolf Creek Tavern		✓				✓	✓	
Youngberg Hill Farm	✓					✓		
Ziggurat			✓	✓				

	Romantic Hideaway	Luxurious	Pets Allowed	No Smoking Indoors	Good Place for Families	Beach Nearby	Cross-Country Ski Trails	Golf Within 5 Miles	Fitness Facilities	Near Wineries	Good Biking Terrain	Skiing	Tennis	Swimming on Premises	Conference Facilities	Hiking Nearby
	✓	✓		✓				✓	✓		✓		✓			
	✓	✓		✓	✓			✓			✓				✓	
			✓							✓						✓
			✓	✓	✓		✓	✓			✓			✓		✓
	✓	✓				✓	✓	✓	✓		✓				✓	
	✓	✓		✓			✓				✓					✓
					✓	✓										
					✓	✓		✓	✓		✓					
					✓	✓					✓					✓
					✓		✓	✓			✓	✓				✓
			✓	✓												✓
	✓		✓	✓	✓						✓			✓	✓	✓
					✓	✓		✓			✓					
					✓											✓
	✓				✓		✓	✓			✓					✓
	✓				✓	✓		✓						✓	✓	
	✓		✓	✓	✓	✓					✓					✓
				✓				✓			✓					✓
				✓			✓	✓			✓			✓		
				✓	✓			✓		✓	✓				✓	
															✓	
	✓	✓		✓	✓		✓	✓			✓			✓	✓	
	✓	✓		✓												

Name of Property	Accessible for Disabled	Antiques	On the Water	Best Value	Car Not Necessary	Full Meal Service	Historic Building	
WASHINGTON								
Alexander's Country Inn	✓	✓				✓	✓	
Anchorage Inn								
Anderson House		✓					✓	
Blackwell House					✓		✓	
Blair House	✓	✓			✓		✓	
Blakely Estates			✓	✓				
Bombay House		✓			✓		✓	
Captain Whidbey Inn		✓	✓				✓	
Cashmere Country Inn		✓					✓	
Chambered Nautilus		✓			✓		✓	
The Channel House		✓	✓				✓	
Chelsea Station		✓			✓		✓	
Clark House on Hayden Lake	✓		✓				✓	
Cliff House and Sea Cliff Cottage			✓					
Coast Watch Bed & Breakfast			✓					
Colonel Crockett Farm		✓	✓				✓	
Country Cottage of Langley	✓	✓			✓			
Country Keeper Bed & Breakfast Inn		✓						
Cricket on the Hearth Bed & Breakfast Inn				✓				
Deer Harbor Inn			✓			✓	✓	
Downey House	✓	✓					✓	
The Duffy House	✓	✓	✓					
Eagles Nest Inn	✓							
Edenwild Inn	✓	✓	✓		✓			

Romantic Hideaway	Luxurious	Pets Allowed	No Smoking Indoors	Good Place for Families	Beach Nearby	Cross-Country Ski Trails	Golf Within 5 Miles	Fitness Facilities	Near Wineries	Good Biking Terrain	Skiing	Tennis	Swimming on Premises	Conference Facilities	Hiking Nearby
✓			✓				✓				✓			✓	✓
	✓		✓			✓				✓		✓			
✓			✓			✓	✓	✓		✓	✓	✓			
						✓		✓							✓
✓			✓	✓			✓	✓		✓			✓	✓	
			✓				✓			✓					✓
✓			✓			✓		✓		✓		✓		✓	
			✓			✓				✓		✓		✓	
✓			✓				✓			✓	✓	✓	✓		✓
✓			✓			✓	✓	✓	✓		✓		✓		✓
✓	✓		✓			✓		✓		✓		✓			
			✓			✓	✓	✓		✓			✓		
✓	✓					✓		✓						✓	✓
✓	✓		✓			✓	✓			✓					
✓			✓			✓		✓							✓
✓	✓		✓			✓	✓			✓					
✓			✓			✓				✓		✓			
✓			✓			✓	✓	✓		✓					
						✓		✓							✓
✓			✓			✓	✓	✓		✓				✓	
✓	✓		✓							✓					
✓			✓			✓	✓	✓		✓					
✓			✓			✓		✓		✓			✓		✓
✓	✓					✓		✓							

Name of Property	Accessible for Disabled	Antiques	On the Water	Best Value	Car Not Necessary	Full Meal Service	Historic Building	
Flying L Ranch	✓	✓						
Fort Casey Inn	✓	✓					✓	
Fotheringham House		✓					✓	
Gallery Bed & Breakfast at Little Cape Horn		✓	✓					
Gaslight Inn		✓			✓		✓	
Gregory's McFarland House		✓					✓	
Guest House Cottages		✓	✓					
Gumm's Bed & Breakfast		✓			✓		✓	
Heather House		✓						
Heritage House	✓	✓			✓		✓	
Heron Inn		✓						
Hillside House		✓	✓		✓			
Home by the Sea Bed & Breakfast and Cottages	✓	✓	✓				✓	
Hotel Planter							✓	
Hous Rohrbach Pensione								
Inn at Ilwaco		✓			✓		✓	
Inn at Langley	✓		✓					
Inn at Penn Cove	✓	✓					✓	
Inn at Swifts Bay		✓			✓			
Inn at White Salmon	✓	✓						
James House		✓			✓		✓	
Kangaroo House		✓			✓		✓	
Kimbrough House		✓			✓		✓	
Lake Crescent Lodge	✓	✓	✓			✓	✓	
Lake Quinalt Lodge		✓	✓			✓	✓	

Romantic Hideaway	Luxurious	Pets Allowed	No Smoking Indoors	Good Place for Families	Beach Nearby	Cross-Country Ski Trails	Golf Within 5 Miles	Fitness Facilities	Near Wineries	Good Biking Terrain	Skiing	Tennis	Swimming on Premises	Conference Facilities	Hiking Nearby
			✓	✓		✓				✓				✓	✓
			✓	✓	✓	✓				✓				✓	
✓			✓									✓			
✓		✓	✓	✓	✓	✓	✓			✓					
✓	✓						✓			✓			✓		
✓	✓		✓			✓	✓								✓
✓	✓					✓	✓	✓		✓			✓		
				✓	✓		✓						✓		✓
✓			✓			✓	✓			✓					
✓	✓		✓			✓	✓			✓		✓			
✓						✓	✓			✓					
✓			✓		✓		✓	✓		✓		✓			
✓		✓	✓	✓	✓		✓			✓	✓	✓	✓		
✓			✓		✓		✓			✓					
			✓	✓		✓	✓			✓	✓	✓	✓	✓	✓
✓				✓	✓		✓			✓		✓		✓	✓
✓	✓		✓		✓		✓			✓				✓	
	✓		✓		✓				✓	✓		✓		✓	
✓	✓		✓		✓		✓			✓					
				✓		✓	✓			✓	✓	✓		✓	
✓	✓		✓			✓	✓			✓		✓			
✓			✓		✓	✓	✓			✓		✓			
			✓						✓			✓			
✓		✓	✓	✓	✓	✓									✓
✓		✓		✓	✓				✓	✓		✓	✓	✓	

Name of Property	Accessible for Disabled	Antiques	On the Water	Best Value	Car Not Necessary	Full Meal Service	Historic Building	
Lakeside Manor			✓					
Land's End		✓	✓					
Lizzie's Victorian Bed & Breakfast		✓					✓	
Log Castle Bed & Breakfast	✓	✓	✓					
Lone Lake Cottage and Breakfast			✓					
Love's Victorian Bed and Breakfast		✓						
MacKaye Harbor Inn		✓	✓				✓	
Majestic Hotel	✓	✓	✓			✓	✓	
Manor Farm Inn		✓				✓	✓	
Maple Valley Bed & Breakfast		✓						
Marianna Stoltz House					✓		✓	
Mazama Country Inn	✓					✓		
Mio Amore Pensione	✓	✓	✓				✓	
Moby Dick Hotel and Oyster Farm			✓				✓	
The Moon and Sixpence		✓					✓	
Moore House Bed & Breakfast		✓					✓	
Mount Meadows Inn		✓	✓				✓	
Mountain Home Lodge		✓				✓		
M. V. Challenger		✓			✓		✓	
My Parents' Estate							✓	
Old Consulate Inn		✓			✓		✓	
Old Honey Farm Country Inn	✓	✓				✓		
Olympic Lights		✓	✓				✓	
Orcas Hotel	✓	✓	✓		✓	✓	✓	
Orchard Hill Inn		✓	✓					

Romantic Hideaway	Luxurious	Pets Allowed	No Smoking Indoors	Good Place for Families	Beach Nearby	Cross-Country Ski Trails	Golf Within 5 Miles	Fitness Facilities	Near Wineries	Good Biking Terrain	Skiing	Tennis	Swimming on Premises	Conference Facilities	Hiking Nearby
			✓		✓	✓				✓	✓				✓
✓	✓		✓		✓		✓			✓					✓
✓			✓		✓		✓			✓		✓		✓	
✓			✓		✓	✓	✓					✓			
✓			✓		✓					✓			✓		
✓			✓			✓				✓					✓
✓			✓		✓	✓	✓			✓					
✓	✓			✓		✓	✓			✓	✓			✓	
✓			✓		✓					✓		✓	✓		
✓			✓	✓	✓		✓			✓	✓	✓			
			✓												
						✓				✓	✓	✓		✓	✓
✓		✓	✓			✓				✓	✓	✓	✓		
		✓	✓		✓	✓	✓			✓				✓	✓
✓			✓		✓		✓			✓		✓			
✓			✓	✓	✓	✓	✓			✓	✓	✓		✓	✓
✓			✓		✓		✓			✓	✓		✓		✓
✓			✓			✓	✓			✓	✓	✓	✓	✓	✓
✓			✓		✓	✓	✓			✓		✓		✓	
			✓			✓		✓		✓	✓				✓
✓	✓		✓			✓	✓			✓		✓		✓	
✓			✓	✓		✓	✓			✓	✓			✓	✓
✓					✓	✓	✓			✓					
✓			✓		✓	✓	✓			✓		✓		✓	
		✓	✓	✓		✓	✓			✓	✓	✓	✓	✓	

Name of Property	Accessible for Disabled	Antiques	On the Water	Best Value	Car Not Necessary	Full Meal Service	Historic Building	
The Portico		✓					✓	
Ravenscroft Inn		✓			✓			
Roberta's		✓			✓		✓	
Run of the River Inn		✓	✓		✓			
Salisbury House		✓			✓		✓	
Salish Lodge	✓	✓	✓			✓	✓	
San Juan Inn		✓	✓				✓	
Schnauzer Crossing	✓	✓	✓					
Shelburne Inn	✓	✓			✓	✓	✓	
Shumway Mansion		✓			✓		✓	
Silver Bay Bed & Breakfast & Guest Cabins		✓	✓		✓			
Sou'wester Lodge				✓			✓	
Starrett House Inn		✓			✓		✓	
Sun Mountain Lodge	✓					✓		
Tudor Inn		✓			✓			
Turtleback Farm Inn	✓	✓					✓	
Villa Heidelberg		✓			✓		✓	
Warwick Inn					✓		✓	
Waverly Place		✓		✓	✓		✓	
Wharfside		✓	✓		✓			
Whidbey Inn		✓	✓					
White Swan Guest House		✓					✓	
Wildflower Inn		✓						
Willows Inn	✓	✓	✓			✓	✓	

	Romantic Hideaway	Luxurious	Pets Allowed	No Smoking Indoors	Good Place for Families	Beach Nearby	Cross-Country Ski Trails	Golf Within 5 Miles	Fitness Facilities	Near Wineries	Good Biking Terrain	Skiing	Tennis	Swimming on Premises	Conference Facilities	Hiking Nearby
				✓				✓			✓					
	✓	✓				✓	✓	✓	✓		✓		✓		✓	
				✓				✓			✓		✓			
	✓	✓					✓	✓			✓	✓	✓		✓	✓
	✓	✓		✓		✓		✓			✓		✓			
	✓	✓					✓	✓	✓		✓	✓			✓	✓
				✓			✓	✓	✓		✓		✓			
	✓	✓		✓		✓		✓			✓		✓		✓	
	✓						✓	✓			✓		✓		✓	✓
	✓	✓		✓		✓	✓	✓	✓		✓		✓		✓	
	✓	✓		✓		✓					✓			✓		✓
	✓			✓	✓	✓		✓			✓		✓		✓	✓
	✓	✓		✓			✓	✓			✓		✓		✓	
					✓			✓		✓	✓	✓	✓	✓	✓	✓
	✓			✓			✓	✓	✓		✓	✓	✓			✓
	✓			✓				✓			✓					
	✓			✓		✓		✓			✓		✓		✓	
	✓						✓	✓	✓							✓
				✓									✓			
	✓		✓	✓	✓	✓		✓			✓		✓			
	✓			✓		✓					✓		✓			
	✓			✓							✓					
	✓			✓			✓	✓	✓		✓	✓	✓			✓
	✓	✓		✓		✓					✓				✓	

California

Northern California

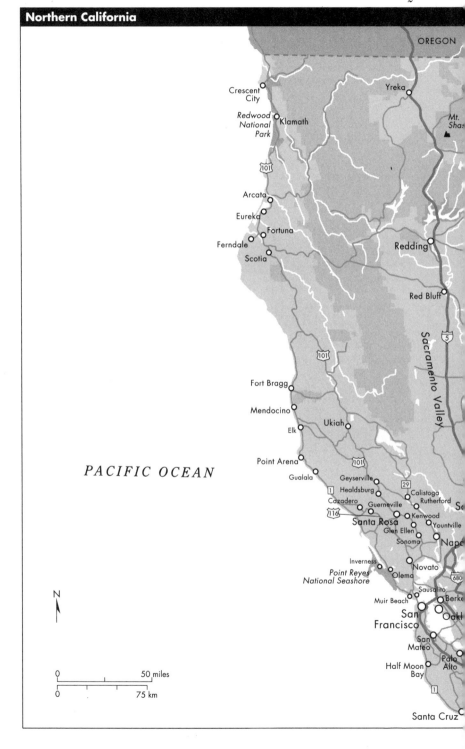

OREGON

Crescent City

Yreka

Redwood National Park Klamath

Mt. Shas·

Arcata

Eureka
Fortuna

Ferndale
Scotia

Redding

Red Bluff

Sacramento Valley

Fort Bragg

Mendocino

Elk Ukiah

Point Arena

PACIFIC OCEAN

Gualala

Geyserville
Healdsburg
Cazadero Guerneville Calistoga
Rutherford
Kenwood
Santa Rosa Yountville
Glen Ellen
Sonoma Nap

Inverness
Point Reyes National Seashore Novato
Olema
Sausalito Berke
Muir Beach
San
Francisco Oakl

San
Mateo
Half Moon Palo
Bay Alto

Santa Cruz

N

0   50 miles

0   75 km

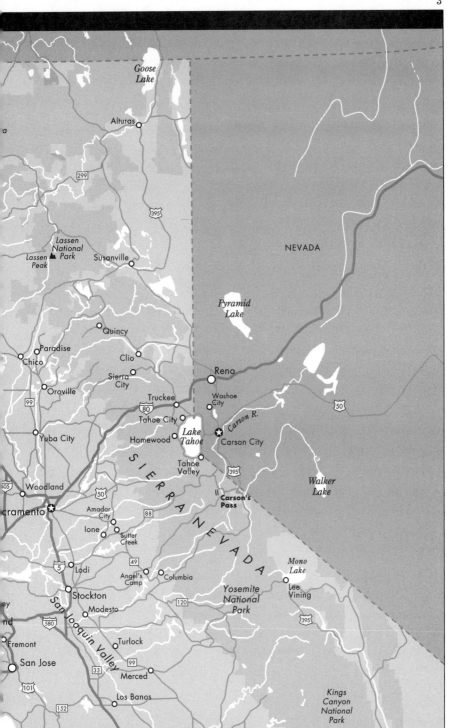

Goose
Lake

Alturas

NEVADA

299

395

Lassen
National
Park
Lassen
Peak
Susanville

Pyramid
Lake

Quincy

Paradise
Chico

Clio

Oroville

Sierra
City

Reno

99

Truckee

Washoe
City

80

Tahoe City

50

Yuba City

Homewood

Lake
Tahoe

Carson R.

Carson City

SIERRA

Tahoe
Valley

505

Woodland

50

395

Walker
Lake

cramento

Amador
City

88

Carson's
Pass

Ione

Sutter
Creek

49

NEVADA

Lodi

Angel's
Camp

Columbia

Mono
Lake

5

Stockton

120

Yosemite
National
Park

Lee
Vining

Modesto

580

395

Fremont

Turlock

San Joaquin Valley

99

San Jose

33

Merced

101

Los Banos

Kings
Canyon
National
Park

152

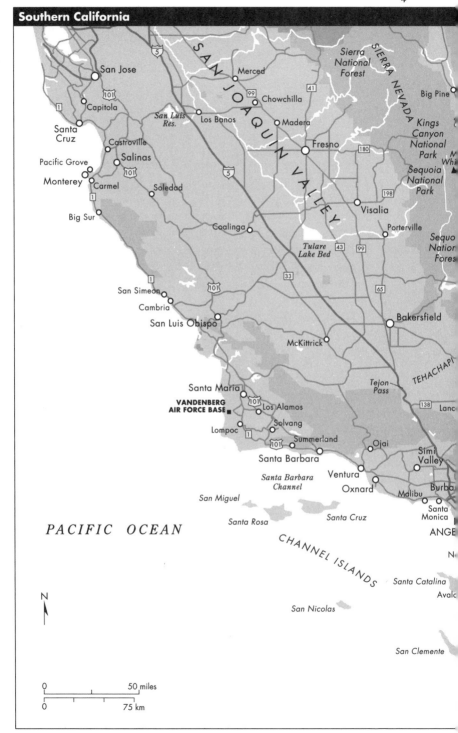

Southern California

PACIFIC OCEAN

N

| 0 | | 50 miles |
| 0 | | 75 km |

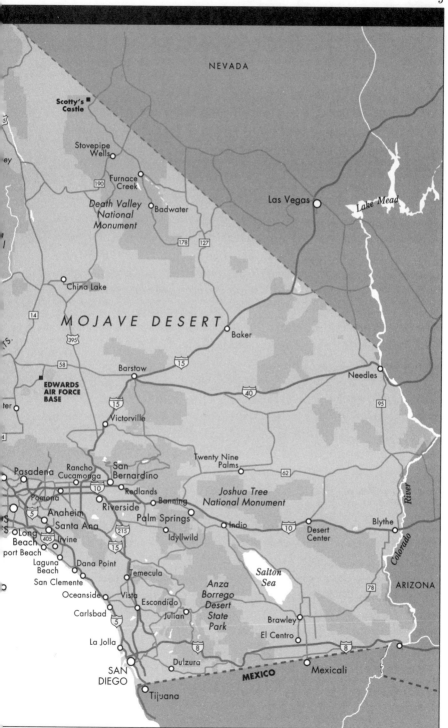

Southern Counties
Including San Diego and Palm Springs

*"From the desert to the sea . . ." is the signature of
longtime southern California TV newsman Jerry Dunphy.
These are the natural boundaries of the vast area known as
the Southern Counties: San Diego, Riverside, Imperial.
Each has its own charms.*

*San Diego hugs the sea, stretching inland 4,255 square
miles over mile-high mountains to the desert at sea level.
Beyond is vast Riverside, the desert resorts of Palm Springs
and Palm Desert, and the date-growing areas surrounding
Indio. To the north are two dozen wineries in the historic
Temecula countryside and a pair of mountains more than
10,000 feet high, San Jacinto and San Gorgonio. Imperial,
ranging along the Mexican border, is the source of most of
the tomatoes, lettuce, and grapefruit consumed by
Americans.*

*The Southern Counties also contain the oldest and newest
communities in California. San Diego is the birthplace of
California; Portuguese explorer Juan Rodríguez Cabrilho
landed here and claimed the area for Spain in 1542. The
burgeoning suburban communities of Riverside County
represent the youngest and fastest-growing in the state.*

*History and geography aside, this is a land of recreation.
Hikes on wooded mountain trails. Sailing the deep green
Pacific or blue inland lakes. Playing golf at one of dozens
of championship courses. Tennis. Bicycling. Ballooning.
Wine tasting. Discovering the lushness of a flower-carpeted
desert in spring. Delving into history at southern
California's only Gold Rush town. Encountering wild
animals at the San Diego Zoo and Wild Animal Park.
Cavorting with the whales at Sea World. Exploring the vast
1,400-acre Balboa Park. Watching thoroughbred racing*

*from the grandstand or elegant clubhouse at Del Mar.
Basking on a long white beach.*

*Culture abounds here, too. San Diego's Old Globe Theater
is world-famous for its performances of classics,
contemporary drama, experimental works, and, of course,
its summer Shakespeare Festival. The San Diego Opera
draws audiences from all over southern California. Art
galleries flourish in seaside La Jolla. Balboa Park's art,
anthropological, natural history, and other museums lure
Sunday afternoon visitors.*

*While this is an area of many splendid resorts, the
Southern Counties also offer the intimacy, individuality,
and personal contact that only bed-and-breakfast lodging
can provide.*

Places to Go, Sights to See

Balboa Park (tel. 619/239–0512). In addition to the *San Diego Zoo*, the
1,074-acre urban park contains 13 museums, including the *San Diego
Museum of Art* (tel. 619/232–7931), *Reuben H. Fleet Space Theater and
Science Center* (tel. 619/238-1168), *Museum of Man* (tel. 619/239–2001),
Museum of Photographic Art (tel. 619/239–5262), and *Centro Cultural de
la Raza* (tel. 619/235–6135). The *Simon Edison Centre for the Performing
Arts* houses three stages, including the famed *Old Globe Theatre* (tel.
619/239–2255), the oldest professional theater in California, which presents
a full season of Shakespearean, classic, and contemporary plays. On
weekends the park fairly sings with fun as street performers, mimes, and
musicians work the crowd on the Prado.

Cabrillo National Monument (tel. 619/557–5450), atop the tip of Point Loma,
commemorates Juan Rodríguez Cabrillo's 1542 exploration of San Diego,
offering exhibits, films, and lectures at the Visitor's Center about the
monument, tide pools, and gray whales migrating offshore. Descriptive signs
line the cliffside walks leading to a promontory that affords stunning views
over the bay as far south as Mexico. You can explore the old Point Loma
lighthouse, replaced in 1891 by one closer to shore.

The Desert. *Indian Canyons* (S. Palm Canyon Dr., tel. 619/325–5673),
ancestral home of the Agua Caliente Indians, begins 5 miles south of
downtown Palm Springs. Inside this Indian-owned sanctuary, visitors can see
relics of ancient American history while wandering through landscapes of
palms and wildflowers, towering rockfaces, and dense growths of sycamores,
willows, and mesquite. *Joshua Tree National Monument* (north of I–10 via

Hwy. 62, 29 Palms, tel. 619/367–7511), about a one-hour drive from Palm Springs, is a colorful preserve illustrating desert life and history, with hiking trails, picnic areas, and naturalist-led walks. This meeting place of the Mojave and Colorado deserts includes such sights as Hidden Valley, a legendary cattle rustlers' hideout, the Oasis of Mara, and Key's View, an outstanding scenic point commanding a superb sweep of valley, mountain, and desert. The southern part of the park is especially beautiful in spring, when wildflowers bloom. *Living Desert Reserve* (17–900 Portola Ave., tel. 619/346–5694) in Palm Desert is a 1,200-acre wildlife park and botanical garden with bighorn sheep, coyotes, birds of prey, reptiles, and other desert wildlife roaming in natural settings. *Palm Springs Aerial Tramway* (1 Tramway Rd., tel. 619/325–1391) is a 2½-mile gondola ride from the desert to an observation area at the 8,516-foot level of Mt. San Jacinto, where there are 54 hiking trails, camping and picnic areas, and a restaurant and lounge. *The Desert Museum* (101 Museum Dr., tel. 619/325–7186) in Palm Springs offers art exhibitions, often Western in flavor, and natural history and science sections illuminating aspects of the surrounding desert. The *Annenberg Theater* there features top-name popular entertainers.

Gaslamp Quarter National Historic District (tel. 619/233–5227). The 16-block area in downtown San Diego, centered around 4th and 5th avenues from Broadway to Market Street, contains most of the city's Victorian commercial architecture, now housing antiques shops, cafés and restaurants, and the San Diego Repertory Theater. Walking tours of the district are conducted on Saturdays at 10 AM and 1 PM starting at the Gaslamp Quarter Association headquarters (410 Island Ave., tel. 619/233–5227). Also located in the area is the Center City East Arts Association (600–1300 G St.), a large concentration of galleries, art studios, boutiques, and coffeehouses.

Hot-Air Ballooning. *Sunrise Balloons* (tel. 800/548–9912) offers 45- to 60-minute balloon flights in the Palm Springs and Temecula areas, with packages that include picnics and ground transportation in antique cars.

Julian (tel. 619/765–1857). East of San Diego and reached by Highway 78–79, this is the site of the only Gold Rush to take place in southern California. The historic mountain town, now known for its apples, has a gold mine that can be visited, *Eagle Mine* (tel. 619/765–0036), an old-fashioned soda fountain in an 1880s drugstore, a historical museum in an old brewery (tel. 619/765–0227), antiques shops, and restaurants.

Old Town State Historic Park (tel. 619/237–6770), just north of downtown San Diego at Juan Street, near the intersection of I–5 and I–8, was the center of San Diego when it was incorporated in 1850. The historic buildings, clustered around California Plaza, include original and reproduction adobe and log houses in a subdued Mexican Colonial style. Bazaar del Mundo is a shopping and dining enclave built to resemble a colonial Mexican square.

Mission Bay, a 4,600-acre aquatic playground, is the largest of its kind in the world, and is devoted to boating, water skiing, swimming, board sailing, and other forms of recreation like cycling and kite flying. There are 27 miles of bayfront beaches with six designated swimming areas and numerous picnic grounds. *Giant Dipper*, a 65-year-old wooden roller coaster at Belmont Park, an abandoned amusement park turned shopping and dining center, has recently been restored and is running again. *Sea World* (1720 S. Shores Rd., tel. 619/226–3901) is a 150-acre ocean-oriented amusement park featuring trained, performing killer whales, seals, dolphins, and sea otters. The Penguin Encounter has a moving sidewalk passing by a glass-enclosed arctic environment, where hundreds of emperor penguins slide over glaciers into icy waters.

San Diego Zoo (Balboa Park, tel. 619/357–3966) is widely recognized as one of the world's best zoos. More than 3,900 animals of 800 species reside in 100 acres of expertly crafted habitats, including the African Rain Forest, Gorilla Tropics, Sun Bear River, and Tiger River. The zoo is also an enormous botanical garden, with one of the world's largest collections of subtropical plants.

San Diego Wild Animal Park (15500 San Pasqual Valley Rd., Escondido, tel. 619/747–8702) is a 1,800-acre wildlife preserve containing more than 2,500 wild animals that roam free over hillsides resembling their native habitats in Asia and Africa.

Scripps Institution of Oceanography (8602 La Jolla Shores Dr., tel. 619/534–6933) in La Jolla has a fine aquarium filled with saltwater fish, and an outdoor tide-pool exhibit with live starfish, anemones, and other shoreline creatures.

Temecula, 60 miles northeast of San Diego off Highway 15, has an Old Town with a number of historic buildings dating from the 1890s, when Temecula was a frontier cow town. Most of the action is on Front Street, where you'll find an ever-changing array of antiques and gift shops. A favorite local restaurant is the *Bank of Mexican Food* (tel. 714/676–6160), housed in a former Bank of America building, dating from 1913–14. The vault has been converted into a small dining room. Thirteen wineries can be found scattered along Rancho California Road, about 5 miles from Old Town. Tours and tastings are offered on weekends. Most prominent is *Callaway Vineyard and Winery* (tel. 714/676–4001), which offers a calendar of tastings, seminars, picnics, chefs' dinners, and festivals. Another popular spot is the *John Culbertson Winery*, which has a champagne bar, gift shop, and the Champagne Restaurant (tel. 714/699–0088).

Beaches

The long beaches of San Diego are one of the county's principal attractions. The turquoise Pacific invites swimming, surfing, and sunbathing while whales, seals, and dolphins frolic. **Imperial Beach,** a classic southern California beach, is the site of the U.S. Open Sandcastle Competition every July. With the famous Hotel Del Coronado as a backdrop, the **Coronado Beach** is one of the largest in the county, and is surprisingly uncrowded on most days. **Sunset Cliffs,** beneath the jagged cliffs on the west side of Point Loma peninsula, is one of the more secluded beaches in the area, popular primarily with surfers and locals. It's not Atlantic City, but the boardwalk stretching along **Mission Beach** is a magnet for strollers, roller skaters, and bicyclists. The south end attracts surfers, swimmers, and volleyball players. **La Jolla Cove** is one of the prettiest spots in the world: A beautifully palm-tree-lined park sits atop cliffs formed by the incessant pounding of the waves. The beach below the cove is almost nonexistent at high tide, but the cove is still a must-see. One of the most overcrowded beaches in the county, **La Jolla Shores** lures bathers with a wide sandy beach, relatively calm surf, and a concrete boardwalk paralleling the beach. Admission to **Mission Bay's** 27 miles of bayfront beaches and 17 miles of ocean frontage is free.

Restaurants

San Diego's gastronomic reputation rests primarily on its seafood. **Red Sails Inn** (tel. 619/223–3030) in Point Loma offers good, simple seafood on a waterfront location. At **Cafe Pacifica** (tel. 619/291–6666), the approach to seafood is moderately nouvelle, with light, interesting sauces and imaginative garnishes. With its extravagant view of La Jolla Cove, **Top O' The Cove** (tel. 619/454–7779) is more or less synonymous with romance, but it also boasts competently prepared luxury fare—beef, fowl, veal, and seafood—dressed with creamy, well-seasoned sauces. So many L.A. natives have second homes "down in the Springs" that local restaurateurs try to match the Big City's standards—and more and more are succeeding. **Bono** (tel. 619/322–6200), owned by Palm Springs mayor Sonny Bono, serves southern Italian cuisine to show biz folk and the curious. **Las Casuelas Original** (tel. 619/325–3213) is a longtime favorite among natives when it comes to great margaritas and average Mexican dishes. It gets very, very crowded during the winter months. Hearty eaters will enjoy **Di Amico's Steak House** (tel. 619/325–9191), an early California–style restaurant featuring such dishes as prime Eastern corn-fed beef, liver steak vaquero, and son-of-a-gun stew.

Tourism Information

Julian Chamber of Commerce (Box 413, Julian, CA 92036, tel. 619/765–1857); **Palm Springs Desert Resorts Convention and Visitors Bureau** (69930 Hwy. 111, Suite 201, Rancho Mirage, CA 92270, tel. 619/770–9000); **San Diego Convention and Visitors Bureau** (1200 3rd Ave., Suite 824, San Diego, CA 92101–4190, tel. 619/232–3101); **Temecula Valley Chamber of Commerce** (40945 County Center Dr., Suite C, Temecula, CA 92591, tel. 714/676–5090).

Reservation Services

Bed and Breakfast Innkeepers of Southern California (Box 15425, Los Angeles, CA 90015–0385, tel. 800/424–0053).

Bed and Breakfast Inn at La Jolla

L a Jolla is Spanish for "the jewel," the perfect description of this seaside village in northern San Diego. Located across from the Museum of Contemporary Art and just a three-minute walk from the ocean is the Bed and Breakfast Inn at La Jolla. The building, an outstanding example of the stripped-down architecture locals call cubist, was designed by Irving Gill. "We should build our houses simple, plain and substantial as a boulder, then leave the ornamentation to nature," Gill wrote.

The inn, built as a home for George Kautz in 1913, follows those tenets. A simple white stucco box with the occasional arched window or doorway, it has huge diamond-pane windows opening like shutters onto Pacific views. Additional natural "ornamentation" (helped along by famous horticulturalist Kate Sessions) takes the form of a crimson bougainvillea-filled garden with fountain and Japanese pine.

Set in a quiet neighborhood near the town's commercial district, the inn was masterminded by Betty Albee and her daughter, Ardath, who saved the house from demolition, renovated and restored it, and added a sympathetic annex in the rear, which now houses six guest rooms. The inn is managed by Bill Timmerman and his French-born wife, Pierette.

Each room is individually decorated, from rattan-and-white-iron bedsteads to American country pine, and stocked with fresh fruit and sherry. The lion's share of the antiques are in the old part of the house. The pricier rooms have the most sought-after views. The most spacious rooms are the Holiday Room and the Irving Gill Penthouse, a duplex with its own deck.

Pierette has added Gallic specialties to the Continental breakfast: French pear cake, *gâteau marbré*, and other traditional French cakes. (And, yes, there are always croissants.) In fine weather, guests may opt to dine outside on the raised garden deck or on the terrace off the sitting room.

Address: *7753 Draper Ave., La Jolla, CA 92037, tel. 619/456-2066.*
Accommodations: *14 double rooms with bath, 1 double room with public bath, 1 suite.*
Amenities: *Robe in room, phone available, hairdryers in several rooms, fireplace in 3 rooms, refrigerator in 4 rooms, TV in suite and sitting room; afternoon refreshments; picnic baskets available; off-street parking.*
Rates: *$85–$225; Continental breakfast. MC, V.*
Restrictions: *Smoking in guest rooms only, no pets; 2-night minimum on weekends and holidays.*

Julian Hotel

When Steve and Gig Ballinger moved to Julian in 1976 to take over the Julian Hotel, they had a major undertaking ahead of them: restoring the oldest continuously operating hotel in southern California to its former glory. Set at the top of the mountains east of San Diego, Julian was the site of a major gold rush during the 1870s. When the mines played out, the argonauts moved on, leaving a few farmers who planted apple trees. Now Julian, with its gently rolling, oak tree–studded hills, is a popular weekend getaway for southern Californians.

The hotel was founded in 1897 by a freed Georgia slave, Albert Robinson, and his wife, Margaret. Purists, Steve and Gig refused to compromise with history as they undertook the process of restoring the "modernized" hotel to its original Victorian appearance. Rooms were small then; they have not been enlarged. In this mining town few luxuries were available, and thus the rooms are simply furnished; some pieces, most of them oak, are original to the hotel from its earliest days, and other furnishings date to the same period. Beds are of brass, iron and brass, or wood with applied decoration. Each room has an oak dresser with a beveled glass mirror. The bathrooms are called Necessary Rooms, in deference to Victorian modesty, and three have claw-foot tubs. Two cottages can be rented:

one a suite with a lady's vanity room, the other a single bedroom with bath and its own porch.

The Victorian theme starts in the hotel's comfortable lobby, furnished with a settee, black leather armchairs with carved lions' heads, a boldly patterned rose-print carpet, and a Kayton tiger oak piano dating from 1910. It's a busy place in the late afternoon, when guests return from touring the town's historic sites. In cool weather a fire crackles in the wood stove, lending a warmth to the entire room. Guests can also relax in a wicker-filled sun room or in the parlor, which also has a stove.

If you're interested in local history, ask to see the ancient guest register with its many famous signatures, including those of British prime minister David Lloyd George, Admiral Chester Nimitz, members of the Copley and Scripps publishing families, and Ulysses S. Grant, Jr.

Address: *2032 Main St., Box 1856, Julian, CA 92036, tel. 619/765-0201.*
Accommodations: *4 double rooms with bath, 12 double rooms and 1 single room share 4 baths, 1 suite.*
Amenities: *Afternoon tea, private veranda off 1 room, fireplace and dressing room in suite.*
Rates: *$82–$94, suite $145; full breakfast. AE, MC, V.*
Restrictions: *No pets; 2-night minimum on weekends.*

Loma Vista
Bed and Breakfast

The first bed-and-breakfast accommodations in California were the 21 missions built during the 18th century by the Spanish padres, providing lodging and food along El Camino Real. The missions are also the inspiration for the design—and the hospitality—of the Loma Vista Bed and Breakfast.

The inn, which sits like a terra-cotta crown atop a hill in the Temecula wine country, about an hour's drive north of San Diego, is the creation of Betty Ryan, who designed it from the ground up. The look is more like a hacienda than a mission. Carefully tended rose gardens border red-tiled patios. A fountain gurgles. Hummingbirds poke their long beaks into the hearts of fragrant flowers.

Inside, the inn is cool and inviting, with ceiling beams and other oak details. Objects collected from years of world travel, from African brasswork to Thai silk-screen hangings, are displayed throughout the house. Large picture windows in the common rooms reveal gardens and vineyard-covered hillsides. The views from the bedrooms upstairs are more dramatic, unfolding in a broad panorama of citrus groves, distant mountains, and even Mt. Palomar observatory.

The guest rooms are named for varietal wines, but the connection ceases there. Zinfandel is swathed in green and peach, with Colonial reproduc-

tions that include a handsome Chippendale-style secretary bookcase with bonnet top. Chardonnay is furnished in oak and has a Laura Ashley look. Art Deco describes Champagne, with a black lacquer bed, tubular steel chairs, and photographs of Marilyn Monroe and Fred Astaire on the walls. Each room is stocked with fresh fruit and port.

Whatever room you select, the setting is lovely. Don't miss the chance to spend some time sitting on the veranda sipping local wine, enjoying the fresh, cooling breezes, colorful gardens, or setting sun.

Champagne at breakfast, served family style in the inn's large dining room, makes it a festive meal. Betty has a large repertoire of Southwestern favorites, such as *huevos rancheros.*

Address: *33350 La Serena Way, Temecula, CA 92390, tel. 714/676–7047.*
Accommodations: *6 double rooms with bath.*
Amenities: *Air-conditioning; afternoon refreshments; fire pit.*
Rates: *$85–$115; full breakfast. D, MC, V.*
Restrictions: *Smoking outside only, no pets; 2-night minimum on weekends.*

Britt House

In a city not known for its Victorian architecture, the Britt House is a standout. Visitors and San Diegans frequently go by the 1887 Queen Anne house just to gawk at its remarkable two-story stained-glass window and to admire its many gables. A look inside reveals a wealth of gingerbread, hand-carved golden oak staircase, milled and hand-carved oak wainscoting and woodwork, huge double-pocket doors, and ornate scrolling everywhere.

The Britt House is located on a busy corner two blocks from an entrance to Balboa Park in a neighborhood that's undergoing gentrification. Innkeeper Elizabeth Lord, who came to San Diego in 1983 after running a preschool in Saudi Arabia, has slowly been upgrading the inn since she acquired it in 1989. Her large collection of Eastlake furnishings graces nearly every room. The enormous bedrooms are bright and airy, with diaphanous lace curtains, lots of quilts, stuffed animals and dolls, and 19th-century photographic portraits.

Address: *406 Maple St., San Diego, CA 92103, tel. 619/234–2926.*
Accommodations: *9 double rooms share 4 bath, housekeeping cottage with bath.*
Amenities: *Fireplace in 2 rooms, robe in room, afternoon refreshments, phone available.*
Rates: *$95–$110; full breakfast. AE, MC, V.*
Restrictions: *Smoking outside only, no pets.*

Brookside Farm

Edd and Sally Guishard have created a tree-shaded mountain retreat out of an old dairy farm in Dulzura, just a 30-minute drive southeast of San Diego. Although it's no longer a commercial farm, Brookside provides much of the produce and eggs for the B&B, and there's a typical menagerie of goats, chickens, pigs, and ducks. You'll fall asleep to the gurgling sounds of a year-round stream that meanders through the four-acre property.

Rooms are scattered throughout the property: in the main house, built in 1928; in the stone dairy barn; and in two cottages, one of which, the Hunter's Cabin, hangs right over the brook. Sally has made quilts for all the rooms and painted designs on many of the beams, borders, and even pedestal sinks. Edd, a former chef, prepares dinner for guests on weekends. At $15 the four-course meal is a bargain.

Address: *1373 Marron Valley Rd., Dulzura, CA 91917, tel. 619/468–3043.*
Accommodations: *8 double rooms with bath, 2 double rooms share bath, 1 suite.*
Amenities: *Fireplace in 4 rooms, refrigerator available, weekend and holiday dinners on request, cooking classes available, catering; outdoor hot tub, badminton, horseshoes, croquet.*
Rates: *$65–$80; full breakfast. MC, V.*
Restrictions: *Smoking outside only, no pets; 2-night minimum on weekends.*

Heritage Park Bed & Breakfast Inn

This turreted Victorian is the ideal headquarters for touring San Diego's Old Town, just across the street. An 1889 Queen Anne, the inn possesses a wraparound spindlework veranda, roof cresting, stained-glass windows, and ornate millwork. The front parlor, like the rest of the house, is completely furnished with antiques. Especially noteworthy are the Eastlake-style tile fireplace, the William Morris reproduction wallpaper, and the 1914 player piano.

One of the most popular rooms is the Turret, which has a tower alcove with a table set for two; many guests who book this room order dinner, served by a liveried butler.

When Angela and Don Thiess purchased the inn in 1990, they wisely kept on most of the staff, including head innkeeper Rhonda Holmes, whose cheerfulness and helpful advice will greatly enhance your stay.

Address: *2470 Heritage Park Row, San Diego, CA 92110, tel. 619/295-7088.*
Accommodations: *5 double rooms with bath, 4 double rooms share 2 baths.*
Amenities: *Fireplace in 3 rooms, afternoon refreshments, catered dinners available; offstreet parking.*
Rates: *$80–$120; full breakfast. MC, V.*
Restrictions: *No pets; 2-night minimum on weekends.*

Ingleside Inn

Garbo slept here—so did Elizabeth Taylor, Marlon Brando, and diva Lily Pons. Ingleside Inn has been a Palm Springs hideaway for celebrities, Hollywood and otherwise, since the 1930s. The reasons become obvious when you step inside this unpretentious hacienda-style inn and meet innkeeper Babs Rosen, who has watched over the property like a mother hen for many years. Located on a quiet street just a few blocks from Palm Canyon Drive, the inn is a tranquil and private enclave surrounded by lush gardens and a high adobe wall. Individually and elegantly decorated villas and cottages are scattered around the property. All rooms have whirlpool tubs and steam showers. Some are furnished with valuable antiques; the suite occupied by Pons

for 13 years features her Louis XV bedroom set.

Address: *2000 W. Ramon Rd., Palm Springs, CA 92264, tel. 619/325-0046, 800/772-6655, fax 619/325-0710.*
Accommodations: *27 double rooms with baths, 2 double suites.*
Amenities: *Air-conditioning, TV with VCR, phone, stocked refrigerator, whirlpool bath, and steam shower in rooms, fireplace in 14 rooms, room service; restaurant, lounge, limousine pickup at local airport; meeting facilities; outdoor swimming pool and hot tub.*
Rates: *$95–$295, suites $450–$550; Continental breakfast. AE, D, MC, V.*
Restrictions: *2-night minimum on weekends Oct.–May.*

Pelican Cove Inn

The beachfront town of Carlsbad has long been a popular summer destination for southern Californians seeking sand and sun. Those are the lures of Pelican Cove Inn, which is located just two short blocks from the beach. This contemporary inn, vaguely Cape Cod in style, was built by Robert and Celeste Hale. Both from Los Angeles, he's a semiretired attorney, while she continues to work part-time as a court reporter.

Guest rooms, all with private outside entrances, are furnished with a mix of antiques, period reproductions, and modern pieces. The most striking room is the La Jolla Room, where tall, arched bay windows, two-story cathedral ceiling, and elegant champagne color scheme can best be appreciated from the turn-of-the-century French fainting couch. Guests can take breakfast in the parlor, or take a tray outside to the garden gazebo, sun deck, or wraparound porches. Beach chairs, towels, and picnic baskets waiting to be filled are provided for those heading for the surf.

Address: *320 Walnut Ave., Carlsbad, CA 92008, tel. 619/434-5995.*
Accommodations: *8 double rooms with bath.*
Amenities: *TV and fireplace in room, phone available, whirlpool tub in 2 rooms, afternoon refreshments, railroad station pickup.*
Rates: *$85–$150; Continental breakfast. AE, MC, V.*
Restrictions: *No pets, 2-night minimum on weekends.*

Strawberry Creek Inn

Idyllwild is a tiny hamlet high on Mt. San Jacinto, where hiking and exploring hundreds of miles of forested trails are the main activities. Jim Goff and Diana Dugan, San Diego city planners, had been visiting the mountains for years when they discovered that the rambling shingled house located on the banks of Strawberry Creek was for sale. They purchased it and by 1985 had turned it into the Strawberry Creek Inn.

The heart of the inn is a big, comfortable living room with a fieldstone fireplace filling one wall, and a glass-enclosed dining porch. Guests can select from antiques-filled rooms in the main house, many displaying quilts; one of the four skylighted theme rooms added later; or the recently completed Cottage on Strawberry Creek, which has a sitting area, kitchen, whirlpool tub, and a Murphy bed in the living room for overflows.

Address: *26370 Banning-Idyllwild Hwy., Box 1818, Idyllwild, CA 92549, tel. 714/659-3202.*
Accommodations: *9 double rooms with bath, 1 housekeeping suite.*
Amenities: *Evening refreshments, fireplace and refrigerator in 5 rooms, TV and VCR in suite.*
Rates: *$85–$125; full breakfast (except in suite). MC, V.*
Restrictions: *No smoking, no pets; 2-night minimum on weekends, 3-night minimum on holidays.*

Villa Royale

Chuck Murawski has conjured up a European-style country inn in the desert. Villa Royale in Palm Springs is a walled, flower-filled oasis with pilasters, glazed terracotta walls, marble and tile floors, open-beam ceilings, French doors, canopied and painted beds, heavy carved-wood furnishings, and delicate flowered upholstery. All are set beneath the red-tiled roofs of eight buildings on 3½ acres of grounds.

Rooms surround a series of three gardens of bougainvillea, where guests lounge around one of two swimming pools or the outdoor hot tub. The inn has a noted garden restaurant, The Europa, which serves lunch and dinner (except during the summer).

Address: *1620 Indian Trail, Palm Springs, CA 92264, tel. 619/327–2314, 800/245–2314, fax 619/322–4151.*

Accommodations: *23 double rooms with bath, 9 housekeeping suites, 3 double housekeeping suites.*

Amenities: *Restaurant, air-conditioning, TV and phone in rooms, fireplace in 15 rooms, whirlpool tub in 8 rooms, kitchen in 9 double rooms, VCR and tape rental; massage and facials available; room service during restaurant hours; 2 outdoor swimming pools, outdoor hot tub, bicycles.*

Rates: *$65–$270; Continental breakfast. AE, MC, V.*

Restrictions: *No pets; 2-night minimum on weekends, 3-night minimum on holidays.*

Los Angeles and Orange County

Set off from the rest of the continent by mountains and desert, and from the rest of the world by an ocean, this incredible corner of creation has evolved its own identity that conjures envy, fascination, ridicule, and scorn—often all at once.

Los Angeles is a city of ephemerals, of transience, and above all, of illusion. Nothing here is quite real, and that's the reality of it all. The lure that "anything can happen"— and it often does—is what keeps thousands moving to this promised land each year and millions more vacationing there. Not just from the East or Midwest, but from the Far East, Down Under, Europe, and South America. It's this influx of cultures that's been the lifeblood of Los Angeles since its Hispanic beginning.

The first immigrants were the Spanish padres who, following a dream of finding wealth in California, founded their Pueblo de la Reina de Los Angeles in 1781. Oil and oranges helped the town shed its image as a dusty outpost, but the golden key to success came on the silver screen: the movies.

The same sunshine that draws today's visitors and new residents drew Cecil B. DeMille and Jesse Lasky in 1911, who were searching for a new place to make movies outside of New York City. The silent-film era made Hollywood's name synonymous with fantasy, glamour, and, as the first citizens would snicker in disgust, with sin. Outrageous partying, extravagant homes, eccentric clothing, and money, money, money have been symbols of life in Los Angeles ever since. Even the more conservative oil, aerospace, computer, banking, and import/export industries on the booming Pacific Rim have enjoyed the prosperity that inevitably leads to fun living. But even without piles of money, many people have found a kindred spirit in Los Angeles for their colorful lifestyles, be they spiritually, socially, or sexually unusual.

No city embraces the romance of the automobile as does Los Angeles. Cars announce the wealth, politics, and taste of their drivers. Vanity license plates, a California innovation, condense the meaning of one's life into seven letters (MUZKBIZ). Sun roofs, ski racks, and cardboard windshield visors sell better here than anywhere else. You are what you drive—a thought worth remembering when you rent a car. Yes, Lamborghinis are available—even by the hour.

The distance between places in Los Angeles explains the ethnic enclaves that do not merge, regardless of the melting-pot appearance of the city. The tensions between racial and ethnic groups learning to share Los Angeles have been well publicized. More notable for visitors, however, is the rich cultural and culinary diversity this mix of peoples creates.

You can laze on a beach or soak up some of the world's greatest art collections. You can tour the movie studios and stars' homes or take the kids to Disneyland, Magic Mountain, or the Queen Mary/Spruce Goose. *You can shop luxurious Beverly Hills' Rodeo Drive or browse for hipper novelties on boutique-lined Melrose Avenue. The possibilities are endless—rent a boat to Catalina Island, watch the floats in Pasadena's Rose Parade, or dine on tacos, sushi, goat cheese pizza, or just plain hamburgers, hot dogs, and chili. You can experience the best in theater, music, and dance; world-class spectator sports; and a great outdoors that beckons nearly 365 days a year.*

Places to Go, Sights to See

Catalina Island, the island of song and legend, lies a bit more than 20 miles across the sea from Los Angeles. The island is known for the clear-blue waters surrounding it, warm sunny beaches, and the crescent-shaped harbor of Avalon. Inland there's hiking and mountain-bike riding over virtually unspoiled mountains and canyons, coves, and beaches. You reach the island via a two-hour cruise. Contact *Catalina Express* (tel. 800/257-2227) for departure schedules from San Pedro, Long Beach, and Redondo Beach.

Disneyland (Harbor Blvd. exit, I-5, tel. 714/999-4000), Walt Disney's land of fantasy, is even grander than it was when it opened in Anaheim in 1955. New rides, adventures, and attractions are added every year. From Fantasyland to Tomorrowland, Disneyland has many different shops, restaurants, and entertainment areas, but lines for rides can be long; to reduce the wait, plan to arrive early or late, midweek or off-season. A highlight for many visitors is the Electrical Parade and fireworks display presented on summer evenings.

Ethnic Los Angeles. As a major port of entry to the United States, Los Angeles boasts more ethnic diversity than any other city in the country. While every aspect of life here is colored by the culture brought by the newcomers—Hispanics from various Latin American countries, Filipinos, Japanese, Chinese, Vietnamese, Koreans—some communities are more accessible than others. Olivera Street, in the heart of downtown Los Angeles, now boasts a colorful Mexican marketplace, restaurants, and several historic buildings—including Old Plaza Church, Old Plaza Firehouse, and Avila Adobe. Little Tokyo, between 1st and San Pedro streets, is the cultural and commercial center for the Japanese community, with restaurants, sushi bars, shops, and Buddhist temples. Koreatown, Chinatown, Monterey Park (another Chinese community), Fairfax (the Jewish neighborhood), and East Los Angeles (one of the Latino neighborhoods) all have a wide variety of ethnic restaurants, shops, and cultural events.

Hollywood. It may not be the glitter town it once was, but even the name still evokes a bygone era of glamour and legendary movie stars. The corner of Hollywood and Vine *does* exist. The Walk of Fame lines both sides of Hollywood Boulevard from Gower to Sycamore and on Vine from Yucca to Sunset; the walk glitters with terrazzo and brass stars engraved with the names of more than 1,800 entertainment personalities. *Mann's Chinese Theater* (6925 Hollywood Blvd.), originally Grauman's, is where you'll find the names, foot, hand, hoof, or leg prints of famous stars eternalized in concrete in the entryway. To see how movies are made, there are two opportunities: *Paramount Pictures* (860 N. Gower St., Los Angeles, tel. 213/956-1777) offers two-hour weekday guided tours of production facilities and has a limited number of free tickets to shows being produced there. *Warner Bros. Studios* (4000 Warner Blvd., Burbank, tel. 818/954-1744) offers personalized VIP tours during the week, permitting visitors to watch live shooting wherever possible.

Knott's Berry Farm (8039 Beach Blvd., tel. 714/220-5200), in Buena Park, is one of the West's most popular attractions, with more than 165 rides, shops, and shows. Don't miss Mrs. Knott's Chicken Dinner Restaurant—it's as popular now as it was during the 1930s, when Walter Knott built the original "ghost town" to entertain diners waiting for a table.

Melrose Avenue between Highland Avenue and Doheny Drive is the best street for people watching in Los Angeles. The hippest of the hip hang out here in one-of-a-kind boutiques, chic restaurants, theaters, and exclusive clubs.

Rodeo Drive is the famed Beverly Hills shopping street. You'll find international stores such as Chanel, Gucci, Giorgio, and Alfred Dunhill, among many other luxury boutiques. *South Coast Plaza* (Bristol and Sunflower Sts., Costa Mesa, tel. 714/241–1700), in Orange County, has one of the largest concentrations of upscale retail stores in the world.

The Queen Mary (Pier J, tel. 310/435–3511), sitting smugly in Long Beach Harbor, can be quite disarming at first glance. The permanently moored *Queen Mary* is the largest passenger ship ever built. Restored to a semblance of her pre–World War II grandeur, she is available for tours and contains several restaurants. Visitors may even spend the night in the first-class cabins, now the *Queen Mary Hotel.* Housed in a 12-story aluminum dome a short walk away from the *Queen Mary* is the largest wooden aircraft ever built. Designed by Howard Hughes in 1942, *Spruce Goose* made its first and only flight in 1947. Displays surrounding the plane explain its history. Also on view are Hughes memorabilia and *Time Voyager,* a "multi-sensory entertainment."

Universal Studios Hollywood (100 Universal Pl., Universal City, tel. 818/508–9600) stretches across 400 acres, many of which are crossed in the enthusiastically narrated tram tour that takes visitors through a re-creation of the largest television and movie studio's backlots. Meet King Kong, the shark from *Jaws,* and E.T., or experience an earthquake or the parting of the Red Sea.

Museums

Craft and Folk Art Museum (5814 Wilshire Blvd., Los Angeles, tel. 213/937–5544) features changing exhibitions of contemporary crafts and traditional folk art from around the world. Six to eight major shows are planned each year.

George C. Page Museum of La Brea Discoveries (5801 Wilshire Blvd., Los Angeles, tel. 213/936–2230) contains fossils and bones recovered from La Brea Tar Pits, the world's richest source of Ice Age mammal and bird fossils. The glass-enclosed Paleontological Laboratory permits observation of the ongoing cleaning, identification, and cataloguing of fossils excavated from the nearby asphalt deposits.

Hollyhock House (4800 Hollywood Blvd., Hollywood, tel. 310/485–2433), built in 1921, was the first of a number of houses that Frank Lloyd Wright designed in the Los Angeles area. Now owned by the city (as is Barnsdall Park, where it is located), it has been restored and furnished with originals and reproductions of Wright's furniture.

Huntington Library, Art Collections, and Botanical Gardens (1151 Oxford Rd., San Marino, tel. 818/405–2100) displays 18th- and 19th-century British art, including Gainsborough's *Blue Boy.* The library exhibits rare books, prints, and manuscripts. Parklike grounds display more than 14,000 varieties of plants.

J. Paul Getty Museum (17985 Pacific Coast Hwy., Malibu, tel. 310/458–2003) is a re-creation of a 1st-century Roman villa, with formal gardens, major collections of Greek and Roman antiquities, paintings ranging from the 13th century to the late 19th century, and decorative arts. Parking reservations are required.

Los Angeles County Museum of Art (5905 Wilshire Blvd., Los Angeles, tel. 213/857–6222) is a complex of five buildings on the site of the La Brea Tar Pits that houses fine collections of paintings, sculpture, textiles, costumes, and decorative arts. Of particular interest to movie fans is the film series presented in the Leo S. Bing Theater featuring classic films.

Museum of Contemporary Art (250 S. Grand Ave., Los Angeles, tel. 213/626–6222) is a unique below-ground-level museum, designed by Arata Isozaki, featuring modern art from 1940 to the present. Originally designed by Frank Gehry as a temporary home for MOCA, the *Temporary Contemporary* (152 N. Central Ave., tel. 213/626–6222), in Little Tokyo, is now a permanent part of MOCA. A free shuttle bus runs between the two buildings.

Norton Simon Museum of Art (411 W. Colorado Blvd., Pasadena, tel. 818/449–3730) houses many famous Old Master artworks, including paintings by Rembrandt, Rubens, Raphael, and Goya. Highlights of the collection include bronze ballet dancers and horses by Degas, and works by Cézanne, Toulouse-Lautrec, Renoir, and van Gogh.

Southwest Museum (234 Museum Dr., Los Angeles, tel. 213/221–2163) contains extensive collections of Native American art and artifacts housed in a 1914 Mission Revival building. Exhibits include Navajo blankets, an incredible array of baskets, and a full-size Blackfoot tepee.

Performing Arts

Hollywood Bowl (2301 H Highland Ave., Los Angeles, tel. 213/850–2000), a 17,680-seat amphitheater, offers a summer season of outdoor concerts ranging from pop and jazz to classical. Elegant picnics are part of the experience here; bring your own or purchase one when you get there.

Music Center of Los Angeles (135 N. Grand Ave., Los Angeles, tel. 213/972–7211) is a three-theater complex: the large Dorothy Chandler Pavilion, where classical concerts, ballet, and opera are presented—resident companies include the Los Angeles Philharmonic Orchestra, the Los Angeles Music Center Opera, the Joffrey Ballet Los Angeles/New York, and the Los Angeles Master Chorale; the Mark Taper Forum, an intimate theater featuring regional productions, some of which land on Broadway; and Ahmanson Theater, which stages large musical productions.

Orange County Performing Arts Center (600 Town Center Dr., Costa Mesa, tel. 714/556–ARTS) presents musical theater, opera, dance, and classical and jazz concerts.

Spectator Sports

Baseball. The Los Angeles Dodgers play in *Dodger Stadium,* close to downtown Los Angeles (tel. 213/224–1500). The California Angels play at Anaheim Stadium (tel. 714/634–2000).

Basketball. The Los Angeles Lakers play in the *Great Western Forum* (tel. 310/419–3182) in Inglewood. The Los Angeles Clippers play at the *Los Angeles Sports Arena* (tel. 213/748–8000, ext. 339) in Exposition Park. University of California at Los Angeles plays in *Pauley Pavilion* (tel. 310/825–8699) on the UCLA campus; University of Southern California plays at the *Los Angeles Sports Arena* (tel. 213/743–GO–SC).

Football. The Los Angeles Raiders play in the *Memorial Coliseum* (tel. 310/322–5901) in Exposition Park. The Rams play at *Anaheim Stadium* (tel. 714/277–4748). The University of California at Los Angeles Bruins play at the *Rose Bowl* (tel. 818/449–4100) in Pasadena. The University of Southern California Trojans play in the *Memorial Coliseum* (tel. 213/743–GO–SC). A limited number of Rose Bowl tickets are available each year.

Hockey. The Los Angeles Kings play at the *Great Western Forum* (tel. 310/673–6003).

Horse Racing. Thoroughbred horse racing takes place at two local tracks: *Santa Anita* (tel. 818/574–7223) and *Hollywood Park* (tel. 310/419–1574).

Tourist Information

Anaheim Area Visitor and Convention Bureau (800 W. Katella Avenue, Box 4270, Anaheim, CA 92802, 714/999–8999); **Long Beach Area Convention and Visitors Council,** (3387 Long Beach Blvd., Long Beach, CA 90807, tel. 310/426–6773 or 800/4–LBSTAY); **Los Angeles Visitor and Convention Bureau** (699 S. Figueroa at 7th St., Los Angeles, CA 90017, tel. 213/689–8822).

Reservation Services

Bed & Breakfast Innkeepers of Southern California (Box 15425, Los Angeles, CA 90015–0385, tel. 800/424–0053); **Bed & Breakfast Los Angeles** (32074 Waterside Lane, Westlake, CA 91361, tel. 818/889–8870); **CoHost America's B & B** (Box 9302, Whittier, CA 90608, tel. 213/699–8427); **Eye Openers** (Box 694, Altadena, CA 91003, tel. 213/684–4428 or 818/797–2055).

Blue Lantern Inn

The Blue Lantern Inn is brand new, but it already has quite a following. This Cape Cod–style hotel is perched on a bluff above the Dana Point Marina in southern Orange County. One of the only inns around, it offers sweeping marina and ocean views from almost every room. You can watch as the more than 2,000 small boats move in and out of their slips, or keep an eye on the children as they explore a replica of the tall ship *Pilgrim*, immortalized by Richard Henry Dana in his book *Two Years Before the Mast*.

The Blue Lantern is operated by Four Sisters, which owns a number of inns and small hotels, mostly in northern California. Each guest room contains an unusually spacious bathroom; most have double sinks, showers, and whirlpool baths. The decor is contemporary; light mauve with accents in soft green and cream is a favorite color scheme. There's a tall mahogany four-poster bed in the Tower Suite; other rooms have brass, sleigh, or rattan beds. Wicker side chairs, small boudoir chairs, and a Queen Anne–style desk can be found in nearly every room, as well as armoires that conceal TV sets, and refrigerators stocked with complimentary soft drinks.

The lobby is set up with tables for two and four for the buffet-style breakfast. French doors lead to an outdoor sitting area, where many guests take coffee and the morning paper. The library, which contains a collection of books you might actually want to read, is where guests gather in the afternoons for wine and hors d'oeuvres.

Although visitors might be tempted to spend an entire weekend enjoying the beauty and comfort of the inn, the marina complex offers a number of activities. Bicycles are available for exploring the many trails that crisscross the surrounding hills. The innkeepers will make arrangements for sail- or powerboat charters or whale-watching excursions in season. They will also prepare a picnic basket for guests to enjoy at one of the two parks within walking distance of the inn. Guests also enjoy visiting the mission and the chic boutiques, art galleries, and antiques stores at San Juan Capistrano, just a 10-minute drive away.

Address: *34343 St. of the Blue Lantern, Dana Point, CA 92629, tel. 714/661–1304, fax 714/496–1483.*
Accommodations: *29 double rooms with bath.*
Amenities: *Robes, whirlpool tubs, refrigerators, TV, and phone in rooms, afternoon refreshments; fitness center; conference facilities; bicycles.*
Rates: *$125–$275; full breakfast. AE, MC, V.*
Restrictions: *No smoking, no pets.*

Casa Tropicana

Rick Anderson, a young building contractor, had a dream: to turn the somewhat seedy oceanfront of San Clemente into a showplace. The centerpiece would be his unique bed-and-breakfast inn. Casa Tropicana, the inn and restaurant he created and opened in 1990, has a young, beach-bum-casual ambience—the kind of place where guests are more likely to be parking their boogie boards than their BMWs.

The five-story, whitewashed Mediterranean-style inn sits on a narrow hillside across the street from the historic San Clemente pier. On a clear day, the view from some rooms goes all the way to Catalina Island. Right across the street is a prime surfing beach where most of the year surfers can be seen riding the breakers to shore. With the Tropicana Grill occupying the ground floor, guest rooms are located on the second, third, and fifth floors (Rick is on the fourth), each level with its own deck overlooking the ocean.

Every room offers the fulfillment of a different tropical fantasy. Out of Africa is the most popular. The oversize room easily fits a step-up four-poster bed topped with faux mosquito netting, and guests can soak in the double whirlpool tub while watching TV or enjoying the view through a peekaboo window. Other rooms are equally fantastic. Coral Reef has a bed with a peach rattan-clamshell headboard. Emerald Forest is cool and green with vines hanging from the ceiling. The Penthouse has a three-sided fireplace and a deck with outdoor Jacuzzi. Only the rooms facing the ocean have a view or much outside light; if you tend to be claustrophobic, take one of these.

The laid back atmosphere carries through to the Tropicana Grill, whose bar is tucked under a thatched roof. The reasonably priced menu offers Cabo swordfish tacos, chicken fajita salad, and Ragin' Cajun garlic ribs. Room service is available to guests from the restaurant beginning at 7:30 in the morning. Guests can select breakfast from the restaurant menu, have it delivered to their rooms or outdoor deck, or join early morning diners in the café.

Address: *610 Ave. Victoria, San Clemente, CA 92672, tel. 714/492–1234.*
Accommodations: *7 double rooms with bath, 2 housekeeping suites.*
Amenities: *Restaurant; TV, refrigerator, and phone in rooms, double whirlpool tub in 8 rooms, fireplace in 8 rooms; complimentary champagne, room service.*
Rates: *$120–$180, suites $240, penthouse $350; full breakfast. AE, MC, V.*
Restrictions: *Smoking outside only, no pets; 2-night minimum on weekends.*

Channel Road Inn

Originally the home of Thomas McCall, a pioneering Santa Monica businessman, this house was moved from a hilltop site to its current location tucked in a hillside of Santa Monica Canyon, one block from the beach. With the help of the local historical society, innkeeper Susan Zolla saved the Colonial Revival building from demolition and turned it into a gracious inn, one of the only within view of the beach in Los Angeles County.

The house is sheathed in blue shingles, a rarity in Los Angeles and for a Colonial Revival house. The architectural decoration inside is pure Craftsman. Windows are very large and abundant to take advantage of cool ocean breezes and bright sunlight. The honey-colored woodwork in the living room is unusually elegant, with moldings and baseboards carefully milled. Other woodwork has been painted white, which Susan says is historically accurate.

The decor covers a variety of styles, with a common thread of wicker throughout, including the dining room, library, and several of the guest rooms. Beds are the focal point: four-poster beds, pencil-post canopy beds, or sleigh beds. Special attention has been paid to the needs of guests, particularly business travelers who require phones or writing surfaces. Not all rooms, however, have comfortable chairs for extended sitting.

Several rooms have access to balconies or decks with views of the flowering hillside and a glimpse of the ocean. There's an attractive garden sitting area for people who want to relax at the inn, as well as robes and oversize towels for beachgoers or spa users.

The broad white-sand beach is just across Pacific Coast Highway; it's bordered on one side by a 30-mile-long bicycle path that stretches north to Malibu and south to Venice beach. The Venice portion of the path is a colorful carnival on weekends as crazily clad street musicians beat out tunes, vendors sell everything from food to art, and skaters zip by. The J. Paul Getty Museum, with its lovely gardens and superb collection specializing in ancient and French 18th-century art, is only a five-minute drive away.

Address: *219 Channel Rd., Santa Monica, CA 90402, tel. 310/459–1920, fax 310/454–9920.*
Accommodations: *12 double rooms with bath, 2 suites.*
Amenities: *Cable TV and phone in rooms, refrigerator in 2 rooms, VCR in 6 rooms; afternoon refreshments; outdoor hot tub, bicycles.*
Rates: *$95–$130, suites $165–$195; full breakfast. AE, MC, V.*
Restrictions: *Smoking outside only, no pets.*

Anaheim Country Inn

This 1910 "Princess" Anne, located on a quiet residential street, is convenient to Disneyland and the Anaheim Convention Center. It's the only inn in Anaheim, offering an intimate alternative to the hotels in the area. Innkeepers Marilyn Watson and Lois Ramont are longtime Anaheim residents who operated a restaurant here before opening the inn in 1983.

The architecture of the Princess Anne is less ornate than the earlier Queen Anne, so the innkeepers have kept the decor very simple. Furnishings are country style, with some oak pieces dating from the turn of the century. A spool bed, an old-fashioned sewing machine, a brass bed, and Oriental rugs on the floors help sustain the comfortable country atmosphere. The rooms upstairs connect with each other, so combinations are possible for families or couples traveling together. The inn is surrounded by a spacious garden, planted with roses and other flowers.

Address: *856 S. Walnut, Anaheim, CA 92802, tel. 714/778–0150 or 800/755–7801.*
Accommodations: *6 double rooms with bath, 4 double rooms share 2 baths.*
Amenities: *Afternoon refreshments; air-conditioning in 1 room, phone available in 3 rooms; hot tub; croquet; parking.*
Rates: *$55–$100; full breakfast. AE, MC, V.*
Restrictions: *Smoking outside only, no pets.*

Christmas House

Built by wealthy ranchers in 1904, this Queen Anne mansion was known as the Christmas House because of the many lavish holiday parties held there. Indeed, when Jay and Janice Ilsly opened the inn in 1985, they followed tradition and held a Christmas party of their own.

This is an inviting mansion, with turrets, gables, red and green stained-glass windows, wide sweeping verandas, and seven fireplaces. Dark wood paneling is prominent inside, with a grand staircase leading to the second floor. There are some impressive antiques, such as a 150-year-old brass bed. Many business travelers find the inn a convenient address— it's near the Ontario airport—but Christmas House also attracts leisure travelers with its special events: murder-mystery weekends, annual Christmas parties, and a follow-the-actors production of *A Christmas Carol.*

Address: *9240 Archibald Ave., Rancho Cucamonga, CA 91730, tel. 714/980–6450.*
Accommodations: *2 double rooms with bath, 3 double rooms share bath, 2 suites.*
Amenities: *Air-conditioning; fireplace in 4 rooms, TV available in rooms; afternoon refreshments; private outdoor hot tubs.*
Rates: *$55–$125; full breakfast on weekends, Continental breakfast weekdays. AE, D, MC, V.*
Restrictions: *Smoking outside only, no pets.*

Eiler's Inn

Henk Wirtz and his family came to the United States from Germany 12 years ago expressly to open one of the first bed-and-breakfast inns in southern California, in the artsy town of Laguna Beach. He chose a building that had a checkered life dating from the 1930s, when families visiting the beach used its small rooms as headquarters for the day. Later, during the '60s and '70s, it became a rooming house for hippies—including Timothy Leary.

Henk made a lot of changes, creating a very proper European-style inn, complete with lace curtains and a flower-filled courtyard where breakfast is served. The rooms, surrounding the courtyard on two levels, are small, simply furnished and decorated, usually with a double bed and a chair or two; there's an occasional carved armoire or dresser. The bathrooms are small and functional.

Henk came, he said, for the same reasons that guests continue to come—for the town's lovely beachside setting, for the ambience of an artists' colony, and because it's a good place to nourish a creative spirit.

Address: *741 S. Coast Hwy., Laguna Beach, CA 92651, tel. 714/494–3004.*
Accommodations: *11 double rooms with bath, 1 housekeeping suite.*
Amenities: *TV in suite.*
Rates: *$100–$175; Continental breakfast. AE, MC, V.*
Restrictions: *No pets; 2-night minimum on weekends.*

Inn on Mt. Ada

Chewing gum magnate William Wrigley, Jr., built this impressive Georgian Colonial mansion in 1921 as his Catalina Island summer home. The highest residential spot on the island, it has a stunning view of Avalon Harbor, the coastline, and the mountains beyond from nearly every room.

For all its grandeur, Wrigley furnished the home so his family and guests would feel comfortable. Susie Griffin and Marlene McAdam, who transformed the millionaire's mansion into an inn in 1986, maintained that feeling. Furnishings are comfortable rather than elegant: overstuffed sofas and wing chairs in the living room, natural wicker in the downstairs den. The rooms range from spacious to small, but all offer a sea view. Full meal service is included. The inn offers not only a stunning location but also the sort of pampering that a millionaire would require: privacy and discreet attention to detail. Since no private cars are permitted on the island, guests are provided with golf carts for transportation.

Address: *398 Wrigley Rd., Box 2560, Avalon, CA 90704, tel. 310/510–2030.*
Accommodations: *4 double rooms with bath, 2 suites.*
Amenities: *Fireplace in 4 rooms, robes, TV available.*
Rates: *$290–$490, suites $490–$580; AP. AE, MC, V.*
Restrictions: *Smoking outside only, no pets; 2-night minimum on weekends and holidays.*

Little Inn on the Bay

This inn with a New England ambience is located right alongside the marina in Newport Harbor. The two-story building dates from the 1950s, when it was the Lido Shores Hotel—thus the inn wraps around the pool in period style; the wind-protected pool area is inviting even on warm winter days. Many guests opt to spend their entire stay at the Little Inn poolside, from the moment they pick up their breakfast trays until evening, when owner Herrick Hanson serves refreshments.

The rooms are decorated with an eye toward comfort. There are plaid wingback chairs and sofas, dark wooden game tables and chairs, all with a slightly nautical theme. The inn, by the way, is the best place in town from which to watch the annual Newport Harbor Christmas boat parade; the flotilla of brightly lit boats turns right in front of the building.

Address: *617 Lido Park Dr., Newport Beach, CA 92663, tel. 714/673-8800, 800/538-4466, 800/438-4466 in CA, fax 714/673-1500.*
Accommodations: *21 double rooms with baths, 8 housekeeping suites.*
Amenities: *Air-conditioning, TV and phones in rooms; outdoor swimming pool, free bay cruises.*
Rates: *$98–$180; Continental breakfast. AE, D, DC, MC, V.*
Restrictions: *Smoking outside only, no pets; 2-night minimum on holidays.*

Salisbury House

For their new home, Jay and Sue German chose a 1901 Craftsman with some Victorian touches: a curved bay window in the dining room and an abundance of stained-glass windows. There are lots of firwood moldings, a built-in china closet in the dining room, dark polished floors, and wainscoting.

All the guest rooms are quite large and comfortable. There is a white iron bed in the Blue Room and a brass bed and braided rugs in the Attic Suite, which is finished with redwood siding. It also has a clawfoot tub positioned so that the bather can look out over the bird-filled trees. The inn's common areas include a living room, where a fire crackles most of the year, and a striking formal dining room, where Sue serves an imaginative breakfast featuring zucchini pancakes or potato frittata. A self-described "foodie," she says that the local Chinese, Korean, Mexican, Vietnamese, and Italian restaurants inspire her in the kitchen.

Address: *2273 W. 20th St., Los Angeles, CA 90018, tel. 213/737-7817.*
Accommodations: *2 double rooms with baths, 2 double rooms share bath.*
Amenities: *Phone, TV, and air-conditioning in attic room, refrigerator in all rooms; afternoon refreshments.*
Rates: *$70–$95; full breakfast. AE, MC, V.*
Restrictions: *Smoking outside only, no pets.*

Terrace Manor

This inn has a history that's intertwined with that of Los Angeles and Hollywood. The house had been the 1920s home of Los Angeles mayor John C. Porter and later actress Susan Seaforth. The face of innkeeper Sandy Spillman may be familiar to TV viewers; he's an actor who has appeared in numerous shows and commercials. A striking Tudor on the outside, the inn has Craftsman-style tiger oak wainscoting in the common rooms. The heavy beamed ceilings, and walls painted deep shades of green, red, and pink, give the house a cool, dark ambience. Windows contain original green-and-red stained glass. The bedrooms on the second floor are unusually large, with ample-size bathrooms. Sandy, who is also a magician, will make arrangements for guests to visit the Magic Castle, a private club for magicians.

The Spillmans recently acquired the historic Powers House next door; it's now home to Salisbury Manor, a restaurant that's popular locally for its unusual California cuisine and gracious service.

Address: *1353 Alvarado Terrace, Los Angeles, CA 90005, tel. 213/381-1478.*
Accommodations: *4 double rooms with bath, 1 suite.*
Amenities: *Air-conditioning in 1 bedroom; passes to Magic Castle.*
Rates: *$70-$100; full breakfast. AE, DC, MC, V.*
Restrictions: *Smoking outside only, no pets.*

Central Coast
From Santa Barbara to San Simeon

The drive along California's Central Coast is one of the most rewarding in the state, and is the scenic California that most visitors have come to see. Except for a few smallish cities—Ventura and Santa Barbara in the south and San Luis Obispo in the north—this is a rural excursion of nearly 200 miles of rolling golden oak-studded hills and wave-washed beaches.

Highway 101, one of the state's great north–south thoroughfares, is also one of its most historic. The route follows the original El Camino Real (Kings Road) forged by the Spanish padres that leads from one mission to another and is now marked by a series of roadside bells.

Starting in the south the highway passes through Ventura, gateway to the Channel Islands National Park. It hugs the coast as it moves north toward Santa Barbara. With its Spanish-style architecture, fine restaurants, and collection of outstanding bed-and-breakfast inns, Santa Barbara has become a popular weekend destination for work-weary Angelinos. Santa Barbara strives to preserve its Mediterranean ambience, as a walk among the red-tile-roofed shops along State Street reveals.

From Santa Barbara the highway heads north along the coast, skirting a number of lovely beaches at El Capitan, Refugio, and Gaviota. Moving inland at San Marcos, it passes through the lovely Santa Ynez Valley, where wine tasting and bike riding on tranquil country lanes are two popular pursuits. This is also home of ultratouristy Solvang, which has a Danish theme and an array of bakeries and gift shops.

The highway touches the coast again at a place locals call the Five Cities. Here visitors can explore miles of wide hard-packed beaches and fluffy white sand dunes; these beach communities are popular with clam diggers, skin divers, and anglers.

San Luis Obispo, just a few miles up the coast, offers a number of surprises. A laid-back university town, it's the home of California Polytechnic University and has an attractive old-fashioned downtown that reveals its Spanish heritage. Like the area north of Santa Barbara, this is wine country.

Cambria, a few miles north along the coast, is the gateway to Hearst Castle and has long been a stopover for visitors to La Cuesta Encantada. It's also developed as an artists' colony, with many local artists specializing in creating luminous glass objects. Cambria also boasts a number of bed-and-breakfast inns as well as a collection of fine restaurants.

No trip to the Central Coast would be complete without a visit to William Randolph Hearst's castle on the hill at San Simeon. With money from his vast publishing empire, Hearst devoted more than 30 years to building the Italian-Spanish-Moorish-French-style castle with its acres of paintings, sculptures, and other European artwork; gardens; marble swimming pools; lavish dining room; and guest houses that are almost as opulent.

Places to Go, Sights to See

Channel Islands National Park (1901 Spinnaker Dr., Ventura 93001, tel. 805/658–5730) consists of five offshore islands and a visitor center at Ventura Harbor. *Island Packers* (tel. 805/642–1393) offers day-long boat trips to the islands.

Hearst San Simeon Historical Monument (San Simeon State Park, 750 Hearst Castle Rd., San Simeon 93452, tel. 805/927–2020; for tour reservations, tel. 800/444–7275) consists of the famed castle on the hill, 123 acres of pools, gardens, terraces, and guest houses built over three decades by William Randolph Hearst. Half- and three-hour tours are available year-round; the garden tour is offered April through October.

Missions. *La Purisima Mission* (2295 Purisima Rd., Lompoc 93436, tel. 805/733–3713) is the most completely restored mission in the state, illustrating secular as well as religious life at the missions. In this remote setting, which vividly evokes the lives of early settlers, costumed docents demonstrate crafts, including weaving and bread and candle making. *Mission Santa Barbara* (Laguna and Los Olivos Sts., Santa Barbara 93105, tel. 805/682–4149) is known as the Queen of the Missions for its Spanish Renaissance architecture, serene gardens, quiet courtyard, and exhibits of embroidered vestments and illuminated manuscripts.

Santa Barbara County Courthouse (Anacapa and Anapamu Sts., Santa Barbara 93101, tel. 805/962–6464) is a Spanish-Moorish palace with murals, painted ceilings, massive doors, balconies, and Tunisian tiles. Tours are given Tuesday through Saturday.

Santa Barbara Wine Country (Santa Barbara County Vintner's Association, Box 1558, Santa Ynez 93460–1558, tel. 805/688–0881) is actually located in the rolling hillsides of the Santa Ynez Valley. More than 20 wineries along Highways 154 and 176 offer tours and tastings; many also have picnic facilities and schedule special dinners.

Restaurants

Ian's (tel. 805/927–8649) in Cambria offers elegant dining and an eclectic menu featuring light California cuisine. Santa Barbara's **La Super-Rica Taco** (tel. 805/963–4940) is an unsigned corner taco stand where the line always stretches out the door. Also in Santa Barbara, **Louie's** (tel. 805/963–7003) offers patio dining at the Upham Hotel, convenient to many inns. The menu features classic French and nouvelle California cuisines. **Pane E Vino** (tel. 805/969–9274) in Montecito has generated a following for sophisticated Italian cuisine, especially pasta. **Paoli's Italian Country Kitchen** (tel. 805/688–9966) in Solvang serves pasta, pizza, chicken, and seafood.

Tourist Information

San Luis Obispo County Visitors and Convention Bureau (1041 Chorro St., Suite E, San Luis Obispo 93401, tel. 800/634–1414); **Santa Barbara Conference and Visitors Bureau** (510A State St., Santa Barbara 93101, tel. 800/927–4688).

Reservation Services

Bed and Breakfast Innkeepers of Southern California (Box 15425, Los Angeles 90015–0385, tel. 800/284–INNS); **Santa Barbara Bed and Breakfast Innkeepers Guild** (Box 90734, Santa Barbara 93190–0734, tel. 800/776–9176).

The Blue Whale Inn

Like many southern Californians, Fred Ushijima had been visiting the town of Cambria regularly for years, attracted by the laid-back beachfront atmosphere, good restaurants, and the shops and galleries of a growing artists' colony. Cambria's proximity to the Hearst Castle at San Simeon has always meant large numbers of visitors, but the village hasn't become touristy or overdeveloped.

Fred decided to sink roots in Cambria, and he found the perfect location on a triangular point of land jutting out to the sea along Moonstone Beach Drive. A visual delight, the Blue Whale consists of six guest rooms stepped back from the ocean at such an angle that each captures a bit of the view (the best views, surprisingly, are from the rooms farthest back). At the front of the inn is a spacious living room furnished with overstuffed sofas and chairs and a wood-burning stove; it adjoins the dining area, and the two together create a great room with a wall of windows revealing the everchanging ocean vista.

A tiny Japanese-style garden, created by Fred, separates the guest rooms from the parking lot. Planted with a colorful selection of native plants—including lupine, coreapsis, thyme, and westringa—the garden is punctuated by a series of stepping-stones that lead from the parking area to the decks in front of the guest rooms. Guests often contemplate the beauty of nature while sitting on the garden's wooden bench or watching its tumbling waterfall.

In sharp contrast to the expansive views of sea and sky outside, the inn's interior is a riot of wallpapers and flowered fabrics, mostly in shades of blue. Appointments are comfortable: step-up canopy beds, love seats, desks, a coffee table and side chair in each room. Skylights punctuate each vaulted ceiling. Bathrooms, also skylit, have adjacent dressing areas complete with a sink set into a long vanity.

Although Fred is often at the inn sharing his dining suggestions with guests ("a walking menu," one guest observed), John and Nancy Young are the day-to-day innkeepers. John has earned quite a reputation for his breakfasts, particularly the gingerbread pancakes with lemon sauce.

Address: *6736 Moonstone Beach Dr., Cambria, CA 93428, tel. 805/927-4647.*
Accommodations: *6 double rooms with bath.*
Amenities: *Fireplace, refrigerator, TV, phone; afternoon refreshments; gift shop.*
Rates: *$130–$165; full breakfast. MC, V.*
Restrictions: *Smoking outside only; no pets; 2-night minimum on weekends and holidays.*

Old Yacht Club Inn

When former school administrators Nancy Donaldson and Lu Caruso and teacher Sandy Hunt opened Santa Barbara's first bed-and-breakfast in 1980, they set out to provide a homey atmosphere in which guests would feel comfortable putting their feet up—and so pampered that they'd want to return again and again. In addition, there would be the outstanding food prepared by Nancy, a member of the American Wine and Food Institute.

Initially the inn consisted of only the historic 1912 Craftsman house with its broad porches, tiny balcony across the front, redbrick fireplace, and colorful gardens. Just a block from the beach, it had been built as a private home, and during the 1920s served as the headquarters for the Santa Barbara Yacht Club. In 1983 the innkeepers acquired the more spacious house next door, which they transformed into the Hitchcock House.

The Hitchcock is a monument to the families of the innkeepers, with its four rooms named and decorated to honor parents and grandparents. The Julia Metelmann is decorated with life-size photographs of the mother of a former inn partner. The photographs depict Julia as a young pioneer in South Dakota, and furnishings include a red lacquer Chinese chest that once belonged to her.

There are five rooms in the main house, four on the second floor, and one downstairs. The upstairs rooms offer a light and airy ambience. In the two front-facing rooms French doors open onto a balcony where guests can sip wine while taking in the afternoon sun. Downstairs, the sunny Captain's Corner opens onto a private patio.

Breakfast and Saturday night dinners are served in the inn's dining/living room. Nancy uses fresh local ingredients in her five-course gourmet dinners: shrimp from the bay, artichokes from nearby fields, and sorrel grown in the backyard. Breakfast, usually prepared by Sandy, features the lightest of light omelets, home-baked breads, and fresh fruit.

Address: *431 Corona del Mar Dr., Santa Barbara, CA 93103, tel. 805/962–1277.*
Accommodations: *8 rooms with bath, 1 suite.*
Amenities: *Phone in rooms, TV on request, evening refreshments, whirlpool tub in 1 room; dinner served to guests on Sat. nights (about $25); golf privileges at local country club; bicycles, beach towels, chairs.*
Rates: *$75–$135; full breakfast. AE, D, MC, V.*
Restrictions: *No smoking in guest rooms, no pets; 2-night minimum on weekends.*

The Parsonage

Hilde Michelmore is something of a pioneer: In 1981, she opened one of Santa Barbara's first bed-and-breakfasts. "At the time there weren't many around, and nobody was sure exactly what they were." A realtor showed her the 1892 onetime home of the parson of nearby Trinity Episcopal Church. It had recently been renovated, but it looked awful. "It was a school for problem children," Hilde explained. But the big, boxy, hillside three-story Queen Anne worked its magic on her. "I couldn't stop thinking about the house. I loved the floor-to-ceiling windows in the living room, the many bay windows in the upstairs rooms with their beautiful views, the light and airy feeling about the place. Within a month, I'd moved in."

Hilde had been collecting antiques for years, picking up French and English pieces from dealers in Los Angeles, and many of them now grace the rooms of The Parsonage: a Louis XIV dresser and mirror, two side tables, and some unusual wall sconces in the Versailles Room; a Victorian settee in the Los Flores Room; the antique washstand and unusual pedestal sink in the Honeymoon Suite. There are Oriental carpets in nearly every room.

The Honeymoon Suite at The Parsonage may be one of the most romantic accommodations in Santa Barbara. A huge three-room suite that wraps around a front corner of the house, it offers stunning views of the ocean, the city, and the mountains; it also has a separate solarium. Good ocean views can be had from the bay windows of the Las Flores, and the other two second-story rooms have good mountain views.

Common areas consist of the large, bright living room, where Hilde's prize green and purple Oriental rug graces the floor. This room is filled with an ever-changing parade of antiques from her collection. "I like to move things around," she explained.

Weather permitting—which is most of the time—breakfast is served on bone china on the outdoor deck or in the gazebo. The fairly formal meal might consist of Hilde's special French toast, jelly–cheese soufflés, or blueberry pancakes.

Address: *1600 Olive St., Santa Barbara, CA 93101, tel. 805/962-9336.*
Accommodations: *5 rooms with bath, 1 suite.*
Amenities: *Afternoon refreshments.*
Rates: *$85–$115, suite $160; full breakfast. AE, MC, V.*
Restrictions: *Smoking outside only, no pets; 2-night minimum on weekends, 3-night minimum on holidays.*

Union Hotel/ Victorian Mansion

In the tiny Old West outpost of Los Alamos, some 50 miles north of Santa Barbara, these two inns present a study in fantasy fulfillment. The Union Hotel, a onetime Wells Fargo stagecoach station dating from 1880, was renovated by Dick Langdon in 1970 and turned into one of the first bed-and-breakfasts in California. The whimsical Old West atmosphere, which begins in the lobby peopled with mannequins costumed in frontier finery, is carried into the saloon with its mahogany ping-pong table supported by marble statues, and continues in the bedrooms with their French and patriotic wallpapers.

In the neighboring yellow three-story 1864 Mansion, mere whimsy gives way to flat-out fantasy. Dick has created a sort of Disneyland for adults here. Take the Egyptian Room, designed to make a couple feel like Antony and Cleopatra camping out in the desert. A step-up white bed, canopied with gauze, stands in the middle of the room facing a wall-size mural of a desert. Walls are draped with Near East–motif fabrics, there's a step-up hot tub, and a marble-faced fireplace flanked by floor cushions. The bathroom door is a life-size statue of King Tut, opened by tugging his beard, and the bathroom itself resembles the inside of a pyramid. Dick supplies hooded desert robes, backgammon, computer-controlled background music, video-

tapes of *Lawrence of Arabia* and *The Wind and the Lion.*

Other rooms are in equally fantastic style: Roman, Gypsy, Pirate, '50s Drive-In, and French—each with fitting murals, bed, theme robes, music, movies, games, and menus. Breakfast is delivered to the theme rooms through lockers concealed in the walls.

Dick, who moved to Los Alamos 20 years ago, has built a community of artists and artisans who continue to give life to his fantasy. Many live at the inn while working on new projects: a hedge-maze connecting the two inns; a dry-docked 67-foot Danish yawl; and a tree house.

Address: *362 Bell St., Box 616, Los Alamos, CA 93440, tel. 805/344–2744.*
Accommodations: *Hotel: 3 rooms with bath, 10 rooms with sinks share 2 baths. Mansion: 6 rooms with bath.*
Amenities: *In mansion: TV with VCR, tapes, phone, hot tub, fireplace, robes, refrigerator in rooms; restaurant, saloon; shuffleboard, ping-pong, swimming pool; spa in gazebo; maze.*
Rates: *Hotel $80–$100, mansion $200; full breakfast. AE, MC, V.*
Restrictions: *No pets, hotel and restaurant open Fri., Sat., Sun. only.*

Ballard Inn

T his gray and white updated Cape Cod–style inn looks out of place in the Santa Ynez Valley, home of sprawling horse ranches and the up-and-coming wineries of Santa Barbara County. Standing on a corner in the tiny town of Ballard, the Ballard Inn was built in 1985 by a group of Hollywood celebrities and is now owned by Santa Barbara restaurateur Steve Hyslop and partner Larry Stone.

Each room is decorated to illustrate different aspects of local lore. One room feels like a frontiersman's mountain cabin, with a rough stone fireplace and rustic wooden furnishings; another recalls stagecoach days, with a collection of cowboy hats and early photographs of local cattle ranches; another room honors a pair of sister schoolteachers, with a platform rocker, wing chair, and brass chandelier. The common rooms feature comfortable, overstuffed sofas in the living room; and Old West ambience prevails in the Stage-coach room.

Address: *2436 Baseline Ave., Ballard, CA 93463, tel. 805/688–7770 or 800/638–2466.*
Accommodations: *15 double rooms with bath.*
Amenities: *Air-conditioning, fireplace in 7 rooms; afternoon wine tasting; bicycle rentals, carriage rides extra.*
Rates: *$155–$185; full breakfast. MC, V.*
Restrictions: *Smoking outside only, no pets; 2-night minimum on weekends.*

Bath Street Inn

A t first glance, the Bath Street Inn, an 1870s Victorian cottage on a quiet street a few blocks off Santa Barbara's main drag, looks deceptively small. There's no clue that it's so much larger than it appears, thanks to a recent renovation and expansion.

Guest rooms are located upstairs, with those on the third floor filling odd-shaped spaces created by the steep pitch of the roof and its many eaves and gables. The decor throughout is predominantly Victorian, with comfortable, overstuffed sofas, wing chairs, canopy beds, reading nooks, and cabbage-rose wallpaper patterns. "People say it reminds them of their mother's house," remarks Bath Street's creator, Susan Brown, one of Santa Barbara's first innkeepers.

Guests have the use of the entire house, including the garden out back. As pleasant as it is to linger in, this inn makes a convenient home base for excursions to the beach, or for exploring the chic shops that line nearby State Street.

Address: *1720 Bath St., Santa Barbara, CA 93101, tel. 805/682–9680 or 800/788–BATH; 800/549–BATH in CA.*
Accommodations: *7 rooms with bath.*
Amenities: *Afternoon refreshments; bicycles.*
Rates: *$90–$115; full breakfast. AE, MC, V.*
Restrictions: *Smoking outside only, no pets; 2-night minimum on weekends.*

Bayberry Inn

Carlton Wagner, a renowned interior designer, color consultant, and one of the owners of the Bayberry, has created an inn reminiscent of the gilded age just after World War I within this shingle-covered late-19th-century building in Santa Barbara. Throughout you'll find an abundance of silk, crystal, and porcelains. The dining room ceiling is draped in yard after yard of soft pink silk with folds brought together in the center by a crystal chandelier. The walls in the dining room are covered by beveled mirrors. Beds are canopied in heavy fabric, with a crystal chandelier in the center of the canopy. The rooms tend to be cozy, with the dramatic bed as the main feature; lighting in most rooms is subdued, creating a romantic mood.

Wagner and his partner Keith Pomeroy specialize in pampering guests. Pomeroy, whose background is in catering, prepares breakfasts as pretty as they are tasty, served on fine china in the opulent dining room.

Address: *111 W. Valerio St., Santa Barbara, CA 93101, tel. 905/692–3199.*
Accommodations: *8 double rooms with bath.*
Amenities: *Robes, fireplace in 3 rooms, whirlpool tub in 1 room, phone in 4 rooms; afternoon refreshments; guest refrigerator; TV on request; bicycles, croquet, badminton.*
Rates: *$85–$135; full breakfast.*
Restrictions: *No smoking; 2-night minimum on weekends.*

Garden Street Inn

Nostalgia is the theme at this Stick Style Italianate inn just a block from Mission San Luis Obispo and only a few steps from the town's Old California–style downtown. Innkeepers Dan and Kathy Smith retained the 1887 structure's high ceilings, skylighted grand staircase, 8-foot-tall wooden doors, stained glass, and squared bay windows. The thematic decor draws from the Smiths' family histories as well as that of the community. The Field of Dreams Room is dedicated to Kathy's sportswriter father and contains baseball memorabilia; Walden, sporting family wood carvings and New Zealand art, honors Dan's dad, who loved the outdoors; and the Ah Louis Room, containing an antique Oriental curio cabinet, celebrates an early Chinese labor leader

who organized Central Coast railroad workers.

The couple are a good source of information about local history, beaches, restaurants, and the Thursday night farmers' market that takes place nearby.

Address: *1212 Garden St., San Luis Obispo, CA 93401, tel. 805/545–9802.*
Accommodations: *9 double rooms with bath, 4 suites.*
Amenities: *Afternoon refreshments; air-conditioning, radio with tape deck in rooms, fireplace in 5 rooms, whirlpool tubs in 6 rooms.*
Rates: *$80–$120, suites $140–$166; full breakfast. AE, MC, V.*
Restrictions: *Smoking outside only, no pets; 2-night minimum on holiday weekends.*

Inn at Summer Hill

The best-known landmark in Summerland, a small seaside town just south of Santa Barbara, has long been the Big Yellow House restaurant, but the recent opening of the Inn on Summer Hill may change the status quo. Built as a showcase for the talents of interior designer Mabel Schults, the newly constructed Craftsman-style inn consists of two long, narrow buildings with rooms on the first and second floors, each with a motel-style private entrance.

All rooms have private balconies and ocean views, and are lavishly decorated—practically overflowing with furniture, much of it rattan with floral fabrics. White pine is used in the ceilings, wainscoting, paneling, and most of the furniture. Guest rooms on the second level have pine-paneled vaulted ceilings, feel larger, and seem to get less highway noise.

Address: *2520 Lillie Ave., Box 376, Summerland, CA 93067, tel. 805/969–9998 or 800/845–5566, fax 805/969–9998.*
Accommodations: *15 rooms with bath, 1 suite.*
Amenities: *Afternoon and evening refreshments; air-conditioning, TV with VCP and 2 phones, fireplace, refrigerator, robes, hair dryer, and ironing board in rooms; spa.*
Rates: *$145–$175, suite $240; full breakfast. AE, MC, V.*
Restrictions: *Smoking outside only, no pets; 2-night minimum on weekends and holidays.*

J. Patrick House

This inn is set on a pine-shaded acre above East Village Cambria, in an area known as lodge hill, and is convenient to shops, galleries, and restaurants, though it's some distance from the beach. The inn consists of two buildings connected by a garden and a trellised arbor. The front building is a contemporary log cabin, where innkeeper Molly Lynch greets guests, tends to the living room fireplace, and cooks up the unusual breads served at breakfast.

There is one bright, spacious guest room upstairs, and the remaining rooms and a separate guest sitting room are in the cedar-sided two-story building out back. Each of the rooms is named for a county in Ireland: Cork, Clare, Galway, Dublin.

Furnishings are simple and eclectic. Beds are of wicker, willow, or painted wood, and guest rooms are adorned with floral wallpapers and spreads. Flowers abound, and woodland bouquets are tucked into every corner throughout the inn—in rooms, on tables in hallways, on windowsills. Each room has a window seat with a garden view.

Address: *2990 Burton Dr., Cambria, CA 93428, tel. 805/927–3812.*
Accommodations: *8 rooms with bath.*
Amenities: *Fireplace or wood-burning stove in rooms; afternoon refreshments; guest refrigerator.*
Rates: *$100–$120; Continental breakfast. MC, V.*
Restrictions: *No smoking, no pets.*

La Mer

La Mer offers a bit of European ambience in a distinctly southern California seaside setting. Presided over by German-born Gisela Baida, the inn is visible from afar on its perch high up on a hillside and is decorated with a collection of European flags. The inn has five rooms, each decorated in a theme of a different European country. The French Room is powder blue, with an antique carved walnut bed and a ceiling-tall ficus tree. The Norwegian Room has a nautical theme, with a ship's bed, wood paneling, and brass fixtures in the bathroom. The bright and airy rooms are surrounded by balconies and porches.

Gisela serves a sumptuous Bavarian-style breakfast in the parlor, with its view of the ocean; the buffet features cheeses and Black Forest ham in addition to fruit, pastries, and beverages. She promotes the inn as a romantic midweek getaway by offering attractive packages that include dinners, visits to nearby Wheeler Hot Springs, and therapeutic massages.

Address: *411 Poli St., Ventura, CA 93001, tel. 805/643–3600.*
Accommodations: *5 rooms with bath.*
Amenities: *Old-fashioned radio in rooms, fireplace in 1 room; afternoon refreshments; beach towels; antique carriage rides extra, picnic baskets extra.*
Rates: *$105–$155, full breakfast. MC, V.*
Restrictions: *Smoking outside only, no pets.*

Rose Victorian Inn

Roses and romance are the dual themes at the Rose Victorian Inn, a striking 1885 Stick Style house that has become a hideaway for many Hollywood celebrities. On the outskirts of Arroyo Grande, a small farming community about 100 miles north of Santa Barbara, the inn offers seclusion, comfortable rooms, a popular restaurant, and the warm family feeling created by innkeeper Diana Cox. The building is surrounded by lush gardens containing a 30-foot rose arbor and a gazebo. The five rooms in the main house make up the original inn and are simply furnished, decorated in earth tones. The rooms in the carriage house are sunnier and more contemporary in decor, featuring big, bright floral-bouquet prints on the walls and furnishings.

Breakfast features ample servings of eggs Benedict and mimosas. A popular wedding site, this inn is not only a good place for hiding out, but also for exploring, since it's near Pismo Beach, where there's good clamming, and is close to Oceano, known for its massive white sand dunes.

Address: *789 Valley Rd., Arroyo Grande, CA 93420, tel. 805/481–5566.*
Accommodations: *7 rooms with bath, 4 rooms share 2 baths.*
Amenities: *Restaurant, afternoon refreshments.*
Rates: *$130–$175 MAP. MC, V.*
Restrictions: *Smoking outside and in restaurant only, no pets; 2-night minimum on weekends. Inn closed Mon.–Wed.*

Simpson House Inn

The very Victorian Simpson House Inn seems a bit out of place in Spanish-style Santa Barbara. This 1870s Folk Victorian house is deliberately British in character because Scotsman Robert Simpson built it to remind him of his homeland. Now presided over by innkeeper Gillean Wilson, a native of England, the house is set amid an acre of English gardens. Guests especially enjoy the wraparound verandas furnished with white wicker, which is adorned with blue linens and cushions.

The rooms are surprisingly large, bright, and appealing; two have big private decks reached through lace-curtain-covered French doors. The color scheme throughout the inn is bright and bold, particularly the electric blue in the sitting rooms and the deep, dark mauve walls in the dining room. Antiques abound: tapestry settees and chaise longues, Victorian armchairs, brass or iron beds, a collection of china teacups.

Address: *121 E. Arrellaga St., Santa Barbara, CA 93101, tel. 805/963-7067 or 800/676-1280.*
Accommodations: *6 rooms with bath.*
Amenities: *Air-conditioning in 1 room, robes; afternoon refreshments; bicycles, beach chairs, towels; croquet.*
Rates: *$95–185; full breakfast. AE, MC, V.*
Restrictions: *Smoking outside only, no pets; 2-night minimum on weekends, 3-night minimum on holidays.*

Monterey Bay

A semicircle about 90 miles across, Monterey Bay arcs into the California coast at a point about two hours' drive south of the San Francisco Bay area. Santa Cruz sits at the northern end of the curve, and the Monterey Peninsula, containing Monterey, Pacific Grove, and Carmel, occupies the southern portion. In between, Highway 1 cruises along the coastline, passing windswept beaches piled high with sand dunes. Along the route are fields of artichoke plants, the towns of Watsonville and Castroville, and Fort Ord, the army base where millions of GIs got their basic training.

A beneficent climate, stunning scenery, and the sweep of history have combined to bring visitors to this area for hundreds of years. Although evidence suggests that Native Americans lived here 10,000 years ago, the first written records date from 1542, when Portuguese explorer Joao Rodrigues Cabrillo sighted the beaches and pine forests where Carmel now lies. The Spanish later settled here, building missions in Carmel and Santa Cruz, and eventually naming Monterey the capital of Alta California. Monterey remained the center of government for California until 1850, when Sacramento became the state capital upon California's admission to the Union.

During the late 1800s, the cool summers attracted a seasonal colony of Methodists who came to Pacific Grove on retreat; they later built the Victorian homes for which the town is now famous. At about the same time, wealthy Easterners discovered Monterey's splendid scenery and mansions sprang up along Pacific Grove and Pebble Beach.

The Monterey Bay area has attracted artists and writers for more than a century. The best known on the long list of names include novelists Robert Louis Stevenson, Mary Austin, and John Steinbeck; poet Robinson Jeffers; and photographers Edward Weston and Ansel Adams. Carmel's heritage as an art colony lives on in dozens of art galleries scattered throughout the town.

As Monterey was becoming a mecca for artists and the wealthy, Santa Cruz was developing as a working community with logging, fishing, tanning, and farming the major industries. The arrival of the railroad brought visitors from San Francisco and the hot inland valleys to the seaside pleasures of Santa Cruz and Capitola, and the establishment of the University of California at Santa Cruz added yet another dimension to the town's character.

Monterey Bay is one of the loveliest spots on the West Coast. With its combination of rugged natural beauty and sophisticated local culture, this remarkably diverse area offers fine restaurants, bed-and-breakfast inns, tourism attractions (both natural and man-made) that reflect and respect its history and heritage, a lively arts community, and varied shopping.

Places to Go, Sights to See

Big Sur. A 26-mile drive south of Carmel via Highway 1 yields breathtaking views at every turn: The rugged Santa Lucia Mountains rise sharply on one side of the highway, and the Pacific pounds against the shore on the other. Big Sur's intractable landscape was home to author Henry Miller and many famous artists.

Cannery Row (765 Wave St., Monterey, tel. 408/649–6690) is a restored area of shops, restaurants, and galleries where the 16 sardine canneries immortalized in John Steinbeck's novel *Cannery Row* once stood.

Carmel Mission (3080 Rio Rd., Carmel, tel. 408/624–3600). With beautifully landscaped gardens, this is one of the loveliest of the 21 California missions. It is the burial place of Father Junipero Serra, founder of nine of the missions.

Monterey Bay Aquarium (886 Cannery Row, Monterey, tel. 408/648–4888.) The centerpiece of Cannery Row, this sealife museum houses more than 6,500 marine creatures. Exhibits include a 28-foot-tall kelp forest, a shark display, and examples of the undersea life of Monterey Bay.

Monterey State Historic Park (525 Polk St., Monterey, tel. 408/649–7118). This is a collection of adobe structures and other historic buildings from the Spanish and Mexican eras, when Monterey was the capital of California.

Point Lobos State Reserve (Hwy. 1, Carmel, tel. 408/624–4909) is an outdoor museum of unmatched beauty. Nearly 10 miles of trails weave along the shoreline, and there are 750 acres of underwater reserve, a portion of which is open to scuba and skin divers with permits. The many tide-pools contain starfish, anemones, and other examples of marine life; sea lions, otters, and harbor seals are in residence most of the time.

Seventeen Mile Drive. Running along the outer rim of the Monterey Peninsula, this scenic drive offers some of the most photographed ocean vistas in the world. The drive passes through the famous Pebble Beach and Cypress Point golf courses, Lone Cypress, Restless Sea, and numerous magnificent estates. Entrance gates are at Lighthouse Avenue in Pacific Grove, and off Highway 1 and North San Antonio Avenue in Carmel.

Tor House (26304 Ocean View Ave., tel. 408/624–1813) is the unique house and tower built by poet Robinson Jeffers during the early 1900s from stones gathered on Carmel beach. Docent-led tours cover the early history of Carmel as an artists' colony.

Restaurants

Central 159 (tel. 408/372–2235), in Pacific Grove, is known for its eclectic menu featuring the lighter side of New American cuisine. Also in Pacific Grove, **El Cocodrilo** (tel. 408/655–3311) features spicy Central American and Caribbean cuisines. **Fresh Cream** (tel. 408/375–9798), in Monterey, is acclaimed for its classic French cuisine, as well as for its outstanding service. In Santa Cruz, **Gilbert's on the Wharf** (tel. 408/423–5200) offers casual seafood dining with an ocean view. **Shadowbrook Restaurant** (tel. 408/475–1511), in Capitola, serves Continental cuisine. Locally popular for its atmosphere, it is reached by cable car.

Tourist Information

Monterey Peninsula Chamber of Commerce and Visitors & Convention Bureau (380 Alvarado St., Box 1770, Monterey, CA 93942–1770, tel. 408/648–5354, fax 408/649–3502).

Reservation Services

Santa Cruz County Conference and Visitors Council (701 Front St., Santa Cruz, CA 95060, tel. 408/425–1234 or 800/833–3494).

Babbling Brook Inn

Presided over by the vivacious Helen King, this inn offers a combination of romantic setting, California history, and a convenient location for business travelers. In the heart of Santa Cruz, the inn's wooded grounds and gardens make it appear to be worlds away from the city.

The inn consists of four cedar-shingle-sided buildings set on different levels of the hillside property. Portions of the main house's stone foundation date from 1796, when the mission fathers built a gristmill for grinding corn. In 1981, when it became a bed-and-breakfast inn, three cottages were added.

The rooms are decorated in a country-French style: soft colors, floral print curtains, and iron beds covered with floral spreads. Some guest rooms are just big enough for a bed and a chair; others have a spacious sitting area. The most charming guest rooms are in the main house: The Honeymoon Suite is a hideaway tucked under the main house, with a private deck that overlooks the waterfall. The expansive Garden Room has a wood-burning stove, a great garden view, and complete privacy. The rooms in the outbuildings get more street and parking lot noise, but they also have decks facing the garden. The Babbling Brook's gardens are often the setting for weddings, with the big wrought-iron white gazebo as the centerpiece, the

brook meandering through the property and flowers adorning every inch of hillside.

Helen King, a onetime organizer of international tours, is acutely aware of business travelers' needs; she accommodates them by offering an early breakfast, late check-in, and copies of the *Wall Street Journal*. And in the afternoon, Helen hosts a congenial wine-hour gathering in front of the fire in the comfortable living room.

The buffet-style breakfast of frittata, fresh fruits, and croissants with jam is set out in the living room, although guests can go either into the adjacent dining room or outside to enjoy their meal in the shade of the redwood trees.

Address: *1025 Laurel St., Santa Cruz, CA 95060, tel. 408/427-2437 or 800/866-1131, fax 408/427-2457.*
Accommodations: *12 double rooms with bath.*
Amenities: *Cable TV and phone in rooms, fireplace in 10 rooms, whirlpool tub in 2 rooms; picnic baskets available; afternoon refreshments.*
Rates: *$85–$135; full breakfast. AE, D, MC, V.*
Restrictions: *Smoking outside only, no pets; 2-night minimum on weekends.*

Green Gables Inn

The Green Gables Inn, a striking landmark along the oceanfront of Pacific Grove, dates from 1888, when Los Angeles businessman William Lacy built the two-story half-timbered and gabled Queen Anne for his lady friend, Emma Murdoch.

Lacy was also an amateur architect, and he probably designed this elegant house in which nearly every room has a three-sided bay window that takes in the ocean view just across the street. Framed entirely of redwood, it has solid maple floors, countless angles, slopes and nooks, exposed ceiling beams, intricate moldings, woodwork and arches, and even stained-glass windows framing the fireplace and set into pocket doors dividing rooms in what's now the Lacy Suite. The windows, fixtures, and woodwork all date from the original construction.

Roger and Sally Post bought the house as a family home for their four daughters. The Posts began renting out rooms to summer visitors, and in 1983 the Green Gables became a full-time inn (and the cornerstone of the Four Sisters collection of seven large inns in California, operated by the Roger Post family).

Guest rooms in the carriage house, perched on a hill out back, are larger than those in the main house, have more privacy, and views of the ocean. They also offer more modern amenities, but the rooms in the main house, with their intricately detailed molding and woodwork, have more charm. The Lacy Suite on the main floor, doubtless a converted parlor and library, has a fireplace, built-in bookshelves, and a claw-foot tub in the bathroom. Upstairs in the Gable Room, a window seat under leaded-glass windows overlooks the ocean. The Balcony Room is like a sleeping porch, and the Chapel Room actually resembles a church, with a vaulted ceiling and a pewlike window seat stretching across the front of the room.

The food, always fresh, is served in a family-style setting. The ample buffet breakfast includes frittata, a fruit plate, an assortment of breads and scones, and apple pancakes. Afternoon refreshments include wine and hors d'oeuvres. The young staff is gracious and can offer assistance with dinner reservations and sightseeing information.

Address: *104 5th St., Pacific Grove, CA 93950, tel. 408/375–2095.*
Accommodations: *6 double rooms with bath, 4 double rooms share 2 baths, 1 suite.*
Amenities: *Fireplace in carriage-house rooms; afternoon refreshments, picnic baskets available; bicycles, some parking spaces.*
Rates: *$100–$160; full breakfast. AE, MC, V.*
Restrictions: *No smoking in main house; no pets.*

"T hings are not always as they seem," observes Alice in *Through the Looking Glass.* That's certainly the case at this delightful inn, perched on a quiet residential street in the hills above Monterey Bay and just a short walk from Cannery Row and the Aquarium. Take breakfast, for example, where you're likely to sit down to a repast of Sharkleberry Flumptios or Brundt Blumbleberry. Or have a look at the clocks, all of which run backward. Guest rooms have names from the pen of Lewis Carroll. If you need to make a phone call, you'll find the instrument in the Burbling Room.

This fantasy is the creation of Jim and Barbara Allen, who left jobs in Los Angeles as a fire fighter and in the hotel business, respectively, in 1982 to open an inn in "a better climate." Towered and turreted, the 1911 building they bought had seen better days, but the Allens tackled the needed restoration with the humor that now pervades the inn.

In short order, they had the place fixed up, with rooms as comfortable as they are engaging. Momerath, for example, has a superking-size bed with an elaborately carved mahogany headboard as its centerpiece; the private bathroom has a claw-foot tub. Borogrove is a huge corner room with an expansive ocean view, and a telescope for scanning the horizon, a Victorian settee, and

a fireplace. The best view can be had from the third-floor tower, where two rooms share a bath and a small sitting area. The Mimsey room is tiny, but it has wall-to-wall windows and the oldest piece of furniture in the house, a wood-frame bed bought in 1886 for $6.45.

One of the most pleasant spots is the huge wraparound sun porch, from which guests can watch otters and sea lions frolicking in the bay.

Guests usually drift into the comfortable living room after dinner to discuss their dining adventures and sample the milk and cookies guarded by Vorpal Bear, who warns, "Before bedtime . . . not dinner. Vorpal Bear attacks if you cheat."

Jim and Barbara keep up to date on the local restaurants. Fresh Cream, for example, is described as "where Jim takes Barbara when he's in trouble."

Address: *598 Laine St., Monterey, CA 93940, tel. 408/372-4777.*
Accommodations: *3 double rooms with bath, 4 double rooms share 2 baths.*
Amenities: *Afternoon refreshments; off-street parking.*
Rates: *$95–$170; full breakfast. No credit cards.*
Restrictions: *Smoking outside only, no pets; 2-night minimum on weekends, 3-night minimum on holidays.*

Old Monterey Inn

Ann and Gene Swett have elevated the business of innkeeping to a high art, offering their guests quietly elegant accommodations in a historic home—and the type of pampering that anticipates every need. Just a few blocks from downtown Monterey, a woodsy, flower-lined driveway leads to the English Tudor–style home built in 1929 by Carmel Martin, then the mayor of Monterey.

When Gene Swett was transferred to Monterey from the Bay Area in 1968, the family needed a house that was big enough for eight. Although the Martin house was rundown, the Swetts purchased it, renovated it, and created what would become one of the loveliest inns in California.

Outside, Gene created a verdant oasis of year-round color. The house was Ann's domain. She began haunting flea markets as well as garage and yard sales. The quest continues, and the themes and color schemes of guest rooms are always subject to change. Thus the room once known as "Madrigal" is now "Serengeti," evoking a turn-of-the-century African safari, with mosquito netting over the bed, rattan chairs, pith helmets, antique leather hatboxes, and a brass-elephant bird-cage stand. In the Library Room, floor-to-ceiling bookshelves contain volumes of nostalgic children's literature. The Garden Room feels almost like a tree house set in the upper branches of

the massive oak just outside the window.

Guests have the option of having breakfast in bed. But unless you're honeymooning, don't take it. Breakfast takes place in front of the fireplace in the formal dining room, at a table set for 14 with exquisite Oriental china. Guests dine on fruit, breads, quiche, or stratta served course by course. Gene is the consummate host, mingling and getting to know each and every guest to determine their food preferences before sending them off to dinner. He can recommend a half dozen romantic picnic spots, and can advise guests on which galleries and shops are musts and which should be avoided.

The Swetts offer guests a chance to get away from it all. "You come to our inn to talk to each other . . . to get your life back together," explains Gene.

Address: *500 Martin St., Monterey, CA 93940, tel. 408/375–8284.*
Accommodations: *8 double rooms with bath, 1 suite, 1 cottage suite.*
Amenities: *Fireplace in 8 rooms, afternoon and evening refreshments, picnic baskets available.*
Rates: *$150–$210; full breakfast. No credit cards.*
Restrictions: *Smoking in garden only, no pets; 2-night minimum on weekends, 3-night minimum on holidays. Closed Christmas Day.*

Cliff Crest Bed and Breakfast Inn

Innkeeping may seem an unlikely retirement career choice for an aerospace engineer and a recipe tester for Carnation foods, but it's the one Bruce and Sharon Taylor made when they moved from Los Angeles to this seaside town in 1986, purchasing Cliff Crest.

A smallish, modest Queen Anne, Cliff Crest was the home of William and Jenny Jeter. William was a mayor of Santa Cruz, lieutenant governor of California from 1895 to 1899, and founder of a local bank. Historic photographs on the walls illustrate the active life the Jeters led.

Like the Jeters, the Taylors enjoy visiting with guests in the parlor or in the sunny solarium. The guest rooms on the first and second floors contain antiques from the Taylors' personal collection: an Eastlake bedroom suite, an original Morris chair, an antique walnut dresser.

Sharon's penchant for experimenting with recipes continues, and results in such unusual breakfast entrées as chili egg puff, one of her most popular creations.

Address: *407 Cliff St., Santa Cruz, CA 95060, tel. 408/427-2609.*
Accommodations: *5 double rooms with bath.*
Amenities: *Robes, fireplace in 1 room; evening refreshments.*
Rates: *$80–$135; full breakfast. AE, MC, V.*
Restrictions: *Smoking outside only, no pets; 2-night minimum on weekends.*

Gatehouse Inn

This Italianate Victorian house has a somewhat literary history. John Steinbeck, whose grandparents lived across the street, used to visit with owner Alice Langford to discuss poetry and King Arthur. The house dates from 1884 and is one of the oldest in Pacific Grove.

The original decor has either been retained or re-created: lincrusta on walls, Bradbury and Bradbury silkscreen wallpapers and antique white wicker furnishings, lending a bright and airy ambience in both the main house and the sympathetic addition. About half of the rooms are faithfully decorated in the Victorian style; the others are done up in fantasy themes: One is like a sultan's tent, with Persian carpet, brass headboard with inlaid mother-of-pearl, and a chair made from a camel saddle. Some rooms have claw-foot tubs set in their corners or alcoves.

Ann Young, a longtime resident of Pacific Grove, presides. A fount of information on local history, she can provide sightseeing assistance and advice.

Address: *225 Central Ave., Pacific Grove, CA 93950, tel. 408/649-1881 or 800/753-1881.*
Accommodations: *8 double rooms with bath, 1 suite.*
Amenities: *Fireplace, radio/tape player, and phone in rooms; guest kitchen; afternoon refreshments.*
Rates: *$95–$170; full breakfast. AE, MC, V.*
Restrictions: *Smoking outside only; 2-night minimum on weekends.*

Gosby House

The Gosby House is a gabled and turreted landmark dating from 1887, when J. E. Gosby built one of the first boardinghouses in town. The addition of the turret tower, a bay window with stained glass, white spindled gingerbread adorning the front porch, and the shingled exterior transformed the homely building—ugly duckling-style—into a graceful Queen Anne Victorian.

Guest rooms vary in size, and all are decorated with late Victorian antiques and period reproductions. The inn has an informal, country air about it, and at breakfast guests feel comfortable choosing among the buffet offerings of cinammon rolls, quiche, muffins, scones, omelets, or Mexican eggs, and taking them out to the garden; in the afternoon, they can enjoy a glass of wine in the parlor. The young innkeepers are knowledgeable and can offer tourism or restaurant suggestions.

Address: *643 Lighthouse Ave., Pacific Grove, CA 93950, tel. 408/375-1287.*
Accommodations: *20 double rooms with bath, 2 double rooms share bath.*
Amenities: *Phone in rooms, kitchen in 2 rooms, fireplace in 12 rooms; afternoon refreshments; picnic baskets and wine available; bicycles.*
Rates: *$85-$130; full breakfast. AE, MC, V.*
Restrictions: *Smoking in rooms with outside entrance only; no pets.*

Happy Landing Inn

This 1920s inn is a collection of pastel-colored Hansel and Gretel cottages set in a sea of flowers. Flagstone paths wind through the gardens, which include a beckoning lily pond and a lattice gazebo. Stone benches and lawn statuary abound.

Designed by Hugh Comstock, the architect responsible for much of Carmel, the two master suites and five bedrooms share the gardens, the great room, and the kitchen. The rooms have cathedral ceilings, lace curtains, brass beds, and an eclectic assortment of antiques. Each room has its own garden entrance, and a full breakfast will be served to the rooms when "you raise the shade to let us know you're ready," according to owner Dick Stewart.

Coffee and tea are served by a great stone fireplace. The inn is within easy walking distance of the beach, shops, and art galleries of Carmel.

Address: *Monte Verde St. between 5th and 6th Aves., Box 2619, Carmel, CA 93921, tel. 408/624-7917.*
Accommodations: *5 double rooms with bath, 2 suites.*
Amenities: *Cable TV in rooms; fireplace in suites and 1 room; afternoon refreshments.*
Rates: *$90-$145; full breakfast. MC, V.*
Restrictions: *Smoking outside only, no pets; 2-night minimum on weekends.*

Inn at Depot Hill

Suzanne Lankes and Dan Floyd transformed this 1901 railroad depot into an elegant bed-and-breakfast inn, with opulent turn-of-the-century European decor inspired by the legendary *Orient Express.*

In the dining room there's a trompe l'oeil mural depicting the view from a train's dining car. In one bedroom there's a handcrafted metal bed resembling a grapevine. All have marble bathrooms and walls lavishly upholstered with brocades that match curtains and bedspreads, linens trimmed with handmade lace, English cutwork lace canopies, and Oriental rugs.

The inn's ambience is most fully displayed in the Railroad Baron's Suite: bordello-red and gold rooms, with an oversize bed covered with damask and silk, the sitting area separated by heavy gold-tasseled drapes, and a deep soaking tub beneath a skylight in the bathroom.

Address: *250 Monterey Ave., Box 1394, Capitola by the Sea, CA 95010, tel. 408/462–3376, fax 408/458–0989.*
Accommodations: *4 double rooms with bath, 4 suites.*
Amenities: *TV, VCR, stereo, phone with modem, hair dryer, steamer, coffeemaker, and fireplace in rooms, hot tub in 5 rooms; afternoon refreshments.*
Rates: *$145–$225; full breakfast. AE, MC, V.*
Restrictions: *Smoking outside only, no pets; 2-night minimum on weekends.*

Martine Inn

Elegance and grace are the keynotes of the Martine Inn, a nearly century-old mansion perched above the tiny cove of Monterey Bay that frames Pacific Grove. A 1920s remodeling turned the house into a white stuccoed Mediterranean with enormous bay windows. In 1984 Don Martine and his wife, Marion, opened it as an inn.

The house is filled with American antiques, most notably, matching bedroom suites dating from 1840 to 1890: an Eastlake suite, a mahogany suite exhibited at the 1893 Chicago World's Fair; and Academy Award–winning costume designer Edith Head's bedroom suite.

Breakfast is a feast of pastries, salmon Wellington, crab and spinach crepes, and Monterey eggs, all served on antique china and Sheffield silver in the dining room with a wall-to-wall ocean view.

Address: *255 Ocean View Blvd., Pacific Grove, CA 92950, tel. 408/373–3388, fax 408/373–3896.*
Accommodations: *20 rooms with bath.*
Amenities: *Phone and refrigerator in rooms, fireplace in 7 rooms; afternoon refreshments; conference facilities; picnic meals available; outdoor whirlpool tub; off-street parking.*
Rates: *$115–$225; full breakfast. MC, V.*
Restrictions: *Smoking in fireplace rooms only, no pets; 2-night minimum on weekends, 3-night minimum on holidays.*

Sea View Inn

A few blocks from the madding crowd that sometimes overwhelms Carmel, the Sea View typifies what longtime visitors to Carmel come for: peaceful seclusion amid stunning natural beauty. Diane Hydorn and husband Marshall, a former airline pilot and now a writer and artist (whose paintings grace many of the inn's rooms), have been the hosts here since 1975.

Inside the Craftsman cottage there's lots of dark woodwork in open-beam ceilings, paneled walls, milled moldings, hardwood floors topped with Oriental and braided rugs, overstuffed chairs, sofas in subdued colors, and brick fireplaces that keep the living room and game room warm on cool days (which is most of the time). Books, magazines, and games abound, and classical music plays softly in the background.

Breakfast, which consists of quiche, home-baked breads, fruits and cheeses, is served by candlelight.

Address: *Camino Real between 11th and 12th Aves., Box 4138, Carmel, CA 93921, tel. 408/624–8778.*
Accommodations: *6 double rooms with bath, 2 double rooms share bath.*
Amenities: *Afternoon refreshments; rental bicycles.*
Rates: *$80–$110; Continental breakfast. MC, V.*
Restrictions: *Smoking outside only, no pets; 2-night minimum on weekends, 3-night minimum on holidays.*

Seven Gables Inn

T his inn is actually a collection of four yellow gabled clapboard buildings that share a corner lot and a breathtaking view of the ocean. The main house was built in 1886, one of the first of the many showy Victorian homes in Pacific Grove; the three outbuildings were put up during the 1910s and 1940s.

The Flatley family (who opened the Green Gables Inn during the 1950s) has filled the buildings with a collection of European antiques from various periods, marble statues, and bric-a-brac. Gold-leaf mirrors, picture frames, a Tiffany window, crystal chandeliers, inlaid wood furnishings, beveled-glass armoires, and Oriental rugs and marble statues create a formal European atmosphere. Susan Flatley, who manages the inn day to day, grew up in this house and is quite knowledgeable about the area; she happily provides advice and insight on visiting nearby Cannery Row, the Aquarium, and various Monterey historic sites.

Address: *555 Ocean View Blvd., Pacific Grove, CA 93950, tel. 408/372–4341.*
Accommodations: *14 double rooms with bath.*
Amenities: *Afternoon tea; refrigerators.*
Rates: *$95–$185; full breakfast. MC, V.*
Restrictions: *Smoking in garden only; 2-night minimum on weekends, 3-night minimum on holidays.*

San Francisco

Sailboats gliding past Alcatraz Island, the hand-tooled finial of a restored Victorian, the clang of a cable-car bell, the aroma of Italian roast coffee, the spices of Szechuan cooking, the old '60s holdover and the new '90s individualist—San Francisco dazzles, provokes, and never disappoints. A jewel on the tip of a peninsula, the city is surrounded by water—the Pacific to the west of the Golden Gate Bridge, San Francisco Bay to the east. Victorian "painted ladies" cling to hills so steep they rival any roller coaster. Although driving can be nerve-racking and walking challenging, panoramic views reward at every turn.

Many visitors begin their tour of San Francisco at the vibrant waterfront. On a sunny weekend day, tourists and residents alike throng the unique shops, T-shirt stands, historic and hokey museums, and bay-view restaurants. Pier 39, a two-story wooden boardwalk of boutiques, eateries, and an old-fashioned carousel, juts into the ocean. Just up the street are The Cannery and Ghiradelli Square, a former chocolate factory, with more fun shops and restaurants. Along the way, you'll be enticed by the catch of the day cooked and sold at sidewalk stalls along Fisherman's Wharf. This is the northern terminus of the cable car, the nation's only moving National Historic Landmark.

The cable car climbs and dips over the city's hills to North Beach, the Italian neighborhood. Open-air cafés, pastry shops, delis, coffee-roasting companies, bakeries, and pizza parlors ensure that visitors never go hungry as they explore the Italian import shops and the Romanesque/ Gothic cathedral of Saints Peter and Paul. Many of these businesses have been run by the same Italian family that started them for generations. On the adjacent Telegraph

Hill, residents have some of the best views of San Francisco
as well as the most difficult ascent to their aeries.

The next stop is Chinatown, alive and exotic with crowds of
Chinese and more recently arrived Southeast Asians
scrutinizing the abundant vegetable stands and snapping
up bargains on embroidered linens, jade, and ceramics in
the import shops along Grant Avenue. Roast ducks hang in
restaurant windows, Chinese characters cover marquees,
and teahouses offer cups of steaming ginseng, reputed to
induce good health. Nearby is Union Square, the heart of
downtown and the city's premier shopping district. Within
a few blocks are I. Magnin, Neiman-Marcus, F.A.O.
Schwarz, Gump's, Shreve Co., a spate of world-famous
retailers, and many smaller, exclusive boutiques. Chances
are that many of the shoppers who frequent these pricey
establishments live in Pacific Heights, where many-
splendored mansions and town houses dominate some of
San Francisco's most expensive real estate.

Continuing on the west side of the city, you'll find the
stunning Golden Gate Park, home to world-class museums
and delightful gardens. Although the park stretches from
Stanyan Street to the sea, several highlights are clustered
in one section. The M. H. de Young Memorial Museum,
known for its American works, and the renowned Asian
Art Museum share the same building. Next door is the
serene four-acre Japanese Tea Garden, with its winding
paths, a 200-year-old Buddha, a bonsai forest, and the
always-busy Tea House, where fortune cookies were
invented. Across the street, the Strybing Arboretum is
a microcosm of the plant kingdom, divided into such theme
plantings as the New World Cloud Forest and the Scent
Garden. The California Academy of Science and its
magnificent aquarium are across the concourse.

Due north is another urban oasis, the 1,500-acre Presidio,
an area of rolling hills, majestic woods, and attractive
redbrick army barracks. Just outside its eastern boundary

*is the rosy and rococo Palace of Fine Arts, which houses
the Exploratorium, an innovative science museum.
Crowning the Presidio is the Golden Gate Bridge.*

*Since its bawdy, boomtown birth in the wake of the 1848
Gold Rush, San Francisco has pulsed with ethnic diversity,
free enterprise, a thirst for the good life, and a love for the
natural beauty of the West. Take a stroll away from the
tourist spots and you'll discover that this spirit still very
much alive. Although occasional earthquakes may rattle
the city temporarily, San Francisco remains unsinkable.*

Places to Go, Sights to See

Alcatraz Island. Al Capone, Machine Gun Kelly, and Robert Stroud, the
"Birdman of Alcatraz," were inmates at this former maximum-security
federal penitentiary. You can walk through the prison and grounds on
a self-guided tour. Seating on the ferries of the Red and White Fleet (tel.
415/546–2882), which leave from Pier 41, is in great demand and should be
reserved in advance.

Asian Art Museum (Golden Gate Park, tel. 415/668–8921). With an estimated
12,000 works spanning 6,000 years, this is the largest museum outside Asia
that is devoted to Asian art. Highlights include the Magnin Jade Room and
the Leventritt collection of blue-and-white porcelain. The adjoining *M. H. de
Young Memorial Museum* (tel. 415/750–3600) is especially strong in
American art, including works by Sargent, Whistler, Cassatt, and Remington.

Cable Car Museum (Washington and Mason Sts., tel. 415/474–1887) displays
the brawny inner workings of the cable-car system, scale models, and
memorabilia.

California Academy of Sciences (Golden Gate Park, tel. 415/750–7145). One
of the five top museums of natural history in the country, the Academy
encompasses the first-rate *Morrison Planetarium*, featuring star and laser
shows; the *Steinhart Aquarium*, with its 100,000-gallon Fish Roundabout
that's home to 14,000 creatures; and such exhibits as an "earthquake floor,"
which enables visitors to ride a simulated California quake.

Coit Tower (atop Telegraph Hill, tel. 415/274–0203). An elevator to the top of
this Art Deco monument, decorated with murals dedicated to the workers of
California, offers panoramic views of the city and the bay.

Exploratorium (Bay and Lyon Sts., tel. 415/561–0360). This science museum
at the end of the marina, packed with more than 600 hands-on exhibits, gives
children a chance to run off excess energy. You can create a giant soap

bubble, freeze your shadow, or play computerized musical instruments. Be sure to include the pitch-black, crawl-through Tactile Dome in your visit.

Golden Gate Bridge. For the best views of this 54-year-old symbol of San Francisco, see it from Lincoln Boulevard, which forms the western boundary of the Presidio, or drive across the bridge to the parking lot on the Marin side.

Golden Gate Park. The best way to see this 1,000-acre park is by car. Highlights include the *Conservatory* (tel. 415/666–7077), an elaborate Victorian crystal palace that was designed after one in London's Kew Gardens, and the *Japanese Tea Garden* (tel. 415/752–1171), a four-acre village of small ponds, streams, and flowering shrubs created for the 1894 Mid-Winter Exposition. Visitors especially enjoy paddleboating on Stow Lake, the expansive picnic grounds, and the first-class museums located in the eastern section of the park (*see* above).

Hyde Street Pier (just west of The Cannery, tel. 415/556–6435). Climb aboard and explore a 19th-century three-masted schooner, paddle-wheel ferry, steam tug, and other historic ships that have been restored to look as though they just reached port.

Lombard Street (between Hyde and Leavenworth Sts.). Cars line up to zigzag down this "crookedest street in the world," where pedestrians negotiate stairs instead of sidewalks.

Mission Dolores (16th and Dolores Sts., tel. 415/621–8203). The sixth of 21 missions founded in California by the Franciscans and the oldest building in the city, this structure, dating from 1776, retains the appearance of a small-scale outpost, dwarfed by the towers of the adjacent basilica.

Tourist Information

San Francisco Convention and Visitors Bureau (lower level of Hallidie Plaza at Powell and Market Sts., tel. 415/391–2000).

Reservations Services

Bed & Breakfast Innkeepers of Northern California (Box 7150, Chico, CA 95927, tel. 800/284–4667); **Bed & Breakfast International** (Box 282910, San Francisco, CA 94128–2910, tel. 415/696–1690, fax 415/696–1699); **Bed & Breakfast San Francisco** (Box 349, San Francisco, CA 94101, tel. 415/931–3083 or 800/452–8249, fax 415/921–2273); **Lodging San Francisco** (421 North Point, San Francisco, CA 94133, tel. 415/292–4500 or 800/356–7567, fax 415/771–8309).

Archbishops Mansion

The Archbishops Mansion is an elegant European manor reborn in San Francisco. The Second Empire–style residence, built in 1904 for Archbishop Patrick Riordan, faces Alamo Square and its "postcard row" of restored Victorians. Designers Jonathan Shannon and Jeffrey Ross have restored the home to that era of opulence. Everything about it—the scale, the ornamentation, the Napoleon III antiques—is extravagant.

Early morning coffee and complementary wine are served in the front parlor, dominated by a massive redwood fireplace with fluted Corinthian columns. Ornate Belle Époque furnishings and reproductions fill the rooms, such as the crystal chandelier that hung in Scarlett O'Hara's beloved Tara in the movie *Gone With the Wind*. While you sip your wine, you'll be serenaded from the hall with a 1904 ebony Bechstein piano once owned by Noël Coward.

A three-story redwood staircase rises majestically from the coffered foyer. Above, sunlight filters through a 16-foot-wide oval stained-glass dome, which miraculously survived the 1906 earthquake.

Inspired by the Opera House six blocks away, guest rooms are overtly romantic. The gold-hued Don Giovanni Suite conveys a Renaissance formality, and, not surprisingly, has a huge bed (yes, Jonathan and Jeff

decorate with a sense of humor). The zebrawood canopied four-poster bed found in a castle in southern France was masterly carved during the Napoleonic period.

The Carmen Suite's outstanding feature is its bathroom: A claw-foot tub sits in front of a fireplace with, naturally, a tubside champagne stand. A second fireplace warms the Carmen's bedroom, where the 1885 settee has its original horsehair covering. Billowing draperies, canopied beds, and ceramic-tile fireplaces are routine here.

A breakfast of bakery muffins, scones, and tea or coffee is brought to your room in a picnic basket, or you can join the other guests in a formal dining room.

Address: *1000 Fulton St., San Francisco, CA 94117, tel. 415/563–7872 or 800/543–5820, fax 415/885–3193.*
Accommodations: *10 double rooms with bath, 5 suites.*
Amenities: *Phone and cable TV in rooms, fireplace and robes in many rooms, whirlpool tubs in 2 suites; evening refreshments, elevator; laundry service; room service for wine, beer, and snacks; conference facilities; off-street parking.*
Rates: *$100–$169, suites $189–$285; Continental breakfast. AE, MC, V.*
Restrictions: *No smoking in common areas, no pets; 2-night minimum on weekends.*

Mansion Hotel

If inns were awarded prizes for showmanship, the Mansion Hotel would win top honors. First, there's the decapitated head of the resident ghost who reads minds. And where else can you see the innkeeper, clad in sequined dinner jacket, play the saw? They're just part of the live "magic extravaganzas" held every weekend at the Mansion.

The inspiration behind this zaniness is the aforementioned innkeeper, Bob Pritikin. The author of *Christ Was an Adman*, Pritikin isn't afraid of innovation in his hotel, two adjacent Queen Anne Victorians a short walk from the chic boutiques and eateries of Pacific Heights. The cabaret, free to overnight guests, also draws diners from the highly praised restaurant.

The Mansion Hotel is as visually flamboyant as its entertainment, although the west wing (a hotel bought two years ago) has a simpler, country-inn look. In the public areas no surface has been left unembellished. Objets, wall murals, curios (a selection of ugly ties, for example), and sculptures, many by Beniamino Bufano, are everywhere. The porcine theme in the breakfast dining room is tough to miss, surrounded as you are by an old wooden carousel pig and wall painting depicting a swine-filled picnic in progress.

All of the west-wing rooms have murals that depict the famous San Francisco personage for whom the room is named. The authentic and Victorian reproduction decor might include a rolltop desk, four-poster canopy bed, and Tiffany-style lamp. The west-wing rooms have Laura Ashley flower-print wallpaper and matching bedding, with a preponderance of pine furniture. Particularly lavish is the Louis IV room, where such guests as Barbra Streisand, Robert Stack, and Michael York have enjoyed the immense gold-leaf half-tester bed and wardrobe and private redwood deck.

A full breakfast of fresh fruit, cereal, eggs cooked to order, crumpets, bangers, potatoes, and juice can be delivered to your room. In your room you'll find a replica of a Victorian silk rose to take home—and a little chocolate version of the Mansion, which, chances are, will never leave the premises.

Address: *2220 Sacramento St., San Francisco, CA 94115, tel. 415/929–9444, fax 415/567–9391.*
Accommodations: *27 double rooms with bath.*
Amenities: *Restaurant, evening entertainment, phone in rooms, TV on request, fireplace in some rooms, whirlpool tub in 1 room, complimentary newspaper, coffee, and sherry, 24-hour room service, laundry service, billiard table.*
Rates: *$89–$225; full breakfast. AE, D, DC, MC, V.*
Restrictions: *None.*

Victorian Inn on the Park

Overlooking the so-called panhandle of Golden Gate Park, this Queen Anne Victorian is a riot of gables, finials, and cornices. The most unusual feature is the open belvedere in a cupola, one of only two existing in the city; it's a private retreat for guests in the Belvedere Suite.

Renowned San Francisco architect William Curlett designed the mansion in 1897 for a prominent lawyer. In 1980, attorneys Lisa and William Benau, looking for a way to raise their children while working at a job they love, transformed the house into one of San Francisco's first bed-and-breakfasts.

If you've ever wanted to experience the more luxurious aspects of life in the Gay Nineties, this is the place in which to do it. Step across the threshold to a grand entrance of rubbed mahogany paneling and oak parquet floors; they look even more burnished when a fire is lit in the immense brick fireplace framed by a sculpted wood mantel. The parlor is rather formal, with a graceful Rococo Revival fainting couch in floral brocade and a velvet settee. Wine is served here in the evening by the white-tile and painted-wood hearth, which almost touches the ceiling. Light filters through period fringed and embroidered lampshades.

Guest rooms, decorated with Rococo Revival and Eastlake antiques and peppered with modern reproductions, are most noteworthy for their wall treatments. The wallpapers, combining different floral motifs in rich blues, purples, greens, and gold, are reproductions of William Morris designs, meticulously hand silk-screened by Bradbury and Bradbury, a local firm.

Piles of pillows, marble bathroom counters, Victorian-era prints and photos, and a decanter of sherry in every room are some of the inn's special touches. The rooms on the street level are quiet and removed but a bit dark, and noise from the busy street can be heard in the upper-story rooms. These, however, are small complaints that never overshadow the friendly ambience and elegant presentation at the Victorian Inn on the Park.

Address: *301 Lyon St., San Francisco, CA 94117, tel. 415/931–1830, fax 415/931–1830.*
Accommodations: *12 double rooms with bath, 1 suite, 1 double suite with 2 baths.*
Amenities: *Phone and clock radio in rooms, some rooms with fireplace, TV available; meeting facilities.*
Rates: *$88–$144, suites $144–$280; Continental breakfast. AE, D, DC, MC, V.*
Restrictions: *No smoking in breakfast room, no pets; 2-night minimum on weekends, 3-night minimum on holiday weekends.*

White Swan Inn

Fireplaces in every room, romantic furnishings, delicious food, top-notch amenities, and a location just two blocks from Union Square make the White Swan Inn one of the premier bed-and-breakfasts in San Francisco. This circa-1908 building has the look of a London town house, and the decoration is studiously English. Walk into the library, and you'll think you've been admitted to an exclusive gentleman's club, with tufted wing chairs; rich, dark wood; sparkling brass fixtures and hardware; hunting scenes on the pillows; and a red tartan couch.

The guest rooms, predominantly green and burgundy with touches of yellow and rose, have a more informal look than the public rooms. All are similarly furnished with reproduction Edwardian pieces in cherry and other dark woods. Four-poster beds, wingback or barrel chairs, TVs enclosed in an armoire or a cabinet, wooden shutters, and Laura Ashley-style floral wallpaper are standard. A bedside switch allows you to control the gas fireplaces.

The hotel is one of the Four Sisters Inns, owned and operated by the Post family, and each evening and morning, a family member greets guests in the common rooms. At the White Swan, it's usually Kim, one of the four Post sisters for whom their family business was named. Their trademark teddy bears cuddle in the reception area, peeking through banisters and perched on the mantel over the perpetually lit fire. A plush bear also adorns each guest room.

The Four Sisters properties are known for their food, so you're urged to find an excuse to be back at the White Swan in the afternoon. You'll be rewarded by such complimentary snacks as lemon cake, vegetables with curry dip, stuffed grape leaves and specialty cheeses, accompanied by wine, sherry, and other drinks. Typical breakfast fare includes Mexican quiche, soda-bread toast, Swiss oatmeal, fresh fruit, granola, and doughnuts. Everything is homemade. Guests have made so many requests for the recipes that the family has released its own cookbook.

Address: *845 Bush St., San Francisco, CA 94108, tel. 415/775–1755, fax 415/775–5717.*
Accommodations: *26 double rooms with bath, 1 suite.*
Amenities: *TV, wet bar, refrigerator, hair dryer, robes, and phone in rooms; afternoon refreshments, laundry service, wine-only room service, complimentary newspaper and shoe-shine service; valet parking available; conference and catering facilities.*
Rates: *$145–$160, suite $250; full breakfast. AE, MC, V.*
Restrictions: *No smoking in common areas, no pets.*

The Alamo Square Inn

This inn spans three buildings encircling a flower-filled patio overlooking a small garden. The most attractive of the three is the 1895 Neo-Classical Revival Baum House, with delicate reliefwork in the form of wreaths and ribbons.

In the guest rooms, innkeepers Wayne Morris Corn and Klaus Ernst May have opted for reproduction and contemporary furnishings. One upstairs suite features an ultramodern black-laminate bedroom set and a sunken whirlpool bath. Another bright attic suite with dormers has white wicker furniture and opens onto a rooftop sun deck. Several rooms overlook Alamo Square.

The second building is an 1896 Tudor Revival, but the rooms are darker, with small windows. The third house features a modern garden apartment with full kitchen.

Address: *719 Scott St., San Francisco, CA 94117, tel. 415/922-2055 or 800/345-9888, fax 415/931-1304.*
Accommodations: *9 double rooms with baths, 3 suites, 1 housekeeping suite.*
Amenities: *Phone in rooms, 1 suite with Jacuzzi, 4 rooms with TV, 6 rooms with fireplace, refreshments, conference room; off-street parking.*
Rates: *$85–$125; suites $175; full breakfast. AE, DC, MC, V.*
Restrictions: *Smoking outdoors only, no pets; 2-night minimum on weekends, 3-night minimum on some holidays.*

The Bed and Breakfast Inn

This 1885 Italianate Victorian row house is nestled in a quiet mew just off Union Street. The Bed and Breakfast Inn, which also includes an adjacent house, may be the closest you'll come to staying in a native's home. Although owners Bob and Marily Kavanaugh don't reside here—they live across the street—most of the furniture and cherished antiques have descended through the two families.

Guest rooms are cozy, with traditional pieces (some of them love seats), the family china on display, and impressionistic landscape paintings by Marily. Fresh flowers perfume each room. One spacious suite, decorated ' with comfortable contemporary furnishings, boasts a living room, dining area, full kitchen, and a latticed balcony overlooking the deck. A narrow spiral staircase climbs to a sleeping loft. Most rooms that have private bathrooms also have phones and TVs. Pension rooms that share a bath are simple but affordable.

Address: *4 Charlton Ct., San Francisco, CA 94123, tel. 415/921-9784.*
Accommodations: *3 double rooms with bath, 4 double rooms share 3 baths, 2 suites, 1 housekeeping suite.*
Amenities: *Phone in 6 rooms, TV in 5 rooms, complimentary coffee, sherry in rooms with baths, sherry in parlor.*
Rates: *$70–$140, suite $215; Continental breakfast. No credit cards.*
Restrictions: *No smoking except on deck, no pets.*

Chateau Tivoli

his elaborate Queen Anne/
Chateauesque home in the historic Alamo Square district,
built in 1890, is painted in no fewer
than 22 colors, from raisin brown to
turquoise, with ornamentation picked
out in 23-karat gold leaf.

Owners Rodney Karr and Willard
Gersbach have carried the flamboyant appearance of the exterior inside, filling every room, hallway, and
wall with antique furnishings and
art (some from the estates of Corne-
lius Vanderbilt and Charles de
Gaulle), housewares, and knickknacks. Competing for attention is
the carved oak paneling, cornices,
and Ionic columns of the entrance
hall, double parlor, and staircase.
Some of the guest rooms are equally
elaborate, each one devoted to

a particular style: Empire, American
Renaissance, Arts and Crafts,
French-Renaissance Revival. Several
have ceilings "frescoed" with a riot-
ous pattern of different wallpapers.

Address: *1057 Steiner St., San
Francisco CA 94115, tel. 415/776–
5462 or 800/228–1647, fax 415/776–
0505.*
Accommodations: *1 double room
with bath, 4 double rooms share 2
baths, 1 suite, 1 double suite.*
Amenities: *Phone in rooms, complimentary wine, fireplaces in 2
suites.*
Rates: *$80–$125; suites $200; Conti-
nental breakfast, full breakfast on
weekends. AE, MC, V.*
Restrictions: *No smoking; 2-night
minimum on holiday weekends.*

Golden Gate Hotel

he family-run Golden Gate
Hotel is ideal for budget-
conscious visitors. With rooms
as low as $55 for a shared bath (and
a sink in each guest room), this
circa-1913 Edwardian is just two
blocks from Union Square. Hosts
John and Renata Kenaston provide
complimentary afternoon tea and
cookies, served in the hotel's cozy
parlor, which is simply decorated
with ivory-sponged walls, gray-blue
carpeting, a contemporary, "decon-
structivist" fireplace, and Rococo Revival love seat and coffee table.
Coffee lovers can look forward to
what is billed as "the city's strongest coffee."

Guests reach their rooms by riding
the town house's original birdcage
elevator. The rooms are small, clean,

and reasonably quiet given the
hotel's downtown location. Each is
cheerfully furnished, with white or
blue wicker chairs, wicker headboards, and 19th-century mahogany
wardrobes. Laura Ashley floral-print
wallpaper with matching curtains
and comforters are featured in all
rooms with private baths (some of
these have antique claw-foot tubs).

Address: *775 Bush St., San Francisco, CA 94108, tel. 415/392–3702 or
800/835–1118.*
Accommodations: *14 double rooms
with bath, 9 double rooms share 3
baths.*
Amenities: *TV in rooms, phone in
10 rooms, afternoon refreshments.*
Rates: *$55–$79; Continental breakfast. AE, DC, MC, V.*

Inn San Francisco

The Inn San Francisco, in Mission Hill, is quintessential northern California: a beautifully restored 1870s Italianate Victorian with a hot tub out back. Feather beds, 19th-century British and American furnishings throughout, a delightful garden and cottage, and a rooftop patio complete the picture.

The spacious double parlor is elegantly decorated in true Victorian fashion with forest-green walls, rubbed redwood trim, velvet side chairs, a tapestried fainting couch, and Oriental rugs. One popular guest room opens onto a private, sheltered deck with its own traditional redwood hot tub. Another room has a double whirlpool bath beneath a stained-glass skylight. Manager Jane Bertorelli adds her own special touches: fresh flowers and truffles by San Francisco's best-known chocolatier in every room.

Address: *943 S. Van Ness Ave., San Francisco, CA 94110, tel. 415/641–0188 or 800/359–0913, fax 415/641–1701.*
Accommodations: *17 double rooms with baths, 5 double rooms share 2 baths.*
Amenities: *Phone, TV, refrigerator and clock radio in room, hot tub on deck of 1 room, whirlpool tubs in 5 rooms, fireplace in 4 rooms, complimentary tea, coffee, and sherry; hot tub in garden; limited off-street parking.*
Rates: *$75–$175; Continental breakfast. AE, D, DC, MC, V.*
Restrictions: *No smoking in parlor; no pets in public areas.*

Inn at Union Square

A half block west of Union Square, the Inn at Union Square is a friendly, more personal alternative to the area's skyscraping hotels. Interior designer Nan Rosenblatt has endowed the guest rooms and parlors with the rich, inviting ambience of a gracious country home.

At the end of each of five floors is a cozy sitting area warmed by a wood-burning fireplace. High tea, complete with a generous selection of cucumber sandwiches, cakes, and cookies is served here.

Guest rooms feature furniture in Chippendale and Federal styles, heavy draperies, and floral print canopies and half-canopies. Don't expect a view in this crowded part of town, where buildings are squeezed next to each other.

Address: *440 Post St., San Francisco, CA 94102, tel. 415/397–3510 or 800/288–4346, fax 415/989–0529.*
Accommodations: *23 double rooms with baths, 7 suites.*
Amenities: *Phone and TV in room; fireplace in 2 rooms; wet bar in 2 rooms; whirlpool bath, sauna, and refrigerator in 1 suite; refreshments, complimentary newspaper and shoe-shine service, laundry service, room service, honor bar, catered dinner in room available; valet parking.*
Rates: *$120–$180, suites $145–$300; Continental breakfast. AE, DC, MC, V.*
Restrictions: *No smoking.*

Petite Auberge

Just two blocks from Union Square, this circa-1915 Baroque Revival inn is a romantic retreat with a small garden patio in the heart of downtown. Owned and operated by the Four Sisters Inns (*see* the White Swan Inn, above), the Petite Auberge features dainty floral wallpaper, country-French oak armoires and matching headboards carved in flower and vine reliefs, and fireplaces framed with hand-painted floral tiles. Other French touches include glazed terra-cotta tiles in the lobby and some of the rooms in Pierre Deux fabrics.

The lace-curtained guest rooms, predominantly peach, country-French blue, and rose, have thoughtful features such as reading lights above each side of the bed, a selection of old books, fresh apples, hair dryers, and a wine list. Color TVs are tucked away in armoires. Some rooms have bay windows with sitting areas; others have charming tables with hand-painted flowers.

Address: *863 Bush St., San Francisco, CA 94108, tel. 415/928–6000, fax 415/775–5717.*
Accommodations: *26 double rooms with baths.*
Amenities: *Phone in rooms, fireplace in many rooms, whirlpool tub in 1 room; laundry service, afternoon refreshments, wine-only room service, catered dinner in room available; valet parking.*
Rates: *$105–$155, suite $215; full breakfast. AE, MC, V.*
Restrictions: *No smoking in common areas, no pets.*

Spencer House

A short walk from Golden Gate Park and the hippie haven of Haight-Ashbury, this classic 1887 Queen Anne Victorian once was residence of a San Francisco milliner and gold-mine speculator.

Innkeepers Barbara and Jack Chambers purchased the Spencer House as their home in 1984 and spent two years painstakingly restoring it before opening it as an inn in 1986. The French château influence can be seen in the elegant silk wall coverings, Louis XVI antiques, and half-canopied beds suitable for royalty. Rooms are also outfitted with clawfoot tubs, old-fashioned light fixtures, and linens trimmed with antique lace. Many of the original features of the house can be enjoyed, including faceted stained-glass windows, and combination gas-and-electric brass chandeliers. Guests are greeted as if they were long-lost friends, and many of them are. The Spencer House doesn't have a listed telephone number; instead, Barbara and Jack rely on word of mouth and repeat business.

Address: *1080 Haight St., San Francisco, CA 94117, tel. 415/626–9205, fax 415/626–9208.*
Accommodations: *6 double rooms with baths.*
Amenities: *Fireplace in parlor; off-street parking.*
Rates: *$95–$155; Continental breakfast. No credit cards.*
Restrictions: *Smoking in kitchen only; 2-night minimum on weekends, 3-night minimum on holiday weekends.*

Union Street Inn

Window-shopping in San Francisco's most fashionable shopping district, one would never guess that it possesses a garden carriage house, the favorite retreat of Diane Keaton and other celebrities when they visit the city. Of course, guests needn't stay in the cottage to have a view of Union Street Inn's beautiful backyard English-style garden.

The parlor of this 1901 Edwardian features a brick and redwood gas fireplace and padded salmon-colored velvet walls with wainscoting; French doors open onto a gardenside redwood deck. Certainly the cottage accommodations are the most sybaritic: In the center of the 300-square-foot room is an indulgent double whirlpool tub glowing beneath a skylight and hemmed by greenery. The Holly Room has a 19th-century brass bed, wedding-ring quilt, and an English walnut dresser with three hinged, beveled mirrors. The Wild Rose Room features a white wicker bed, striped chaise and ottoman and classic modern posters.

Address: *2229 Union St., San Francisco, CA 94123, tel. 415/346–0424.*
Accommodations: *6 double rooms with baths.*
Amenities: *Phone and robe in rooms, TV on request, whirlpool tubs in 2 rooms; evening refreshments; off-street parking.*
Rates: *$144–$175, carriage house $225; Continental breakfast. AE, MC, V.*
Restriction: *Smoking in garden only, no pets.*

Washington Square Inn

One of San Francisco's prettiest small, modern hotels, this inn overlooks verdant Washington Square and the cathedral of Saints Peter and Paul in North Beach.

Co-owner and interior designer Nan Rosenblatt has captured the ambience of a gracious country home with dramatic floral draperies, half-testers, bedspreads, sofas, and bay-window seats. There isn't a bad view to be had: Some rooms look over Washington Square, while others face an inner patio filled with potted plants and flowers.

In the afternoon, complimentary high tea with cucumber sandwiches is served by the fireplace in the downstairs parlor, followed by evening wine and hors d'oeuvres. Breakfast is served in your room or at the dining table in the parlor, from which you can watch the Chinese residents performing their morning *t'ai chi* exercises in the square.

Address: *1660 Stockton St., San Francisco, CA 94133, tel. 415/981–4220 or 800/388–0220.*
Accommodations: *10 double rooms with baths, 5 double rooms share 2 baths.*
Amenities: *Phone in rooms, complimentary paper and shoe-shine service, afternoon refreshments, laundry service, room service for beer, wine, and soft drinks; off-street parking.*
Rates: *$85–$180; Continental breakfast. DC, MC, V.*
Restrictions: *No smoking, no pets.*

Bay Area
Marin, East Bay, and the Peninsula

Like a twilight fog, the Bay Area beyond San Francisco's city limits defies set boundaries. The peninsula, the East Bay, and Marin are names used knowingly by locals and terms dictated somewhat by geography, but they tell only part of the story. These three areas, all within a 30-mile radius of downtown San Francisco, encompass forested coastal mountains, high-tech industrial centers, majestic shorelines, enclaves of academia, quiet, seaside villages, sunny inland suburbs, and one-of-a-kind nature preserves.

The peninsula stretches south from San Francisco, through Silicon Valley and down to San Jose, and is the only part of the Bay Area that's reachable from the city without crossing a bridge. Along the Pacific coastline here, the air is often moist with fog in the morning and late afternoon but bright with sunshine during midday. Commercial florists and backyard gardeners make much of this mild climate. In South San Francisco you can take a greenhouse tour at Rod McClellan's, the world's largest hybridizer of orchids, and around Half Moon Bay you'll find one of the most prolific flower-growing regions in the world. Here, too, you can shop in boutiques or head to the beach for a picnic or horseback ride on the sand. Swimmers, however, will find the Pacific waters goose-bumpingly cold at any time of the year. To the southeast is Filoli, whose magnificent estate and gardens were used as the setting for the TV series "Dynasty."

San Jose is inland, just below the southern curve of San Francisco Bay. High-tech industry has pumped new life into this city, and a museum called The Garage offers a fun, hands-on peek into computers, including a simulated "clean room" where silicon chips are made. From San Jose north along the bay toward San Francisco there's a string of high-tech–oriented towns, including

Mountain View, where you can take tours of wind tunnels and prototypical aircraft at the Ames Research Center, and Palo Alto, home to Hewlett-Packard, Apple, and the elegant Spanish Revival–style campus of Stanford University.

The East Bay is just that: the area east of San Francisco Bay beginning at Oakland and Berkeley. The University of California at Berkeley holds a long-standing rivalry with Stanford in both football and academics. Berkeley's reputation as a hotbed of radical thinking has always spilled off campus, and during the past decade the city has become known for spawning a generation of innovative young chefs of the "California Cuisine" school, their inspiration being Alice Waters and her Chez Panisse restaurant.

Oakland boasts such attractions as the Oakland Museum, a microcosm of the Golden State's cultural heritage, art, and natural history. The parks and gardens around Lake Merrit, pleasant hillside and bayside neighborhoods, shopping at Jack London Square along the revitalized waterfront, and generally-warmer-than-San Francisco weather offer as much to the visitor as to the commuting resident.

North of the Golden Gate Bridge is Marin, with its redwood forests, well-preserved coastline, and golden-brown hills, interspersed with clusters of suburban towns. Artsy, upscale Sausalito, just across the bridge, is a favorite getaway for both locals and tourists. Whimsical shops and art galleries line the main street, and restaurants cantilevered over the water offer panoramic views of San Francisco Bay and the skyline. Curving mountain roads lead west to the tallest living things on earth—redwood trees—in Muir Woods. Nearby is Muir Beach, a secluded cove along the Pacific, and Stinson Beach, one of the most popular—and crowded—strips of shore in northern California. Point Reyes National Seashore is an expansive

*coastal preserve encompassing rolling hills, long, nearly
deserted sandy beaches, a lighthouse built in 1870,
a re-created Miwok Indian village, an interpretive walk
along the San Andreas Fault, and a free-roaming herd of
tule elk. Many consider Point Reyes to be northern
California at its best.*

Places to Go, Sights to See

Filoli (Canada Rd., Woodside, tel. 415/366–4640). This 654-acre estate is one
of California's best-loved gardens and is open by tour only. Advance
reservations are required.

Muir Woods National Monument (off Hwy. 1, 17 miles northwest of San
Francisco, tel. 415/388–2595). This awe-inspiring grove of coastal redwoods,
the tallest living things on earth, has some specimens that are 250 feet high,
with diameters of more than 12 feet.

Oakland Museum (10th and Oak Sts., Oakland, tel. 510/273–3401). The
museum is devoted to California's natural history, man-made heritage, and
art.

Point Reyes National Seashore (off Hwy. 1, Point Reyes, tel. 415/663–1092).
Encompassing 74,000 acres of rolling hills, forests, pastureland, estuaries,
and beaches, the preserve has a visitor center, re-created Miwok Indian
village, the Morgan Horse Ranch (where horses are bred and trained for the
National Park Service), and Earthquake Trail, which traces the San Andreas
Fault.

Rod McClellan's Acres of Orchids (El Camino Real, South San Francisco,
tel. 415/871–5655). Orchid cultivation is explored in daily tours through this
35-acre complex of greenhouses.

Winchester Mystery House (525 S. Winchester Blvd., San Jose, tel. 408/247–
2101). The eccentric heiress to the Winchester Arms fortune designed this
mansion to baffle evil spirits with 160 rooms, 2,000 doors, 10,000 windows,
blind closets, secret passageways, and 40 staircases.

Beaches

You can stop at virtually any spot along Highway 1 within an hour's drive
north or south of San Francisco for some spectacular coastline scenery. The
beaches tend to be fairly narrow strips of sand, backed either by craggy
bluffs or rolling hills. The water is often much too cold for swimming;
sunbathing is catch-as-catch-can and usually possible only very early in the
afternoon.

Point Reyes, Muir Beach, and **Stinson Beach,** to the north, are well-kempt and popular; to the south, the beaches along **Half Moon Bay** skirt quaint seaside villages.

Restaurants

In Marin County, the small town of Inverness has more than its share of outstanding Eastern European restaurants, the best of which is **Manka's** (tel. 415/669–1034), where Czech cuisine is served up in a dining room warmed by a huge fireplace. Restaurants and cafés line Sausalito's main street, and seafood, plain or fancy, is the specialty in most. **The Spinnaker** (tel. 415/332–1500) offers fresh seafood and homemade pasta dishes in a spectacular setting near the yacht club. Devotees of California cuisine pay homage at Berkeley's landmark **Cafe at Chez Panisse** (tel. 510/548–5525) for fresh and innovative light lunches and dinners from a daily changing menu of grilled dishes, pastas, pizza, and salads. Near the magnificent Filoli estate in Woodside, the **Village Pub** (tel. 415/851–1294) features Continental fare, including a variety of main-course salads and seafood. San Jose may be the fast-food franchise capital of California (no mean feat), but at **Sebastian's** (tel. 408/377–8600), a restaurant on the 17th floor of an office building in the Pruneyard shopping center, you'll find classic and innovative French and Italian dishes.

Tourist Information

Half Moon Bay Coastside Chamber of Commerce (225 S. Cabrillo Hwy., Box 188, Half Moon Bay, CA 94019, tel. 415/726–5202); **San Jose Convention and Visitors Bureau** (333 W. San Carlos St., Suite 1000, San Jose, CA 95110, tel. 408/295–9600); **Sausalito Chamber of Commerce** (333 Caledonia St., Sausalito, CA 94965, tel. 415/332–0505); **West Marin Chamber of Commerce** (Box 1045, Point Reyes Station, CA 94956, tel. 415/663–9232).

Reservation Services

Bed & Breakfast Innkeepers of Northern California (Box 7150, Chico, CA 95927, tel. 800/284–4667); **Bed & Breakfast International** (Box 282910, San Francisco, CA 94128–2910, tel. 415/696–1690, fax 415/696–1699); **Bed & Breakfast San Francisco** (Box 349, San Francisco, CA 94101, tel. 415/931–3083); **Inns of Point Reyes** (Box 145, Inverness, CA 94937, tel. 415/663–1420).

Casa Madrona Hotel

The Casa Madrona was a decaying 1885 Italianate Victorian mansion that was on the verge of tumbling from its steep hillside perch above the Sausalito Marina until John Mays renovated and reopened it as a hotel during the late 1970s. The New Casa, a multilevel addition, is stepped down to the street below like an Italian hill town.

The New Casa's guest rooms all share a magnificent view of the marina across the street, Belvedere and Angel islands, and the forested hills of Tiburon beyond. Many rooms have private balconies. Each room of the New Casa has a distinct personality. The Renoir Room, hung with prints of the artist's work, has a window seat, large deck, fireplace and, in the bathroom, a claw-foot tub surrounded by an impressionistic mural of a flower garden. In the Artist's Loft, an easel and watercolor paints set beneath a skylight await your talents.

Guest rooms in the original Victorian building are decorated in period style, with high ceilings, Victorian-era American furniture, and four-poster or brass beds. Rooms facing east or south have views. There are also three private cottages done up as rustic mountain cabins.

Casa Madrona is more small hotel than homey bed-and-breakfast, and except for a large outdoor deck of the New Casa, the Victorian's parlor and balcony are the inn's only common areas. In the evening, wine, cheese, and fruit are served in the parlor, and guests can relax in the antique settees or in the balcony's wicker chairs while taking the night air. A buffet-style breakfast is served in the sunny Casa Madrona Cafe, at street level, amid the arcade of boutiques next door to the hotel.

The award-winning Casa Madrona restaurant is attached to the original building, and in warm weather the glass walls and ceiling of this terrace dining room slide open to enhance the already panoramic view, which on a clear day can include the San Francisco skyline. The sophisticated American cuisine makes much of the area's ethnic influences, and specialties include rack of lamb with roasted garlic glaze and minted *gremoulata* ice, and dry-aged New York steak with caramelized onion flan.

Address: *801 Bridgeway, Sausalito, CA 94965, tel. 415/332–0502 or 800/288–0502, fax 415/332–2537.*
Accommodations: *32 rooms.*
Amenities: *Phone in rooms, TV in 23 rooms, fireplace in 14 rooms, minibar in 17 rooms, room service during restaurant hours, conference facilities; outdoor hot tub.*
Rates: *$95–$200; Continental breakfast. AE, MC, V.*
Restrictions: *No smoking in restaurant; 2-day minimum on weekends.*

The Mill Rose Inn

Set amid a lush flower garden, The Mill Rose Inn is one of the most indulgent, romantic hostelries in northern California. The word *pampered* takes on new meaning here—guests are provided virtually everything they need for a carefree stay. Most of the guest rooms have Eastlake and Arts and Crafts antique furnishings, brass beds, down comforters, billowing draperies, and fireplaces framed with hand-painted tiles. All come equipped with a stereo, TV, and VCR, refrigerator stocked with beverages, fruit and nut basket, candies, coffeemaker with herb teas and cocoa, sherry and brandy, hairdryer, and more. Sinfully rich desserts are always available in the parlor, and you'll wake to a generous champagne breakfast.

The Mill Rose Inn is 30 miles south of San Francisco, in the oceanside hamlet of Half Moon Bay. Innkeepers Eve and Terry Baldwin both hold degrees in horticulture and take full advantage of the gentle climate. The front garden is an explosion of color, with more than 200 varieties of roses, lilies, sweet peas, daisies, Iceland poppies, irises, delphiniums, lobelias, and foxgloves, all framed by the inn's crisp white exterior. Tourists and local residents stop by just to photograph the spectacular floral displays. Located in the town's historic district, the inn is five blocks from Half Moon Bay and a short drive to Pacific coast beaches.

In contrast to the building's spare exterior, virtually no corner of the guest rooms has gone undecorated. Each is done in rich, deep tones with floral-patterned wall coverings, burgundy carpeting, custom-made brass chandeliers and wall sconces, and watercolor paintings. All have private entrances opening to a balcony that faces the back courtyard, with its hanging potted flowers, brick patio, and whirlpool spa secluded in an old-fashioned gazebo.

In the breakfast room, bouquets on each table and a fire in the hearth, with its hand-painted tiles reading "Welcome All to Hearth and Hall," set the stage for evening desserts and sumptuous breakfasts. Courses might include an orange-banana frappé, fresh fruit, raspberry, crème fraîche soufflé, crisp bacon, enormous croissants, local champagne, and Mexican hot chocolate made with cinnamon and almonds.

Address: *615 Mill St., Half Moon Bay, CA 94019, tel. 415/726-9794.*
Accommodations: *4 rooms with baths, 2 suites.*
Amenities: *Phone, TV, VCR, and stereo in rooms, fireplace in 5 rooms, afternoon wine and snacks, conference facility.*
Rates: *$175–$275; full breakfast. AE, MC, V.*
Restrictions: *No smoking; 2-day minimum on weekends.*

The Pelican Inn

Upon first seeing The Pelican Inn, you may think you've taken a wrong turn and somehow stumbled into the English countryside. Just off Highway 1 in Marin County, The Pelican Inn is fronted by a formal English garden and set in an expanse of lush lawn. This whitewashed Tudor with black timbers is a replica of a 16th-century British inn—the realized dream of Englishman Charles Felix, who built it in 1977.

Now run by Englishman Barry Stock, the hostelry is a favorite stopping place for San Franciscans out to celebrate a special occasion, and for tourists visiting the nearby Muir Woods. Muir Beach is just a short walk from the inn.

Guests are especially drawn to the Pelican's pub. Amiable bartenders, a dart board, an assortment of beers, stouts, and ales, and an inviting selection of ports, sherries, and British dishes create a convivial setting. The aptly named Snug is a parlor set aside for registered guests only. English country antiques, old books, prints and curiosities that Stock has brought back from his homeland, and a comfortable sitting area by the woodburning fireplace make this an ideal sanctuary.

The inn's restaurant is right out of Merry Olde England, with heavy wooden tables, and a dark, time-worn atmosphere, enhanced by foxhunt prints and an immense walk-in hearth with large cast-iron fittings. During dinner and breakfast, the room is lit only by the fireplace, the tall red tapers on each table, and cut-tin lanterns on the walls. Tasty, moderately priced meals include beef Wellington, prime rib, and chicken dishes. Breakfast, served here or in your room, is hearty fare, with eggs cooked to order, breakfast meats, and a variety of toasted breads. In the backyard beer garden, sunlight filters through a greenery-entwined trellis, and a brick fireplace keeps things cozy.

Planked doors with latches open to the guest rooms, some of which are decorated with antiques from different periods. Each room has leaded, multipane windows, Oriental scatter rugs, English prints, heavy, velvet draperies, hanging tapestries, and half-tester beds. Even the bathrooms are special, with Victorian-style hardware and hand-painted tiles in the shower.

Address: *Star Rte. (Hwy. 1), Muir Beach, CA 94965, tel. 415/383-6000.*
Accommodations: *7 rooms with baths.*
Amenities: *Restaurant on premises.*
Rates: *$130–$150; full breakfast. MC, V.*
Restrictions: *Closed Christmas Eve and Christmas Day.*

Blackthorne Inn

The Blackthorne Inn is an adult-size fantasy treehouse. A four-story spiral staircase winds its way to the guest rooms, secluded private balconies nest in the treetops, and the adventurous can slide down a fireman's pole from the inn's deck to the driveway.

Handcrafted in 1978 by owner Bill Wigert, the imaginative structure is highlighted by a 2,500-square-foot deck with ramps to higher decks. A single, 180-foot Douglas fir was milled to create the planks in the living room's vaulted ceiling. Boulders in the room's fireplace were gathered from eight counties. The solarium was made with timbers from San Francisco wharves; the outer walls are salvaged doors from a railway station. The inn is crowned with a glass-sheathed octagonal tower called the Eagles Nest. Guests there pay a price for the drama: They must traverse an outdoor walkway to reach the private bath. They are, however, near the inn's hot tub. Guest rooms are uncluttered, with redwood trim, and floral-print comforters.

Address: *266 Vallejo Ave., Box 712, Inverness, CA 94937, tel. 415/663-8621.*
Accommodations: *3 rooms with baths, 2 rooms share a bath.*
Amenities: *Afternoon dessert and tea; outdoor hot tubs.*
Rates: *$105–$175; full breakfast. MC, V.*
Restrictions: *Smoking on decks only; 2-day minimum on weekends, closed Christmas.*

Cowper Inn

The Cowper Inn encompasses two homes, their front porches connected by a wide wooden deck. One is an 1893 Queen Anne Victorian, and the other is an 1897 Craftsman house. Many guests choose the Cowper for its location, a 10-minute walk from downtown Palo Alto and a half mile to the train to San Francisco.

Innkeeper Peggy Woodworth has created a home away from home for frequent visitors to nearby Stanford University and Silicon Valley; they appreciate the quiet neighborhood and unfussy atmosphere inside. The largest common room is in the Craftsman house: an open living room that's arranged so guests can either join each other in conversation or settle into a secluded corner.

A long dining table is set near a row of windows overlooking the elaborately restored Queen Anne Victorian across the street.

The guest rooms in both houses are furnished simply, decorated in cool, light tones, and have wicker chairs, unobstrusive floral wallpaper, and Amish quilts on the beds.

Address: *705 Cowper St., Palo Alto, CA 94301, tel. 415/327-4475, fax 415/329-1703.*
Accommodations: *12 rooms with baths, 2 rooms share a bath.*
Amenities: *Phones and TV in rooms, kitchenettes in 3 rooms, conference facility.*
Rates: *$55–$98; Continental breakfast. AE, MC, V.*
Restrictions: *No smoking; no pets.*

Gramma's Inn

A five-minute walk from Berkeley's university campus, this inn is a complex of five buildings. The two oldest, the 1903 Shingle-Style Fay House, and the Main House, an 1899 half-timber, sit at a corner, and a garden area connects them with the other buildings.

The inn is a blend of well-worn comfort and more upscale luxury. The common rooms, in the Main House, have a lived-in feel. The parlor's pink-and-white checkered wing chairs and floral-print overstuffed sofas face the fireplace. The breakfast room resembles a greenhouse, and opens to the patio, with umbrella-covered tables and the garden beyond. A full breakfast of omelets and fresh-baked breads is served here.

The newer buildings are somewhat quieter. Rooms in the Garden House get a lot of sunlight and have modern bleached-wood furnishings, tile fireplaces, brass beds, private entrances, and overlook the patio. The Carriage House rooms all have fireplaces, but lack the character of the older buildings. The Cottage House offers larger rooms, all with fireplaces, desks, and sitting areas.

Address: *2740 Telegraph Ave., Berkeley, CA 94705, tel. 510/549-2145, fax 510/549-1085.*
Accommodations: *38 rooms with baths.*
Amenities: *Phones and TV in rooms, fireplace in 20 rooms.*
Rates: *$85-$175; full breakfast. MC, V.*
Restrictions: *No smoking.*

The Hensley House

T his 1884 Queen Anne Victorian, with its steeply pitched roof and witch's hat tower, is a short walk to the light rail for the five-minute ride to downtown San Jose.

A stately grandfather clock graces the entryway, and in the parlor, velvet brocade high-back chairs, a rosewood settee, and red velvet side chairs surround an ivory-hued grand piano. The room leads out to a sunny backyard deck. The full breakfast includes such entrées as eggs Florentine or waffles, and is sometimes served in the library, dominated by an 11-foot-high walnut vestment cabinet from a Jesuit monastery, and a 500-year-old stained-glass window.

Deep, cool color schemes, and Victorian antique and reproduction wardrobes highlight the guest rooms. The largest room is in the tower, and features a corner gas fireplace, whirlpool tub, half-canopy bed, and a bay-window sitting area.

Address: *456 N. 3rd St., San Jose, CA 95112, tel. 408/298-3537, fax 408/298-4676.*
Accommodations: *5 rooms with baths.*
Amenities: *Phone, clock radio, hairdryer, robes in rooms; fireplace, whirlpool tub, and refrigerator in 1 room, air-conditioning, conference facility.*
Rates: *$75-$95; full breakfast. AE, D, DC, MC, V.*
Restrictions: *Smoking outside only.*

Old Thyme Inn

This understated Queen Anne house's rosy hues and white picket fence set a tone of comfort and good cheer. Innkeepers Anne and Simon Lowings lovingly restored the house and enjoy sharing it with their guests.

Anne's pride and joy is her herb garden, where more than 80 varieties of herbs sweeten the air, some imported from the couple's native England. Fresh herbs garnish the inn's breakfast specialties, and guests are invited to take cuttings home with them.

The Garden Suite features a four-poster bed and whirlpool tub beneath skylights. The Thyme Room has a whirlpool, fireplace, and a half-canopy bed. Even with such up-to-the-minute luxuries, the inn retains a genuine air of old-fashioned friendliness and hospitality.

A full breakfast of home-baked breads, fruit, yogurt, granola, a hot item such as English crumpets, and a dessert of, say, hot cherry flan is served family style.

Address: *779 Main St., Half Moon Bay, CA 94019, tel. 415/726–1616.*
Accommodations: *6 rooms with baths, 1 suite.*
Amenities: *Phone available, refreshments, fireplace, whirlpool tub in 2 rooms, TV, VCR, fireplace, whirlpool tub, refrigerator in suite; health club next door.*
Rates: *$90–$135, suite $210; full breakfast. AE, D, MC, V.*
Restrictions: *Smoking in garden only.*

Roundstone Farm

My hillside haven" is how owner Inger Fisher describes Roundstone Farm. Nestled among the hills near Point Reyes National Seashore, this farmhouse was constructed in 1987. From the rambling shed-style building, you'll see pastoral scenes of Inger's horses grazing by the pond, meadows stretching to wooded hillsides, and a glimmer of Tomales Bay.

A 16-foot-high skylighted and beamed cathedral ceiling and tall windows keep the living room bright. The wood stove, country-casual furniture, and stone floors confirm that you've gotten away from it all. The decor throughout the inn is low-key, in keeping with—perhaps creating—the relaxed atmosphere. Guest rooms are uncluttered, with floral-print curtains and bedspreads, a Windsor side chair or two, and white wood headboards fashioned after garden gates, all harmonizing with antique armoires from England and Denmark.

Breakfast is served family style in the dining room, whose sliding glass doors lead to a patio and garden.

Address: *9940 Sir Francis Drake Blvd., Box 217, Olema, CA 94950, tel. 415/663–1020.*
Accommodations: *5 rooms with baths.*
Amenities: *Fireplace in 4 rooms.*
Rates: *$115–$125; full breakfast. AE, MC, V.*
Restrictions: *Smoking on deck only; 2-night minimum on weekends, closed first 2 weeks of Dec.*

Ten Inverness Way

Veteran innkeeper and columnist Mary Davies has created a coastal country-style bed-and-breakfast in Inverness, on Tomales Bay. The weathered 1904 Shingle-style house is convenient to the Point Reyes National Seashore, and close to the fine Czechoslovakian or French restaurants in town.

The inn's living room is warmed by a large stone fireplace, and the walls are lined with bookshelves. Windows look out onto the trees and gardens.

The atmosphere is country-cottage casual, and the decor takes its cues from the stone fireplace, redwood interior, and Oriental rugs. Hand-sewn quilts enhance the guest rooms. There's nothing fancy or fussy here but, then again, people come to get *away* from fancy and fussy.

Breakfasts feature banana-buttermilk buckwheat pancakes and chicken-apple sausage.

Address: *10 Inverness Way, Box 63, Inverness, CA 94937, tel. 415/669–1648.*
Accommodations: *4 rooms with baths, 1 suite.*
Amenities: *Hot tub, complimentary beverages.*
Rates: *$110–$160; full breakfast. MC, V.*
Restrictions: *Smoking in garden only; 2-day minimum on weekends, 3-day minimum on holidays.*

Wine Country

Less than an hour north of the cosmopolitan streets of San Francisco lies the gateway to California's wine country, the premium grape-growing region in the United States. Well-traveled highways gradually give way to country roads that meander through lush valleys, along hillsides dotted with orchards, and past thousands of acres of vineyards whose color and character change dramatically with the season.

The counties of Napa and Sonoma, which garner the lion's share of wine-tasting awards, are separated by the majestic Mayacamas Mountains. The 21-mile-long Napa Valley, which stretches from the top of San Francisco Bay to the unassuming town of Calistoga, boasts more than 200 wineries. But it is dwarfed by its neighbor to the west. Sonoma's 1,600 square miles consist of rolling hills, scenic valleys, and five distinct wine-growing regions, including one that straddles the dynamic Russian River as it wends its way west to meet the waters of the Pacific Ocean.

It has been said that Napa is reminiscent of parts of the French countryside, while Sonoma resembles Italy, especially Tuscany. The analogies with Europe are particularly apt, given the local emphasis on fine wines and extraordinary cuisine. Moreover, many of the region's earliest wineries were established during the 1800s by immigrants from France and Italy as well as from Germany and Hungary. Gradually orchards of apples, pears, walnuts, and plums were replanted with grapes, though Sonoma is still famous for its apples and other produce. Sonoma's numerous ranches and farms produce everything from beef and poultry to strawberries and melons, and it's all available at the hundreds of produce stands scattered along the county's 1,450 miles of roadsides.

The wine country's abundant open space is endangered, however, by encroaching development. The county seat itself has mushroomed, making it difficult to travel easily between the Sonoma Valley and the Russian River area.

Despite recent urban growth, particularly in the vicinity of Santa Rosa, the wine country is still largely rural—fertile ground for dozens of small inns that attract a constant stream of visitors year-round. In Napa, summer weekends find cars snaking along Highway 29, the main north–south thoroughfare. An increasingly popular option is the Silverado Trail, a two-lane road that parallels the highway on the eastern side of the valley.

Sonoma bears myriad reminders of the county's mission heritage; in Napa, the hot springs and mud baths bear testimony to the valley's volcanic history. Napa has a reputation for elitism, whereas Sonoma remains close to its agricultural heritage. Combined, the two areas constitute one of California's prime attractions.

Places to Go, Sights to See

Horseback Riding (tel. 707/996–8566). The *Sonoma Cattle Company* offers guided one- and two-hour excursions at Jack London State Historic Park and Sugarloaf Ridge State Park.

Hot-Air Ballooning. *Sonoma Thunder* (4914 Snark Ave., Santa Rosa, tel. 707/538–7359 or 800/759–5638, fax 707/538–3782) operates hot-air balloons above the vineyards and west along the Russian River, allowing visitors to view the coastline.

Jack London State Historic Park (2400 London Ranch Rd., Glen Ellen, tel. 707/938–5216). Memorabilia from the life of the prolific author–sailor–farmer are displayed in a museum home. The remains of Wolf House, London's dream home that burned down mysteriously in 1913, can be seen through a grove of redwood trees.

Luther Burbank Memorial Gardens (Santa Rosa and Sonoma aves., Santa Rosa, tel. 707/576–5115). The renowned horticulturist Luther Burbank chose this area for his extensive plant-breeding experiments. He is remembered in this well-maintained National Historical Landmark home, carriage house, and greenhouse, all of which can be seen on docent-guided tours.

Mud Baths. Nineteenth-century settlers discovered the health benefits of the natural mineral waters and volcanic ash of Mt. St. Helena. Establishments on

Lincoln Avenue in Calistoga tout health regimens ranging from immersion in mud baths to soaking in hot baths to full massage treatments.

The Petrified Forest (4 mi west of Hwy. 128, between Calistoga and Santa Rosa, tel. 707/942–6667). Ancient trees, some more than 100 feet tall, were covered by volcanic ash 6 million years ago when nearby Mt. St. Helena erupted. Also visible are petrified seashells, clams, and other remains of marine life.

Russian River (between Hwy. 101 and the Pacific Ocean along the Russian River Rd., tel. 800/253–8800). Secluded beaches, angling spots, and boats, canoes, and inner tubes for rent can all be found along the shady banks of this popular resort area.

Sonoma State Historic Park (Sonoma, tel. 707/938–1578). Facing the plaza in the center of the old city is *Mission San Francisco Solano* (First St. and Spain St. E), the site where the original flag of California was first flown in 1846. Barracks, an old hotel, and other historic structures, including *La Casa Grande* (General Mariano Vallejo's former home), are part of this complex.

Sugarloaf Ridge State Park (Hwy. 12, just outside Kenwood, tel. 707/833–5712). Some 25 miles of trails lead through grassy meadows and groves of redwood and laurel trees within this 2,500-acre park, where bird-watching, picnicking, camping, and horseback riding are popular.

Wineries

Choosing which of the 400 or so wineries to vist will be difficult, and the range of opportunities makes it tempting to make multiple stops. The wineries along the more frequented arteries of the Napa Valley tend to charge nominal fees for tasting, but in Sonoma County, where there is less tourist traffic, fees are rare. In Sonoma, you are more likely to run into a wine-grower willing to engage in convivial conversation than you are along the main drag of the Napa Valley, where the waiter serving yards of bar has time to do little more than keep track of the rows of glasses.

One of California's first premier wineries, **Buena Vista Winery** (18000 Old Winery Rd., Sonoma, tel. 707/938–1266) was built in 1857 by Hungarian Count Agoston Harazthy, who enclosed his limestone caves within large stone buildings that still house barrels of wine. The Napa Valley cousin of France's Moët et Chandon label, **Domaine Chandon** (California Dr., Yountville, tel. 707/944–2280) offers a close-up of how sparkling wines are produced and bottled. **Hakusan Sake Gardens** (1 Executive Way, Napa, tel. 707/258–6160) is a refreshing change from winery tours; you can taste both warm and cold sake in the Japanese garden. No tour of the Napa Valley would be complete without a visit to **Robert Mondavi** (7801 St. Helena Hwy., Oakville, 707/963–9611), the winery owned by one of the most famous and admired winemakers in the United States. Set atop a hill at the northern end of the Napa Valley, **Sterling Vineyards** (1111 Dunaweal La., Calistoga, tel. 707/942–5151) features an aerial tramway. In 1990 Vicki and Sam Sebastiani opened the Tuscan-style **Viansa Winery** (Hwy. 12, Schellville, tel. 707/945–4747) overlooking the Sonoma Valley.

Restaurants

The Diner (tel. 707/944–2626) in Yountville is a homey American-Mexican diner specializing in hearty, simply prepared dishes that range from waffles or huevos rancheros at breakfast to seafood tostadas at dinner. North of Yountville is **Mustards Grill** (tel. 707/944–2424), an unpretentious roadside restaurant serving such fresh, flavorful fare as roast rabbit, grilled fish, and a long list of noteworthy appetizers. In the El Dorado Hotel in Sonoma, **Ristorante Piatti** (tel. 707/996–2351), like its namesake in the Napa Valley, is known for its homemade pastas, calzones, and pizzas prepared in a wood-burning oven; grilled meats are another specialty. In St. Helena, **Tra Vigne** (tel. 707/963–4444) has high ceilings, gilded moldings, and hearty Italian fare. **Big 3** (tel. 707/938–9000) in Boyes Hot Springs is a casual restaurant at the Sonoma Mission Inn & Spa known for fresh local produce, poultry, and seafood. The breakfast and Sunday brunch menus feature spa dishes as well as eggs, waffles, and Sonoma sausages.

Tourist Information

Healdsburg Chamber of Commerce (217 Healdsburg Ave., tel. 707/433–6935 or 800/648–9922 in CA; **Napa Valley Visitors Bureau** (4260 Silverado Trail, Yountville, CA 94599, tel. 707/258–1957); **Sonoma County Visitors and Convention Bureau** (10 4th St., Santa Rosa, CA 95401, tel. 707/575–1191); **Sonoma Valley Visitors Bureau** (435 E. 1st St., Sonoma, CA 95476, tel. 707/996–1090).

Reservation Services

Bed & Breakfast Inns of Sonoma County (Box 51, Geyserville, CA 95476, tel. 707/433–4667).

Auberge du Soleil

Partially obscured by groves of gray-green olive trees, the "inn of the sun" is nestled into a hillside on the eastern edge of the Napa Valley. Claude Rouas, the French-born restaurateur who made San Francisco's L'Etoile the virtual headquarters of the society set, opened a restaurant on this site in 1981. "The restaurant took off immediately," recalled Rouas. "But I had always dreamed of opening an inn in the style of the country inns in Provence, like La Colombe d'Or. I wanted something with that Provence feeling but also something that would be fitting in the Napa Valley."

The guest accommodations also had to suit the existing restaurant, a stunning structure with light-colored walls and an extended balcony entwined with grapevines. To this end, Rouas went back to the original design team—architect Sandy Walker and designer Michael Taylor. Together they built nine "maisons" (each named for a French region) on the 33-acre site below the restaurant; two others were added in 1987. The result is a low-rise blend of southwestern French and adobe-style architecture.

Each room has its own entrance and a trellis-covered veranda facing the valley. The rooms have a fresh, streamlined look with smooth, hand-glazed terra-cotta tiles on the floors and framing the fireplaces. The

walls are a soothing pale stucco, and tall double doors, covered with white wooden shutters, open onto the balcony. High ceilings and air-conditioning fight the summer heat; on winter nights, however, guests may want to pull the soft leather chairs close to the fireplace for warmth.

The Auberge du Soleil is eminently suited to honeymooners, who can remain sequestered, thanks to room service. But the inn also has ample public spaces where groups can gather. The restaurant, whose reputation suffered after the departure of the original chef, is now one of the valley's most popular. Although Rouas is often on the premises, the day-to-day business of management is left to George A. Goeggel, another European, who came to the inn from the Rosewood Hotel Group.

Address: *180 Rutherford Hill Rd., Rutherford, CA 94573, tel. 707/963–1211, fax 707/963–8764.*
Accommodations: *27 rooms with baths, 21 suites.*
Amenities: *Air-conditioning; fireplace and refrigerator in room, whirlpool baths in 12 rooms, outdoor pool and whirlpool bath, tennis courts, tennis pro, massage room, restaurant, conference facilities.*
Rates: *$275–$325, suites $425–$525; Continental breakfast. AE, D, MC, V.*

Kenwood Inn

Terry and Roseann Grimm deserve an award for transforming a ramshackle antiques shop into a romantic Italian-style retreat. Since the inn, which faces the vineyards on the hills across Highway 12, is separated from the two-lane road by a large flagstone patio, a swimming pool, and extensive grounds (landscaped with dozens of rosebushes as well as persimmon, fig, apple, and—most appropriately—olive trees), there is little traffic noise.

The inn's most seductive features are the smallest details, from the down mattresses covered with Egyptian cotton sheets to the aromatic sprigs of fresh-from-the-garden herbs used to garnish breakfast dishes. Innkeeper Sandra Ellis, who speaks with a British accent from her native Kenya, gives guests the impression that no request is too much trouble, whether it's preparing an afternoon fruit and cheese platter or arranging a specially catered dinner for private parties.

Room No. 3, decorated in dark greens and lush burgundies, has a queen-size bed as well as a private patio and a garden entrance. The paisley wallpaper and moss-colored draperies make it a cozy place for enjoying a fire. It is set off from the other two ground-floor accommodations by a large living room furnished simply with glass and wrought iron console tables along the walls, ebony straight-back chairs imported from Mozambique, and two overstuffed sofas upholstered in Italian prints and flanking the fireplace. Room No. 6, located upstairs, claims the most privacy and the best view, as well as a four-poster king-size bed canopied in mango, burgundy, and black.

Sandra, whose background includes a stint as manager of a commercial fishing marina and an importer of African furniture, has found her métier in the kitchen. Breakfast may consist of a plate of fresh fruit, a slice of rock-shrimp quiche, and a poached egg served on a square of polenta drizzled with pesto; other specialties include blintzes and crêpes.

Address: *10400 Sonoma Hwy, Kenwood, CA 95442, tel. 707/833–1293.*
Accommodations: *2 double rooms with baths, 2 suites.*
Amenities: *Fireplace, feather mattress and down comforter and pillows in room; pool, off-street parking.*
Rates: *$125–$170, suites $135–$225; full breakfast. AE, MC, V.*
Restrictions: *No smoking; 2-night minimum on weekends.*

Madrona Manor

A fraction of its former size, this estate dates from 1881, when San Franciscan John Paxton commissioned a mansion to be built on 240 acres on the outskirts of Healdsburg. To the Eastlake-style architecture he added gingerbread flourishes, steeply pitched dormers, gables, a mansard roof, and a wraparound porch. He filled it with massive furniture; many pieces, including a rosewood square grand piano, are still in use.

Today the estate comprises an eight-acre wooded knoll. In 1981 it was bought by Carol and John Muir, who had been living in Saudi Arabia. After redecorating the Carpenter Gothic carriage house, they added four third-floor guest rooms in the main house for a total of nine. Instead of duplicating the turn-of-the-century California decor of the lower floors, they chose Portuguese reproductions. Still, the newer rooms are more modern in tone than the original five. The bedroom suite in no. 203 is American Victorian Renaissance, with circular mask crests on both the chest and the double bedstead. The only guests who might feel crowded are those in the first-floor room, where more than one visitor has reported seeing a ghost during the night.

Less successful are the accommodations in the outbuildings, which lack the elegance of the original rooms.

The Meadow Wood Complex, with its very private bedroom and deck, is headquarters for travelers with children and dogs.

The Garden Suite has recently been redecorated with rattan furniture and a marble fireplace. Because of its seclusion beyond the garden, it is third in popularity only to the veranda rooms. The carriage house, with its massive Nepalese hand-carved rosewood door, houses eight rooms, as well as the new Suite 400, which has contemporary French furnishings and a Grecian marble bathroom. The whirlpool bath has shutters that open onto the sitting room, facing the fireplace.

Herbs and some vegetables from the inn's extensive gardens find their way to the dinner menu at Madrona Manor. Local fish, poultry, and game are often smoked on the premises, and the marmalade at breakfast is made from mandarin oranges picked from several trees on the property.

Address: *1001 Westside Rd., Healdsburg, CA 95448, tel. 707/433-4231 or 800/258-4003.*
Accommodations: *18 double rooms with baths, 3 suites.*
Amenities: *Air-conditioning; fireplace in 18 rooms, restaurant; pool.*
Rates: *$125-$200; full breakfast. AE, D, MC, V.*
Restrictions: *Smoking outdoors only.*

Beltane Ranch

Beltane Ranch is a century-old farmhouse that commands sweeping views of the Sonoma Valley vineyards. Innkeeper Rosemary Wood, whose family has owned the surrounding ranch for the past 55 years, converted the property into an inn back in 1981.

The two-story wraparound balcony, furnished with hammocks, a wooden swing, and plenty of chairs and tables, is an ideal spot for relaxing after a long day outdoors. Two of the three upstairs rooms extend the entire width of the building, with both front and back access to the porch. Ceiling fans, floral fabrics, comfortable reading chairs, and window shutters remain from the days when this was a cherished family retreat. Some furnishings, including a massive carved-wood marble-top dressing table, are antiques. The somewhat drab bathrooms are offset by cozy dressing areas. Despite a wood-burning stove and plenty of reading material, the public rooms are undistinguished. The inn's greatest glory is its gardens, which are occasionally the scene of various charity fund-raisers.

Address: *11775 Sonoma Hwy., Box 395, Glen Ellen, CA, 95442, tel. 707/996-6501.*
Accommodations: *4 double rooms with baths.*
Amenities: *Private hiking trails, horseshoes, tennis court, off-street parking.*
Rates: *$95–$120; full breakfast. Personal checks accepted.*
Restrictions: *Smoking outside only.*

Cross Roads Inn

A better view of the area could be found only on a hot-air-balloon tour of the valley. It's no wonder that the most requested accommodations are the Puddle Duck Room, where from the corner whirlpool bath one can take in views of both the valley and the hillside in back. Named for Beatrix Potter characters, all the extra-large rooms (such as the one with the king-size pine four-poster bed Sam and Nancy Scott commissioned for the house) are decorated with pastel colors, lace tablecloths, delicate floral wallpaper, and mahogany, cherry, or pine furniture. The smallest and most private room is the Mrs. Ribby Room, the only guest room that's on the lower floor.

Breakfast can be taken privately or on the spacious decks. Guests can gather later in the living room, where a circular glass fireplace warms the room on chilly evenings.

Address: *6380 Silverado Trail, Napa, CA 94558, tel. 707/944-0646.*
Accommodations: *3 double rooms with baths.*
Amenities: *Whirlpool baths, ceiling fan in 1 room; afternoon and evening refreshments; hiking trails.*
Rates: *$175–$200; full breakfast. MC, V.*
Restrictions: *No smoking; 2-night minimum on weekends and holidays.*

The Gaige House

The Gaige House is not the most stunningly furnished bed-and-breakfast in the wine country. Most of the pieces are oak or mahogany reproductions, but what it lacks in luxury, the house makes up for in spacious accommodations and an excellent location. Built during the 1890s, the Italianate Queen Anne graces the tree-lined main street of one of Sonoma's most endearing villages. The former estate of author Jack London sits nearby at the top of a winding road.

After languishing as a boardinghouse and a school, The Gaige House was restored in 1980 by the previous innkeepers. Steve Salvo, a former agricultural researcher in the Central Valley, moved here with his wife, Michol, five years ago.

They are adding a room in the Carriage House in the back of the 1.2-acre property, which encompasses a pool and an enormous oak-shaded deck overlooking Calabezas Creek. Afternoon wine is served in the parlor amid the Salvos' interesting art collection, which includes a bejeweled carousel horse carved during the 1920s and a huge Bakatiara rug.

Address: *13540 Arnold Dr., Glen Ellen, CA 95442, 707/935-0237.*
Accommodations: *8 double rooms with baths.*
Amenities: *Fireplace in 2 rooms, afternoon refreshments; off-street parking, pool, bicycle rentals.*
Rates: *$85-$150; full breakfast.*
Restrictions: *Smoking outside only.*

Hope-Merrill House

The north Sonoma town of Geyserville has at least two things going for it: location and this fastidiously restored Eastlake/Stick Style manse. Bob and Rosalie Hope had been collecting Victoriana long before they moved here to open a pair of inns—the 1904 Queen Anne cottage (now the Hope-Bosworth House) and the older house across the street, named for J. P. Merrill, the original resident. The latter, built during the 1880s, offered ample space, including a sitting room large enough to accommodate a five-piece Eastlake walnut parlor set.

In a building that has won recognition from the National Trust for Historic Preservation for outstanding restoration, it is not surprising to find the original Lincrusta Walton wainscoting, Bradbury & Bradbury silkscreen wallpapers, striped chaise longues, wicker settees, and other Victorian features. Rosalie and Bob, whose hospitality befits his North Carolina drawl, have recently opened a third inn in Mexico.

Address: *21253 Geyserville Ave., Box 42, Geyserville, CA 95441, tel. 707/857-3356 or 800/825-4233.*
Accommodations: *7 double rooms with baths.*
Amenities: *Fireplace in 3 rooms, whirlpool baths in 2 rooms; outdoor pool, gazebo.*
Rates: *$95-$125; full breakfast. AE, MC, V.*
Restrictions: *Smoking outside only, no pets, 2-night minimum on weekends. Mar.–Dec., 3-night minimum on holidays.*

Magnolia Hotel

I f the rooms in this inn are on the small side, write it off to authenticity. The three-part inn was built of brick and fieldstone in 1873. Originally a hotel, it served as a bordello, a bastion of bootlegging, and a 4-H Club meeting place before being restored during the late 1960s. Bruce and Bonnie Locken took it over in 1977, abandoning their careers as general manager of San Francisco's Clift Hotel and a professional dietitian, respectively, and bringing aboard their sons Craig and Lars.

The seven rooms in the main building are decorated similarly: Bedstands are brass and/or iron, windows are hung with pink organdy curtains, and occasional tables are topped with marble. The rooms in the Garden Court and Carriage House, which were remodeled a decade ago, are more spacious, especially Camellia, which has bay windows and a private entrance. Connected by open-air walkways and surrounded by aromatic shrubbery, the ivy-covered buildings are flanked by vineyards and are only a block away from the commercial district of tiny Yountville.

Address: *6529 Yount St., Drawer M, Yountville, CA 94599, tel. 707/944-2056.*
Accommodations: *11 double rooms with baths, 1 suite.*
Amenities: *Air-conditioning; gaslog fireplace in 5 rooms, wine cellar; pool, outdoor hot tub.*
Rates: *$89–$169; full breakfast. Personal checks or cash only.*
Restrictions: *No smoking.*

Quail Mountain

T he private road off Highway 29 winds up, up, and up through a forest of redwood, Douglas fir, madrona, and oak trees to a site 300 feet above the valley floor. Wild quail scurry about, disappearing into wild lilac, ferns, berry bushes, and wildflowers. Don and Alma Swiers chose this 23-acre parcel more than a decade ago, intending to open an inn after long careers in education and the oil industry.

The two smaller accommodations feature small semiprivate decks facing the forested slopes above the inn, but the best choice is the Fern Room, a minisuite with a small sun room facing the valley. The decor is unstudied country-style, with handmade quilts set atop white linen duvets. Furnishings are minimal: an attractive pine bureau, two bedside tables, and a rocking chair.

Afternoon wine and cheese and morning meals are served in the brick-floored solarium. The enormous breakfasts can range from a dish of pureed rhubarb (home-grown) topped with crème fraîche to a colossal apple pancake.

Address: *4455 N. St. Helena Hwy., Calistoga, CA 94515, tel. 707/942-0315 or 942/0316.*
Accommodations: *3 double rooms with baths.*
Amenities: *Afternoon tea; pool, hot tub.*
Rates: *$90–$110; full breakfast. MC, V.*
Restrictions: *Smoking outside only; 2-night minimum on weekends.*

Sonoma Hotel

Few American town squares evoke a sense of place and history as well as the plaza in the heart of old Sonoma. Flanked by old adobes and false-front buildings, the eight-acre square was laid out in 1835 by General Mariano Vallejo. Many of the buildings have been restored and converted into restaurants, shops, and hotels, the most historic of which is the Sonoma Hotel.

An old-fashioned feeling pervades this three-story, century-old adobe structure (the high-gabled top floor was added around 1880). Only when you leave the hotel do you realize that you are in the 1990s, not the 1890s.

There are challenges to furnishing a hotel without a single reproduction—mattresses had to be custommade to fit the oddly shaped beds. Turn-of-the-century English and French bedroom sets furnish all but one of the accommodations; that one, named in honor of Vallejo, boasts the Italianate hand-carved burled walnut furniture that belonged to the general's sister.

Address: *110 W. Spain St., Sonoma, CA 95476, tel. 707/996-2996.*
Accommodations: *6 double rooms with baths; 10 double rooms share 2 baths, 1 suite.*
Amenities: *Restaurant, bar.*
Rates: *$62–$105; Continental breakfast. AE, MC, V.*

Thistle Dew Inn

Steps away from historic Sonoma Square, this inn is actually two in one, with accommodations in both the main house, built in 1869, and in a 1905 cottage relocated to these grounds from three blocks away. Most of the Arts and Crafts–style furniture, original to the house, is a suitable match for the relatively simple design of the buildings. The six-leaf dining-room table and matching sideboards, for instance, are Gustav Stickley creations. There are also gallery-quality pieces of Mission furniture, such as the chest of drawers signed by Charles Limbert. In the cottage, where four rooms share a parlor, Navajo rugs and Amish quilts complement the early 1900s decor. The Rose Garden and the Cornflower rooms in the main house have walls that were sponge-painted

in their namesake colors vividly enough to keep some guests awake at night.

After they bought the inn in 1990, Norma Barnett, a practicing psychologist, redecorated all of the guest rooms; Larry tends the kitchen and the English-style garden that borders the inn.

Address: *171 W. Spain St., Sonoma, CA 95476, tel. 707/938-2909.*
Accommodations: *6 double rooms with baths.*
Amenities: *Air-conditioning; afternoon refreshments; Jacuzzi, bicycles, access to local health club.*
Rates: *$80–$100; full breakfast, AE, MC, V.*
Restrictions: *Smoking outside only.*

Vintners Inn

In a few years, this 44-room country inn may acquire the patina of an established *auberge* in the south of France. When it opened in 1981, however, it stood out like a cactus in a vineyard. Surrounded by mostly open land, the Vintners Inn consists of four two-story Mediterranean-style villas, topped with red-tiled roofs and set off with arched windows, patios, walkways, and fountains. Clever landscaping makes the nearby freeway much less noticeable.

The decor consists of homey floral-print wallpapers and some antique furnishings, including turn-of-the-century pine chests, desks, and armoires in a country-French style. The suites are huge, and the upstairs corner rooms feature vaulted ceilings and windows on two sides. Instead of closets, there are hanging rods in the dressing room. Buffet breakfast is served in a casual dining room. California cuisine is available at the adjacent John Ash & Co., one of the county's top restaurants.

Address: *4250 Barnes Rd., Santa Rosa, CA 95403, tel. 707/575-7350 or 800/421-2584 in CA; fax 707/575-1426.*
Accommodations: *39 double rooms with baths, 5 suites.*
Amenities: *TV, radio, and telephone in room, fireplace in 18 rooms, refrigerator in suites, conference facilities; outdoor hot tub.*
Rates: *$128-$185; full breakfast. AE, DC, MC, V.*
Restrictions: *2-night minimum on weekends Mar. 15-Oct. 31.*

North Coast and Redwood Country

The northwestern corner of California lies in splendid isolation. This land of scenic beauty and serene majesty— some 400 miles south to north, 50 east to west—has long lured the independent thinker, the artist, and occasionally the roadside entrepreneur.

California's magical Highway 1 hugs the coast until, about 50 miles north of Mendocino, it turns east, climbs over the Coast Range, connects with U.S. 101, and meanders through the redwoods to the Oregon border. Along the way it passes deep fern-filled gulches where streams and waterfalls flow, golden rolling hills dotted with oak trees, farms and sheep ranches, and the quaint fishing villages of Noyo, Albion, and Elk—century-old hole-in-the-wall ports where steamers navigated craggy inlets to pick up loads of lumber.

The redwoods, which once covered the hillsides, lured New Englanders here a century ago. The new settlers built houses just like the ones they had left back home, hence the clapboard architecture of most of the towns. They also brought the region a sense of community that's difficult to find in other, more urban parts of California. And now the fiercest protectors of the redwood forests are descendants of the immigrants who came to fell the trees.

It takes time to explore the North Coast, not only because the roads are narrow, twisty, and slow but also because so many sights require you to get out of your car and walk. But the region is worth exploring at leisure. Step up to a headland above a cove and watch the waves crash over the rocks. Take in the wildness of the ocean; maybe you'll be lucky enough to spot a whale in the distance, sounding and spouting. Take a walk among the redwoods and savor the silence, the scent of the flowers, the sweetness of the wood, the near-darkness created by the dense canopy of trees.

*The shopkeepers, gallery owners, and restaurateurs along
the North Coast are always ready to chat. Ask them what
lured them to this isolated part of California and most will
tell you it's the stunning beauty of the coast and the
freedom of the isolation, the chance to be part of a community that shares their values. The world they've created
is rich for the visitor in both natural beauty and man-
made luxuries. Good accommodations in historic bed-and-
breakfast inns, outstanding cuisine made from superb
local ingredients, and recreation and relaxation await you.*

Places to Go, Sights to See

California Western Railroad's Skunk Trains (Fort Bragg, tel. 707/964–6371)
offer full- and half-day scenic excursions through the redwood forest to
Willits.

Fort Ross State Historic Park (12 mi north of Jenner on Hwy. 1, tel.
707/847–3286) is a reconstruction of the outpost founded in 1812 by Russian
seal and otter hunters from Alaska. The visitor center has interpretive
exhibits; there is also a Russian chapel, battlements, and picnic facilities.

Kruse Rhododendron State Reserve (10 mi north of Fort Ross on Hwy. 1,
tel. 707/847–3221) provides 5 miles of hiking trails among 1,317 acres of wild
pink flowering rhododendrons, redwood forest, and bridges over fern-filled
canyons. The flowers are at their peak from April through June.

Mendocino, the largest of the villages along the coast, perches on headlands
with spectacular ocean views. If the frame buildings of this former lumber
port, dating from 1852, look familiar, it's because so many New England–set
movies have been shot here. Now a thriving artists' colony, Mendocino offers
galleries, boutiques, and such unusual shops as Wind and Weather (weather
instruments) and Out of this World (astronomical items). The Mendocino Arts
Center (tel. 707/937–5791) offers classes year-round. The town sponsors
a summer art fair, a music festival, and two performing-arts companies. You
get good views (and good picnicking) in Mendocino Headlands State Park,
which surrounds the town.

Mendocino Coast Botanical Gardens (south of Fort Bragg, tel. 707/964–
4352) covers 17 acres and includes heather, perennials, succulents, ivies,
roses, camellias, and dwarf rhododendrons.

Point Arena Lighthouse and Museum (1 mi south of Point Arena, tel.
707/882–2777) is a former whaling station and lumber port. The lighthouse,
built in 1870, has been automated; it now contains a museum of lighthouse
history.

Redwoods. Redwoods once covered the hillsides above the Pacific from San Francisco all the way north to the Oregon border. Most of the trees have been logged, but a few outstanding groves remain preserved in state parks and in the Redwood National Park. *Armstrong Redwoods State Reserve* (tel. 707/869–2015), near Guerneville, is a 752-acre virgin-redwood grove with hiking trails and picnic facilities. *Humboldt Redwoods State Park* (tel. 707/946–2311), 45 miles south of Eureka on U.S. 101, contains the largest stand of virgin redwoods in the world; Avenue of the Giants, a 33-mile scenic highway; a visitor center and picnic areas; and the Founder's Trail in Rockefeller Forest, which leads to Founder's Tree, one of the tallest of the trees. *Richardson Grove State Park* (tel. 707/247–3318), south of Garberville on U.S. 101, is a 1,000-acre grove of big trees; the favorite scenic walks there are Lookout Trail and Tourney Trail.

Roadside attractions are part of the redwood experience. The *Drive-Thru Tree* at Myers Flat (tel. 707/943–3154) has a base with a diameter of 21 feet, wide enough for a car to drive through. Scotia is the home of *Pacific Lumber Company,* the world's largest redwood lumber mill; a museum displays tools, equipment, and photographs of early logging operations and provides free passes for a tour of the mill. At *Trees of Mystery* (tel. 707/482–5613), near Klamath, a giant statue of Paul Bunyan invites visitors to view unusual redwood formations, as well as a large collection of Native American artifacts.

State Parks. Much of the coast up through Sonoma and Mendocino counties belongs to California state parks. Two of the largest are *Sonoma Coast State Beach,* a 10-mile stretch from the mouth of the Russian River south to Bodega Bay, and *Salt Point State Park,* a 6,000-acre beach lover's paradise of wave-sculpted shoreline. Farther north, near Mendocino, *Russian Gulch State Park* offers redwoods, fern glens, and a waterfall, while *Westport Union Landing Beach* has beautiful picnic sites.

Victoriana. In *Eureka's Old Town*—an ongoing project to preserve the city's many splendid Victorian buildings, the most striking of which is the Carson Mansion—visitors will find art galleries, boutiques, and antiques and specialty stores, as well as horse-drawn carriage rides. *Ferndale,* an architecturally authentic Victorian village, has been designated a state historic landmark. The town consists of colorful Victorians; the ones along Main Street have been converted into shops, restaurants, and inns. You can get a walking-tour map from the Chamber of Commerce (tel. 707/786–4477).

Restaurants

Several of the inns described here have exceptional restaurants. In addition, the following are recommended: **Cafe Beaujolais** (tel. 707/937–5614) in Mendocino may be the best restaurant in this part of California. Owner Margaret Fox's innovative breads and confections are famous. **Carter House** (tel. 707/445–1390) in Eureka has gained a reputation for sophisticated cuisine using many ingredients from the hotel's own gardens. The **Samoa Cookhouse** (tel. 707/442–1659), on Humboldt Bay in Eureka, the last surviving lumber-camp cookhouse in the West, serves up hearty meals family style at long tables.

Tourist Information

Redwood Empire Association (785 Market St., San Francisco, CA 94103, tel. 415/543–8334); **Eureka/Humboldt County Convention and Visitors Bureau** (1034 2nd St., Eureka, CA 95501, tel. 800/346–3482, 800/338–7352 in CA); **Russian River Visitors Information Center** (14034 Armstrong Woods Rd., Guerneville, CA 95446; tel. 707/869–9009).

Reservation Services

Bed-and-Breakfast Innkeepers of Northern California (Box 7150, Chico, CA 95927, tel. 800/284–4667); **Bed-and-Breakfast International** (1181-B Solano Ave., Albany, CA 94706, tel. 800/872–4500); **Mendocino Coast Innkeepers Association** (Box 1141, Mendocino, CA 95460, tel. 707/964–0640 or 800/382–7244).

Applewood:
An Estate Inn

Jay Gatsby would feel right at home at this country inn surrounded by forests of giant redwoods in the heart of the Russian River resort area. The creation of two refugees from the Bay Area, Jim Caron and Darryl Notter, The Estate occupies a Mission Revival home built in 1922 by the flamboyant financier Ralph Belden. As you sit in the inn's brightly lit solarium sipping wine, it's possible to imagine the flapper-era parties that went on here: beautiful people, enchanting music, bootleg booze.

Jim and Darryl discovered the house while they were visiting the Russian River on vacation. "The area had long been a popular vacation spot for people from the Bay Area, including my family," Jim explained. "But it had become rundown by the 1960s. One of our goals with The Estate is to restore the former elegance."

At the heart of the inn, on the main floor, are the three connecting common rooms. The bright solarium, with windows on three sides and a full-width skylight, makes a natural gathering place for guests, who enjoy curling up on the huge green-and-white rattan sofas. On cold afternoons a fireplace provides a crackling counterpoint to the room's garden ambience. The living room feels more subdued; with burgundy carpet, a heavy-beamed ceiling, and the back of the two-sided

great stone fireplace, it evokes the feeling of a country lodge. Through a pair of double doors lies the bright dining room; from here, a pair of French doors open onto the pool area.

Guest rooms—located on the main floor and on a lower level (where there's a small library for guests)— are decorated in easy-to-take pastels and furnished with comfort and understated elegance. They all boast sitting areas and plenty of light and are variously furnished with overstuffed love seats, boudoir chairs, chaise longues, and small desks.

The innkeepers pride themselves on their food. Both are accomplished cooks, Jim having learned "at my mother's knee" and Darryl at a cooking school in Bangkok. The fare tends more toward the hearty than the nouveau—eggs Florentine in the morning, steak or leg of lamb at dinner.

Address: *13555 Hwy. 116 (near Guerneville), Pocket Canyon, CA 95446, tel. 707/869-9093.*
Accommodations: *10 double rooms with baths.*
Amenities: *Phone and cable TV in rooms; heated swimming pool, outdoor hot tub.*
Rates: *$100–$175; full breakfast. AE, D, MC, V. Dinner about $30.*
Restrictions: *No smoking, no pets; 2-night minimum on weekends.*

Gingerbread Mansion

The Gingerbread Mansion is a tourist attraction in and of itself; visitors are constantly making the detour from U.S. 101 to the Victorian village of Ferndale so they can photograph its bright-orange-and-yellow exterior and its flower-filled English gardens. The Gingerbread, with its spindle roof ridges and icicled eaves, its bay windows and its shingled turret, must be one of the most photographed buildings in California. Pity those who never get inside to indulge a bit of whimsy in the fantasy rooms, or to enjoy the warm hospitality of innkeeper Ken Torbert and his staff.

The Gingerbread Mansion has served many different purposes in the years since 1899, when it was built as a doctor's residence. A 1920s expansion converted the Queen Anne/Eastlake mansion into a hospital. Over the years it turned into a rest home and later an American Legion hall; when Ken purchased it in 1981, it had become an apartment house. "Alice's experiences in Wonderland guided my renovating ideas," he explained. Thus the inn is full of surprises—pleasant ones, such as rooms with mirrors for people of all heights, and a pair of claw-foot tubs set toe to toe on a white-fenced platform.

The whimsical bathrooms are a special delight. The Fountain Suite bath has side-by-side claw-foot tubs facing a mirrored wall in which the fire in the Franklin stove can be seen flickering. The claw-foot tub on a platform in the Rose Suite bathroom is surrounded by floral wallpaper under a mirrored ceiling; bathing there gives you the feeling of being in a garden. The actual gardens are Ken's pride and joy. Narrow brick paths meander through sculptured boxwood and past blossoming rhododendrons, camellias, and azaleas in winter, and fancy fuchsias throughout the summer and fall.

There are thoughtful surprises, too. Rooms are straightened, the lamps and shades adjusted at turndown each evening. Umbrellas stay at the ready for protection when it rains. Morning coffee is prepared to order for each guest before breakfast, which is served at two large tables in the dining room. This is the time for conversation over a variety of home-baked breads, a selection of unusual local cheeses, and fruit.

Address: *400 Berding St., Box 40, Ferndale, CA 95536, tel. 707/786–4000.*
Accommodations: *9 double rooms with baths.*
Amenities: *Franklin stove in 3 rooms; afternoon refreshments, bathrobes, guest refrigerator; bicycles.*
Rates: *$85–$175; Continental breakfast. AE, MC, V.*
Restrictions: *Smoking outside only, no pets; 2-night minimum on weekends and holidays.*

Harbor House

Some of the guests who arrive at Harbor House never want to leave. Some don't: Innkeepers Helen and Dean Turner fell in love with Harbor House and purchased it in 1985.

Those who love the ever-changing character of the sea find themselves mesmerized by the view from this country inn perched right on the edge of the coast. If you have booked one of the inn's red-and-white cottages, you'll be able to savor the view from your own furnished deck. In some rooms you can warm yourself by a fireplace while studying the sea. If you want to see the ocean close up, you need only descend the steep path to the inn's private beach; although swimming might be dangerous, this is a good place for a picnic.

Harbor House's magnificent setting is just one of its attractions. The rustic-elegant lodge dates from 1916, when it was built as an executive residence for the Goodyear Redwood Lumber Company, which shipped the lumber it logged out of the cove below. The main building—an enlarged version of the Home of Redwood, designed by Louis Christian Mullgardt for the 1915 Panama-Pacific Exposition in San Francisco—was constructed entirely of virgin redwood.

The living room is a stunning example of the carpenter's craft. The floors, walls, and vaulted ceilings are made of old-growth redwood; they were rubbed with beeswax, a natural preservative, to achieve the luster they still have today. This comfortable room beckons you to curl up on one of the overstuffed sofas flanking the enormous stone fireplace.

The guest rooms, also furnished with overstuffed chairs and sofas, are equally comfortable. The Cypress and Harbor rooms, occupying corners on the first and second floors respectively, are both large enough to hold two large beds plus two sitting areas. Both have sea views, as does the Lookout—the smallest room in the inn, on the second floor—which also has its own private deck. Its white cast-iron bed is spread with a wedding-ring quilt.

Breakfast and dinner are served in the dining room. Menus feature fresh local seafood and meats as well as organically grown vegetables.

Address: *5600 S. Hwy. 1, Box 369, Elk, CA 95432, tel. 707/877–3203.*
Accommodations: *10 double rooms with baths.*
Amenities: *Restaurant, fireplaces in 5 rooms, wood-burning stove in 4; private beach.*
Rates: *$150–$220; MAP. No credit cards.*
Restrictions: *No smoking in restaurant, no pets; 2-night minimum on weekends, 3- or 4- night minimum on some holidays.*

Joshua Grindle Inn

ike much of Mendocino, the Joshua Grindle Inn looks as if it was imported directly from New England and plunked down on the California coast. And in a way it was. Joshua Grindle, like many of the area's settlers, hailed from Maine. A raftsman for the Mendocino Lumber Company, he built the two-story redwood farmhouse for his bride in 1879; it stayed in the family until 1967.

The inn displays many of Mendocino's best qualities: functional New England architecture, a respect for the land, and a casual, relaxing ambience. It stands on a two-acre hilltop near the turnoff into town from Highway 1. The original farmhouse has five guest rooms, a parlor, and a dining room. Three bedrooms upstairs are bright and airy, with either ocean or treetop views. The guest room called the Library is particularly appealing. A small, cozy room, it has its own seating area, a four-poster queen-size bed, and floor-to-ceiling bookcases flanking a fireplace decorated with hand-painted tiles depicting Aesop's fables. In the late afternoons you'll find guests in the farmhouse parlor, reading or playing backgammon, sipping sherry, or fingering the antique pump organ.

There are two outbuildings. The weathered redwood Watertower has three rooms, including one on the second level with windows on four sides and, naturally, a splendid view of the ocean and town as well as the mountains to the east. The Cottage, which has two rooms, is shaded by cypress trees that Joshua Grindle planted 100 years ago. Furnishings throughout the inn are simple but comfortable American antiques: Salem rockers, wing chairs, steamer-trunk tables, painted pine beds.

Innkeepers Arlene and Jim Moorehead, who purchased the inn in 1989, came to innkeeping after careers with Bechtel in San Francisco. "It was a natural move," Jim said. "We love old houses, good food, and people." At breakfast guests gather around a long 1830 harvest-pine table. Although the table isn't big enough to accommodate everyone when the inn is full, no one seems to mind enjoying a prebreakfast cup of coffee on the veranda. After breakfast, guests frequently take the short walk into town to shop for antiques or explore the art galleries.

Address: *44800 Little Lake Rd., Box 647, Mendocino, CA 95460, tel. 707/937-4143.*
Accommodations: *10 double rooms with baths.*
Amenities: *Fireplace in 6 rooms, guest refrigerator.*
Rates: *$80–$130; full breakfast. MC, V.*
Restrictions: *Smoking outside only, no pets; 2-night minimum on weekends and in Aug., 3-night minimum on holidays.*

St. Orres

T his inn is the creation of a man who loves to build. With its copper-plated Russian-style onion domes, it's also a landmark along the northern California coast. Eric Black, like many others, moved to Gualala in an effort to get back to the earth; he had been working as a master carpenter in the Bay Area. Eric purchased a run-down loggers' motel, razed it, and created a hotel that reflects the coast's Russian heritage.

St. Orres offers three types of accommodations. The main hotel, which fronts the highway, has eight rooms upstairs; they're very small, but beautifully embellished with such woodwork touches as mitered redwood paneling and handcrafted doorless armoires with clothes hooks and shelves. Two groups of cottages scattered about the property offer more comfortable accommodations. The Meadows includes three cottages with elevated bedrooms, private decks through French doors, wood-burning stoves, and sun decks. The rustic Wildflower Cabin has an outdoor, but private and protected, shower. The seven Creekside cottages are more luxurious and— scattered on a wooded hillside away from the hotel—quite private. Pine Haven, the largest, has its own skylighted pair of onion domes, one of which holds the blue-and-white tiled bathroom. These cottages share a complex with hot tub, sauna, and sun deck.

The dining room, filling an enormous domed corner of the hotel, has three-story-high leaded-glass windows and rough-hewn open beams. It's a first-class establishment, luring "foodies" all the way from San Francisco. The fixed-price menu offers quail, rabbit, venison, wild boar, and occasionally wild turkey; accompaniments are equally exotic—cream of sorrel or cold strawberry soup, or pâté with sun-dried blueberries. Breakfast is served in the dining room to guests staying in the hotel rooms and delivered in a specially designed wooden box to cottage guests.

Gualala, an 1860s lumbering port, is a lively arts center with plenty of galleries. In addition, the Gualala River is a popular spot for swimming and steelhead fishing.

Address: *36601 S. Hwy. 1, Box 523, Gualala, CA 95445, tel. 707/884–3303.*
Accommodations: *11 double rooms with baths, 8 double rooms share 3 baths.*
Amenities: *Restaurant, 3 rooms with fireplace, 5 with wood-burning stove; spa complex in Creekside section with hot tub and sauna.*
Rates: *$50–$180; full breakfast. MC, V.*
Restrictions: *No smoking in restaurant, no pets; 2-night minimum on weekends, 3-night minimum on holidays.*

Timberhill Ranch

The two couples who created Timberhill Ranch were seeking a refuge from their harried, urban, corporate lives; they found it on 80 acres of rolling hills in Sonoma County—just a stone's throw from the coast, but worlds apart. Tarran McDaid and Michael Riordan and Barbara Farrell and Frank Watson admit that they created Timberhill mainly for their own pleasure. It has the kind of features they enjoy: privacy, expansive views of rolling hills (green in winter and spring and gold the rest of the year), tennis courts, a swimming pool, miles and miles of trails for quiet strolls in the woods, an excellent dining room, and outstanding and discreet service.

With 15 cottages tucked beneath trees on the hillside above a small pond, the focal point of the ranch is the quietly elegant lodge. The lodge contains an expansive living room with a Sonoma fieldstone fireplace and floor-to-ceiling windows with a view of the pool and the hills beyond.

The dining room is a point of pride. Candlelit and formal in the evenings, it's a marked contrast to the casual atmosphere of the rest of Timberhill. A six-course dinner featuring California cuisine is served nightly. A typical menu features such entrées as ahi tuna with a wasabi beurre blanc and pickled ginger, and New Zealand lamb with cabernet and black currants. There's also a care-fully selected wine list, including after-dinner port, sherry, and champagne.

The cottages are identical in design but differ in decor. Small log cabins built of sweet-scented cedar, they have tall windows and decks where many guests enjoy the Continental breakfasts the innkeepers deliver. The beds are dressed with handmade quilts, the walls tastefully decorated with original oils, and the fireplaces stocked up and ready to light. Timberhill provides terry-cloth bathrobes and huge fluffy towels.

This is a ranch, so there are animals: horses in the white-fenced paddock close by; ducks and geese cruising the pond in formation; a pair of llamas; and two dogs—Banger, an Australian shepherd, and Bridgette, a Shih Tzu, who trot behind the innkeepers as they make their daily rounds.

Address: *35755 Hauser Bridge Rd. (Timber Cove Post Office), Cazadero, CA 95421, tel. 707/847-3258, fax 707/847-3342.*
Accommodations: *15 double rooms with baths.*
Amenities: *Fireplace, minibar, refrigerator, and coffeemaker in rooms; swimming pool, outdoor hot tub, tennis courts, hiking trails.*
Rates: *$325–$350; MAP; picnic lunches, $15–$25. MC, V.*
Restrictions: *No smoking in dining room, no pets.*

Carter House

A deep brown four-story Victorian, Carter House dominates Eureka's upscaling Victorian Old Town. Though it may look old, Carter House is anything but. The creation of local builder-turned-innkeeper Mark Carter, the bed-and-breakfast was built in 1982 following a floor plan for a San Francisco mansion. Inside, the inn is as bright and airy as the exterior is dark and brooding. The inn doubles as a gallery for local artists.

The guest rooms on the top floor have the best views, while those on the basement level offer more privacy. The furnishings are simple, mostly antiques, with one dresser dating from the 18th century. There are beds with carved headboards, Victorian settees, and dormer windows with mountain views. Decorations include contemporary art and fresh flowers.

Breakfast is a four-course meal featuring local seafood, fruits, vegetables, and herbs.

Address: *1033 3rd St., Eureka, CA 95501, tel. and fax 707/445–1390 or 800/235–1552.*
Accommodations: *3 double rooms with baths, 3 double rooms share bath, 1 suite.*
Amenities: *Restaurant at adjacent Carter Hotel, fireplace and whirlpool tub in suite, afternoon and evening refreshments.*
Rates: *$75–$185; full breakfast. AE, D, DC, MC, V.*
Restrictions: *Smoking in parlors only, no pets.*

"An Elegant Victorian Mansion"

An 1888 Stick Style Queen Anne, "An Elegant Victorian Mansion" stands on a quiet street several blocks from downtown Eureka. Hosts Doug and Lily Vieyra, who welcome guests into their home with bright, warm smiles, are likely to be wearing turn-of-the-century costumes. Doug may invite you for a spin in one of his antique Fords.

The four rooms upstairs are smallish but comfortably furnished with antiques; the Senator, for example, contains a bedroom set that Lily used as a child in her native Beligum. Common areas include an enormous double parlor furnished with Louis XV reproductions, a game room/library containing an old convent desk from Lily's school in Belgium, and a comfortably furnished family room with a TV/VCR and stereo.

Lily, whose cooking has gained an excellent reputation locally, serves a breakfast that features Belgian specialties in the formal dining room.

Address: *1406 C St., Eureka, CA 95501, tel. 707/444–3144 or 707/442–5594.*
Accommodations: *1 double room with bath, 3 double rooms share 3 baths.*
Amenities: *Bathrobes, Swedish massage ($45 per hour), afternoon ice-cream sodas; sauna, bicycles.*
Rates: *$85–$125; full breakfast. MC, V.*
Restrictions: *No smoking, no pets.*

Grey Whale Inn

From the outside, the Grey Whale Inn looks exactly like what it used to be: the Redwood Coast Hospital, in the heart of Fort Bragg's commercial district.

The rooms range from small to enormous; the largest contains enough space for two queen-size beds, a sitting area, and a minikitchen. A former delivery room still has the sink in which newborns were bathed.

Innkeepers Colette and John Bailey, who opened the inn in 1978, have been sprucing up the decor, some of which dates from the 1960s. Their freshly decorated rooms are definitely of the '90s, with soft, light colors, extensive redwood paneling, and bright, flowered quilts. The larger of the two penthouse rooms has

a spacious outdoor deck and a big modern bathroom with a whirlpool tub; the other has a smaller deck and bathroom but a splendid ocean view.

Address: *615 N. Main St., Fort Bragg, CA 95437, tel. 707/964-0640 or 800/382-7244.*
Accommodations: *14 double rooms with baths.*
Amenities: *Phone in rooms, cable TV and kitchenette in some rooms.*
Rates: *$70-$150; full breakfast. D, MC, V.*
Restrictions: *Smoking outdoors only, no pets; 2-night minimum on weekends, 3- to 4-night minimum on holidays.*

The Headlands Inn

Although The Headlands Inn offers the best ocean views in town, the gracious hospitality of hosts Rod and Pat Stofle is every bit as big a lure. A tall, slender pair, they perfectly complement their three-story saltbox-style inn.

The hosts greet their guests in a bright parlor furnished with antiques that include a rosewood square piano from the 1830s. Two bedrooms open onto a comfortable antiques-filled parlor that's reserved for guests; its centerpiece is an antique French carousel pig. Two rooms set into the third-floor gables have dormer windows; their bathrooms, though private, open onto a small parlor/landing. There's also a cottage (at one time it was a cookie bakery) behind the main

house; it comes with a cannonball four-poster, a small refrigerator, and a fireplace. The lavish breakfasts might include Florentine ham rolls, basil-seasoned baked eggs, or Welsh sausage pies.

Address: *Howard and Albion Sts., Box 132, Mendocino, CA 95460, tel. 707/937-4431.*
Accommodations: *5 double rooms with baths.*
Amenities: *Afternoon refreshments, refrigerator available.*
Rates: *$98-$150; full breakfast in room. No credit cards.*
Restrictions: *Smoking outside only, no pets; 2-night minimum on weekends, 3- or 4-night minimum on holidays.*

Rachel's Inn

Although Rachel's Inn stands right on the highway, it's surrounded by more than 100 acres of parkland where you frequently see deer grazing. Rachel Binah greets her guests with an invitation to take a 20-minute stroll to the bluffs above the Pacific. "That way you'll know why I'm passionate about saving this coast from offshore oil development," she explains.

The inn consists of two buildings: a renovated 1860s farmhouse, the Main House, and the new Barn. The Main House has bedrooms and guest parlors on both floors. The Barn has two bedrooms and a parlor downstairs, and two very bright suites upstairs. The furnishings throughout are simple—white wicker, country French, contemporary, and a few antiques—with sunlight flowing in through the many large windows. A caterer by profession, Rachel serves a hearty full breakfast.

Address: *Hwy. 1 (2 mi south of Mendocino at Little River), Box 134, Mendocino, CA 95460, tel. 707/937-0088.*
Accommodations: *2 triple rooms, 5 double rooms, all with baths, 2 suites.*
Amenities: *Fireplace in 5 rooms, wet bar and refrigerator in suites; beach access.*
Rates: *$96–$165; full breakfast. No credit cards.*
Restrictions: *No pets; 2-night minimum on weekends, 3- or 4-night minimum on holidays.*

Scotia Inn

The Scotia Inn provides an inside look at the world's largest redwood-lumber mill operation. The hotel dates from 1923, when it replaced an earlier structure that had served stagecoach travelers to the Pacific Lumber Company. The inn still provides lodging for people who do business with the company, as well as for visitors who want to find out about the business side of the redwoods.

Although the inn (like the town) is owned by the Pacific Lumber Company, Gerald Carley took over the management of the hotel in 1985. The rooms are fairly spartan (though the furnishings include carved and canopied beds and Art Deco sofas). However, the exceptionally grand dining room and lobby demonstrate how truly beautiful polished redwood paneling, flooring, and woodwork can be. (Guest rooms on the second floor are reached via a gleaming redwood staircase.) The dining room is particularly pleasant, its tables set alongside closely spaced double-hung windows, with huge plants everywhere.

Address: *Main and Mill Sts., Box 248, Scotia, CA 95565, tel. 707/764-5683.*
Accommodations: *10 double rooms with baths, 1 suite.*
Amenities: *Restaurant with banquet facilities, lounge, cable TV in 8 rooms.*
Rates: *$55–$150; Continental breakfast. MC, V.*
Restrictions: *Smoking allowed but discouraged, no pets.*

Sacramento and Gold Country

The reason California is called the Golden State is found right here, on a long, narrow expanse of land about 150 miles inland from San Francisco, stretching from Mariposa in the south to Sierra City in the north. The hills in these parts are often the color of spun gold, but it was the riches hidden inside that set off the biggest gold rush in history, endowed California with its buoyant economy— and earned the state its 18-karat nickname.

Sacramento is just west of those mineral-loaded hills, but it, too, got its wealth from gold. Before gold was discovered in 1848, just 30 miles away in the foothills of Coloma, Sacramento was little more than a settlement of fur trappers and farmers. By 1852, however, it had become the bustling supply center for the Veta Madre, or Mother Lode, as the Mexican prospectors dubbed this gilded region.

For the next few decades, Sacramento boomed and bloomed. When the West Coast was linked to the East Coast by rail, Sacramento was the obvious place to put the station (these days, the site of the old Central Pacific Railroad is a flourishing museum, naturally). And in 1854, when Sacramento was selected as the permanent capital of the new state of California, no one blinked. Los Angeles? Nothing but a dusty dot down south. Even San Francisco was merely a Second City.

All this history is worth noting because, aside from some eye-popping vistas and an admirable collection of rivers and lakes, history is largely what this area has to offer these days. It's a lot, of course, particularly in a state where a 1935 bungalow qualifies as a municipal treasure.

This rip-roaring history also makes the area's relative anonymity and laid-back pace so seductive. Sacramento, an artless metropolitan sprawl with nearly 1.5 million people—and almost as many cars—is a big city now. Under its new patina of sophistication, however, Sacramento is still a small town. People ride bicycles on its busiest streets, big trees shade its many parks, and just a short drive away, you'll still see the tomato and asparagus farms that shaped central California's economy for years.

The Gold Country is one of the few parts of California that haven't had a population explosion in recent years. The locals like it that way. Up in the foothills of the Mother Lode, Jackson, with around 3,000 inhabitants, is considered big. And although visitors pour into these tiny townlets on hot summer weekends, this is still a splendid place for fleeing the crowds.

The Mother Lode is also a magnificent backdrop for motoring. Driving along Highway 49 (doubtless a reminder of 1849, the year 80,000 prospectors flooded the area), you'll see gently rolling hills, sheep and cows, lazy streams—and just when you need some relief from the bucolic, up pops a Gold Rush town, such as Drytown, Volcano, or Jackass Hill. Each is outfitted with old wooden buildings, a rustic spot for a picnic, and a pretty little creek. And if that's not enough, the names alone should keep you amused.

Places to Go, Sights to See

Amador County Museum (225 Church St., Jackson, tel. 209/223–6386) offers a glimpse of mining history with a large-scale reconstruction of the famous headframe-hoisting equipment, stamp mill, and wheels used during the 1920s at Jackson's Kennedy Mine, the largest gold mine from the turn of the century until it closed in 1942.

California State Capitol (10th and L Sts., Sacramento, tel. 916/324–0333) was completely gutted in 1972 and rebuilt to look as it did at the turn of the century. The enormous white, gold-domed building in downtown Sacramento houses the governor's offices, both divisions of the California State Legislature, and a museum, with re-creations of early 20th-century government offices. The Senate chamber, where visitors can watch debates from the gallery, is particularly flamboyant, with gilded columns, massive crystal chandeliers, and a magnificent crenellated ceiling.

California State Railroad Museum (2nd and I Sts., Sacramento, tel. 916/445–4209) has a collection of more than two dozen vintage engines and cars, which visitors can walk through and inspect. The Sonoma, a late-19th-century high-tech masterpiece, is widely regarded as the finest restored example of an American Standard locomotive. The Gold Coast private car, with its marble fireplace and swagged curtains, offers a glimpse of how passengers traveled in high style, circa 1895.

Coloma. The Gold Rush, and all the fuss, started on January 24, 1848, in this unassuming town. *Marshall Gold Discovery State Historic Park* (Hwy. 49, tel. 916/622–3470) immortalizes the big event. The town also has a pleasing collection of buildings, including an 1850s Chinese store.

Columbia State Park (off Hwy. 49, tel. 209/532–0150). Dozens of the Mother Lode's boomtowns are now ghost towns, but Columbia never became deserted. In 1945, the state of California turned this tiny hamlet into a historic state park where only horses, stagecoaches, and pedestrians are allowed on the unpaved streets. Bartenders and shopkeepers don Wild West attire. And visitors who tire of scouring Main Street's museums and candy stores can try panning for gold at the nearby creek. There's also an excellent nature trail and polished theatrical productions at the Fallon Theater.

Crocker Art Museum (216 O St., Sacramento, tel. 916/449–5423) houses an appealing, if uneven, collection of European and American art in a richly restored Italianate Victorian mansion. The collection is particularly strong in Old Master prints and drawings and in California paintings from the late 19th century and the post-1945 period.

Daffodil Hill. In mid-March this four-acre ranch just north of the tiny town of Volcano, near Jackson, becomes a vibrant display of color with more than 500,000 spring blooms, including, of course, daffodils.

Frog Jumping Jubilee. Held the third weekend in May at the Calavaras County fairgrounds just south of Angels Camp, this much-touted international competition inspired by Mark Twain's story "The Celebrated Jumping Frog of Calavaras County" allows visitors to "rent a frog."

Governor's Mansion of California (1526 H St., Sacramento, tel. 916/324–0539), an opulent white Victorian (and one of California's first homes to have indoor plumbing), was home to the state's governors and their families until 1966, when Ronald Reagan requested a newer residence. The eclectic furnishings include a handsome four-poster bed that was extended to 7 feet to accommodate Governor Earl Warren's height, and an old-fashioned claw-foot bathtub with red fingernail polish on its toenails.

Moaning Cavern (off Rte. 4, on Parrot's Ferry Rd., Vallecito, tel. 209/736–2708) is California's largest public cavern. In addition to taking a guided tour of the main chamber, adorned with minerals and prehistoric bones, visitors who don't mind descending by rope can explore deeper chambers.

Murphys. Known as the Queen of the Sierras, this picturesque Gold Rush town has a tree-shaded Main Street lined with rustic wooden buildings. The *Old Timers Museum* (Main St., tel. 209/728–1160), which displays Gold Rush and town memorabilia, occupies the old Wells Fargo office built in 1856; it's a miracle building, the locals say, because it has survived three fires and several earthquakes. Across the street, *Murphys Hotel* (457 Main St., tel. 209/728–3444) has a guest book signed by Mark Twain, Black Bart, and Ulysses S. Grant. Upstairs is a reconstruction of the room where Grant stayed in 1880. A few blocks away is *Mercer Caverns* (Sheepranch Rd., tel. 209/728–2101), a collection of unusual natural crystalline formations in wildly varied sizes and textures. Several nearby vineyards are open to the public, including the *Stevenot Winery* (2690 San Domingo Rd., tel. 209/728–3436) and *Milliaire Winery* (276 Main St., tel. 209/728–1658).

Sutter Creek. The Mother Lode's classiest little town, this is an ideal place to survey the wooden buildings, narrow streets, and rolling hills that make the Gold Country so appealing. Main Street and Hanford Street boast some of the area's most intriguing antiques and gift shops. The *Stoneridge Winery* (13862 Ridge Rd., tel. 209/223–1761) is also nearby.

Restaurants

Sacramento's best restaurants are a pleasing blend of sophistication and health consciousness. Adventurous northern Italian food is served with style at **Biba** (916/455–BIBA), a spacious, white-walled restaurant owned by cookbook author Biba Caggiano. The menu of California–Continental offerings changes each month at **Mitchell's Terrace** (tel. 916/488–7285), where reservations are a must. **Chanterelle** (tel. 916/442–0451), a California French restaurant, is a popular place for catching state legislators tucking into beef with lingonberries or quail with chestnuts. The **Imperial Hotel** in Amador City (tel. 209/267–9172) has a well-earned reputation for its elegant American-style food. But it's getting competition from **Ballads** (tel. 209/267–5403), its new next-door neighbor. In nearby Sutter Creek, **Pelargonium** (tel. 209/267–5008) offers a different menu nightly, including a vegetarian entrée.

Tourist Information

Amador County Chamber of Commerce (Box 956, Jackson, CA 95642, tel. 209/223–0350); **Calavaras County Chamber of Commerce** (Box 111, Angels Camp, CA 95222, tel. 209/736–4444); **Sacramento Chamber of Commerce** (917 7th St., Sacramento, CA 95814, tel. 916/443–3771).

Reservations Services

B&B International (Box 282910, San Francisco, CA 94128–2910, tel. 415/696–1690 or 800/872–4500); **Eye Openers B&B Reservations** (Box 694, Altadena, CA 91003, tel. 213/684–4428 or 818/797–2055, fax 818/798–3640); **The Inns of Amador County** (tel. 209/296–7778 or 800/726–4667).

Culbert House Inn

Paul and Theresa Rinaldi are pure thirtysomething in the nicest way. She's an engineer (mechanical), and he's an engineer (on trains). But when they had their second child, they vowed day care wasn't for them and decided to work at home. After months of hunting in California and Oregon, they found the old Culbert residence in tiny Amador City (population 150), a Gold Rush town best known these days for its antiques shops and restaurants.

The sprawling gray Culbert House, owned for years by a prominent Amador City lumber family, was built in stages, the western half in 1860, the eastern half in 1894. Vacant for seven years, it seemed just right for the Rinaldis, with its French windows, lush garden, and mighty trees (the showpiece is a skyscraping sequoia). After months of renovation, the Culbert House Inn opened on Memorial Day weekend in 1990.

The inn, soon to have a fourth guest room, is a skillful blend of simplicity and sophistication. Paul and Theresa have kept the best parts of the old two-story house, including the wall moldings, high ceilings, and handsome hardwood floors. They've updated the rest, notably the bathrooms, which have either sizable stall showers or old-fashioned pedestal tubs. The decor is country French, with swagged window dressings in polished cotton prints, carved armoires from Belgium, and lots of blue, white, and red.

The Gallic color scheme is particularly appealing in the light-filled sitting room, which has an upright piano, navy blue-and-white checked sofas, and a view of the garden. Each afternoon Theresa sets out her blue and white Royal Doulton china and serves fruit, cheese, and drinks, including herbal teas (the Rinaldis are organic-food enthusiasts).

All guest rooms open onto a wraparound porch outfitted with white wicker rockers. The prettiest is probably the Mulberry Suite, a spacious, somewhat formal room with salmon pink walls, lush flower prints on the bed, Louis XV–style chairs, throw pillows, and a 19th-century love seat covered in red moiré beside the glass-fronted fireplace. But the pale pink Magnolia Suite, with an iron and brass bed and adjoining sun room, is a close second.

Address: *10811 Water St., Amador City, CA 95601, tel. 209/267–0750.*
Accommodations: *1 double room with bath, 2 suites.*
Amenities: *Fireplace in 1 room, afternoon refreshments; croquet.*
Rates: *$80–$95 weekdays, $90–$105 weekends; full breakfast. MC, V.*
Restrictions: *Smoking outside only, no pets; 2-night minimum on weekends.*

The Foxes Bed and Breakfast Inn

The simple white two-story structure that houses The Foxes Bed and Breakfast Inn in Sutter Creek was built during the Gold Rush, but while its 19th-century origins are intriguing, this elegant six-room inn owes its chief appeal to the late-20th-century pampering of guests. Min Fox, who has owned the inn with her husband, Pete, since 1980, sits down with guests each evening and discusses the next day's breakfast. (There's an airy French toast made with apple juice and egg white for the cholesterol-conscious.) Breakfast is served in your room on an antique wooden table with Queen Anne reproduction chairs, the coffee or tea in an ornate silver pot. The place mats are crocheted, as is the little round doily that is slipped over the base of the stemmed orange-juice glass. And tape decks in each room provide a little background Mozart or, oh well, Mantovani.

For years Pete and Min ran an antiques shop that specialized in Victorian pieces. When they decided to turn the house into an inn, they rearranged the unsold tables, armoires, and carved Victorian beds (one headboard is 9 feet tall) and—voilà—the place was practically furnished. Guest rooms in the inn have grown increasingly romantic over the years, particularly the three newer rooms in the carriage house out back. The big Blue Room, with ice-blue floral print wallpaper, has a large bed with a carved headboard and a white Mar-

seilles spread. A wooden canopy with pale blue curtains is suspended overhead. The armoire, which looks country French, was actually made in Argentina more than a century ago. Silk flowers sit in a pot atop a dark wooden pedestal, its base carved in the shape of a griffin. And on the wall there's a print of two baby foxes. (Every room has a foxy touch, such as a fox-head pillow or print, which just misses being twee.)

The house also has a peach-colored front parlor, with a spool-based table and plenty of Rococo Revival love seats for curling up with a good book or flipping through Min and Pete's menu collection (a spicy potpourri sweetens the air). Or you may prefer to sit in the gazebo out back and admire the lush garden, particularly enticing in the spring when the big pink dogwood is in bloom.

Address: *77 Main St., Sutter Creek, CA 95685, tel. 209/267–5882, fax 209/267–0712.*
Accommodations: *6 double rooms with baths.*
Amenities: *Air-conditioning, radio, and tape deck in rooms, fireplace and TV in 3 rooms; off-street parking.*
Rates: *$90–$115 weekdays, $105–$130 weekends; full breakfast. D, MC, V.*
Restrictions: *No smoking, no pets; 2-night minimum on weekends.*

The Old Victorian Inn

At first glance The Old Victorian Inn has three big strikes against it. It's in hot, dusty Stockton, 49 miles south of Sacramento and slightly west of Gold Country, a nice enough place to live but hardly a lure for visitors. It's also situated on a busy corner in a charmless old residential district. But although most of the seven rooms share baths, this three-story house, a flamboyant California-style Queen Anne Victorian built in 1890, is enchanting from bottom to top. Meticulously restored in 1985 by owner Rex Buethe, a Stockton native, the inn is like a turn-of-the-century time capsule (with late-20th-century plumbing, fortunately).

The mood begins in the burnt-orange front parlor, where a fire is likely to be flickering in the tile-framed fireplace. On a nearby wall hangs a portrait of Dr. Lester E. Cross, the home's original owner. The parlor's Victorian platform rocker and magnificent carved courting chair are appealing and genuine; like many of the house's antiques, they hail from the Haggin Museum, Stockton's fine museum and art gallery a short drive away. In the hallway near the dining room there's an unusual brass intercom—like the kind seen on old ships—that Mrs. Cross used to converse with her kitchen staff.

Dr. Cross's bourgeois Victorian taste can be seen in the three second-floor bedrooms, all furnished with the house's original armoires, mirrors, and elaborately carved wooden beds. The Canterbury Room, the prettiest, has a wonderful walnut fireplace mantel, an old wicker chair, and lots of satiny pillows. It seems staid, however, compared with the brilliantly colored attic parlor and guest rooms. Papered in Victorian shades of turquoise and rust with lots of gilt swirls, the attic's Grand Gable Room boasts a big brass bed and exquisite oak wainscoting. The bathroom is equally fanciful, with an antique copper tub edged in wood. A candle holder now sits on a nearby table, ever since a guest asked to bathe by candlelight.

Rex, who serves a breakfast of fresh-squeezed orange juice and homemade muffins, is a social worker–turned–antiques addict. He restored the house with an eye to selling it, but once it was done he, understandably, couldn't bear to part with it. Architecture and antiques buffs should be glad he's still in charge.

Address: *207 West Acacia, Stockton, CA 95203, tel. 209/462–1613.*
Accommodations: *1 double room with a half bath, 6 double rooms share 4 baths.*
Amenities: *Air-conditioning, robes, afternoon refreshments; off-street parking.*
Rates: *$65–$105; Continental breakfast. No credit cards.*
Restrictions: *No smoking, no pets.*

Wine & Roses Country Inn

In her high-necked white lace blouse, Kris Cromwell, the personable owner of Wine & Roses Country Inn, looks as though she stepped straight out of *Victoria* magazine. It's no surprise, then, that her inn on three acres of rich farmland in Lodi, a grape-growing, winemaking community south of Sacramento, is unabashedly romantic. The curtains are of white lace, a fire crackles in the sitting room, and fresh, fragrant flowers are everywhere. Ribbons and bows, too, are ubiquitous.

Kris's Victorian touches nicely complement this rambling two-story country house, built in 1903 and a short ride from the Lucas Winery, which offers tours to guests. The sitting room is large and airy, with two walls of windows, rose-colored carpeting, and cushiony sofas. A treadle sewing machine stands in a corner, and family photographs grace the mantel.

Wine & Roses, which opened in 1988, is very much a family affair. Kris, a former real estate agent, runs the place with her son Del Smith and his wife, Sherri, whom he met when she was hired as the inn's chef. The couple recently had a baby daughter, so the Wine & Roses dynasty continues (more photos for the mantel).

Comfort, coziness, and strong colors seem to have been Kris's priorities

while decorating the nine guest rooms. Eidelweiss, which overlooks the garden, is typical, with deep green walls, pale mauve carpeting, and a green and white floral print duvet on the big brass bed. A dried-flower wreath hangs over the bed. The bathroom has a claw-foot tub with a shower. A clock radio awakens you if the chickens don't.

Breakfast, Sunday brunch, and a four- or seven-course dinner (weekends only) are served in the large pink dining room, overlooking the rosebushes. On warm days and nights, guests can eat outside on big round tables. Or you can sip coffee or wine in the sitting room with Kris, who likes to chat with her guests. These days she's likely to discuss expansion plans for 20 new cottages tucked among the trees and a pool, all to be completed sometime this year.

Address: *2505 West Turner Rd., Lodi, CA 95242, tel. 209/334–6988, fax 209/333–0716.*
Accommodations: *9 double rooms with baths.*
Amenities: *Restaurant, afternoon and evening refreshments, airconditioning, TV, phone, clock radio in rooms; free use of health club, croquet, badminton, horseshoes.*
Rates: *$85 weekdays, $105 weekends; full breakfast. AE, MC, V.*
Restrictions: *No smoking, no pets.*

Aunt Abigail's

There's no Aunt Abigail, but Susanne Ventura, who owns this light-filled 1912 Colonial Revival house with her husband, Ken, is as warm and welcoming as a favorite aunt. She leaves her guests homemade cookies on a carved wooden sideboard at night, and the dining-room breakfast table is set with sterling silver flatware and draped with a lacy cloth.

Susanne first visited Aunt Abigail's as a paying guest in 1985. A year later, she quit her job with an insurance company and bought the place, which is situated in what was once one of Sacramento's toniest neighborhoods. (After years of decline, the area is gradually becoming gentrified.) Aunt Abigail's six rooms, named for Susanne's and Ken's relatives, include Margaret, in shades of beige and green, with a big photograph of Ken's flapperish Aunt Margaret. Uncle Albert boasts neat burgundy and gray-striped Victorian wallpaper. The prettiest, however, is the front parlor, with a big Art Deco light fixture from the Alhambra, a much-missed Sacramento movie palace, circa 1927.

Address: *2120 G St., Sacramento, CA 95816, tel. 916/441–5007.*
Accommodations: *4 double rooms with baths, 2 doubles share a bath.*
Amenities: *Afternoon refreshments, air-conditioning in room, TV available; outdoor hot tub, off-street parking.*
Rates: *$70–$115; full breakfast. D, DC, MC, V.*
Restrictions: *No smoking, no pets.*

Bear Flag Inn

The Golden Bear, the grisly centerpiece of the California State flag, is the official emblem for Jim and Linda Anderson's Bear Flag Inn in Sacramento. But his cuddly cousin, the teddy bear, is the real mascot at this spotless 1910 Craftsman bungalow, located on an undistinguished residential block a short drive from the State Capitol. A family of vintage teddies, garbed in jackets and hats, fills a dining room window. And a little round pillow shaped like a bear's head sits on each bed.

The Andersons, who both worked for a Bay Area industrial tool company before buying the inn in 1988, also collect turn-of-the-century high-tech toys; among them is an Edison Victrola they'll crank up for visitors.

The two-story house boasts a staircase that's textbook Arts and Crafts, an arc-shaped rose quartz fireplace in the sitting room, and a porch swing. The rooms include Meadow, with a four-poster pine bed, and Fireside, which has a skylight, a four-poster cherrywood bed, and of course a fireplace. On sunny days Linda serves breakfast in the tree-lined garden.

Address: *2814 I St., Sacramento, CA 95816, tel. 916/448–5417.*
Accommodations: *5 double rooms with baths.*
Amenities: *Afternoon refreshments, air-conditioning, fireplace in 1 room; bicycles, off-street parking.*
Rates: *$75–$125; full breakfast. AE, MC, V.*
Restrictions: *No smoking, no pets.*

Cooper House

In 1865, Mark Twain came to Angels Camp and immortalized the food served there: "Beans and dishwater for breakfast, dishwater and beans for dinner, and both articles warmed over for supper." Twain's spirit still resonates through this tiny mining town, but, fortunately, the food's improved. Each morning Chris Sears, who owns Cooper House, cooks something such as meatless eggs Benedict with a honey-mustard and dill sauce, or semi-guilt-free French toast made with homemade whole-wheat bread.

This rambling board and batten Craftsman bungalow has a big stone fireplace, polished wood beams, and, like many foothills homes, a corrugated tin roof. The three carpeted guest rooms all open onto either a porch or veranda. The furnishings are more comfortable than costly, though Chris has a few striking pieces, such as an early 19th-century dining table with carved legs, originally owned by Archie Stevenot, an early mine developer. The watercolors and pastels on the walls are local, too, done by Chris and several area artists.

Address: *1184 Church St., Box 1388, Angels Camp, CA 95222 tel. 209/736-2145.*
Accommodations: *1 double room with bath, 2 suites.*
Amenities: *Afternoon refreshments, air-conditioning; off-street parking.*
Rates: *$80–$95; full breakfast. MC, V.*
Restrictions: *Smoking outside only, no pets.*

The Driver Mansion Inn

First things first: The bathrooms in the five largest rooms at the Driver Mansion Inn are fabulous, with whirlpool tubs and stall showers with glass doors and acres of marble. Yet step out of the tub and you're in a three-story turn-of-the-century Colonial Revival house with a sloping lawn and a sprawling wraparound porch, set far back on a busy, semicommercial street near downtown Sacramento. Richard and Sandi Kann, former Los Angelinos, bought the house in 1984.

The guest rooms feel luxurious, with reproduction Queen Anne and Empire furniture and a smattering of new and Victorian pieces. And the enormous pink "penthouse," which occupies the entire top floor, has a marble-top dining table and a big brass and iron bed. Two caveats, however: The rooms can seem a little cold, since they lack the books, fresh flowers, and assorted quirky collectibles found in many inns, and the handsome parlor isn't always open to guests.

Address: *2019 21st St., Sacramento, CA 95818, tel. 916/455-5243 or 800/456-2019, fax 916/455-6102.*
Accommodations: *7 double rooms with baths, 2 suites.*
Amenities: *Afternoon refreshments, air-conditioning, cable TV, phone, clock radio in rooms, fireplace in 4 rooms, whirlpool tub in 5 rooms, refrigerator in 1 suite.*
Rates: *$85–$225; full breakfast. AE, DC, MC, V.*
Restrictions: *No smoking, no pets.*

Fallon Hotel

From 1850 to 1858, Columbia was a classic boomtown, with more than $87 million in gold discovered in its reddish hills. Back then, Owen Fallon's hotel was *the* place to stay. Things calmed down once the gold disappeared.

These days, Columbia is a booming state park, and the state-owned Fallon, sensitively restored to its 1890 appearance, is its shiniest showpiece. The front guest rooms are huge, with reproductions of Arts and Crafts wallpapers, velvet drapes, and headboards in carved wood or iron from the 1890s. The smaller rooms are painted instead of papered. All but No. 15 have tiny private bathrooms with old-fashioned chain-pull toilets.

Just as appealing (though the Fallon's bathrooms are better) is the nearby nine-room City Hotel (tel. 209/532–1479), also owned by the state and dating from 1870.

Address: *Columbia State Park, Box 1870, Columbia, CA 95310, tel. 209/532–1470.*
Accommodations: *1 double room with wheelchair-accessible bath, 1 double room and 12 double rooms with half baths share 5 showers.*
Amenities: *Ice-cream parlor, air-conditioning, bathrobes, slippers, nonworking fireplace in 1 room; off-street parking.*
Rates: *$50–$85; Continental breakfast. AE, MC, V.*
Restrictions: *No smoking, no pets. Closed Mon.–Wed. second week in Jan.–third week in Mar.*

The Heirloom

You don't see a lot of homes reminiscent of the Old South in California's Gold Country. But The Heirloom in Ione, a one-street foothills mining town, occupies a gracious two-story house built for a Virginia farmer in about 1863. And it's got columns atop columns, a two-story veranda, wisteria and magnolia—the antebellum works.

The Heirloom is peaceful and old-fashioned. The dining room, where owners Patricia Cross and Melisande Hubbs serve breakfast, is decorated with china plates and copper kettles. The front parlor includes a handsome grand piano once owned by Lola Montez, the Madonna of the Gold Rush era. Guest rooms in the main house are snug, with tall windows, lace curtains, and quilts. The biggest has a fireplace, a four-poster bed, and a balcony. Out back, a rustic adobe cottage houses two guest rooms with wood-burning stoves and fragrant cedar, redwood, and pine beams.

Address: *214 Shakeley La., Ione, CA 95640, tel. 209/274–4468.*
Accommodations: *4 double rooms with baths, 2 double rooms share a bath.*
Amenities: *Afternoon refreshments, air-conditioning in rooms, fireplace in 1 room, wood-burning stove in 2 rooms; bicycles, croquet.*
Rates: *$58–$90; full breakfast. No credit cards.*
Restrictions: *No smoking, no pets; 2-night minimum on weekends.*

High Sierra
Including Lake Tahoe

"The Range of Light" is the name the naturalist John Muir applied to the Sierra Nevada, the mile-high mountains that form two-thirds of California's eastern border. Stretching from Lassen Peak in the north past Yosemite, Kings Canyon, and Sequoia (the site of 14,494-foot Mt. Whitney) national parks to the Tehachapi range in the south, the Sierra Nevada contains mile after mile of snowcapped peaks encircling alpine lakes, flower-filled meadows, towering waterfalls (including Yosemite Falls, which drops nearly a half mile), and endless forests, including the giant sequoias.

The mountains have played a significant role in the state's history. Initially, they formed an all but impenetrable barrier to explorers and pioneers. (The tragic story of the Donner party—trapped in the brutal Sierra winter of 1846–47 and driven by starvation to madness and cannibalism—became engraved in American legend.) To this day some high passes are closed during the winter, and snow and ice force others to close intermittently. And the tracks across Donner Summit still pass through a series of snowsheds so that the railroad can stay open through the winter.

While much of the Gold Rush took place at lower elevations, the forty-niners mined the mountainsides north of Lake Tahoe as well. Gold Lake Recreation area, in the Lakes Basin, is said to have gotten its name from nuggets found strewn on its beaches.

During the Gold Rush and later, when the transcontinental railroad was built, the mountains yielded up the timber needed to shore up the mine shafts, brace the hillsides, and tie tracks together; thus towns like Truckee and Quincy sprang up to serve the needs of loggers, miners, and builders.

Today the lures of the Sierra Nevada are gorgeous scenery and endless possibilities for recreation. In the southern portion, the scenic splendor of the three national parks draws millions of visitors each year. Yosemite is the most famous, with its glacier-carved canyon, giant granite monoliths, thundering waterfalls, and pristine acres of alpine wilderness. The Ahwanhee Hotel, with its cathedral ceilings, great stone hearth, and richly decorated Indian rugs, stands in a choice spot, with a stunning view of Half Dome. Sequoia, a strip of rugged natural beauty at 8,000 feet, gets its name from the world's largest living thing, the giant sequoia. This park and the adjacent Kings Canyon National Park offer more than 1,000 miles of high-country trails.

Lake Tahoe—at 12 by 22 miles (and with an average depth of nearly 1,000 feet)—is itself a scenic wonder: The largest alpine lake in North America has water so pure that you can spot a dinner plate 75 feet beneath the surface. Lake Tahoe is a two-season paradise. Winter brings 300–500 inches of snow to the upper elevations, along with some of the finest skiing in the West and some of the best facilities: cross-country trails, snowmobile trails, snow play areas, and 212 lifts and tows. During the summer, the recreation shifts from ice to water: boating, fishing, waterskiing, along with biking and hiking.

North of Lake Tahoe is a largely undiscovered portion of the High Sierra, which includes the Lakes Basin Recreation Area, a gentle wilderness of pristine lakes, trails, and peaks. Historically this is gold country; today it's timber country. Visitors will discover a sparse population and several well-placed bed-and-breakfast inns amid mile upon mile of tranquil, scenic beauty.

Cross-country Ski Centers. *Sorensen's* (Hope Valley, CA, tel. 916/694–2203) provides 20 kilometers of groomed trails and 100 kilometers of marked, unimproved trails, rentals, lessons, and day tours. *Spooner Lake Cross Country Ski Area* (Glenbrook, NV, tel. 702/749–5349) divides 101 kilometers among 21 groomed trails and offers rentals, lessons, and moonlight tours. *Tahoe Nordic Center* (Hwy. 28, Tahoe City, CA, tel. 916/583–9858) provides 65 kilometers of groomed trails as well as rentals, lessons, races, and full-moon tours. *Royal Gorge Cross Country Ski Resort* (off I–80 at Donner Summit, Soda Springs, CA, tel. 916/426–3871) has 317 kilometers of groomed track, 77 trails, as well as rentals, lessons, warming huts, trailside cafés, and a ski patrol. *Tahoe Donner Cross Country* (3½ mi off I–80 at Donner State Park exit, tel. 916/587–9484) has 65 kilometers of track, 32 trails, and offers rentals, lessons, and night skiing (Wed.–Sat.).

Donner Memorial State Park and Museum (Donner Pass Rd., 2 mi west of Truckee, tel. 916/587–3841) lies beneath the granite wall of Donner Summit, where 22 feet of snow trapped the Donner party during the winter of 1846–47. The *Emigrant Trail Museum* contains exhibits recounting their tragedy and illustrating the history of the Central Pacific Railroad. *Donner Lake*, with 7½ miles of alpine shoreline, offers swimming, fishing, sailing, sunbathing, horseback rentals, and hiking trails.

Genoa, Nevada (Foothill Rd., off Hwy. 207), the first settlement in the state, retains its historic flavor; the town's Victorian Gothic homes are of particular interest. The Carson Valley Chamber of Commerce and Visitors Authority (Box 1200, Minden, NV 89423, tel. 702/782–8144) offers tourist information.

Lake Tahoe Cruises. Several companies offer cruises on the lake. The *Tahoe Queen* (Box 14327, South Lake Tahoe, CA 95702, tel. 800/238–2463) is a glass-bottom stern-wheeler that departs on a variety of excursions from Emerald Bay and includes lunch and sunset dinner/dance cruises. *North Tahoe Cruises* (700 N. Lake Blvd., Tahoe City, CA 95730, tel. 916/583–0141) takes visitors on champagne Continental-breakfast cruises, shoreline cruises, and sunset cocktail cruises. *Woodwind Sailing Cruises* (Box 1375, Zephyr Cove, NV 89448, tel. 702/588–3000) operates a 41-foot catamaran on regular excursions (daily Apr. 1–Oct. 31). *M.S. Dixie* (Box 1667, Zephyr Cove, NV 89448, tel. 702/588–3508) offers daily dinner and cocktail cruises to Emerald Bay.

Lake Tahoe 72-Mile Shoreline Drive (guide from Lake Tahoe Visitors Authority, Box 16299, South Lake Tahoe, CA 95706, tel. 916/544–2386). This stunning scenic drive includes many of Tahoe's high points: deep green Emerald Bay, the 38-room Scandinavian castle called Vikingsholm, the beautiful beaches at Meeks Bay and D.L. Bliss State Park, and the early 19th-century homes at the Tallac Historic Site.

Plumas–Eureka State Park (5 mi west of Blairsden on Hwy. A–14, tel. 916/836–2380), which summons up the gold-mining era in California, contains

Johnsville, which verges on being a ghost town, a partially restored stamp mill, and a museum illuminating hard-rock mining and early pioneer life.

Portola Railroad Museum (Box 608, Portola, CA, tel. 916/832–4131) illustrates the history of the Western Pacific Railroad with 25 diesel locomotives as well as freight cars and track and maintenance equipment. You can even drive the train here; one-hour lessons are available.

Sierra County Historical Park and Museum at the Kentucky Mine (Hwy. 49, 1 mi east of Sierra City, CA, tel. 916/862–1310). The mine operated on and off from the 1850s until 1953. The museum contains a collection of local mining memorabilia; tours include a restored stamp mill, tunnel, blacksmith shop, and trestle. Concerts of all kinds are held here on Friday evening in July and August.

Ski Areas. North Lake Tahoe alone has 108 lifts serving 16,500 skiable acres in 12 alpine ski areas. Most areas are served by a single lift ticket, the Ski Tahoe North Interchangeable Lift Ticket. A brief sampling includes *Alpine Meadows* (2600 Alpine Rd., off Hwy. 89, outside Tahoe City, CA, tel. 916/593–4232); *Diamond Peak* (Incline Village, NV, tel. 702/832–1177); *Homewood* (West Shore, Lake Tahoe, CA, tel. 916/525–7256); *Mount Rose* (Mt. Rose Hwy., outside Reno, NV, tel. 702/849–0704); *Northstar-at-Tahoe* (off Hwy. 267, 6 mi from Lake Tahoe, CA, tel. 916/562–1010 or 800/533–6787); and *Squaw Valley USA* (1960 Squaw Valley Rd., off Hwy. 89, Olympic Valley, CA, tel. 916/583–6985).

Sleigh rides are popular during the winter. Contact: *Borges Carriage and Sleigh Rides* (Hwy. 50 and Parkway at Lake Tahoe, NV, tel. 916/541–2953); *Camp Richardson Corral* (Hwy. 89 at Camp Richardson, CA, tel. 916/541–3113); *Kirkwood Ski Resort* (Hwy. 89 at Carson Pass, CA, tel. 209/258–RIDE), or *Northstar* (Hwy. 267 between Truckee and Lake Tahoe, CA, 916/562–1010).

Tahoe Trailways is a network of bicycling and walking paths edging the lake. The trail extends north from Tahoe City along Highway 89 toward Truckee, then east as far as Dollar Point and south along the West Shore to Meeks Bay. Bicycles can be rented from *Olympic Bike Shop* (620 N. Lake Blvd., Tahoe City, CA, tel. 916/581–2500), *Tahoe Gear* (5095 W. Lake Blvd., Homewood, CA, tel. 916/525–5233), and *Wray Rental* (315 W. Lake Blvd., Tahoe City, CA, tel. 916/583–2023).

Virginia City, Nevada (Hwy. 341, off Hwy. 50 east of Carson City, tel. 702/847–0177), site of the Comstock Lode, is the nation's most famous mining boomtown. Retaining its century-old rustic flavor, the town contains old-time saloons, Piper's Opera House, a frontier cemetery, shops, museums, mine and mansion tours, gambling, and the offices of the *Territorial Enterprise,* where Mark Twain once worked.

Restaurants

Two of the inns listed below, **Sorensen's** in Hope Valley and **Busch and Heringlake Country Inn** in Sierra City, have restaurants. **Le Petit Pier** (tel. 916/546–4694) offers lakeside dining and is one of the best French restaurants in the area. **Sunnyside** (tel. 916/583–7200) has a lakeside dining room with a charming old-boating atmosphere and serves seafood and prime rib. **O.B.'s Pub and Restaurant** (tel. 916/587–4164) is popular for its old-fashioned lace curtains, stained glass, and old-time atmosphere, and for its California cuisine.

Tourist Information

California Highway Information (tel. 916/445–2820); **Lake Tahoe Visitors Authority** (Box 16299, South Lake Tahoe, CA 95706, tel. 916/544–5050, 800/288–2463 for lodging information, or 900/776–5050 for local entertainment and events information at a $1-per-minute rate); **Nevada Highway Information** (tel. 702/289–0250); **North Lake Tahoe Chamber of Commerce** (Box 884, Tahoe City, CA 96145, tel. 916/583–2371); **South Lake Tahoe Chamber of Commerce** (3066 Lake Tahoe Blvd., South Lake Tahoe, CA 96150, tel. 916/541–5255).

Reservation Services

Bed-and-Breakfast Innkeepers of Northern California (Box 7150, Chico, CA 95927, tel. 800/284–INNS).

High Country Inn

With the craggy Sierra buttes in the background, High Country Inn offers arguably the most stunning view to be had at any lodging in the area. The inn is located in the remote Lakes Basin Recreation Area, where more than 30 jewel-like lakes nestle against the craggy mountains.

High Country Inn is the creation of Marlene and Cal Cartwright. Cal, whose roots in this region date from the 1850s, when his ancestors traveled from Maine around Cape Horn to reach the fields and hillsides of the Gold Rush, wanted to settle here upon retirement. When he and Marlene found a ranch-style mountain house on a 2½-acre corner, they snapped it up.

The house was built in 1961; a new section, added in 1981, offers the best room, the second-floor Sierra Buttes Suite. Tall cathedral windows across one wall frame the buttes; you can laze in bed and watch the morning sun creep down them. There's a wood-burning stove in one corner, a modern bath/dressing room with a 6½-foot tub, a good collection of books, and contemporary art on the walls. The furnishings reflect Calvin's and Marlene's family history. The cane-seat chairs in the Golden Pond Room came from the East with Calvin's family in 1852. Marlene, a midwesterner, has decorated the rooms with the quilts her mother made.

The heart of the inn is a big, open space that serves as living room, dining room, and kitchen. Guests gather here in front of a huge stone fireplace to admire the view, curl up on the big brown sectional with a book (the Cartwrights' library is especially good on local history), or just watch the buttes through the windows.

The inn has a special brand of entertainment in its trout pond. Marlene invites guests to feed the fish—more than 300 nibblers come right up to shore to get a bite.

You can expect a delicious breakfast here. Marlene sets up places at a long table fronting the window wall, so everyone has breakfast with a view; in good weather she serves on the deck. She collects unusual recipes, so corn bread and quiche might come spiced up southwestern style. Despite its remote location, the inn is close to some good dining spots, such as the lodges at nearby Sardine Lake and Packer Lake.

Address: *Hwy. 49 at Bassets, HCR 2, Box 7, Sierra City, CA 96125, tel. 916/862–1530, fax 916/862–7689.*
Accommodations: *2 double rooms with baths, 2 double rooms share a bath.*
Amenities: *TV and VCR in living room; trout pond, river.*
Rates: *$70–$110; full breakfast. MC, V.*
Restrictions: *Smoking outside only, no pets.*

Sorensen's

I f you ever wanted to go camping in the High Sierra and couldn't take the idea of sleeping on the ground, Sorensen's is a good alternative. A historic mountain resort lying alongside the Carson River, at the 7,000-foot level just east of Carson Pass, open year round, Sorensen's offers access to 600 square miles of public land: mountain scenery, hiking trails, fishing streams, star-laden nighttime skies, and fields of summer wildflowers. The inn provides comfortable accommodations ranging from the fairly primitive to the classy, in bed-and-breakfast units and housekeeping cabins, some of which date from the turn of the century, when Martin Sorensen, an immigrant Danish shepherd and his wife, Irene, began camping here. For more than 50 years, the place was a summer hangout for wilderness folk, fishing people, and family friends. In 1970, the family sold the business, beginning a decade of decline during which the Sorensen's came to be known locally as The Last Resort.

Enter John and Patty Brissenden, community activists from Santa Cruz, who purchased The Last Resort for 1,000 ounces of gold and set about to revitalize it, renovating some of the cabins and building others from scratch.

The result is an eclectic collection connected by a network of trails: log cabins in the woods, rustic cedar-sided cabins, even a replica of a 13th-century Norwegian house. Most of the cabins have kitchens; many have separate sitting areas and sleeping lofts. Cabins are offered on a housekeeping basis, but there are small, simply furnished bed-and-breakfast rooms as well. Guests select breakfast from the menu at the Country Café, housed in a log cabin and open for all three meals.

Not only do John and Patty offer accommodations for outdoor lovers; they also try to enhance your understanding of it all with classes in fishing and fly-tying. Guests can hike along the historic Emigrant Trail (which passes through the property), study the stars, and cross-country ski throughout the winter.

Address: *14255 Hwy. 88, Hope Valley, CA 96120, tel. 916/694-2203 or 800/423-9949, fax 916/694-2204.*
Accommodations: *1 double room with bath, 2 double rooms share a bath, 25 housekeeping cabins, each accommodating 2–8 persons.*
Amenities: *Restaurant, wood-burning stoves, pets permitted in 2 cabins; convenience store, sauna, trout pond, picnic tables, barbecues, children's play area.*
Rates: *$60–$100, cabins $45–$225; Continental breakfast. MC, V.*
Restrictions: *No smoking; 2-night minimum on weekends, 4-night minimum on holidays.*

White Sulphur Springs

Travelers have been stopping at the big white farmhouse called White Sulphur Springs since the 1850s, when it was built as an overnight lodge for the Quincy Mohawk Stage Line. But today's visitors will have a tough time picturing the thousands of prospectors who once ranged over the now-tranquil tree-covered hillsides and gentle valleys that surround this inn. For this is a quiet place. On a still summer night you can hear a car coming down the highway long before its headlights become visible.

Although the character of the surrounding countryside has changed from bustling to calm, the ambience of the inn remains much the way it was when George McLear operated it as a stage-coach stop. Many of the furnishings are original to the inn: a pump organ in the parlor, an antique piano, brocade-covered Victorian settees, a pine bedroom set handcrafted by McLear himself. Other pieces, including crystal chandeliers and an extra-large dining-room table, came later.

The inn also contains an ancient wood stove (today it sits in an upstairs bathroom) with the name "Clio" on the door. "Originally the bustling town nearby was called Wash, but people kept confusing it with Washington a few miles away," explained Linda Vanella, whose family has long owned the property. "The folks who gathered at the store in town were trying to come up with a new name when someone spotted the stove and said, 'That's it! Clio.' They named the town after the wood stove."

There are guest rooms in the main house and in two cottages, the Dairy House and the Hen House (the original chicken coop). All are bright and airy, with expansive views of meadows and mountains; a balcony across the front of the main house extends the view for guests on the second floor. The Victorian furnishings include a fainting couch, antique washstands, dry sinks, and rocking chairs.

The inn has a warm spring–fed Olympic-size swimming pool. With four championship courses in the area, golf is popular with visitors, too.

Address: *Hwy. 89, Box 136, Clio, CA 96106, tel. 916/836-2387 or 800/854-1797.*
Accommodations: *1 double room with bath, 5 double rooms share 2 baths, 1 housekeeping and 1 double housekeeping suite.*
Amenities: *Terry-cloth robes; outdoor pool, picnic area, barbecue, facilities for horses.*
Rates: *$70–$140; full breakfast. D, MC, V.*
Restrictions: *Smoking outside only, no pets (except horses); 2-night minimum on summer weekends.*

Busch and Heringlake Country Inn

L ike many High Sierra and Gold Country inns, the Busch and Heringlake Country Inn was originally a stagecoach stop. Guests will find reminders of the building's history in the 2-foot-thick walls, the exposed stone wall behind the bar, and the brick facade, as well as in the antique safe and old boiler in a corner.

But the accommodations on the second floor are thoroughly modern, with four guest rooms comfortably furnished to reflect an earlier era: brass and four-poster beds, exposed woodwork, and original art on the walls. The inn is the creation of the engaging Carlo Giuffre, who bought the long-neglected property in 1986. Carlo is full of information about the exploits of local adventurers and of-

fers plenty of advice on where to see what they discovered.

Carlo has turned the ground floor of the inn into a Gold Rush–era saloon and restaurant serving moderately priced Italian food. The restaurant operates during the summer but may have year-round hours by the time you read this.

Address: *Main St., Box 68, Sierra City, CA 96125, tel. 916/862–1501.*
Accommodations: *4 double rooms with baths.*
Amenities: *Restaurant and bar (seasonal), whirlpool tub in 2 rooms, fireplace in 1 room.*
Rates: *$75–$110; full breakfast. MC, V.*
Restrictions: *No smoking, no pets.*

Chaney House

T his stone building fronting the west shore of Lake Tahoe is a striking example of what's known locally as Old Tahoe. Constructed by the same Italian stonemasons who built Vikingsholm, the 38-room Scandinavian estate at Emerald Bay, it has a King Arthur ambience, with 18-inch walls, carved Gothic arched doors, cathedral ceilings, and a massive stone fireplace in the living room. Initially it was the family home of Gary and Lori Chaney, who opened it as an inn in 1989. The family feeling is still very much present. "This is my daughter's room, just as she left it," Lori is quick to mention.

The inn's lakefront location is a big plus for summertime activities: sunning, boating, fishing, and swimming

(in the cold, cold water). The innkeepers are full of advice about evening cruises, hiking and biking trails, and winter skiing.

Address: *4725 W. Lake Blvd., Box 7852, Tahoe City, CA 96145, tel. 916/525–7333, fax 916/525–4413.*
Accommodations: *1 double room with bath, 2 double rooms share 1 shower, 1 housekeeping suite.*
Amenities: *TV in suite and living room, afternoon refreshments; private pier with boat dock and barbecue pit, gardens, grill, hammock, volleyball, horseshoes; paddleboat and mountain bike rentals.*
Rates: *$85–$110; full breakfast. No credit cards.*
Restrictions: *Smoking outside only, no pets; 2-night minimum on weekends and July–Aug.*

Cottage Inn at Lake Tahoe

These lakeside cottages have lured visitors to Tahoe for more than 50 years. The Old Tahoe–style cottages and the main lodge, called the Pomin House, are sun-spotted under a parklike canopy of trees and surrounded by walkways and sitting areas. Inside, guests find streamlined pine furnishings, traditional Tahoe knotty-pine walls, and bright Scandinavian color schemes. The rooms are generally small, but the suites—two to each cottage—all have separate sitting rooms. The Family Suite is well named: A separate housekeeping unit that can be rented with or without the upstairs, it has a brass trundle bed in the parlor, a queen-size brass bed in a separate bedroom, and a TV/VCR.

The inn stands right on a busy highway and is convenient to all the Tahoe attractions—beaches, ski slopes, and restaurants.

Address: *1690 W. Lake Blvd., Box 66, Tahoe City, CA 95730, tel. 916/581-4073.*
Accommodations: *6 double rooms with baths, 8 suites, 1 housekeeping suite.*
Amenities: *Afternoon refreshments, wood stoves in 2 cottages, fireplace in 1 cottage; beach access, docks, sauna, barbecues, shuffleboard, croquet, ski lockers.*
Rates: *$90–$150; full breakfast. Family Suite $150–$225; no breakfast. MC, V.*
Restrictions: *No smoking, no pets; 2-night minimum on weekends, 3- or 4-night minimum on holidays.*

The Feather Bed

Innkeepers Chuck and Dianna Goubert acquired the 1893 Queen Anne–style Huskinson House in 1979. They've created a comfortable inn, decorating the spacious rooms with vintage wallpapers and a few well-chosen Victorian antiques. Guests tend to gravitate to the porch or the parlor to chat with the gregarious innkeepers. Chuck, who for years ran the inn himself while Dianna went off to her secretarial job at the Plumas County Office of Education every day, is full of ideas about what to see and do in this remote area. Quincy—population 6,000—is the only real city in this corner of California. Chuck will direct you to the small Plumas County Museum, just a few steps away, where displays illustrate Gold Rush–era history in the Feather River country. Or he'll offer advice on the best ways to enjoy Mt. Lassen, an hour's drive away. Ardent theater lovers, Chuck and Dianna generally have some theatrical project going on at the inn—usually a summer-evening melodrama presented by a local repertory company.

Address: *542 Jackson St., Box 3200, Quincy, CA 95971, tel. 916/283-0102.*
Accommodations: *6 double rooms with baths, 1 suite.*
Amenities: *Air-conditioning in 4 rooms, phones, cable TV in sitting room, afternoon refreshments; bicycles.*
Rates: *$60–$90; full breakfast. AE, DC, MC, V.*
Restrictions: *Smoking outside only, no pets.*

Rockwood Lodge

When you step inside the Rockwood Lodge, innkeepers Lou Reinkens and Connie Stevens ask you to remove your shoes—"in the Dutch tradition." Actually, the request may have more to do with the white carpet, which sets the tone for this quietly elegant, antiques-filled inn on the west shore of Lake Tahoe. The beautiful stone building—one of the last to be constructed in the Old Tahoe style, with knotty-pine paneling—was built in 1939 by Bay Area dairyman Carlos Rookwood with winnings from the Irish Sweepstakes. The adornments are as lovely as the architecture: original Dalí and Boulanger prints, an 18th-century cobbler's bench in the Rubicon Bay Room, and a 7-foot soaking tub and shower for two in the shared bathroom. The inn makes a good headquarters for a Tahoe visit. It stands across the street from a public beach and marina, where boats can be rented, and is a short distance from ski lifts and bicycle and cross-country trails.

Address: *5295 W. Lake Blvd, Box 226, Homewood, CA 96141, tel. 916/525-5273, fax 916/525-5949.*
Accommodations: *2 double rooms with baths, 2 double rooms share a bath.*
Amenities: *Terry-cloth robes, afternoon refreshments, mud room with ski storage; barbecue.*
Rates: *$100–$150; full breakfast. No credit cards.*
Restrictions: *Smoking outside only, no pets; 2-night minimum on weekends, 3-night minimum on holidays.*

Winters Creek Ranch

The Winter Creek Ranch, situated on 10 acres on the eastern slope of the Sierra Nevada, midway between Reno and Carson City, offers an Old West, ranch-style experience with the comforts of a bed-and-breakfast inn. Built in 1980, it offers three accommodations with Victorian furnishings—a cherrywood sleigh bed, an 1865 carved bed and nightstand, and a collection of 19th-century clothing. Innkeepers Michael and Patty Stockwell encourage guests to hike, ride horses, or mountain-bike on the many trails around the inn. Horses are a big attraction; the inn's stable includes eight for riding, plus a pair of wild Mustangs. Winter guests have an equally wide selection of pursuits: ice-skating on the pond, sleigh riding, cross-country skiing, sledding down the hillside. Because of the inn's rural location, many guests opt to order dinner from a local caterer and sup in their rooms. Michael and Patty sometimes do barbecues for guests as well.

Address: *1201 Hwy. 395, Washoe Valley, NV 89704, tel. 702/849-1020.*
Accommodations: *1 double room with bath, 2 suites.*
Amenities: *Fireplace in 1 room, afternoon refreshments, picnic lunches and catered dinners available; rental horses, trout pond, sleigh rides, barbecues, special events.*
Rates: *$85–$105; full breakfast. AE, MC, V.*
Restrictions: *Smoking outside only, no pets.*

Oregon

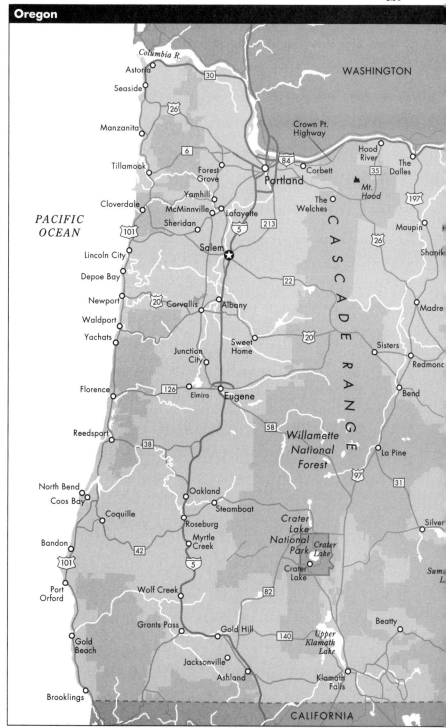

Oregon

WASHINGTON

Columbia R.

Astoria

Seaside

Manzanita

Tillamook

Cloverdale

PACIFIC
OCEAN

Lincoln City

Depoe Bay

Newport

Waldport

Yachats

Florence

Reedsport

North Bend

Coos Bay

Coquille

Bandon

Port
Orford

Gold
Beach

Brooklings

30

26

6

Forest
Grove

Yamhill

McMinnville

Sheridan

Lafayette

101

20

Corvallis

Junction
City

126

Elmira

38

Oakland

Steamboat

Roseburg

Myrtle
Creek

42

5

Wolf Creek

Grants Pass

Jacksonville

Ashland

Gold Hill

Crown Pt.
Highway

84

Portland

Corbett

Salem

213

22

Albany

Sweet
Home

20

Eugene

58

Willamette
National
Forest

Crater
Lake
National
Park

Crater
Lake

82

140

Hood
River

The
Welches

Mt.
Hood

35

The
Dalles

197

Maupin

26

Shanik

Madre

Sisters

Redmonc

Bend

La Pine

97

31

Silver

Crater
Lake

Sum
L

Beatty

Upper
Klamath
Lake

Klamath
Falls

CALIFORNIA

C A S C A D E   R A N G E

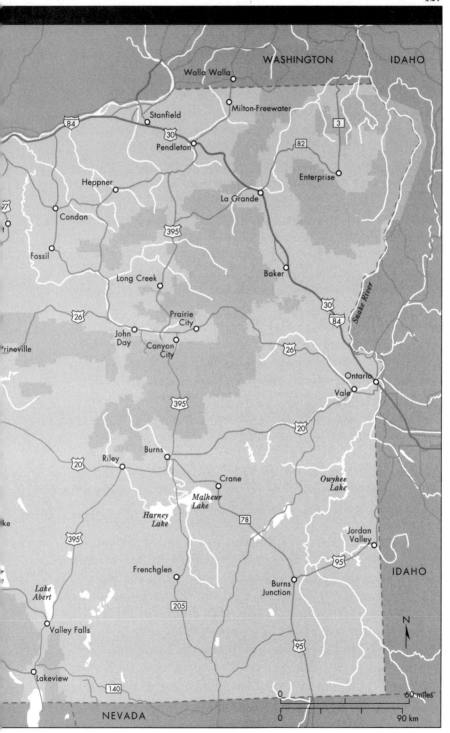

South Coast

Thanks to the foresight of the state legislature, Oregon's nearly 300-mile coastline is preserved for "free and uninterrupted use" by the public, preventing commercial corruption of its awe-inspiring beauty. Only the mighty Pacific has changed its profile, leaving it looking as untamed and natural as it did a hundred years ago. The southern half of the coast—from points south of Newport down to Brookings on the Oregon/California border—is a kaleidoscopic landscape of rugged offshore monoliths, sweeping dunes, towering cliffs, and quiet coves dotted with bayfront communities and an extensive network of state parks connected by Highway 101, often said to be the most scenic highway in the United States.

Winter is the time for storm- and whale-watching here; spring is cool and breezy enough for kite festivals; summer brings sunny beach days; and autumn is dependably warm and calm, perfect for viewing blazing fall foliage. Photographers will have a field day with the many old-fashioned-looking (though automated) lighthouses that dot the southern coast, including Heceta Head Lighthouse (Devil's Elbow State Park north of Florence), Coquille River Lighthouse (Bullards Beach in Bandon), Umpqua River Lighthouse (south of Winchester Bay), Yaquina Bay Lighthouse (south of Newport), and Cape Blanco Lighthouse (north of Port Orford), Oregon's tallest. Also picture perfect are the offshore seal rookeries, favorite sea lion sunning spots, rocky bird hatcheries, and numerous tidal pools. Avid bikers probably won't mind the many steep hills and cliff-hugging passes of the well-marked Oregon Coast Bike Trail, parallel to Highway 101 and running from Astoria in the north all the way to Brookings. They'll certainly appreciate the special campgrounds in Bullards Beach, Cape Arago, Cape Blanco, Samuel Boardman, Harris Beach, Humbug Mountain, William Tugman, and Umpqua River state parks.

As in the north coast, the economy concentrates on fishing, shipping, and lumber, though tourism continues to grow in importance. Small coastal towns such as Bandon, Cranberry Capital of Oregon, and Gold Beach have blossomed into resort communities, with year-round activities and festivals to entertain visitors.

Newport, a busy harbor and fishing town of some 8,500 residents, lures travelers with its high-masted fishing fleet, well-worn buildings, art galleries and shops, fragrantly steaming crab kettles, and the finest collection of fresh seafood markets on the coast. The tiny burg of Yachats has acquired a reputation that's disproportionate to its size, offering a microcosm of all the coastal pleasures: bed-and-breakfasts, excellent restaurants, deserted beaches, surf-pounded crags, and fishing and crabbing. It is also one of the few places in the world where the silver smelts come inland, celebrated by a community smelt fry each July.

Just past Heceta Head, Highway 101 jogs inland, and as you head south, you'll notice that the headlands and cliffs give way to endless beaches and rolling dunes. Nearby is Florence, a popular destination for both tourists and retirees and the gateway to the Oregon Dunes National Recreation Area. The picturesque waterfront Old Town has restaurants, antiques stores, fish markets, and other wet-weather diversions. The largest metropolitan area on the Oregon coast, Coos Bay is the world's largest lumber shipping port. But the glory days of the timber industry are over, and Coos Bay has begun to look in other directions, such as tourism—the Golden and Silver Falls State Park is close by—for economic prosperity.

Starting at Gold Beach, where the Rogue River, renowned among anglers, meets the ocean, is Oregon's banana belt. From here to Brookings, mild California-like temperatures encourage a blossoming trade in lilies and daffodils, and you'll even see a few palm trees growing. Brookings is equally famous as a commercial and sport-fishing port of

*the incredibly clear, startling turquoise-blue Chetco River,
more highly esteemed among lovers of fishing and the
wilderness than is the Rogue.*

Places to Go, Sights to See

Cape Perpetua. The lookout at the summit of this basalt cape, 3 miles south
of Yachats, is the highest point along the Oregon coast, affording
a panoramic view of the dramatic shoreline. Forestry service naturalists lead
summer hikes along trails from the visitor center, on the east side of the
highway, to quiet, sandy coves and fascinating tide pools. During winter
storms and high tide, water shoots up at the rear of the steadily worn chasm
known as Devil's Churn just before the entry to the Cape loop drive.

Darlingtonia Botanical Wayside (Mercer Lake Rd.). Immediately east of
Highway 101, 6 miles north of Florence, a paved half-mile trail with
interpretive signs leads through clumps of rare, carnivorous, insect-catching
cobra lilies (*Darlingtonia californica*), so named because they look like
spotted cobras ready to strike. The park is most attractive in May, when the
lilies are in bloom.

Hatfield Marine Science Center (2030 S. Marine Dr., tel. 503/867–3011).
Inside the Marine Science Center, an extension of Oregon State University
located just south of Newport, are displays of birds and other wildlife native
to the shoreline, the skeletal remains of a whale, and numerous tanks of
local marine life, including a shallow pool where visitors can touch starfish
and anemones. The star of the show is the large octopus in a round, low tank
near the entrance; he seems as interested in human visitors as they are in
him, and he has been known to reach up and gently stroke children's hands
with his suction-tipped tentacles.

Mt. Emily. This mountain northeast of Brookings was the only spot in the
continental United States to be attacked from the air during World War II.
According to local accounts, a single Japanese pilot using a small plane
assembled aboard a submarine offshore dropped an incendiary bomb here in
1942. (You can get to the Bomb Site Trail via forestry service road 1205.)
Decades later the pilot presented his sword to the town as a gesture of
goodwill; the sword is displayed at the Brookings city hall. Recently the
Japanese contributed $2,000 to the town library to promote intercultural
understanding.

Oregon Dunes National Recreation Area (tel. 503/271–3611). Stretching
between Florence and North Bend are 32,000 acres of shifting sand dunes,
said to be the largest oceanside dunes in the world. This enormous park
encompasses beaches, trails, campgrounds, lakes, marshes, and forested
areas. Even though forestry service regulations require mufflers on all
vehicles, the screeching of dune buggies, four-wheelers, and other all-terrain
vehicles careening through the dunes can be overwhelming in some areas.

The quietest spot from which to see the dunes is the Dunes Overlook, off Highway 101 about 30 miles north of Coos Bay.

Redwood Nature Trail. This mile-long hiking trail on the north bank of the Chetco River in Brookings takes you along paths shaded by an immense canopy of giant redwoods ranging in age from 300 to 800 years.

Rogue River Tours. You might see bald eagles fishing for salmon, ospreys perched atop high trees, or black bears and deer roaming the banks of the Rogue on the half- and full-day wilderness trips offered by *Jerry's Rogue Jets* (tel. 503/247–4571 or 800/451–3645) or *Mail Boat Hydro-jets* (tel. 503/247–7033 or 800/458–3511), both of which leave from Gold Beach.

Sea Gulch (east side of Hwy. 101 in Seal Rock, tel. 503/563–2727) is a full-size ghost town inhabited by more than 300 fancifully carved wood figures. Ray Kowalski, a master of chain-saw carving—a peculiar Oregon art form—wields his Stihl chain saw with virtuosity to create his cowboys, Indians, hillbillies, trolls, gnomes, and other mythical figures. Visitors can watch him work in his adjoining studio.

Sea Lion Caves (91560 Hwy. 101, Florence tel. 503/547–3111). During the fall and winter months, hundreds of wild Steller sea lions gather in the warm amphitheater of this huge, multihued sea cavern, 208 feet below the highway and about a mile south of Heceta Head. Visitors ride an elevator down to the floor of the cabin, near sea level, to watch from above the antics of the fuzzy pups and their parents. In spring and early summer, the sea lions move to the rocky sun-warmed ledges of the rookery outside the cave to mate and give birth.

Shore Acres Arboretum and State Park (Hwy. 101 and W. Beaver Hill Rd., tel. 503/888–4902). Once the summer estate of a powerful Coos Bay lumber baron, all that remains of Shore Acres, south of Charleston, are the gardens, which include a Japanese garden and lily pond, rose garden, and formal box-hedged gardens of azaleas, rhododendrons, and flowering annuals and perennials, modeled after those at Versailles. The glass-enclosed gazebo on the sea cliff is a warm and protected spot for whale-watching.

South Slough National Estuarine Research Reserve (Seven Devils Rd., tel. 503/888–5558). Bobcats, raccoons, bears, bald eagles, cormorants, and great blue herons are only a few of the species living in the varied ecosystems (tide flats, salt marshes, open channels, and uplands) of this 4,000-acre reserve 4 miles south of Charleston. More than 300 species of birds have been sighted here. South Slough, the first estuary reserve in the nation, has well-marked nature trails, guided walks, and an informative interpretive center.

Strawberry Hill. A few miles north of Yachats on Highway 101 is one of the best spots along the Oregon coast from which to view harbor seals at rest, on small rocky islands just offshore, and peer at the starfish, anemones, and sea urchins living in the tide pools and exposed at low tide.

Undersea Gardens (250 S.W. Bay Blvd., Newport, tel. 503/265–2206). One of Oregon's most famous tourist attractions, the "gardens" give visitors a glimpse of the world beneath the waves from its glass-walled, nautiluslike viewing chambers. Giant octopuses, salmon, red snappers, crabs, and ferociously ugly wolf eels are among the creatures on display.

Beaches

Virtually the entire coastline of Oregon is a clean, quiet white-sand beach, publicly owned and accessible to all. A word of caution: The Pacific off the Oregon coast is not the mild-mannered playmate it becomes in southern California. It is 45°–55° F year-round, temperatures that can be described as brisk at best and numbing at worst. Tides and undertows are strong, and swimming is not advised. When fishing from the rocks, always watch for sneaker or rogue waves, and never play on logs near the water—they roll into the surf without warning and have cost numerous lives over the years. Above all, watch children closely while they play in or near the ocean.

Everyone has a favorite beach, but Bandon's **Face Rock Beach** is justly renowned as perhaps the state's loveliest for walking, while the beach at **Sunset Bay State Park** on Cape Arago, with its protective reefs and encircling cliffs, is probably the safest for swimming. Nearby, **Oregon Dunes National Recreation area** adds extra cachet to Florence's beaches. Fossils, clams, mussels, and other aeons-old marine creatures, easily dug from soft sandstone cliffs, make **Beverly Beach State Park** (5 miles north of Newport) a favorite with young beachcombers.

Restaurants

Bandon Boatworks (tel. 503/347–2111) on the jetty offers outstanding ocean views, heaping buckets of steamer clams, delectably sweet cranberry bread, and passable Mexican specialties. Creative vegetarian and Mediterranean fare emphasizing organically grown produce and herbs is the focus at the **Sea Star Bistro** (tel. 503/347–9632) in Bandon's Old Town, which also operates a small youth hostel and a romantic, wharf-front guest house. Poor service mars the dining experience at the much-touted **La Serre** (tel. 503/547–3420) in Yachats; clam puffs in fluffy filo pastry are front-runners on the seafood, soup, and salad menu. **Mo's,** a favorite local chain with a well-deserved reputation for outstanding clam chowder and seafood, also serves chicken, salads, and sandwiches. All six editions (Florence, Cannon Beach, Lincoln City, Otter Rock, and two in Newport) are clearly marked on blue state highway signs along Highway 101. **Yuzen** (tel. 503/563–4766) in Waldport is overpriced and understaffed, but it offers the only authentic Japanese cuisine on the south coast.

Tourist Information

Bandon Chamber of Commerce (350 S. 2nd St., Box 1515, Bandon, OR 97411, tel. 503/347–9616); **Bay Area Chamber of Commerce** (50 E. Central, Box 210, Coos Bay, OR 97420, tel. 503/269–0215 or 800/824–8486); **Brookings–Harbor Chamber of Commerce** (Hwy. 101 South-Harbor, Box 940, Brookings, OR 97415, tel. 503/469–3181); **Gold Beach Chamber of Commerce** (510 S. Ellenburg, Gold Beach, OR 97444, tel. 503/247–7526 or 800/542–2334; 800/452–2334 in OR). **Oregon Coast Association** (Box 191, Oregon Coast, OR 97308, tel. 800/98–COAST); **Port Orford Chamber of Commerce** (Box 637, Port Orford, OR 97465, tel. 503/332–8055); **Waldport Visitors Center** (Hwy. 101 & Maple St., Box 669, Waldport, OR 97394, tel. 503/563–2133); **Yachats Area Chamber of Commerce** (441 Hwy. 101, Box 174, Yachats, OR 97498, tel. 503/547–3530).

Reservation Services

Bed and Breakfast Reservations—Oregon (2321 N.E. 28th Ave., Portland, OR 97212, tel. 503/287–4704); **Northwest Bed and Breakfast** (610 S.W. Broadway, Suite 606, Portland, OR 97205, tel. 503/243–7616 or 800/800–6922).

Chetco River Inn

By the time you reach the Chetco River Inn, 17 slow miles inland from Brookings along a twisting, single-lane forest service road that runs beside the Chetco River, you'll feel that you have left the busy world far behind. The large spruce-sided contemporary inn was designed over the phone by owners Clayton Brugger, a contractor, and his wife, Sandra, and the architect, who has never actually visited the property! While it fits well into the rugged surroundings, the inn is thoroughly modern rather than rustic.

Broad covered porches, cross-ventilation windows, and deep-green marble floors keep the inn cool during those occasional hot days of summer, when guests can usually be seen lounging in shaded hammocks, casting a fishing line (the Chetco is just outside the front door), or bobbing in the river in inner tubes. During the evenings, everyone gathers to talk in the airy, vaulted-ceiling common room furnished with Oriental carpets, leather couch, caned captain's chairs, and Chippendale dining ensemble. A collection of wreaths adorns the walls of the open kitchen at the end of the room.

Upstairs are tall shelves of books and games on the banistered landing leading to the guest rooms. A fishing motif dominates the River View Room, with cedar-paneled ceiling, red-and-black plaid bedspread, wicker furnishings, and a collection of

antique creel baskets and duck decoys. The other rooms, which look out on the lush trees surrounding the house, are slightly larger, furnished with Oriental rugs, eclectic antiques, and reproduction brass and iron bedsteads. All rooms have vanity areas and robes. An overflow room that opens onto a private bath can be used by families or friends of guests.

Your best bet for dining is to enjoy Sandra and Clay's five-course meals,which are available by advance notice. Featuring fresh local ingredients, the menu might include smoked salmon pâté, orange-carrot soup with Grand Marnier, grilled game hen, and homemade ice cream.

Address: *21202 High Prairie Rd., Brookings, OR 97415, radio tel. 503/469–8128, or 800/327–2688.*
Accommodations: *3 double rooms with baths.*
Amenities: *Afternoon refreshments, lunch and dinner available; archery, badminton, darts, horseshoes equipment, swimming holes, nature trails, deep-sea charters and hunting or fishing guides by arrangement, fishing and hunting packages.*
Rates: *$75–$85; full breakfast. MC, V.*
Restrictions: *Smoking outside only, no pets. Closed Thanksgiving and Christmas–New Year's Day.*

Cliff House

This large 1930s gable-on-hip-roofed house perched on Yaquina John Point in the coastal town of Waldport is perhaps the closest you'll come on the Oregon coast to the Smithsonian's attic, with pieces by Steuben, Lalique, Tiffany, Dresden, and Rosenthal, among the amazing abundance of objets here. Elaborate lead-glass chandeliers contrast—not unpleasantly—with knotty pine and cedar paneling, modern skylights, and an enormous river-stone fireplace. Window seats on the banistered, wraparound landing above the living room provide a cozy spot for sitting and taking in the sights, both inside and out. The outside is spectacular, a green headland jutting into the sea, with endless white beaches, shore pines, cliffs, and green surf.

Each of the five guest rooms reflects the romantic whims of owners Gabrielle Duvall and D. J. Novgrod. In the bedrooms, guests will find pot-bellied wood-burning stoves, a profusion of fresh-cut flowers, trays of sherry and chocolates, fluffy down comforters, and mounds of pillows on brass or four-poster rice beds. The Bridal Suite, with a positively royal 15th-century French gilt and ice-blue velvet Louis XV bedroom set, and mirrored bathroom with two-person shower and whirlpool tub overlooking the ocean, is by far the most opulent chamber.

Terry robes and thongs are supplied for the short trip from your room to the large Jacuzzi, sauna, and steam room on the broad-back deck overlooking the ocean and the Alsea Bay and bridge.

A run on the beach below or a rigorous game of croquet is a good way to work off the large morning meal, an elegant affair served on fine china with silver or gold flatware and plenty of fresh flowers. Gabby and D.J. are happy to arrange a variety of romantic interludes—including catered dinners, sunset horseback rides, champagne limousine drives into the nearby mountains, or picnic baskets for lunch along the coast.

Address: *Yaquina John Point, Adahi Rd., Box 436, Waldport, OR 97394, tel. 503/563-2506.*
Accommodations: *5 double rooms with baths.*
Amenities: *Cable TV and individual heat controls in rooms, VCR in 2 rooms, wood-burning stoves in some rooms, Jacuzzi in suite, afternoon refreshments, catered meals and masseuse available; Jacuzzi on deck, aviary, rental bicycles.*
Rates: *$95–$125, suite $225; full breakfast. House $75; no breakfast. MC, V.*
Restrictions: *Smoking outside only, no pets; 2-night minimum on weekends, 3-night minimum on holidays. Closed Nov.–Mar.*

The Johnson House

Entering Ron and Jayne Fraese's simple Italianate Victorian in Old Town Florence—the house celebrates its centennial in 1992—guests pass into a different era, accompanied by the sounds of Jack Benny, Fred Allen, and Fibber McGee and Molly emanating from a 1930s Philco radio in the living room. Antique sepia photographs and political cartoons adorn the walls, and vintage hats hang from the entryway coat tree. Furnishings throughout the house date from the 1890s to the mid-1930s, and include marble-top tables and dressers, Queen Anne and Chippendale chairs, walnut armoires, cast-iron beds, and a sprinkling of ornate Victorian pieces. In the bedrooms are lace curtains, crocheted doilies, and eyelet lace-trimmed percale duvet covers on goose-down comforters and pillows. Sadly, the old hardwood floors have been covered over in industrial-brown paint. The best room in the house isn't actually in the house but in the tiny garden cottage, with a claw-foot tub in the sunny bedroom. Although the porch with wicker rockers is billed as private, you'll probably find yourself sharing it with a pair of lazing kittens.

Jayne's green thumb is evident in the same delightful gardens surrounding the cottage, producing the fresh herbs, fruits, and edible flowers that garnish her breakfasts.

The Johnson House is a five-minute walk from ocean beaches and only a block from the quaint antiques shops, crafts boutiques, and eateries on the bay dock. A bowl of chowder at Mo's on the dock will do for a casual meal, but for a more refined atmosphere, head to the Windward Inn Restaurant (3757 Hwy. 101 N, tel. 503/997–8243), a few miles to the north; top choices include broiled scallops, mounds of steamer clams, fragrant veal in Madeira sauce, and a sumptuous chocolate-mocha toffee torte. Also nearby are the Sea Lion Caves, Oregon Dunes National Recreation Area, and the strange carnivorous lilies at the Darlingtonia Wayside.

For those who want to reside smack on the ocean, the Fraeses have a romantic vacation rental 9 miles north on Highway 101. Moonset, an octagonal cedar cabin for two, sits on a high meadow with a spectacular view of the coastline.

Address: *216 Maple St., Florence, OR 97439, tel. 503/997–8000, fax 503/997–6526 (Mon.–Fri. only).*
Accommodations: *2 double rooms with baths, 3 double rooms share 2 baths, 1 cottage suite.*
Amenities: *Individual heat controls in rooms, afternoon refreshments; croquet and boccie ball.*
Rates: *$65–$95; full breakfast. MC, V.*
Restrictions: *Smoking outside only, no pets. Closed Jan.*

Tu Tu Tun Lodge

Fine-dining options in the tiny coastal town of Gold Beach are few, but follow the Rogue River 7 miles inland and your culinary prayers will be answered at Tu Tu Tun (pronounced "too too tin") Lodge. Owners Dirk and Laurie Van Zante, an exceptionally friendly young couple, preside over cocktails and hors d'oeuvres as guests relax on the piazza, enjoying the breathtakingly beautiful river scenery. Then it's on to a multicourse, fixed-price dinner that often features barbecued Chinook salmon or prime rib accompanied by a superior selection of wines. During the busy high season (May–October), there are only four spaces at the table for nonguests at breakfast and dinner (lunch is for guests only), so reservations are highly recommended.

Tu Tu Tun, named after the peaceful tribe of riverbank-dwelling Indians, is an ideal retreat. Surrounded by an abundance of wildlife dwelling in the old-growth timber and the rugged river, you'll quickly get back in touch with nature. In the evenings, guests often sit near the big stone fireplace in the modern, open-beam cedar inn watching for the pair of bald eagles that fly down over the river at sunset. At "O'dark hundred" (the Van Zantes' expression for daybreak), avid anglers are down at the dock raring to tackle the Rogue's mighty steelhead and salmon.

The two-story wing of riverside guest rooms is motel-like in structure and uniformity. However, the wonderful views from the back porch or private balconies, creel and crossed fishing poles (or old logging or mining equipment) hanging above the cedar headboards, and thoughtful touches such as toiletries and fresh flowers set these rooms apart from typical highwayside accommodations. Two suites in the main lodge have stunning river views through wraparound picture windows, fully equipped kitchens, and large living rooms with fireplaces and fans hung from the vaulted ceilings. The sunny, spacious three-bedroom Garden House beyond the orchard has no view of the river but is suitable for larger families or groups.

Address: *96550 N. Bank Rogue, Gold Beach, OR 97444, tel. and fax 503/247-6664.*
Accommodations: *16 double rooms with baths, 2 housekeeping suites, 1 triple housekeeping suite.*
Amenities: *Restaurant, alcoholic beverages available, fireplace in 2 suites, conference facilities; lap pool, four-hole pitch-and-put, horseshoe court, jet-boat tour pickup from dock.*
Rates: *$108–$118, suites $170–$190; breakfast extra. MAP $169.50–$250.50. MC, V.*
Restrictions: *No pets July–Aug. Main lodge and restaurant closed last Sun. in Oct.–last Fri. in Apr.*

Ziggurat

L ike some fanciful dream of ancient Babylon, Ziggurat rises out of the tidal grasslands of the Siuslaw River. Located 7 miles south of Yachats, this terraced, step-pyramid-shaped inn, hand-built with native salt-silvered cedar siding, is without question the most unusual member of Oregon's B&B fraternity. Owner Mary Lou Cavendish soon realized that the interest the pyramid generated would bring a steady stream of visitors and that she and partner Irving Tibro had more than enough room to share, so she opened her amazing home as a bed-and-breakfast after construction was completed in 1987. (A cottage on the property in the shape of a tetrahedron is in the planning stages.)

Inside, an eclectic collection of original artwork—from Indonesian *wayang* puppets to Buddhist paintings from Nepal—and specially commissioned wooden furniture complement the house's sleek, ultramodern lines, stainless-steel trim, black carpeting, slatelike tiles, smooth white walls, and tinted triangular windows. On the ground floor, a narrow solarium surrounds two guest rooms that share a sauna and living room/library, complete with microwave, sink, and refrigerator. One guest room has a modern canopy bed in elm. A library nook, living room with grand piano and wood-burning stove, and dining room, kitchen, and bathroom with steam shower share space on the second floor. Forty feet up

and tucked under the eaves of the pyramid is another guest room, with two balconies and parallelogram windows overlooking the ocean and the arched bridge that spans the Yachats River. Guests residing here have exclusive use of the steam shower two floors below.

A brisk walk to the beach below the house is a good follow-up to the large breakfast served on one of the two glass-enclosed sun porches. Ziggurat is within easy reach of the area's many coastal pleasures, including Cape Perpetua, Sea Lion Caves, Strawberry Hill Wayside, and the boutiques and restaurants of tiny Yachats. Those interested in shells should make a stop at the Sea Rose Gift Shop (95478 Hwy. 101, Yachats, tel. 503/547–3005) to see the displays of rare, exotic, and common shells from around the world.

Address: *95330 Hwy. 101, Yachats, OR 97498, tel. 503/547–3925.*
Accommodations: *1 double room with bath, 2 double rooms share bath.*
Amenities: *Refrigerator in 1 room, sauna and solarium with ocean views shared by 2 rooms, steam shower in private bath.*
Rates: *$75–$85; full breakfast. No credit cards.*
Restrictions: *Smoking outside only, no pets; 2-night minimum on holidays.*

Cliff Harbor Bed and Breakfast

This weathered-cedar contemporary house perched on Coquille Point, a windswept, grassy bluff above the ocean and Bandon's Coquille River, is owned by Katherine Haines, a holistic health practitioner, and her husband, Douglas, a master cabinetmaker.

The redwood-trimmed Harbor Suite, with sunny sitting-room window seats overlooking an enclosed patio and sun deck, is situated at the front of the house opposite the ocean. Douglas's handiwork can be seen in the built-in cedar-and-fir armoire and desk; the wood-and-bamboo headboard and nightstands have an Oriental look. Cliffside Studio, a fully equipped apartment above the garage, affords grand ocean views and has a fireplace. The beach below the house is perfect for long walks.

Not all visitors sample Cliff Harbor's hospitality: A variety of birds and seals migrate to Coquille Point to give birth to their young.

Address: *850 Portland Ave., Box 769, Bandon, OR 97411, tel. 503/347-3956.*
Accommodations: *1 suite, 1 housekeeping suite.*
Amenities: *TV and phone in rooms, private entrances, guests in suite served wine upon arrival, massage available.*
Rates: *$95–$125; full breakfast. No credit cards.*
Restrictions: *No smoking, no pets; 2-night minimum in studio, 2-night maximum in suite.*

Coos Bay Manor

This 15-room Colonial Revival manor house built in 1911 is Coos Bay's newest bed-and-breakfast thanks to the efforts of transplanted Californian and former banker Patricia Williams. Visitors enter through a formal English garden and imposing, wisteria-draped portico to find such original features as glowing hardwood floors and painted wainscoting, and a tasteful mixture of antiques and period reproductions (although the red-and-gold flocked wallpaper is reminiscent of a Victorian bordello). The star of the living room is an 1870 Weber box baby grand piano with ornate lions' heads adorning the legs.

The guest rooms are theme oriented, such as the frilly Victorian Room, with lace-canopy bed; the Cattle Baron's Room, with cowhide bedspread and coyote skin wall hangings; and the Colonial Room, with velvet curtains and four-poster beds. The wharf is only two blocks away; other sights of interest nearby include Shore Acres Arboretum and the South Slough Estuary.

Address: *955 South 5th St., Coos Bay, OR 97420, tel. 503/269-1224.*
Accommodations: *1 double room with bath, 4 double rooms share 2 baths.*
Amenities: *Robes and coffeemaker in rooms, small dogs welcomed, bicycles.*
Rates: *$55–$60; Continental breakfast. MC, V.*
Restrictions: *Smoking in parlor or outside only.*

Heather House Bed and Breakfast

Each spring and summer, mounds of heather surround Bob and Katy Cooper's 1947 Craftsman, perched on a hill overlooking the coast at Gold Beach. It's not Brigadoon, but Katy's Scottish accent and customs might convince you that it's so. Precisely at 4 each afternoon, out comes the tea with finger sandwiches, little tarts, scones, and shortbread.

Each of the guest rooms has a different look: blue-and-green plaids and kilted soldier dolls in the Tartan Room; lace-trimmed rose-print bed linens and curtains and graceful, authentic Queen Anne pieces in the Victorian Room; and geisha doll and samurai helmet on the shiny black alcove dresser in the Oriental Room.

Jet-boat tours on the Rogue are just minutes away from Heather House, as is fun and funky Honeybear Campground (34161 Ophir, Gold Beach, OR 97444, tel. 503/247–2765), where an umpah band and lederhosen-clad waiters liven up the German buffet. Reservations are a must for this weekends-only diner.

Address: *190 11th St., Gold Beach, OR 97444, tel. 503/247–2074.*
Accommodations: *2 double rooms with baths, 2 double rooms share bath.*
Amenities: *Afternoon refreshments.*
Rates: *$48–$65; full breakfast. MC, V.*
Restrictions: *Smoking outside only, no pets.*

The Highlands

By the time you reach this delightful bed-and-breakfast—1½ miles up an old logging road and into the mountains overlooking Haines Inlet and a grassy meadow of grazing cattle in the valley far below—you'll know how it got its name. Hovering high above the fog and cool winds of the coast, Marilyn and Jim Dow's contemporary cedar-and-glass home is immediately welcoming and comfortable.

Guests have the run of the entire lower level, which includes a huge den with enormous picture windows for valley gazing. Tole objets d'art, antique dolls, a delicately stitched whole-cloth quilt, and other family heirlooms give the decor a homey, country feel. The furnishings include wicker, country-pine antiques, and

tasseled canopy pencil-post or cast-iron beds covered with floral or Battenberg lace-trimmed bed linens. Breakfast, served on the upstairs deck above colorful terraced gardens, might feature fresh eggs from the Dows' flock of free-ranging chickens.

Address: *608 Ridge Rd., North Bend, OR 97459, tel. 503/756–0300.*
Accommodations: *2 double rooms with baths.*
Amenities: *Telephone and individual heat controls in room, whirlpool tub in 1 room, fully equipped kitchen available; outdoor enclosed hot tub.*
Rates: *$60–$65; full breakfast. MC, V.*
Restrictions: *Smoking outside only, no pets.*

Home by the Sea

This quirky little B&B on a headland above Battle Rock Park in Port Orford enjoys a most spectacular view of the south Oregon coast. Built by owners Alan and Brenda Mitchell in 1985, the three-story shingled house is decorated with stained-glass hangings and Brenda's handmade quilts (all for sale). The mix-and-match Americana furnishings are comfortable and low-key; the rare myrtlewood bedsteads in both ocean-view bedrooms were specially commissioned. Bathrooms are cramped, but tidy and functional; a washer and dryer (which are available for guests' use) take up space in one bathroom.

Breakfast is served either in the lower-level solarium, which offers a conversation-stopping ocean view, or on the porch. This is a prime spot for watching whales (October–May), winter storms, and birds; the Oregon Islands National Wildlife Refuge is just offshore. The Wooden Nickel (Hwy. 101, Port Orford, tel. 503/332-5201), a nearby myrtlewood factory with weekday tours, is a good spot for picking up souvenirs of the area.

Address: *444 Jackson, Box 606-F, Port Orford, OR 97465, tel. 503/332-2855.*
Accommodations: *2 double rooms with baths.*
Amenities: *Phone available.*
Rates: *$60–$70; full breakfast. MC, V; no personal checks.*
Restrictions: *No smoking, no pets; 2-night minimum on summer weekends.*

The Lighthouse

This 1980 contemporary cedar in Bandon is named for its view of the Coquille River Lighthouse across the estuary. Wide windows in the large sunken living room and a porch off the raised dining room take advantage of the view. The simple, eclectic furnishings throughout—from Art Deco to contemporary—are brightened by painted rainbow supergraphics on the walls, colorful Guatemalan masks, whimsical prints, family photos, huge plants, and battered, neon-colored fishnet floats hanging from the ceiling. Vivacious Linda Sisson, who performs with the local theater group, and her husband Bill, a contractor and former Frisbee champion, no longer live on the property but are usually on hand to meet guests and serve breakfast. The Lighthouse is a great spot from which to watch the timber-rattling storms that draw tourists to the coast in winter; the Bandon Storm Watchers (Box 1693, Bandon, OR 97411) can provide information on storm-watching, whale-watching, and tide-pooling in Bandon.

Address: *650 Jetty Rd., Box 24, Bandon, OR 97411, tel. 503/347-9316.*
Accommodations: *4 double rooms with baths.*
Amenities: *Two-person whirlpool tub and fireplace in 1 room, TV in 1 room, cable TV and wood-burning stove in common area.*
Rates: *$85–$100; Continental breakfast. MC, V.*
Restrictions: *No smoking, no pets; closed July 4.*

Southern Oregon
Including Ashland

Protected by the Klamath and Siskiyou mountain ranges from the extreme weather patterns of the Pacific Ocean, southern Oregon—from points south of Roseburg, past Ashland, to the Oregon/California border—enjoys a much warmer, drier climate than the Willamette Valley to the north and the coastline to the west. As in the valley, the economy centers on farming and ranching, with an additional boost from tourists, lured by the area's many historic sites, natural attractions, and cultural events.

With more than its fair share of national parks and challenging rivers, southern Oregon is a paradise for outdoors enthusiasts. At the Mt. Ashland Ski Area there are plenty of cross-country and downhill courses (4 lifts and 23 runs at 1,150 vertical feet) to keep skiers busy from Thanksgiving through April. There are also cross-country trails in the heights around Crater Lake and snowmobile trails around Diamond Lake. The Pacific Crest National Scenic Trail and the Siskiyou National Forest offer the best hiking and camping in the region. Water adventurers turn to the Klamath or Rogue rivers for recreation.

The Rogue, one of Oregon's most scenic rivers, bores through the verdant Siskiyou National Forest and the coastal mountains, rushing full force to meet the ocean. It is a favorite for jetboat and rafting tours out of Grants Pass, an old stagecoach stop along the Portland–San Francisco route named in 1865 to honor Grant's capture of Vicksburg. Approximately 20 miles north of Grants Pass off busy Interstate 5 is Wolf Creek, another vintage way station, and Golden, an entertaining gold-mining ghost town 3 miles farther east, up Coyote Creek. When gold was discovered in 1851 in Jacksonville, just south of Grants Pass, a wave of saloons, gambling houses, and brothels opened to coax the shiny dust from the hordes of miners;

*today it remains a good example of a Gold Rush
boomtown, with more than 75 historic buildings, many
dating from the late 19th century.*

*Southeast on Highway 99 and one of the state's chief
tourist destinations, Ashland is home to the renowned
Oregon Shakespeare Festival, "festival" being somewhat of
a misnomer, since it runs for nine months out of the year.
Its immense popularity has provided fertile ground for
a flourishing arts community and profusion of boutiques,
galleries, taverns, fine restaurants, and exceptional bed-
and-breakfasts.*

Places to Go, Sights to See

Butte Creek Mill (402 Royal North, tel. 503/826–3531). This historic mill on
the banks of the Little Butte Creek at Eagle Point has been in operation
since 1872. Visitors can watch enormous French-quarried millstones hard at
work making flour. Next door to the mill is an old-fashioned country store
selling a variety of fresh-ground grains and bulk spices, teas, granolas, and
raw honey.

Crater Lake National Park (503/594–2211). Amazingly crystal-clear blue
waters fill this caldera at the crest of the Cascade Range, formed 6,800
years ago when Mt. Mazama decapitated itself in a volcanic explosion. You
can drive, bicycle, or hike the 33-mile rim road. Boat tours leaving from
Cleetwood Cove, on the lake's north side, go to Wizard Island, a miniature
cinder cone protruding above the surface. A lodge offers summer
accommodations, but the cabins at Diamond Lake Resort (Diamond Lake, OR
97731, tel. 503/793–3333) just north of Crater Lake are a better option.

Golden Ghost Town (3482 Coyote Creek Rd., Wolf Creek, tel. 503/866–2685).
Golden is a partially restored, century-old gold-mining town with a general
store, post office, blacksmith shop, schoolhouse, and church. Fake wooden
gravestones planted next to the church were left behind after shooting of
a 1972 episode of the TV series "Gunsmoke." Guided tours, complete with
spicy stories from the Old West, are a bargain at $1.

Jacksonville. This 1850s Gold Rush town, on the National Register of
Historic Places, has dozens of historic homes and buildings, a fascinating
cemetery, a schoolhouse, several saloons, and numerous shops and antiques
stores. The *Jacksonville Museum* (206 N. 5th St., tel. 503/773–6536), located
in the old Jackson County Courthouse, houses an intriguing collection of
Gold Rush–era artifacts and outlines the rich local history. Jacksonville is
also home to the popular *Peter Britt Festival* (Peter Britt Gardens, tel.
503/779–0847), a weekly series of outdoor concerts and theater lasting from

late June to early September that features classical music, jazz, bluegrass, and folk music and dance.

Klamath Basin National Wildlife Refuge (Klamath Falls, tel. 503/884–0666). There are many viewing sites around this protected 80,000-acre habitat of marshland and shallow lakes, home to a wide variety of birds and waterfowl. Visitors can observe hundreds of bald eagles that nest here over the winter or watch the endless legions of ducks and geese fly over during spring and fall migrations.

Minshall Theater (101 Talent Ave., Talent, OR 97540, tel. 503/535–5250 or 503/779–4010). Audiences cheer on the hero, hiss at the villain, and sing along at the Gay Nineties–style revue staged here on weekend evenings from June to September.

Oregon Caves National Monument (on Hwy. 46, 50 miles southwest of Grants Pass, tel. 503/592–3400). Known as the Marble Halls of Oregon, Oregon Caves National Monument, high in the Siskiyou Mountains, entrances visitors with prehistoric limestone and marble formations. Dress warmly and wear sturdy shoes for the chilly, mildly strenuous 75-minute, half-mile subterranean tour. The rustic *Oregon Caves Chateau* (Box 128, Cave Junction, OR 97523, tel. 503/592–3400) offers food and lodging at the monument from June through September.

Oregon Shakespeare Festival (15 S. Pioneer St., Box 158, Ashland, OR 97520, tel. 503/482–4331). A Tony Award-wining repertory company presents 11 different Shakespearean, classic, and contemporary dramas on three different stages during a season that stretches from February through October. The informative Festival Tour, often led by company members, goes behind the scenes of the festival's three theaters, including the Elizabethan, a re-creation of Shakespeare's Globe Theatre that operates only from June to October. The tour also visits the Shakespeare Festival Exhibit Center, exploring the festival's history in costumes, props, set designs, and photographs. In the Fantasy Gallery, visitors can don elaborate robes, gowns, and crowns and pose for pictures on an Elizabethan throne. *The Feast of Will,* held in early June in the lovely neighboring Lithia Park—designed by the man who was responsible for San Francisco's Golden Gate Park—kicks off the lively summer season.

River Rafting. Wet-knuckle enthusiasts flock to the challenging Rogue River, near the California border. Many parts of the river flow through true wilderness, with no road access. Deer, bears, eagles, and other wild creatures are abundant here. Outfitters based in Grants Pass include: *Hellgate Excursions* (953 S.E. 7th St., tel. 503/479–7204 or 800/648-4874) and *Orange Torpedo Trips* (777 Debrick Way, tel. 503/479–5061). *Rogue Wilderness, Inc.* (325 Galice Rd., tel. 503/479–9554 or 800/336–1647) is 2 miles away in Merlin.

Wineries. Top wineries in the region include *Bridgeview Vineyards* (4210 Holland Loop Rd., Cave Junction, tel. 503/592–4698), which also offers B&B–style accommodations; *Rogue River Winery* (3145 Helms Rd., tel 503/476–1051) in Grants Pass; *Valley View Vineyards* (1325 Applegate Rd., tel.

503/488–0888), in Jacksonville; and *Weisinger's* (3150 Siskiyou Blvd., tel. 503/488–5989) in Ashland.

Restaurants

Just as southern Oregon has an abundance of B&Bs, so, too, is there an ample crop of restaurants to choose from, with many concentrated in Ashland. **Chateaulin** (tel. 503/482–2264), in Ashland, serves fine French cuisine in charming ivy-and-brickwork surroundings; after-theater crowds come here for the extensive wine list and light café fare. You can enjoy Texas-style barbecued steaks, ribs, and chicken from the creekside deck of the **Back Porch Barbecue** (tel. 503/482–4131). Just north of Ashland in Talent, the **Arbor House** (tel. 503/535–6817) features an eclectic international menu that includes jambalaya, curries, braised lamb, charbroiled steaks, and seafood. **New Sammy's Bistro** (tel. 503/535–2779), also in Talent, is a pricey, reservations-only diner offering trendy Oregon cuisine that's strictly organic. The best bet in Grants Pass is **Matsukaze** (tel. 503/479–2961) for reasonably priced Japanese fare. A bit farther north, **Buzz'z Blue Heron** (tel. 503/479–6604) in Merlin features steaks and burgers as well as Cajun, Italian, and Oriental specialties and local dinner-theater productions.

Tourist Information

Ashland Chamber of Commerce (110 E. Main St., Box 1360, Ashland, OR 97520, tel. 503/482–3486); **Grants Pass Visitor and Convention Bureau** (1501 N.E. 6th St., Box 1787, Grants Pass, OR 97526, tel. 503/476–5510 or 800/547–5927); **Jacksonville Chamber of Commerce** (185 N. Oregon St., Box 33, Jacksonville, OR 97530, tel. 503/899–8118); **Medford Visitors and Convention Bureau** (304 S. Central, Medford, OR 97501, tel. 503/772–5194).

Reservation Services

Ashland's B&B Reservation Network (Box 1051, Ashland, OR 97520, tel. 503/482–BEDS); **Bed and Breakfast Reservations—Oregon** (2321 N.E. 28th Ave., Portland, OR 97212, tel. 503/287–4704); **Country Host Registry** (901 N.W. Chadwick La., Myrtle Creek, OR 97457, tel. 503/863–5168); **Southern Oregon Reservation Center** (Box 477, Ashland, OR 97520, tel. 503/488–1011 or 800/533–1311).

Chanticleer Inn

Named after a strutting rooster in Chaucer's *Canterbury Tales*, Chanticleer has good reason to crow. This trilevel 1920 Craftsman built into a hill and surrounded by cheerful gardens and a long river-rock porch continues to lead the ranks in personal service. The accommodating nature of owners Jim and Nancy Beaver, who opened the bed-and-breakfast in 1981, is apparent throughout the extremely well-run, tidy inn. Attention to detail—including a stuffed cookie jar and a selection of teas and coffees left out for guests, as well as the option of having breakfast in bed—is a major factor in their success.

The country-French decor seems fresh and new (reproduction pieces *are*, however, interspersed with antiques), from the thick carpets and soft-colored paint and paper on the walls to the shiny Pierre Deux fabrics covering the cushions and pressed white percale-and-lace pillowcases and duvets on the beds. Carved pine armoires function as closets, and fluffy down comforters cover antique brass and wrought-iron beds in the various guest chambers. The Beavers have thoughtfully placed a stack of scripts of the current Oregon Shakespeare Festival plays on your bureau. Other special touches include fresh flowers, alarm clocks, telephones, and individual climate control. The Chanticleer Suite, a self-contained two-bedroom apartment with its own enclosed garden and kitchen, is perfect for families. The only negative among a long list of positives is the rocket-engine sound made by the exhaust fans in the bathrooms.

Italian roast coffees, vegetable latkes topped with apple sauce or sour cream, cheese blintzes, British banger sausages, and lemon-strawberry cake with crème fraîche are among the gourmet breakfast specialties. The inn is just four blocks from the festival theaters and countless boutiques and shops of downtown Ashland; the wonderful Winchester Country Inn (35 S. 2nd St., tel. 503/488–1113) and Primavera (241 Hargadine St., tel. 503/488–1994), a newcomer to the bustling Ashland dining scene, with dramatic decor and light provincial European fare, are also close at hand.

Address: *120 Gresham St., Ashland, OR 97520, tel. 503/482–1919.*
Accommodations: *6 double rooms with baths, 1 double housekeeping suite.*
Amenities: *Phone and individual climate control in rooms, wood-burning stove in suite, stocked refrigerator, evening refreshments.*
Rates: *$105–$135, suite $180; full breakfast. MC, V.*
Restrictions: *Smoking outside only, no pets; 2-night minimum on weekends Feb.–Oct.*

Jacksonville Inn

Gold flecks still sparkle in the mortar of the locally made bricks and quarried sandstone used to construct this two-story building in 1863. Located on the main street of Jacksonville, this historic building has served as a general store, bank, hardware store, professional offices, and furniture repair shop. Purchased in 1976 by Jerry and Linda Evans, it is now an inn and dinner house, with a well-deserved reputation for the best wining and dining around.

Of the eight guest rooms on the top floor, the best and largest is No. 1, with a canopy bed, rolltop desk, wingback chairs, and a settee next to the fireplace. All the rooms have wood trim salvaged from buildings of the same period, and frontier American antiques, including marble-top dressers and blanket-draped rockers. Telephones, minifridges, and TVs hidden away in specially constructed armoires that match the period furnishings are standard features. Tall brass-and-oak bedsteads have been lengthened to accommodate queen-size mattresses. Worn bathroom fixtures that probably date from the 1960s are being replaced as bathrooms are renovated one room at a time.

For breakfast, guests choose from a gourmet menu; entrées might include a chef's choice omelet, spinach and mushroom *gâteau* in Mornay sauce (scrambled eggs with cream cheese and sherry in a puff-pastry cup) or brioche French toast with maple butter and cinnamon sugar, preceded by fresh-squeezed orange juice and a fruit platter. The dining room is open only to inn guests for breakfast and to the general public for lunch, dinner, and Sunday brunch. There's also a quiet bar/lounge with weekend entertainment and a bistro in the basement that features smaller portions from the more formal dining-room menu.

The newest offering in the inn's growing retinue is a large, one-room wood-frame cottage two blocks away. With a canopy pencil-post bed across from a marble fireplace, wet bar, stocked kitchenette, and whirlpool tub and sauna shower in the spacious bathroom, it is a romantic little hideaway. Ashland and its Oregon Shakespeare Festival activities are about 20 minutes away by car.

Address: *175 E. California St., Box 359, Jacksonville, OR 97530, tel. 503/899–1900, fax 503/899–1373.*
Accommodations: *8 double rooms with baths, 1 housekeeping cottage.*
Amenities: *Restaurant, lounge, wine shop, air conditioning, phone, and TV in rooms, whirlpool tub, steam shower, and fireplace in cottage, conference facilities.*
Rates: *$80–$85, $175 housekeeping suite; full breakfast. AE, D, DC, MC, V.*
Restrictions: *Smoking in lounge or on outside porch only.*

Old Stage Inn

In the heart of southern Oregon's Gold Rush territory stands an immaculate white 1857 Greek Revival farmhouse on a quiet country lane a mile or so north of Jacksonville. Owners Hugh and Carla Jones, an amiable, devoutly religious couple who truly believe that "guests who come as strangers should leave as friends" have done an admirable job of refurbishing and decorating this bed-and-breakfast. The inn's elegant decor is the work of Carla, an interior decorator by profession. Eastlake, Rococo Revival, and other period furnishings are surrounded by thick Oriental carpets, polished wood floors, rich brocade swag curtains, and vibrant wallpapers.

Eleven-foot-high ceilings, broad, lace-curtained windows, and plenty of square footage give the bedrooms a spacious, airy feel, complemented by Carla's sense of style. A plump bunny pillow sits on a large four-poster rice bed with silk ivy-entwined canopy in one room. In another room, doors were removed and antique lamps added, turning a shallow pegboard closet into an interesting alcove framing the carved oak headboard of a lace-covered bed. Victorian-style floral wallpaper above penny-tile wainscoting, a Queen Anne reproduction velvet armchair next to the double shower, and a brocade step stool leading to the raised whirlpool bath surrounded by candelabras make you forget that this is a shared bathroom.

A charming cottage with seating alcove offers more privacy and is completely accessible for the disabled.

Carla's breakfasts are magnificent presentations: Fresh flowers and ivy decorate the table, where you'll start with a variety of homemade tea breads and a fruit dish such as poached pears in raspberry puree or baked Alaska grapefruit, followed by an entrée of orange-pecan pancakes or smoked turkey in cream sauce on whole wheat and wild rice waffles. During the summer, guests enjoy sipping lemonade on the side porch as they watch Canadian geese in a nearby pond, or taking part in croquet on the side lawn. All-terrain bicycles as well as an ornate, Cinderella-style opera coach are available for special outings to the Britt Music Festival or for a tour of historic Jacksonville.

Address: *883 Old Stage Rd., Box 579, Jacksonville, OR 97530, tel. 503/899–1776 or 800/US–STAGE, fax 503/899–1776.*
Accommodations: *2 double rooms with baths, 2 double rooms share bath.*
Amenities: *Air-conditioning; fireplace in 2 rooms, afternoon refreshments; coach rides available.*
Rates: *$85–$105; full breakfast. MC, V.*
Restrictions: *Smoking outside only, no pets; 2-night minimum June–Aug. and on holiday weekends.*

The Winchester Country Inn

Of the many Victorian bed-and-breakfasts in Ashland, this 1886 Queen Anne is the only one with a restaurant, and it's the closest to the Festival theaters as well. Painstakingly renovated by Michael and Laurie Gibbs during the early 1980s and listed on the National Register of Historic Places, the Winchester has established a reputation as one of the premier dining spots in Ashland. Open to the public for dinner and Sunday brunch, it offers a seasonal menu plus favorites such as French Vietnamese *teng dah* beef (broiled fillet marinated in a lemon-peppercorn sauce) and duck with orange sauce. The outstanding food makes up for the fact that the small guest sitting room just beyond the gift shop is almost entirely overshadowed by the restaurant.

The decor of the guest chambers maintains the period style of the house without appearing the least bit cluttered in the Victorian fashion. A mixture of American Colonial reproductions and antiques, as well as Rococo Revival and Eastlake reproductions, including tall mirrored wardrobes and brass-and-iron or heavy, carved wooden bedsteads, add distinction, while contemporary wicker or cushioned chairs and wall-to-wall carpeting lend comfort. A handpainted porcelain sink set into an antique dresser serves as a vanity in the bedroom; scented salts in the attached bathroom make for a luxurious soak in the deep claw-foot tub. A crystal decanter of sherry and sinfully rich truffles on a tray on the dresser make a late-night snack irresistible.

Favorite rooms include the Sylvan Room, in sunny shades of peach, and the creamy blue Garden Room, both of which have delightful bay sitting areas overlooking the terraced gardens. The Sunset Room has its own balcony view of the treetops of downtown Ashland. Rooms at the basement level have garden patios or small decks as compensation. With a private entrance, casual wicker furniture, and two beds with curlicue white iron headboards, the Enders Room is most suitable for families. Plans are under way for two new suites in a summer cottage.

During winter and spring, the Gibbs offer a variety of special packages, from winemakers' dinners (showcasing wines of the Northwest) and romantic getaways with dinner for two (plus one night's lodging) to murder-mystery weekends and a popular Dickens Christmas Festival.

Address: *35 S. 2nd St., Ashland, OR 97520, tel. 503/488–1113.*
Accommodations: *7 double rooms with baths.*
Amenities: *Air-conditioning; restaurant, phone in rooms.*
Rates: *$115; full breakfast. MC, V.*
Restrictions: *Smoking outside only, no pets.*

Arden Forest Inn

This early 20th-century cross-gabled farmhouse sits on a small plot of land in Ashland's historic district, within walking distance of the Festival theaters but removed from noisy downtown.

Its eclectically decorated interior reflects the interests of owners Audrey Sochor, an artist, and her husband, Art, a retired English professor and an active theater buff. Contemporary furnishings in the common rooms include rattan and director's chairs and glass-top tables with stacks of art books as pedestals. Bleached fir floors, whitewashed walls, abundant windows, and track lighting form a bright showcase for the Sochors' folk art collection, Audrey's paintings and textiles, and Art's impressive literary library. A dearth of fragile collectibles and antiques makes this bed-and-breakfast a good choice for families.

Guests who generally recoil at the thought of a low-fat, low-calorie vegetarian breakfast come away more than satisfied with the Sochors' fruit platters, cobblers, crêpes, and fresh popovers.

Address: *261 W. Hersey St., Ashland, OR 97520, tel. 503/488-1496.*
Accommodations: *3 double rooms with baths, 1 double suite.*
Amenities: *Air-conditioning; horseshoe court.*
Rates: *$78, $122 suite; Continental breakfast. AE, MC, V.*
Restrictions: *No smoking, no pets; 2-night minimum on weekends.*

Bayberry Inn Bed and Breakfast

This white-trimmed, gray clapboard 1925 Craftsman, located on Ashland's Main Street, is one of the newest in the city's growing corps of B&Bs. Innkeepers Cheryl Lynn Colwell and Marilyn Brittsan Evans selected an English country decor for the interior. Deep green carpeting, mauve floral wallpaper, and a green marble fireplace give the living room and attached dining room a touch of formality. The cozy Sheffield's Room upstairs features dark floral swagged draperies, candlestick lamps, and graceful Louis XV–style chairs and other French reproductions. Two other second-floor rooms are bright and spacious, with broad window seats beneath wide, lace-swathed dormer windows. Downstairs guest rooms are more casually furnished, with lots of white wicker and lighter floral-print bedspreads and curtains.

Marilyn's background in catering is evident in her memorable morning repasts, served in the large, four-table dining room off the kitchen. Breakfast service is also available on the sunny back deck.

Address: *438 N. Main St., Ashland, OR 97520, tel. 503/488-1252.*
Accommodations: *5 double rooms with baths.*
Amenities: *Air-conditioning; afternoon refreshments, dinner available by reservation.*
Rates: *$95; full breakfast. MC, V.*
Restrictions: *Smoking outside only, no pets; 2-night minimum on weekends. Closed Thanksgiving and Christmas.*

Chriswood Inn

I n Grants Pass, the midpoint of the Rogue River, a Union Jack hangs opposite the American flag at the door of this 1927 English Tudor. George and Jeanne Woods spent six months touring B&Bs in Scotland prior to opening their English-style inn near Old Town. The inn's decor leans more toward the casual but refined, with a mixture of antiques, reproductions, and contemporary furnishings, and a sprinkling of fine prints the couple kept from their days as gallery owners.

The surprisingly large bedrooms, equipped with a sink, are country quaint, with Jeanne's handcrafted floppy-ear, fabric-covered bunnies poised on beds and bookshelves, garlands or baskets of dried flowers on walls and tables, and cheerful quilts and comforters on sturdy brass beds. Victorian Rococo wicker chairs placed around small magazine-covered tables in spacious sitting areas invite repose.

In keeping with English tradition, a downstairs publike game room is replete with card table, dart board, and pool table (or is it snooker?).

Address: *220 N.W. "A" St., Grants Pass, OR 97522, tel. 503/474–9733.*
Accommodations: *3 double rooms share 2 baths.*
Amenities: *Air-conditioning, cable TV, and robes in rooms; afternoon refreshments, meeting room.*
Rates: *$65; full breakfast. No credit cards.*
Restrictions: *Smoking outside only, no pets.*

Country Willows Bed and Breakfast Inn

A few miles south of downtown Ashland, this blue clapboard 1896 farmhouse sits on five sylvan acres with graceful willow trees and a babbling brook, overlooking the Siskiyou Mountains. Guests enjoy nestling into rattan furniture on the two-tiered front porch to soak in the farmland scenery.

The spacious guest rooms are appointed with a comfortable mixture of period reproductions and modern pieces, individual air-conditioning, and small private baths. Skylights, a stone fireplace, a two-person oak-framed tub, and a large brass bed in the main room of the new Sunrise Suite in the renovated barn make it the most romantic guest room. There is a potbellied wood-burning stove and full kitchen in the one-room cottage just beyond the swimming pool.

Innkeepers Bill and Barbara Huntley are avid backpackers and are happy to swap hiking tales or give advice on nearby sections of the Pacific Coast Trail.

Address: *1313 Clay St., Ashland, OR 97520, tel. 503/488–1590.*
Accommodations: *1 single room and 3 double rooms with baths, 1 housekeeping double room with bath, 2 housekeeping suites.*
Amenities: *Air-conditioning in rooms; evening refreshments, outdoor swimming pool and hot tub.*
Rates: *$70–$100, $135 suites; full breakfast. MC, V.*
Restrictions: *Smoking outside only, no pets; 2-night minimum on weekends Feb.–Oct.*

Mt. Ashland Inn

I t's just not possible to get closer to the cross-country and downhill skiing on Mt. Ashland or the hiking on the Pacific Coast Trail than the Mt. Ashland Inn, a contemporary cedar-log chalet designed and handcrafted by architect Jerry Shanafelt and his wife, Elaine. A crackling fire in the large stone fireplace in the living room provides a welcome hearth for all who enter this cozy mountain retreat 16 miles south of Ashland in the cool heights of the Siskiyou Mountains. The Shanafelts' attention to decorative detail can be glimpsed throughout the inn, from Jerry's stained-glass entryway panels (incorporating antique German glass), handmade cedar dining table and Windsor chairs, and high reliefwork on the guest room doors, to Elaine's hand-stitched quilts and good eye for quality Eastlake pieces. The gigantic McGloughlin Room, with windows on three sides overlooking the various peaks surrounding the lodge, has the best view, but the new Sky Lakes Suite, with a small waterfall cascading into a two-person whirlpool tub, is the most romantic.

Address: *505 Mt. Ashland Rd., Box 944, Ashland, OR 97520, tel. 503/482-8707.*
Accommodations: *4 double rooms with baths, 1 suite.*
Amenities: *Wet bar and refrigerator in 1 room.*
Rates: *$75-$125; full breakfast. MC, V.*
Restrictions: *Smoking outside only, no pets; 2-night minimum on weekends June–Sept. and holidays.*

River Banks Inn

T his Japanese-style contemporary ranch house on the banks of the Rogue River 15 winding miles outside Grants Pass is a cross-cultural fantasy starting with the Navaho "sweat lodge" and Zen meditation house. Then it's on to the main house, with its skylit and plant-filled Garden Room (part of the Caribbean Dream Suite), where you can soak in a sunken whirlpool tub; and to the Casablanca Room, with its carved Peruvian bed frame and bed stand, Afghani and Kurdish rugs, and sarcophagus lamp.

What sounds funky comes off as fun, especially in the genial company of owner Myrtle Franklin. More than anything, the River Banks Inn carries reminders of different phases of Myrtle's life: The pillow- and fur-covered stone ledge couch in the living room, and the massage room are carryovers from her days as a therapist at the Esalen Institute in Big Sur; the Steinway piano a reflection of her past as a musician; and the restaurant-style kitchen a throwback to her stint as a chef.

Address: *8401 Riverbanks Rd., Grants Pass, OR 97527, tel. 503/479-1118.*
Accommodations: *2 double rooms with baths, 2 suites.*
Amenities: *Phone in rooms, cable TV and VCR in 3 rooms, whirlpool tub in 1 room; outdoor hot tub, children's playhouse.*
Rates: *$95-150; full breakfast. MC, V.*
Restrictions: *Smoking outside only, no pets.*

River's Reach Bed and Breakfast

A year-long tour of bed-and-breakfasts in the United States, followed by a stint managing a lodge at Lake Tahoe—where he met his partner, Kay Johnson—were part of Russ Reichert's preparation for opening this Grants Pass B&B in 1991.

Once you're inside the compound the peaceful surroundings will make you forget that the city is so close by. Both children and adults love the ponds, rambling trails up rolling hillsides, paddocks of horses and llamas, turkeys, cows, and dogs.

Inside the 1986 ranch house, a freestanding brick fireplace and large, hung panels of leaded and stained glass add distinction to the living room. Art prints overshadow the simple but comfortable furnishings in the guest rooms. A large country breakfast features the fresh eggs, sausage, and produce of this self-sustaining ranch.

Address: *4025 Williams Hwy., Grants Pass, OR 97527, tel. 503/474-4411.*
Accommodations: *2 double rooms share bath, 1 suite, 1 housekeeping suite.*
Amenities: *Air-conditioning, evening refreshments, wood-burning stove in 1 room, TV in 2 rooms, VCRs available, whirlpool tub in shared bath; buggy rides available.*
Rates: *$55–$85; full breakfast. No credit cards.*
Restrictions: *Smoking outside only.*

Sonka's Sheep Station Inn

After enjoying numerous sojourns on farms in New Zealand, Evelyn and Louis Sonka decided to open their own ranch and share the experience with others. Their Folk Victorian–style farmhouse sits on a 400-acre working sheep ranch in a cloud-shrouded valley 18 miles south of Roseburg.

The sheep motif is everywhere: in artwork, etched glass, wallpaper, and even trim. Furnishings consist of traditional-style pieces and oak spoolwork antiques. Guest rooms boast patchwork quilts and color-coordinated dust ruffles on iron-and-brass beds. The remodeled bunkhouse holds two double rooms and a full kitchen.

Guests are welcome to join in on the early morning herding, or watch shearing and other seasonal rituals and Louis's border collies herd the sheep about the field. Although Evelyn does offer her guests dinner service, it's a safe bet that those who have been out playing with the woolly babies won't opt for the lamb.

Address: *901 N.W. Chadwick La., Myrtle Creek, OR 97457, tel. 503/863-5168.*
Accommodations: *2 double rooms share bath, 1 double housekeeping suite.*
Amenities: *Satellite TV, dinner available.*
Rates: *$50–$60, $110 suite; full breakfast. MC, V.*
Restrictions: *Smoking outside only, no pets; closed 2 weeks at Christmastime.*

Willowbrook Inn Bed and Breakfast

Gold Hill, a small farming community on the banks of the Rogue River, enjoys a slower pace than the neighboring towns of Grants Pass and Medford, and nowhere is that lifestyle more evident than at the Willowbrook Inn. Guests can sip lemonade while they relax in sturdy willow-branch chairs or in a hammock on the front porch, watching the birds flit among the old trees in the yard.

The interior of this 1905 Dutch Colonial farmhouse echoes the country charm of its setting, with a spinning wheel, bow-back Windsor armchairs, parson's bench, and Colonial reproductions. A peek into the kitchen offers a glimpse into Tom and Joann Hoeber's former lives running a gourmet cookware shop. Guest rooms have coordinated floral wallpaper, curtains, and bed covers, and step-up four-poster beds.

After a robust breakfast of sage-sausage pie and other dishes seasoned with spices from the Hoebers' massive herb garden, guests can enjoy rafting and fishing on the Rogue River or make the half-hour drive to Ashland.

Address: *628 Foots Creek Rd., Gold Hill, OR 97525, tel. 503/582–0075.* **Accommodations:** *2 double rooms with bath, 1 suite.* **Amenities:** *Air-conditioning; outdoor swimming pool.* **Rates:** *$60–$70; full breakfast. MC, V.* **Restrictions:** *Smoking outside only, no pets.*

Wolf Creek Tavern

This handsome Classical Revival inn, located in the tiny town of Wolf Creek, is a nostalgic example of a postal town hostelry in the late 19th century.

The Victoriana-filled ladies' parlor and saloonlike men's Tap Room have fireplaces. The tiny Jack London Room is kept as a showroom, with tattered quilt on the short, narrow beam bed and a candle on the rough-hewn desk table, typical furnishings found in lodgings of the period. The master chamber, the oldest and largest of the guest rooms, is furnished with simple 19th-century folk antiques. The rooms in the south wing are much smaller, with patinated brass beds and oak or mahogany dressers.

The concessionaires currently running the historic tavern for the Oregon State Parks and Recreation Division have many management kinks to work through; service is not what it should be, though the period-costume–clad staff does try.

Address: *100 Front St., Box 97, Wolf Creek, OR 97497, tel. 503/866–2474.* **Accommodations:** *8 double rooms with baths.* **Amenities:** *Restaurant, air-conditioning, conference room.* **Rates:** *$45–$55; breakfast extra. MC, V.* **Restrictions:** *No smoking in some bedrooms, no pets; closed 2 weeks in Jan.*

Willamette Valley
Including Eugene

*Cradled between the Cascade Mountain range to the east
and the Coast Range and Pacific Ocean to the west is the
serene green expanse of land known as the Willamette
Valley. Cloud-shrouded craggy bluffs and sheep-dotted,
pastoral meadows line I–5 and Highways 99W and 99E, the
major arteries through this lush north–south corridor.
Historic stagecoach stops and gold-mining boomtowns,
culture-rich college towns, and small farming communities
dot the valley between Salem, Oregon's state capital in the
north, and Roseburg in the south. For the most part,
industry here revolves around what the fertile land and
mild climate provides: rich, moist soil for hundreds of
thriving farms, orchards, and nurseries; rolling meadows
of pastureland for ranching; and stands of timber for the
logging trade. During harvest season highways and byways
are lined with roadside stands overflowing with colorful
fresh fruits and vegetables, nuts, jams, and flowers.
Vineyards abound as well, producing mainly such cool-
climate varietals as Pinot Noir, chardonnay, and Riesling.*

*Many of Oregon's rivers and streams—including the
Deschutes, McKenzie, North Umpqua, and Willamette
rivers—cut through this valley, providing thrilling rapids
rafting and outstanding fishing for steelhead, sockeye,
trout, and bass. Several of Oregon's remaining 54 covered
bridges, dating from the turn of the century, are scattered
throughout the Willamette Valley.*

*Colleges and universities in the Willamette Valley—
including Oregon State University in Corvallis and the
University of Oregon in Eugene—provide academic and
cultural life to the entire region. With its own ballet,
opera, symphony, and theater companies, Eugene, Oregon's
second-largest metropolitan area, is host to the valley's
strongest arts programs.*

Places to Go, Sights to See

Albany. There are three distinct historic districts in this vintage Victorian
town, each with numerous commercial and residential buildings representing
scores of architectural styles and periods. Albany is also a good jumping-off
point for the covered-bridge circuit through Eugene and Cottage Grove.

Cottage Grove. "Tour the Golden Past," a pamphlet available at the ranger
station on Row River Road, is a good guide to the abandoned mines,
historical buildings, and covered bridges (five in this area) of this nostalgic
Gold Rush boomtown. The rangers can also direct you to public gold-panning
areas. The Bohemian Mining Days festival in July celebrates Cottage Grove's
mining tradition.

Covered Bridges. There are about a dozen covered bridges in the Willamette
Valley, most of which are clustered in and around Cottage Grove and in Linn
County. Contact the Albany Convention and Visitors Commission (*see* Tourist
Information, below) for a touring map. The Covered Bridge Society of
Oregon (Box 1804, Newport, OR 97365, tel. 503/265–2934) can also provide
historical information.

Euphoria Chocolate Company (6 W. 7th St., tel. 503/343–9223). This little
company a few blocks south of the heart of downtown Eugene makes some
of the best-loved chocolate in Oregon.

Finley National Wildlife Refuge (26208 Finley Refuge Rd., Corvallis, tel.
503/757–7236). This refuge is a bird-watcher's paradise, with large fields of
grasses and grains that attract Canadian geese, grouse, pheasants, quail,
wood ducks, and other varieties of birds. The refuge is also home to
numerous deer.

Hult Center for the Performing Arts (1 Eugene Center, Eugene 97401, tel.
503/687–5000). This world-class arts complex in Eugene is an airy confection
of glass and native wood, containing two of the most acoustically perfect
theaters on the West Coast. It hosts everything from heavy-metal concerts to
classical ballets and is the home of Eugene's symphony, ballet, and opera
companies. It is also the site of the renowned two-week Oregon Bach Festival
that takes place in June and July.

Museums. The top museums in the valley include the *University of Oregon
Museum of Art* (1430 Johnson La., Eugene, tel. 503/346–3027), best known
for its Oriental collection; the *Horner Museum* (Gill Coliseum, Oregon State
University, Corvallis, tel. 503/737–2951), featuring artifacts from Oregon's
natural and cultural history; and *Wistec* (2300 Centennial Blvd., Eugene, tel.
503/687–3619), a science and technology museum.

Oakland. The citizens of this small community on the old stage line between
San Francisco and Portland have done a lot to restore their 19th-century
pioneer town, which is on the National Register of Historic Places. Blocks of

refurbished buildings representing styles dating from 1860 include several saloons, the gristmill, livery stable, general mercantile, opera house, icehouse/butcher shop, and pioneer post office, once the distribution center for the West Coast.

Saturday Market (8th and Oak St.). This bustling art, craft, and food market in Eugene attracts big crowds each Saturday from April through December, when farmers sell fresh produce and flowers, chefs create ethnic fare, and entertainers perform in the streets.

Wineries. There are nearly two dozen wineries in the valley, offering tours, tastings, and gorgeous scenery. The Oregon Winegrowers' Association (1200 N.W. Front Ave., Suite 400, Portland 97209, tel. 503/228–8403) can provide information and brochures on the region's wineries.

Restaurants

The region's hands-down-favorite restaurant is chef Rolf Schmidt's **Chanterelle** (tel. 503/484–4065), in Eugene, offering hearty French and other European cuisines and delicious pastries in intimate surroundings. Other top restaurants in Eugene include **Ambrosia** (tel. 503/342–4141) for Italian cuisine and **Scampi's** (tel. 503/485–0601) for Continental fare. **Tolly's** (tel. 503/459–1819), a combination soda fountain/wine library/restaurant/antiques shop/art gallery in Oakland, offers the best dining in town, with bistro fare, standard American favorites, and a dash of Scandinavian cuisine.

Tourist Information

Albany Convention and Visitors Commission (435 W. 1st Ave., Box 548, Albany, OR 97321, tel. 503/926–1517 or 800/526–2256); **Corvallis Convention and Visitors Bureau** (420 N.W. 2nd Ave., Corvalis, OR 97330, tel. 503/757–1544 or 800/334–8118); **Cottage Grove Chamber of Commerce** (710 Row River Rd., Box 587, Cottage Grove, OR 97424, tel. 503/942–2411); **Eugene–Springfield Visitors Bureau** (305 W. 7th Ave., Box 10286, Eugene, OR 97440, tel. 503/484–5307 or 800/547–5445, 800/452–3670 in OR); **Roseburg Visitors and Convention Bureau** (Dept. OT, 900 S.E. Douglas, Box 1262, Roseburg, OR 97470, tel. 503/672–9731 or 800/444–9584).

Reservation Services

Bed and Breakfast Reservations—Oregon (2321 N.E. 28th Ave., Portland 97212, tel. 503/287–4704); **Country Host Registry** (901 N.W. Chadwick La., Myrtle Creek 97457, tel. 503/863–5168); **Eugene Bed and Breakfast Innkeepers** (711 W. 11th Ave., Eugene 97202, tel. 503/345–7799); **Northwest Bed and Breakfast** (610 S.W. Broadway, Suite 606, Portland 97205, tel. 503/243–7616 or 800/800–6922).

Hanson Country Inn

In 1928 Jeff Hanson built this rotund Dutch Colonial on a high knoll overlooking the rolling Willamette Valley as the headquarters for his prospering poultry-breeding ranch. Here, in the egg house opposite the main house he developed his world-famous strain of White Leghorn chickens. After Hanson died, the house stood empty for 13 years. In 1987 it was purchased by Patricia Covey, a friendly Californian looking for escape from the Bay Area who had seen Corvallis listed in *Best Cities to Live in in America*. With plenty of polish and elbow grease, Patricia was able to restore the original grandeur of the house's unique features, including the carefully laid honeycomb tile work in the bathrooms and the intricately carved spindle room divider and sweeping spindle staircase, both made of New Zealand gumwood carved by local craftsmen.

A baby grand piano, 1920s American furniture, assorted sculptures, and a selection of Patricia's own paintings bring understated elegance to the great living room with its massive central fireplace. Sun pours through tall windowpanes, brightening the cozy reading nook where a plump easy chair sits beside floor-to-ceiling bookcases. The sun porch, with sparkling stained-glass windows and casual rattan furniture, looks onto a terraced garden with a stone fountain and a white vine arbor.

The suite, in shades of peach and sea-foam green, has a lovingly polished four-poster bed, an attached sitting room, and a private veranda overlooking a gentle slope to the valley below. The largest double room, a favorite of wedding couples because of its romantic box-canopy bed, has a sitting alcove and windows on three of its sides—providing views of the valley, the terraced garden, and the quiet pasture behind the house. All rooms are appointed with 1920s American furniture and soft bed linens imported from England.

Guests can get acquainted with resident cats, chickens, and sheep, explore the unrestored egg house, or take walks in the gardens and orchards on the five-acre grounds. Wine-tasting at nearby vineyards or a visit to the University of Oregon's Horner Museum are other entertainment possibilities.

Address: *795 S.W. Hanson St., Corvallis, OR 97333, tel. 503/752-2919, fax 503/570-4232.*
Accommodations: *1 double room with bath, 2 double rooms share bath, 1 suite.*
Amenities: *Phone and cable TV in 2 rooms.*
Rates: *$50–$65; full breakfast. AE, DC, MC, V.*
Restrictions: *Smoking outside only, no pets.*

The Lyon and the Lambe

This 2½-story, pitch-roofed home with a wraparound porch was built in 1990 but matches the surrounding homes from the '20s and '30s in this centrally located, older neighborhood in Eugene near the University of Oregon and the Hult Center for the Performing Arts. A whimsical purple door and multilingual bed-and-breakfast sign hint at the unconventional things to come.

Inside, an eclectic collection of modern and folk art is a counterpoint to centuries-old French and Spanish family antiques and ultramodern Italian furniture. Goines (famous for his Chez Panisse menu covers) prints fill one wall of the dining room, a statue of a graceful ballerina rests at the foot of the wide staircase next to the library, and Thai shadow puppets stare quietly across the hall at pictures of lions and lambs.

Guest rooms are furnished with unusual antique pieces: An intricate handmade quilt serves as the headboard in one room, and an open antique steamer trunk serves as the dresser in another. Extra touches include Perrier and water glasses on doily-covered trays, fresh and dried flower arrangements, candles and books of poetry, a choice of pillows (down, poly, or orthopedic), and a selection of current paperbacks that guests are free to take when they leave. The cozy, two-person whirlpool tub room is adorned with

candles, flower arrangements, mirrors, a stereo, and a selection of scented bath salts and oils. The heated towel rack is a rare joy to find in the United States.

Barbara Brod brings previous innkeeping experience and an effervescent personality to this bed-and-breakfast. Her German husband, Henri, lends international flair, from his *Kaiserschmarrn,* a fluffy egg breakfast dish with raisins and nuts, to the *bett hupferl,* a sweet treat left on guests' pillows at bedtime. The Brods can offer sound dining advice and often arrange a free glass of wine with dinner at one of their favored spots. They are also up on the latest art exhibits and cultural events in town and can point the way to nearby Skinner Butte Park for a delightful jog along the Willamette River.

Address: *988 Lawrence St., Eugene, OR 97401, tel. 503/683–3160.*
Accommodations: *4 double rooms with baths.*
Amenities: *Whirlpool tub, phones, ceiling fans, and individual heat control in room, meeting room; well-mannered dogs welcomed.*
Rates: *$60–$75; full breakfast. MC, V.*
Restrictions: *No smoking in 1 bedroom; 2-night minimum during conventions and university functions.*

Steamboat Inn

Deep in the Umpqua National Forest, 38 winding miles east of Roseburg, this 1855 river rock and pine lodge sits alongside the luminous blue North Umpqua River. Fisherfolk from around the globe come here to test their skills against the elusive steelhead and trout. Owners Jim and Sharon Van Loan were themselves frequent visitors and worked as members of the inn's summer crew for three years before buying it in 1975.

While its fishing tradition is still much in evidence—rehabilitated fly-tying cabinets serving as the reception desk and an unobtrusive fly shop—the Steamboat has seen a shift toward a more refined country inn. A few of the eight cozy riverside cabins behind the lodge have yet to be redecorated, but for the most part, all the rough edges of this fishing camp have been delicately hewn down with coordinated pastel bedding, draperies, and carpets, as well as thoughtful decorative touches of dried flowers, botanical prints, and hand-quilted comforters. Knotty pine paneling and rustic Americana furnishings in the guest rooms echo the decor of the main lodge.

Recent additions to the property include two detached suites along the river and five roomy, lofted chalets a half mile down the road. A king-size bed in the master bedroom, twin beds in the loft, a fireplace in the living room, deep-soaking tub in the roomy bathroom, and a kitchenette stocked with dishes and cookware make the chalets perfect for families or small groups. The riverside suites offer intimate seclusion, with large stone fireplaces, two-person Japanese-style soaking tubs, and large private decks looking onto the river.

The Steamboat's famous candlelit "fisherman's dinner" might include Northwest wines, salad spiced with roasted local nuts or garden-fresh herbs, fresh bread, a vegetable dish, and roasted lamb or fresh spring salmon steamed, poached, or grilled.

Nonfishing activities in the area include backpacking and hiking on the trails of the surrounding Umpqua National Forest, soaking in swimming holes, picking wildflowers, or making a day trip to cross-country ski at Diamond Lake or to admire the breathtaking, crystal-blue waters of Crater Lake.

Address: *Steamboat Inn, Steamboat, OR 97447, tel./fax 503/498–2411.*
Accommodations: *8 double rooms with baths, 7 housekeeping suites.*
Amenities: *Dinner available, air-conditioning, meeting room, small pets allowed for extra fee.*
Rates: *$85–$125, riverside suites $195; breakfast extra. MC, V.*
Restrictions: *No smoking in lodge or riverside suites.*

Beckley House

The entire town of Oakland is on the National Register of Historic Places, and this clapboard, Italianate Victorian fits right in. The large, bright living room features diamond-paned windows, oak floors, and whitewashed walls with dusty blue stenciling below the high ceilings. Dark cedar wainscoting, shiny wall sconces, and a large central fireplace give a formal feel to the dining room. Oil paintings and intricately carved wardrobes and bedsteads fill the roomy second-floor guest rooms. The radiantly sunny suite, a converted sun porch, has a white iron bed topped with a canopylike drapery and a colorful quilt.

Sally Wheaton, an interior decorator, and her husband, Floyd, retired from the sheet-metal business, left California and bought Beckley House during the summer of 1991.

A complimentary Continental breakfast is served two blocks away at Tolly's, the combination soda fountain/restaurant/wine library/art gallery/antiques shop that has long been a treasured Oakland fixture.

Address: *338 S.E. 2nd St., Oakland, OR 97462, tel. 503/459-9320.*
Accommodations: *2 double rooms with baths, 1 suite.*
Amenities: *Horse and carriage rides available.*
Rates: *$60–$75, suite $85 weekends, $80 weekdays; Continental breakfast. No credit cards.*
Restrictions: *Smoking outside only, no pets.*

Black Bart's Bed and Breakfast

This is not a pirate's hideaway but a whimsical bed-and-breakfast named after the grand-champion mammoth donkey, Black Bart, the beloved family pet of innkeepers Don and Irma Mode. Happily retired, Bart grazes in a pasture next to the house—a small gable-roofed, two-story, white clapboard farmhouse built during the 1880s, and set back on a dusty rural road. The Modes' passion for collecting colors every inch of the house, beginning with the glassed-in front porch, where guests enter through an unusual assortment of antique toys, an old wood cookstove, and mannequins dressed in long gingham gowns.

Inside, the house may seem cluttered and hokey to some but quaint and charming to others; rooms are filled with every type of collectible imaginable. Second-floor guest rooms follow a country decor, with brass and carved wooden bedsteads, handmade quilts, and more dolls, stuffed toys, and donkey memorabilia.

Address: *94125 Love Lake Rd., Junction City, OR 97448, tel. 503/998-1904.*
Accommodations: *1 double room with bath, 2 double rooms with ½ baths share full bath.*
Amenities: *Air-conditioning; carriage and wagon rides available.*
Rates: *$50–$60; full breakfast. AE, MC, V.*
Restrictions: *Smoking outside only; no pets; 2-night minimum during major conventions in Feb. and Aug.*

The Dome Bed and Breakfast

This modern geodesic dome resting before a group of Douglas firs is certainly conspicuous in the tiny rural community of Elmira, 14 miles west of Eugene. William and Eileen Stadler built the 1,556-square-foot dome themselves in 1983 and decided to open it as a bed-and-breakfast in 1991.

Large picture windows and skylights throw sunlight on the angular walls, giving an airy feel to this open, two-story structure. The decor is comfortable contemporary; the large common room features a raised stone fireplace surrounded by plump, cushioned couches and a dark cherrywood dining table. Soft floral bed linens brighten the generally spartan decor of the bedrooms. A skylight above the bed in the second-floor suite is excellent for late-night stargazing. The downstairs guest room, which is accessible to the disabled, opens onto a deck overlooking an apple orchard.

The Stadlers, who live in a large house near the dome, prepare a full breakfast every morning, including eggs Florentine and Don's own homemade sausage.

Address: *24456 Warthen Rd., Elmira, OR 97437, tel. 503/485-4495.*
Accommodations: *1 double room with bath, 1 suite.*
Amenities: *Air-conditioning, cable TV, clock radio, phone, iron, and ironing board in rooms.*
Rates: *$65; full breakfast. MC, V.*
Restrictions: *Smoking outside only, no pets.*

House of Hunter

A path of roses beside two giant tulip trees leads to the bright red door of this somewhat stern-looking Victorian Italianate overlooking downtown Roseburg. Walt Hunter and his wife, Jean, have done an admirable job of restoring the house they bought in 1989.

The interior is mostly formal, especially in the front dining room where massive cabinets display fine family china and cut glass. The living room, furnished with early 20th-century American chairs and couches, is less stiff and more inviting. Second-floor guest rooms have small vanities, tall armoires, frilly curtains, ruffled bedspreads, and lacy pillows that Jean created.

Each morning trays of steaming coffee and freshly baked breads and muffins await early risers, followed by a large, full breakfast. On the back porch guests can burn calories on the exercise bike and treadmill while looking out onto Walt's developing English flower garden.

Address: *813 S.E. Kane, Roseburg, OR 97470, tel. 503/672-2335.*
Accommodations: *2 double rooms with baths, 2 double rooms with basins share bath.*
Amenities: *Air-conditioning; phone and TV available.*
Rates: *$50-$65; full breakfast. No credit cards.*
Restrictions: *Smoking outside only, no pets.*

McGillivray's Log Home Bed and Breakfast

Whether it's the cozy feeling of being surrounded by wood, or owner Evelyn Mc-Gillivray's congeniality, this bed-and-breakfast is welcoming and homey. Set on five quiet acres just outside the bustle of Eugene, this log home was built by Evelyn and her late husband in 1982.

From the split-log staircase and carefully carved door latches and light-switch plates to the colorful stained-glass windows on the second-floor landing, the McGillivrays did it all. Rough strips of wood frame old photos of burly loggers hard at work, appropriate in this structure of pine, fir, oak, chinquapin (an Oregon hardwood), and other woods. Ruffled curtains, quilted pillows and bedspreads, and hand-hewn wood-slab headboards, bedside tables, dressers, and coffee tables add to the rustic atmosphere.

Breakfast is an event as Evelyn stands before her antique wood-burning cookstove preparing fresh coffee, bacon-wrapped eggs, and her special-recipe buttermilk pancakes. Trimmings might include fresh-squeezed juice, baked fruit, hazelnut-honey butter, and maple or choke-cherry syrup.

Address: *88680 Evers Rd., Elmira, OR 97437, tel. 503/935-3564.*
Accommodations: *2 double rooms with baths.*
Amenities: *Air-conditioning; afternoon refreshments.*
Rates: *$50–$60; full breakfast. MC, V.*
Restrictions: *Smoking outside only, no pets.*

Wine Country
Including Salem

*Years ago, researchers at Oregon State University
concluded that the soils and climate of the Willamette
Valley were unsuitable for the cultivation of fine varietal
wine grapes. Fortunately for oenophiles everywhere, they
were much mistaken. Oregon's first vineyards took root
during the early 1960s. Caressed by moisture-laden breezes
off the Pacific and coddled by Oregon's long, warm
summers and crisp autumns, cool-climate varietals such as
Pinot Noir, Riesling, and chardonnay soon proved the
academics wrong.*

*The vintages of 1983 and 1985 put the stamp of greatness
on Oregon's Pinot Noir, as wines from the Yamhill and
Willamette valleys won numerous gold medals in blind
tastings against the best from California and France.
Perhaps afflicted with Pinot envy, Burgundy's Drouhin
family bought 180 acres here in 1987; they released their
first bottling last year.*

*If you've been to California's famous Napa and Sonoma
wine districts, you'll have an idea of what the Oregon wine
country is not. The state's 88 bonded wineries have about
6,000 acres under cultivation, compared with California's
800 wineries and 700,000 acres of vineyards. Oregon's
wineries tend to be small, personal, and family run. In
fact, if you make a disparaging remark about the Riesling
while you're in the tasting room, you may find yourself
answering to the owner, who, it just so happens, is pouring
out the samples.*

*Oregon's wine country lacks the maturity and sumptuous
splendor of California's—as well as its pretensions. Its
wineries are scattered from the Columbia River Gorge, just
across the river from Washington, all the way south to
Ashland, near the California border. But the greatest*

concentration—nearly 40 in all—is found within an hour's drive of Portland, dotting the hills as far as Salem. Geographically, the wine country occupies a wet, temperate trough between the Coast Range to the west and the Cascades to the east. The landscape is a beguiling one— green and rugged, rich with soothing picture-postcard views that invite picnicking.

The small towns along the way—Forest Grove, McMinnville, Yamhill, Dundee—retain their rural charm. If that means they have yet to succumb to rampant commercialism, it also means you may have to hunt a bit for the best available food, lodging, and other amenities. Oregon's wine country is a quiet district, heavy on bucolic serenity, but lightly endowed with sites of noteworthy historical significance, national parks, or other tourist attractions. Napa Valley it's not, but Oregon's wine country makes a fine side trip from Portland—and it's an even better destination for two to three days of quiet R&R.

Places to Go, Sights to See

Bush House (600 Mission St., S.E., tel. 503/363–4174), situated just south of Salem's downtown district and set in the 105-acre Bush's Pasture Park, is a creaky, gaslit Italianate mansion from 1878 with 10 marble fireplaces. (Next door is the Bush Barn Art Center, a gallery selling works by Northwest artists.) Located a few blocks away, the fanciful 1894 *Deepwood Estate* (1116 Mission St. S.E., tel. 503/363–1825) is in better taste. Built in the Queen Anne style, the estate is noteworthy for its splendid interior woodwork, original stained glass, and formal English-style garden.

The **Lafayette Schoolhouse Antique Mall** (Hwy. 99W, between Newberg and McMinnville, tel. 503/864–2720), a large, freshly restored 1910 schoolhouse, houses Oregon's largest permanent antiques show. It's filled with a vast assortment of collectibles and antiquities—from toys to clothing to furniture, china, glass, silver, and Native American artifacts.

McMinnville is the largest (population 16,000) and most sophisticated of Oregon's wine-country towns. Its central location, excellent restaurants and shops, and collection of top-notch B&Bs make it the headquarters of choice for most wine-country tourers. Founded in 1849, *Linfield College* (tel. 503/472–4121), an oasis of brick and ivy in the midst of McMinnville's farmers' market bustle, hosts Oregon's International Pinot Noir Celebration, which attracts a who's who of international winemakers each July.

Mission Mill Village and Thomas Kay Woolen Mill Museum (1313 Mill St. S.E., tel. 503/585–7012) in Salem offers visitors a vivid glimpse of a late-19th-century woolen mill, complete with waterwheels and mill stream. Teasel gigging and napper flock bins are just two of the processes and machines on display at the museum complex. Everything still works; it looks as if the workers have merely stepped away for a lunch break. The *Marion Museum of History* displays a fine collection of pioneer and Calipooya Indian artifacts. The spare simplicity of the *Jason Lee House, John D. Boone Home*, and the *Methodist Parsonage*, also part of the village, offer a glimpse of domestic life in the wilds of Oregon during the 1840s.

Newberg, a graceful old pioneer town located in a broad bend in the Willamette River a half hour southwest of Portland, is also worth a visit. One of the oldest and most significant of the town's original structures is the *Hoover-Minthorn House* (115 S. River St., tel. 503/538–6629), the boyhood home of President Herbert Hoover. Built in 1881, the beautifully preserved frame house includes many original furnishings and features, as well as the woodshed that no doubt played a formative role in shaping young "Bertie" Hoover's character.

The **Oregon Wine and Food Festival** (Oregon State Fair and Exposition Center, 2330 17th St. N.E., Salem, OR 97310, tel. 503/378–3247) is held each January at the State Fairgrounds in Salem. Dozens of Oregon's top wineries bring their current releases, and wine lovers can taste to their heart's content for a modest fee. For the resilient of palate, it's an excellent opportunity to compare wines, styles, and vintages.

Salem, Oregon's state capital, is located on the 45th parallel about 45 miles south of Portland, precisely halfway between the North Pole and the equator. Even if you have no political ambitions, make time for a visit to the *Capitol* complex (900 Court St., tel. 503/378–4423). The view of the city, the Willamette Valley, and the mountains from its 140-foot-high dome is impressive, there are surprisingly good murals and sculptures inspired by the state's history, and when the legislature is in session you can observe Oregon's political movers and shakers in action. Tours of the rotunda, the House and Senate chambers, and the governor's office leave from the information counter under the dome. Just across State Street are the tradition-steeped brick buildings and immaculate grounds of *Willamette University* (tel. 503/370–6303), the oldest college in the West. Founded in 1842, Willamette has long been a mecca for aspiring politicians. The tall, prim Waller Hall, built in 1841, is one of the five oldest buildings in the Pacific Northwest. The university hosts theatrical and musical performances, athletic events, guest lectures, and art exhibitions year-round.

Wine Touring, by car or bicycle, is obviously the star attraction here. First pick up a copy of *Discover Oregon Wineries*, a free guide available at visitor information centers and at most places where Oregon wines are sold (it's also available from the Oregon Winegrowers' Association, 200 N.W. Front St., Portland, OR 97209, tel. 503/228–8403). The guide is an invaluable companion, with maps to each winery, opening hours, and suggested itineraries.

Day tourers can begin anywhere, but if you're planning a more extended exploration of the wine country, you should choose a base of operations central to the area you intend to explore. McMinnville has the best concentration of restaurants and bed-and-breakfasts. Salem to the south and Forest Grove to the north also make good headquarters.

Opening hours vary widely. The tasting rooms of some wineries are open daily year-round; others are either open only on weekends or closed for lengthy periods during the winter. Some of the state's best wineries, such as Adams, Adelsheim, Cameron, and Eyrie, have no tasting rooms and are open to the public only on special occasions such as Thanksgiving weekend (call the individual wineries for details).

The etiquette of Oregon wine tasting is simple. You select a winery and present yourself at its tasting room. The attendant provides glasses and offers samples of the wines available for tasting that day. There is seldom a charge for tasting, though an exception may be made for particularly rare bottlings. Feel free to try any or all of the available wines; swishing and spitting are allowed, and you're not compelled to buy anything.

Many of the establishments command hilltop views and maintain picnic areas for visitors' use. McMinnville and Hillsboro offer the greatest variety of delis and specialty food shops. During the summer and fall, the wine country's many roadside produce stands yield luscious strawberries, raspberries, marionberries, pears, nectarines, peaches, plums, apples, kiwis, and other local fruits.

Choosing Oregon's top wineries is as subjective as choosing its top wines. It's fair to say that *Adelsheim Vineyard* in Newberg (1922 N.W. Pettygrove St., tel. 503/538–3652), *Cameron Winery* in Dundee (8200 Worden Hill Rd., tel. 503/538–0336), *Eyrie Vineyards* in McMinnville (935 E. 10th St., tel. 503/472–6315), *Knudsen-Erath Winery* in Dundee (Worden Hill Rd., tel. 503/538–3318), *Ponzi Vineyards* near Beaverton (14665 S.W. Winery La., off Schollsbury Rd., tel. 503/628–1227), *Shafer Vineyard Cellars* in Forest Grove (Hwy. 8, tel. 503/357–6604), and *Tualatin Vineyards* in Forest Grove (David Hill Rd., tel. 503/357–5005) are among the state's oldest and most consistently esteemed operations. *Chateau Benoit* in Carlton (6580 N.E. Mineral Springs Rd., off Hwy. 99W, tel. 503/864–2991), *Elk Cove Vineyards* in Gaston (27751 N.W. Olson Rd., tel. 503/985–7760), *Laurel Ridge Winery* in Forest Grove (Rte. 1 and David Hill Rd., tel. 503/359–5436), *Rex Hill Vineyards* in Newberg (30835 N. Hwy. 99W, tel. 503/538–0666), and *Yamhill Valley Vineyards* in McMinnville (16250 S.W. Oldspill Rd., tel. 503/843–3100) have some of the most beautiful winery views and picnic grounds in the area.

Restaurants

The wine country's culinary star is undoubtedly **Nick's Italian Cafe** (tel. 503/434–4471) in McMinnville. A favorite of tourists and local winemakers alike, Nick's serves up spirited northern Italian home cooking in modest surroundings. The five-course, fixed-price menu changes nightly to reflect the region's exquisite seasonal produce. Don't overlook the extensive wine list of Oregon's vintages. **Roger's** (tel. 503/472–0917) is a McMinnville family favorite that emphasizes reasonably priced fresh seafood. The restaurant has a pleasant streamside location, and there's patio dining during the summer. **Lavender's Blue, A Tea Room** (tel. 503/472–4594), in McMinnville, serves up an impeccably English high tea, great homemade desserts, light lunches, and dinners. The **Inn at Orchard Heights** (tel. 503/371–1812), across the river from downtown Salem, is a handsome hilltop restaurant filled with the soothing sounds of rippling water and classical music. The European owner/ chef puts a richly sauced Continental spin on fine local beef, seafood, and game. Salem's **Thompson Brewery & Public House** (tel. 503/363–7286) is a fun, casual outpost of the Portland-based restaurant and pub chain. It serves wonderfully eclectic and inexpensive cuisine, preferably washed down with local "microbrews."

Tourist Information

McMinnville Chamber of Commerce (417 N. Adams St., McMinnville, OR 97128, tel. 503/472–6196); **The Oregon Wine Center** (1200 N.W. Front Ave., Portland, OR 97209, tel. 503/228–8336); **Portland/Oregon Visitors Association** (26 S.W. Salmon St., Portland, OR 97204–3299, tel. 503/275–9750); **Salem Convention & Visitor Center** (Mission Mill Village, 1313 Mill St. S.E., Salem, OR 97301, tel. 503/581–4325).

Reservation Services

Bed & Breakfast Accommodations—Oregon (2321 N.E. 28th Ave., Portland, OR 97212, tel. 503/287–4704); **Bed & Breakfast Northwest** (610 S.W. Broadway, Portland, OR 97205, tel. 503/243–7616).

Flying M Ranch

The mysterious red "M" signs begin in downtown Yamhill—a somnolent town of 700 or so in the very press of the wine country— and continue west for 10 miles into the Chehalem Valley, in the rugged foothills of the Coast Range. Following them alertly will bring you to the 625-acre Flying M Ranch, perched above the Yamhill River.

The centerpiece of this rough-and-ready, Wild West–flavored amalgam of motel, campground, dude ranch, timber camp, and working ranch is the great log lodge, decorated in a style best described as Paul Bunyan Eclectic and featuring a bar carved from a single, six-ton tree trunk. On weekends, this is *the* happening place; the adjoining restaurant serves thick steaks and prime rib, and there are even a few fish dishes on the menu now. Sensitive souls may notice the accusing eyes of dozens of taxidermied trophies watching while they eat.

Guests have a choice of seven secluded cabins and 28 motel units. (Ask about special packages: the Retreat package includes dinner for two with wine, wine and fruit in the room, a full breakfast, and horseback riding.) The motel is modern and clean, but lacks personality. (All the beds, however, do have log frames.) The cabins, a better choice, are equipped with kitchens, living rooms, wood-burning stoves, and decks overlooking the river. All are spacious, and

evoke a rustic, log-cabin charm. The cozy Honeymoon Cabin has a huge stone-and-brick fireplace and a double whirlpool tub.

Be sure to book ahead for a long-time Flying M specialty, the Steak Fry Ride. Participants ride a hay wagon to the ranch's secluded creekside elk camp for a barbecued steak dinner with all the trimmings, including a crooning cowboy. The more adventuresome can ride horses from the ranch's stables, one of the Flying M's many countrified amenities. There are horseshoe pits, a big swimming hole, good fly-fishing, even a family of irascible pet buffalo (please, no petting). As if this weren't enough, the wineries are a half-hour drive away over back-country gravel roads. If you don't make it back by dark, finding the Flying M could be a real challenge.

Address: *23029 N.W. Flying M Rd., Yamhill, OR 97148, tel. 503/662–3222, fax 503/662–3202.*
Accommodations: *28 double rooms with baths, 7 housekeeping cabin suites, 1 double housekeeping cabin suite.*
Amenities: *Restaurant, bar, radios in cabins, TV in 1 cabin, live entertainment, meeting and catering facilities; campsites, fishing, hiking trails, horseback riding, horseshoe pits, swimming hole, tennis court.*
Rates: *$50–$70, cabins $75–$150; breakfast extra. AE, D, DC, MC, V.*
Restriction: *Closed Dec. 24–25.*

Mattey House

Mattey House is a sprawling Queen Anne mansion nestled behind its own little vineyard a few miles north of McMinnville. Its tasteful, distinctively western Victorian ambience and its experienced hosts make Mattey House the area's most accomplished B&B.

The house itself was built in 1892 by Joseph Mattey, a prosperous local butcher and cattle rancher. Gene and Susan Irvin found it in 1984, partially restored but in need of considerable TLC. They finally opened their doors in February 1986.

To wine-country visitors tuckered out by a long day's slurping, Mattey House is an oasis of welcoming warmth. Entering the living room, which is framed by Ionic columns and fretwork, you'll find a cheerful fire in the old carved-wood-and-marble hearth, soothing classical music on the CD player, wallpaper reproducing a William Morris pattern, and beautiful period furnishings that feel as if they're an integral part of the house. There's a porch swing overlooking the vineyard and 10 acres of largely unlandscaped grounds for those in a strolling mood.

Upstairs are the four guest rooms, all named for locally grown varieties of grapes. The Chardonnay Room, with its tall windows and cream-colored decor, is bright and sunny; so is the Blanc de Blancs Room, with its white and off-white tones, white wicker, antique brass bed, and Art Deco posters. Chardonnay has a connecting door to the burgundy-hued Pinot Noir Room, filled with genuine Eastlake furniture; for an added fee it's possible to reserve them as a two-couple suite. These three rooms share two baths. The Riesling Room, with an antique oak bed, more Eastlake pieces, and a 6-foot-long claw-foot tub, is the only room with a private bath. (Note the wine–glycerine soaps in all the bathrooms.)

The Irvins fortify their guests well before launching them on a morning's wine touring. Breakfast features fresh local fruit—perhaps a baked apple or a poached pear in raspberry sauce—followed by fresh-baked breads and the house specialty, scrambled eggs with smoked salmon. At the end of their tour, guests are greeted with hors d'oeuvres and a glass of Oregon wine.

Address: *10221 N.E. Mattey La., McMinnville, OR 97128, tel. 503/434–5058.*
Accommodations: *3 double rooms share 2 baths, 1 double room with bath.*
Amenities: *Afternoon refreshments, robe and clock in room.*
Rates: *$55–$65; full breakfast. MC, V.*
Restrictions: *No smoking, no pets.*

Steiger Haus

"**Z** sa Zsa Gabor slapped here," proclaims the plaque in Steiger Haus's hallway, covered with hundreds of pictures of guests from the inn's early years. Well, actually it says "slept." These little mementos aren't just there for show; they're an illustration of the genuine affection innkeepers Lynn and Doris Steiger feel for their guests. After a weekend at Steiger Haus, you feel like family.

Located on a quiet residential street near downtown McMinnville, the modern cedar-sided and brick structure was built in 1984 as a B&B. Linfield College, the site of Oregon's annual International Pinot Noir Celebration, is just around the corner.

Steiger Haus is a warm, fuzzy sort of place, thanks largely to Doris Steiger's fondness for sheep, wool, spinning, and weaving. Sheep are everywhere, peering from the walls, the tables and shelves, and even from the upholstery. Many of the inn's colorful rugs and place mats were woven by Doris in her cedar-walled solarium/studio.

The inn's public areas have a country-contemporary charm. On the main level are an open kitchen with breakfast bar, brick fireplace, and oak dining suite with Windsor-style chairs built by an Oregon craftsman. There are comfortable, modern TV rooms upstairs and downstairs. In summer and fall, most of the action shifts outdoors.

Steiger Haus's five guest rooms are cool and contemporary, enlivened with woolly artwork, bright florals, fresh paint, and sunlight. (Two of them can be linked to form a suite.) The downstairs room has a brick fireplace, a small, cozy sitting area, a pretty private bath, and opens onto one of the decks. The Treetop Room upstairs features a handmade oak bed with curved head- and footboards of turned spindles, tall windows, and a late-Victorian Wakefield wicker-and-oak desk. It shares a huge skylit bath with a second room, which is equipped with two single beds, goose-down comforters, and a bent-willow settee. An old grape-harvesting bin forms the base of a table in another guest room. Breakfast, served at the guest's convenience, is a hearty affair; Lynn says that he's constantly giving out recipes for their oatmeal-granola hotcakes.

Address: *360 Wilson St., McMinnville, OR 97128, tel. 503/472–0821.*
Accommodations: *3 double rooms with baths, 2 double rooms share bath.*
Amenities: *Fireplace in 1 room, cable TV and VCR on each floor, phone on each floor, evening refreshments.*
Rates: *$55–$75; full breakfast. No credit cards.*
Restrictions: *Smoking on decks only, no pets.*

Youngberg Hill Farm

Like ghostly twilight sentinels, the deer come down to greet guests at Youngberg Hill Farm. They have free run of this 700-acre estate, high in the hills west of Mc-Minnville. Well, nearly free run—guests must remember to close the gate of the deer fence that surrounds the house itself and its 13 acres of young Pinot Noir vines, a favorite midnight snack for these graceful stags. During the fall the deer are more wary, because innkeeper Norm Barnett and his wife, Eve, are keen hunters.

Norm and Eve built the inn from scratch in 1988, a monster-size nine-bedroom replica of a classic American farmhouse commanding breathtaking views over mountain and valley from atop a steep-sided hill. Early spring evenings at Youngberg Hill, a working farm, means dozens of tiny black-faced lambs wobbling through the lush pastureland on knobby knees.

Youngberg Hill is a comfortable place, but needs a bit more time and experience before it achieves a proper, lived-in warmth. The common areas are spacious, modern, and high-ceilinged, with Victorian belly-band molding and bull's-eye corners. The furnishings are largely golden oak period reproductions that are hot from the showroom; the sitting room's deep sofa and settee, upholstered in an unusual grapevine-patterned chintz, are a welcoming touch, as are the suede-covered armchairs and wood-burning stove. Big windows make the most of the hilltop estate's romantic views. The five guest rooms are small to medium in size; furnished with golden oak and Victorian Cottage reproductions, they have a cozy modern ambience.

Breakfast is Eve's province. Her Austrian-influenced specialties—rich, puffy *Kaiserschwarm* served with warm marionberry syrup and smoked pork chops are typical fare—linger on the palate well into the afternoon. Among the inn's special attractions are a nicely stocked, reasonably priced wine cellar and special hunters' weekends in the fall.

Address: *10660 Youngberg Hill Rd., McMinnville, OR 97128, tel. 503/472-2727.*
Accommodations: *5 double rooms with baths.*
Amenities: *Air-conditioning in room, fireplace in 2 rooms, cable TV in common area, wine available, meeting facilities; hiking trails, hunting, swimming hole.*
Rates: *$65–$75; fall hunting packages (including 3 meals) $100 per person per day; full breakfast. AE, MC, V.*
Restrictions: *Smoking on porch only, no pets; 3-day minimum for hunting package.*

Kelty Estate

This simple white-clapboard farmhouse, built in 1872, is located on busy Highway 99 between Newberg and McMinnville, directly across the street from the Lafayette Schoolhouse Antique Mall.

New owners Ron Ross, a former facilities manager, and his wife, JoAnn, a nurse, spent most of 1990 renovating the four-acre estate. The Rosses' hard work is reflected in the house's handsome living areas. Sunlight from tall windows gleams on newly refinished oak floors and tasteful wine-colored patterned rugs; an elegant border of green and blue paisley circles the freshly painted walls.

The two upstairs guest rooms have received similar care. Paint, carpets, and furnishings are all new, and there's an austere, contemporary emphasis on brass and velour. White lace curtains add an old-fashioned note. Both rooms have queen-size beds, hardwood floors, and private baths. If possible, reserve the room at the back of the house; the front room, overlooking Highway 99, is a little noisier. Guests have their choice of Continental or full farmhouse breakfast.

Address: *675 Hwy. 99W, Lafayette, OR 97127, tel. 503/864-3740.*
Accommodations: *2 double rooms with baths.*
Amenities: *Cable TV in living room.*
Rates: *$55; full breakfast. No credit cards.*
Restrictions: *No smoking, no pets.*

Main Street Bed & Breakfast

The first inn in this part of the wine country, Main Street Bed & Breakfast is in Forest Grove, 25 miles west of Portland and hard by such highly regarded wineries as Tualatin, Shafer, and Ponzi.

The B&B occupies a 1913 Craftsman bungalow that has a stone foundation, cross-gabled roof, and a wide front porch with glider. The corner lot, in a quiet residential neighborhood, is filled with flowers and shady trees. Inside, Marie has decorated with a mix of contemporary furnishings and her various collections: owls, kaleidoscopes, and old handmade aprons. Though modern, the carpets, couches, and baths are softened with old-fashioned touches —a lace tablecloth here, a clawfoot tub there.

The two upstairs guest rooms are a little fussy, decorated in florals and lace, with dried flowers and stuffed or painted tole geese in profusion. There's an extra room that, when available, can be used for children. The full breakfasts are hearty, not arty: Rhubarb crisp, smoked pork chops, and fried potatoes are some of Marie's standbys.

Address: *1803 Main St., Forest Grove, OR 97116, tel. 503/357-9812.*
Accommodations: *2 double rooms share bath.*
Amenities: *Afternoon refreshments, phone in 1 room.*
Rates: *$50. MC, V.*
Restrictions: *Smoking on porch only, no pets; 2-night minimum on weekends.*

Orchard View Inn

Two years ago Wayne and Marie Schatter escaped the southern California rat race to run Orchard View Inn. Southern California seems a world away from the long, sunlight-warmed deck of this octagonal redwood house, 1,000 feet up in the Chehalem Mountains west of McMinnville. Birdcalls, the rustle of wind through the evergreen canopy overhead, and the music of water cascading from pool to pool down the hill are the only sounds.

Inside, the inn mixes contemporary vaulted ceilings and velour-upholstered couches with beautiful Chinese antiques. Guest rooms are smallish, modern, and simply furnished. The Antique Room displays a framed collection of Marie's family heirlooms: 19th-century lace gloves,

purses, fans, a silver cane handle that belonged to her mother. The single basement room has a private entrance and bath; its rather startling plaid carpet is redeemed by a series of gorgeous 1930s-vintage Chinese prints on the wall.

Address: *16540 NW Orchard View Rd., McMinnville, OR 97128, tel. 503/472-0165.*
Accommodations: *2 double rooms with baths, 2 double rooms share bath.*
Amenities: *Kitchen and laundry room available; hammock.*
Rates: *$65–$70; full breakfast. MC, V.*
Restrictions: *Smoking outside only, no pets; 3-night minimum during Pinot Noir Celebration.*

Sheridan Country Inn

The lawn that surrounds the Sheridan Country Inn is so expansive that it's impossible not to pity the person who has to mow it. The flower-splashed, birch-shaded serenity of this remote corner of the wine country is marred only by the exterior of the house itself, a World War II–vintage Tudor whose facade is overly busy. It's only one of several nagging contradictions that keep this 11-room inn just below the top tier of wine-country guest houses.

The inn is just outside Sheridan, a farm town nearly 10 miles from the nearest winery. There are seven guest rooms in the big main house, plus four satellite units in two cabins out back. Extensively renovated in 1988, all of the rooms are uniformly spacious, clean, and well appointed;

that's fortunate, because the public areas are cluttered with venerable 1970s-vintage furnishings and vaguely Oriental knickknacks.

The cabin rooms have phones, queen-size brass beds, TVs, decks, refrigerators—and large orange No Smoking signs tacked onto the walls.

Address: *1330 W. Main St., Sheridan, OR 97378, tel. 503/843-3226 or 503/843-3151.*
Accommodations: *11 double rooms with baths.*
Amenities: *Phone, TV, and refrigerator in rooms, air-conditioning in cabin rooms, whirlpool in 1 room, meeting room.*
Rates: *$35–$95; Continental breakfast. AE, DC, MC, V.*
Restrictions: *No smoking, no pets.*

Portland

*The best way to go about describing Portland's appeal
might be to start with what the City of Roses doesn't have.
There are no palm trees (but no droughts either). Freeway
gridlock is almost unknown, major-league baseball is
something you watch on TV, and strollers have a much
better chance of seeing an elk or a cougar than a movie
star. Portland's easy charm rests on twin foundations: its
beguiling urban amenities and its access to a wealth of
recreational treasures. (It may be the only major city in
the world where you can catch 30-pound chinook salmon
downtown.) Within the city limits there are more than
9,400 acres of parkland—home to deer, elk, and what are
probably the last urban old-growth forests in the world.*

*Portland became the City of Roses thanks to the efforts of
Leo Samuel, a turn-of-the-century insurance mogul who
planted a jungle of roses in front of his mansion and hung
out shears so that passersby could help themselves to choice
blooms. The idea readily took root in Portland's friendly,
temperate climate. One legacy is the city's internationally
renowned Rose Test Garden (in Washington Park),
overlooking the downtown skyline, the Willamette River,
and Mt. Hood, whose snowbound 11,235-foot summit towers
50 miles to the east.*

*The first settlers didn't arrive in Portland—then the
highest easily navigable point on the broad Willamette—
until the 1840s. In 1844 pioneers Asa Lovejoy and William
Overton used an ax to mark a few boundary trees in the
dense riverbank forest (near what are now Southwest Front
and Washington streets), paid a 25¢ filing fee, and took
possession of the 640 acres that are now downtown
Portland. A year later Overton sold his share to Francis
Pettygrove for $50 worth of trade goods. Pettygrove,
a Maine native, and Lovejoy, a Bostonian, tossed a coin to*

decide who would name the town-to-be; Pettygrove won, and with homesick fondness chose Portland.

Twenty years ago the New York Times architecture critic described Portland's core area as a bombed-out mess. Today downtown Portland, with its award-winning mix of green public spaces, efficient mass transit, modern skyscrapers, and beautifully restored historic buildings, ranks as one of the best-planned cities in the United States. Many of the fine old structures along the waterfront, some dating from the 1850s, rest on foundations riddled with gloomy tunnels; a hundred years ago these passageways echoed with the moans of shanghaied sailors who were being carted, drugged and drunken, down to the river.

Today the most ominous fate awaiting visitors to the area is overeating—Portland is said to have more restaurants per capita than any other West Coast city. A moribund movie house has been transformed into the glowing new Portland Center for the Performing Arts, home to the Oregon Symphony Orchestra, Shakespearean theater, and touring concerts and arts events. One of the unlovely parking lots that so offended the New York Times is now Pioneer Courthouse Square, a broad brick piazza filled with whimsical art and equally esteemed by conservatively dressed office workers and more exotic citizenry. It's a fine place from which to begin a ramble through the heart of the city, and it's within easy walking or light-railing distance of many of the city's bed-and-breakfasts.

Places to Go, Sights to See

Exploring Portland is easy—and you don't need a car. The city's popular six-year-old light-rail system, *MAX*, makes a loop from downtown Portland to the suburb of Gresham, 13 miles east (tel. 503/233–3511 for ticket and schedule information). Along the way, it forms a handy link between the bed-and-breakfast establishments in Northeast Portland's *Irvington* district and many of the city's most important destinations: *Memorial Coliseum* (1401 N. Wheeler St., tel. 503/235–8771), home of the world-champion *Portland Trailblazers* basketball team; the brand-new *Oregon Convention Center* (777 N.E. Martin Luther King Jr. Blvd., tel. 503/235–7575); the shops, restaurants, and historic districts of the downtown core; *Pioneer Courthouse Square* (bounded by Broadway Ave. and 6th, Morrison, and Yamhill Sts.); the *Portland Art Museum* (1219 S.W. Park, tel. 503/226–2811); and the *Portland Center for the Performing Arts* (1111 S.W. Broadway Ave., tel. 503/248–4335).

Outside the city, the *Columbia Gorge National Scenic Area,* a remarkably unspoiled expanse of waterfalls, hiking trails, and mysterious fern-draped grottoes, enfolds I–84 just 30 minutes east of downtown Portland. Mt. Hood, with its historic *Timberline Lodge* and year-round skiing, is a half hour farther on. Ninety minutes west of Portland, the gray-green Pacific Ocean gnaws ceaselessly at Oregon's rock-fanged coastline. Award-winning wineries along the way help to enliven the journey.

Parks and Gardens. Portland's *Washington and Forest parks* occupy more than 5,000 acres in the city's West Hills, forming the largest contiguous municipal park in the United States. At its southeast end, where Washington Park meets the tony King's Hill neighborhood, is Portland's famed *International Rose Test Garden,* (400 S.W. Kingston Ave., tel. 503/796–5193) which sports more than 10,000 bushes in 400 varieties as well as gorgeous views out over the downtown skyline to Mt. Hood and Mt. St. Helens beyond. On the opposite side of the avenue, the serene expanse of manicured sand, boulders, trees, shrubs, rills, and ponds that form the *Japanese Gardens* (S.W. Kingston Ave., tel. 503/223–4070) are a reminder of Portland's close links with the Pacific Rim. *Hoyt Arboretum* (4000 S.W. Fairview Blvd., tel. 503/228–8732), just up the hill, contains 10 miles of near-wilderness hiking trails and more than 700 species of trees and plants. *Washington Park Zoo* (4001 S.W. Canyon Rd., tel. 503/226–7627), founded in 1887, is one of the world's most prolific breeding grounds for Asian elephants, and contains major exhibits on the Alaskan tundra, the Cascade Mountains, and the African plains.

Powell's City of Books (1005 W. Burnside St., tel. 503/228–4651) may also owe a debt of gratitude to Portland's wet climate. With more than a million volumes, it's one of the world's great bookstores—and a browser's haven on a gray afternoon. Patrons can borrow a volume from the shelves and read over cups of caffè latte or espresso in the commodious Ann Hughes Coffee Room.

Shopping. Powell's is located midway between Portland's two main shopping districts. In the downtown core, affluent clients browse the city's chicest shops, including the glittering new *Pioneer Place* (700 S.W. 5th St., tel. 503/228–5800). Northwest Portland's *Pearl District,* located along N.W. 21st and 23rd streets, is home to an eclectic array of clothing, gift, and food shops as well as art galleries, ethnic eateries, and bookstores.

Wineries and brew pubs are another local amenity that's putting Portland on the map. The Pinot Noir and chardonnay grown in the nearby Yamhill and Tualatin valleys have induced several Burgundian winemakers to buy land here. And the City of Roses is home to more microbreweries and brew pubs—tiny breweries with attached public houses—than any other city outside Europe. Among the most highly regarded are *Bridgeport Brewing Co.* (1313 N.W. Marshall St., tel. 503/241–7179); *McMenamin Brewing* (nearly two dozen Portland locations; call 503/223–0109 or 503/288–9498 to find the closest one); *Portland Brewing Co.* (1339 N.W. Flanders St., tel. 503/222–7150); and *Widmer Brewing Co.* (929 N. Russell St., tel. 503/281–2437). Bridgeport, McMenamin, and Portland Brewing all have attached pubs that serve ales fresh from the brew house as well as hearty pub fare. The *B. Moloch Heathman Bakery and Pub* (901 S.W. Salmon St., tel. 503/227–5700) offers a variety of local brews and sophisticated but inexpensive nouvelle pub cuisine.

Restaurants

For a relatively small city, Portland has a surprisingly rich restaurant scene, particularly for lovers of fresh seafood and exotic ethnic cuisines. There are three contenders for the city's most elegant eatery: the Alexis Hotel's **Esplanade at RiverPlace** (1510 S.W. Harbor Way, tel. 503/295–6166), with its superb service, river views, and intensely rich Northwest cuisine; the intimate and sumptuous northern Italian elegance of **Genoa** (2832 S.E. Belmont St., tel. 503/238–1464); and the impeccable country-French artistry of **L'Auberge** (2601 N.W. Vaughn St., tel. 503/223–3302). But the city's best-known restaurant is undoubtedly **Jake's Famous Crawfish** (401 S.W. 12th Ave., tel. 503/226–1419). Jake's white-coated waiters serve up unimpeachably fresh Northwest seafood from a lengthy sheet of daily specials in a series of bustling wood-paneled dining rooms. The **Café des Amis** (1987 N.W. Kearny St., tel. 503/295–6487) attracts an equally devoted clientele with its low-key elegance; the kitchen adds a country-French spin to the superb local fish, game, and produce.

Tourist Information

Portland/Oregon Visitors Association (26 S.W. Salmon St., Portland, OR 97204–3299, tel. 503/275–9750).

Reservation Services

Bed & Breakfast Northwest (610 S.W. Broadway Ave., Portland, OR 97205, tel. 503/243–7616); **Bed & Breakfast Accommodations—Oregon** (2321 N.E. 28th Ave., Portland, OR 97212, tel. 503/287–4704).

Eastmoreland Bed and Breakfast

Ed and Patricia Ehrhart, the owners of this fir-shaded B&B in Portland's ritzy Eastmoreland neighborhood, don't advertise. And there's no sign outside their 1910-vintage Colonial Revival home. Yet the more they try to keep it quiet, the more popular their establishment becomes.

Ed, a metal-products executive, and Patricia, an MBA, originally hail from Albuquerque. Their low-key, erudite style suits their clientele, most of whom come from nearby Reed College.

The house itself is a joy, filled with Revolutionary-era tiger-maple furniture collected by Patricia's mother and hand-carved duck and goose decoys used by her father and grandfather. Rich, personal touches are everywhere: a tiger-maple cabinet holds whimsical 19th-century shaving mugs collected by her father; a downstairs bathroom is papered with early 1920s *Oregonians* the Ehrharts unearthed during renovation. The old-fashioned screened side porch is much beloved during Portland's long, warm summer evenings. (You'd better guard your drinks around Ginger, a sweet-tempered retriever, who might pad over for a friendly slurp.)

The mother-in-law cottage off the garden, with its private entrance and well-stocked kitchenette, is handy for extended stays or for guests who desire extra privacy. The cottage has a more contemporary feel than the house's three guest rooms, which share a sunny Colonial ambience. The Rutledge Suite, the largest of the three, is a bright, book-filled space with a tiger-maple four-poster bed, lace curtains, and a serene pale blue and cream color scheme.

There are graceful touches in almost every corner of the rooms: a 19th-century Jenny Lind crib; a brush and mirror set of tarnished Victorian silver; a towel warmer and Oriental carpets in the bathroom; pieces of rare hand-painted Damm Nance glass. The two upstairs rooms are smaller but still pleasant; one has Italian enamel twin beds, the other a double with a white wicker headboard.

Breakfasts, served on wonderful Meissen Blue Onion china, belie the Ehrharts' passion for fitness. The Dungeness crab cakes and brown sugar–glazed oatmeal layered with fresh fruit make for prime eating.

Address: *6702 S.E. 29th Ave., Portland, OR 97202, tel. 503/775-7023, fax 503/774-7720.*
Accommodations: *2 double rooms share bath, 1 suite, 1 housekeeping suite.*
Amenities: *Air-conditioning; exercise facilities; outdoor spa.*
Rates: *$70–$95; full breakfast. MC, V.*
Restrictions: *No smoking, no pets.*

Heron Haus

Along flight of wooden stairs leads down from the driveway of this West Hills mansion. At the bottom is a tiny, secluded orchard of pear, apple, and cherry trees. This is just one of the many hidden charms of Heron Haus, arguably the most accomplished B&B in the Rose City.

The house itself is a sturdy Tudor built in 1904 from stucco and Port of Portland ballast stone. It sits high in the hills above Northwest Portland, handy to the hiking trails and old-growth stands of gigantic Forest Park as well as to the shopping and restaurants of the Pearl District. Its effervescent owner, Julie Keppeler, worked in investment real estate, publishing, convention planning, and adult education before settling into the B&B business. Oh, yes—she's also a weaver, potter, and photographer.

Keppeler renovated the 7,500-square-foot house in 1986—and she did it with assurance and charm. The modern touches, such as Southwestern artwork and Scandinavian-flavor furnishings, subtly complement the house's existing features. There's a huge breakfast room with herringbone-patterned oak floors and fireplace; a warm, carpeted sun room overlooking the backyard pool; and a sophisticated entertainment room with a big-screen TV/VCR and deep couches. Most beguiling of all is the mahogany-accented library, its leaded-glass cabinets filled with selections ranging from Isak Dinesen to Audubon, its furnishings sturdy Victorian Eastlake.

Each of the five huge guest rooms has a private bath, a phone, and a work desk—a particular convenience for business travelers. The most splendid of the five rooms is the Kulia Suite, modern and airy with a queen-size bed and a romantic flower-shaped hot tub overlooking the downtown skyline. The Ko Room, just down the hall, is distinguished by its antique seven-headed shower, king-size brass bed, and two well-appointed sitting areas. (These two rooms can be converted into a $175-per-night suite.) At the top of the house, the Manu Room sprawls over a space so large that two average B&B rooms would easily fit into it; the gigantic bathroom sports a graceful eyebrow window looking out over the city.

Breakfast is a luxury Continental affair, with fresh fruits, croissants, pastries, and cereal.

Address: *2545 N.W. Westover Rd., Portland, OR 97210, tel. and fax 503/274-1846.*
Accommodations: *5 double rooms with baths.*
Amenities: *Air-conditioning; phone in rooms; outdoor heated pool.*
Rates: *$85–$175. MC, V.*
Restrictions: *Smoking outside only, no pets.*

Portland Guest House

Northeast Portland's Irvington neighborhood used to be full of neatly kept working-class Victorians just like this one, with its flower-filled yard and window boxes, and its fresh coffee with cream paint and graceful wrought-iron fence. Most of them fell to the wrecking ball when the prosperous 'teens and '20s transformed Irvington into a neighborhood for the nouveau riche.

This house endured decades of neglect until longtime neighborhood residents Susan and Dean Gisvold brought it back to life in 1987. Now, rebuilt from the studs outward, the house oozes a comfortable sense of place and history, from its scarred oak floors to the haunting photographs of once-resident families on the walls. It's not as grand as the nearby Portland White House, but it's hardly a poor relation, and it has a fresh, sunny authenticity all its own.

Each of the five smallish, high-ceilinged guest rooms has some special and memorable touch: an ornately carved walnut Eastlake bed or armoire; an immaculately enameled claw-foot tub; or a shady deck overlooking the back garden.

Outside the four second-floor rooms is a lace-curtained window seat that's perfect for reading or postcard writing. The tasteful mauve and gray walls of the downstairs living and dining rooms are finished with white bull's-eye molding; a gorgeous Oriental carpet cushions the hardwood floor. The ponderous Eastlake living room suite has been reupholstered in pretty rose satin.

Fifteenth Avenue, which runs by the etched-glass front door, can be busy in the mornings and afternoons, but this is barely noticeable in the freshly soundproofed house. The conveniently central Northeast Portland neighborhood, with its broad tree-shaded avenues lined with stately old homes, offers plentiful charms of its own. The MAX light-rail line is a 10-minute walk to the south. Closer to home, neighborhood shops yield Oregon wines and produce, imported cheeses, and fresh-baked breads for picnics in the landscaped yard.

The Gisvolds don't live on the premises, but they're often around, and a full-time manager occupies a downstairs apartment. Breakfast is served in front of the cheerful dining room fireplace.

Address: *1720 N.E. 15th Ave., Portland, OR 97212, tel. 503/282-1402.*
Accommodations: *3 double rooms with baths, 2 double rooms share bath.*
Amenities: *Phone in room.*
Rates: *$45–$75; full breakfast. AE, DC, MC, V.*
Restrictions: *Smoking outside only, no pets.*

Portland's White House

The chirping of the resident canaries, Quayle and Bush, and the splash of falling water provide a melodious welcome for guests at this memorable Northeast Portland B&B. Listed on the National Register of Historic Places, the house was built in 1912 in Southern Federal style. Except for the tiled roof, it bears an uncanny resemblance to its District of Columbia namesake—a resemblance indicative of the chief-executive personality of its builder, timber tycoon Robert Lytle. Its sweeping circular driveway, carriage house, and Greek columns all whisper of bygone elegance.

This White House's neighborhood, Irvington, may lack the grandeur of Pennsylvania Avenue, but its location makes it handy to downtown, Memorial Coliseum, the MAX light-rail line, and the new Oregon Convention Center. Owners Larry Hough, an electrician by profession, and his Dublin-born wife, Mary, a former antiques dealer, bought the house in 1984 and have since lavished more than 8,000 hours on its restoration. The public areas gleam with hand-rubbed Honduran mahogany and ornately inlaid oak. (Even the old servants' quarters are finished with mahogany.) The sweeping hand-carved stairway is lit by exquisite Pulvey stained-glass windows. Outside, the sunny rose-hung decks make fine places for relaxing with a spot of summer tea. Downstairs is a cavernous ballroom.

The six spacious, high-ceilinged guest rooms are furnished with a tasteful mix of antiques, period pieces, and reproductions. The Canopy and Baron's rooms feature ornate canopy beds and huge claw-foot soaking tubs. In the Garden Room, French doors open onto a private veranda trellised with flowers. The Balcony Room has an ornate brass bed, tiled Art Deco bathroom, and a small balustraded balcony overlooking the courtyard fountain.

The Houghs are hardworking resident innkeepers who attack their duties with charm and zest. Mary's mother kept boardinghouses during her Irish childhood; her blood ties to the lodging business are evident in her immaculate housekeeping and hearty breakfasts. Eggs Benedict are a morning standby. The tea kettle is always on the hob, and the pantry is well stocked with fresh-baked chocolate chip cookies and a brimming basket of local apples.

Address: *1914 N.E. 22nd Ave., Portland, OR 97212, tel. 503/287-7131.*
Accommodations: *4 double rooms with baths, 2 double rooms share bath.*
Amenities: *Afternoon tea; phone in rooms.*
Rates: *$68–$98; full breakfast. MC, V.*
Restrictions: *Smoking in ballroom only, no pets.*

RiverPlace
Alexis Hotel

The downtown Portland skyline towers above the rotunda roof and turrets of the RiverPlace Alexis on the banks of the Willamette River. A forest of sailboat masts crowds the complex's marina; the green ribbon of 2-mile-long Waterfront Park begins almost at the hotel's front door. The Alexis anchors a crescent of shops, restaurants, condominiums, and offices that went up in 1985 and breathed new life into downtown Portland's front door.

Thoroughly modern though it is, observers disagree on the overall feel of the hotel. Some say it looks vaguely Dutch; to others it has a clean Cape Cod ambience. One thing they all agree on, however, is its elegance; since the hotel opened its doors, it has become the residence of choice for visiting celebrities and CEOs.

Inside, the Alexis has the feel of an intimate European hotel. The subtle luster of teak as well as green Italian marble is everywhere, and the staff provides a level of service seldom seen in this casual western city. (The 150 employees outnumber the guest rooms nearly two to one.) The lobby, bar, and restaurant are handsome spaces, luxuriously appointed with wood-burning fireplaces, rich fabrics, and Oriental carpets.

The 84 guest rooms overlook river, skyline, and courtyard, but they lack some of the elegance of the public areas. Thick carpeting and well-soundproofed walls are a given; the paint is a subtle pale yellow that makes the most of Portland's often wan sunlight. Furnishings are modern and comfortable, but they have a cookie-cutter uniformity. The rooms are medium in size and spare. Junior suites have huge tiled bathrooms and comfortable sitting areas. Fireplace suites are larger, with marble-top wet bars, king-size beds, small whirlpool baths, and two color TVs each.

Dinner at the Esplanade Restaurant off the lobby is an experience to savor. The nightly menu may include such delicacies as Dungeness crab with artichokes, warm rabbit and wild green salad with a star-anise vinaigrette, or medallions of elk with a savory currant-caramel sauce.

Address: *1510 S.W. Harbor Way, Portland, OR 97201, tel. 503/228–3233 or 800/227–1333, fax 503/295–6161.*
Accommodations: *39 double rooms with baths, 35 suites, 10 condominiums.*
Amenities: *Restaurant, bar, air-conditioning; cable TV and phone in rooms, 24-hour room service; sauna; pets by prior arrangement.*
Rates: *$165–$180, suites $180–$500, condominiums $250–$350; Continental breakfast. AE, D, DC, MC, V.*

The Clinkerbrick House

Stately chestnut trees and a facade bristling with the fancifully twisted and fused bricks that give the house its name lend personality to this countrified 1908 Dutch Colonial structure in Northeast Portland's convenient Irvington neighborhood. Innkeepers Peggie and Bob Irvine opened this small, comfortable B&B in 1987.

The house's public spaces have an American-country feel without the clutter. Beautiful old quilts spill from pine cabinets; an intriguing V-shaped corner bench invites fireside conversation. With its whimsical brickwork, unusual tin wainscoting, and lovely leaded-glass cabinetry, the house itself is a curiosity.

The three upstairs guest rooms have their own entrance, as well as a common area with a kitchen. In the sunny Strawberry Room, dark green carpeting, a crewel-embroidered wingback chair, and a pine pencil-post bed pull the room together. The Rose Room, decorated with pink roses and white wicker, has an antique crocheted bedspread and a lace-finished day bed.

Address: *2311 N.E. Schuyler St., Portland, OR 97212, tel. 503/281–2533.*
Accommodations: *1 double room with bath, 2 double rooms share bath.*
Amenities: *Full kitchen.*
Rates: *$50–$60; full breakfast. AE, MC, V.*
Restrictions: *Smoking outside only, no pets.*

General Hooker's B&B

Ebullient owner Lori Hall, a movie buff, former fashion designer, and special-ed teacher turned spinner and innkeeper, sets the tone at this Southwest Portland B&B. The house, an 1888 Queen Anne five minutes from downtown Portland, was extensively renovated in 1978; now its antique facade belies its gallerylike interior and modern furnishings.

There's a single guest room in the basement, a white-walled chamber with a loft bed: double below, twin above. On the top floor, a tree-shaded deck with views of river, skyline, and mountains provides the perfect place for sipping a beer or glass of wine from Hall's well-stocked guest refrigerator. All guests have access to it, but it communicates directly with the Rose and Iris rooms—the former a spacious chamber with a superking-size bed and a skylighted bathroom, the latter a comfortable space with a Civil War–era armoire.

Address: *125 S.W. Hooker St., Portland, OR 97201, tel. 503/222–4435 or 800/745–4135, fax 503/222–4435.*
Accommodations: *1 double room with bath, 3 double rooms share 2 baths.*
Amenities: *Air-conditioning; complimentary beer and wine in guest refrigerator; cable TV/VCR in rooms; half-price YMCA passes.*
Rates: *$70–$110; Continental breakfast. MC, V.*
Restrictions: *Smoking on deck only, no pets.*

The Georgian House

Greek columns flank the front door of this striking redbrick Georgian Colonial, and legend has it that there are 20 $20 gold pieces in its foundation to ward off ill fortune. The Irvington neighborhood house was a broken-windowed wreck when the present young innkeepers, Willie and Mike Ackley, bought it in 1987. It now gleams anew behind manicured lawns, flower beds, and wrought-iron fences.

Downstairs, a cheerful solarium overlooks the small formal garden, as do a broad vine-canopied deck and the gazebo. Each of the three guest rooms has a personality of its own. The smallish Maid's Room feels English, from the century-old cherrywood Eastlake bed to the marble-top dresser and dark burgundy walls.

The Pettygrove Room has an outdoorsy, masculine ambience, with 150-year-old German-pine twin beds that, pushed together beneath a stunning handmade quilt, form a king-size bed. The Lovejoy Suite, the largest and sunniest of the three, has hardwood floors, a tiled fireplace, an ornate brass canopy bed, and its own TV and chaise-equipped sitting room.

Address: *1828 N.E. Siskiyou St., Portland, OR 97212, tel. 503/281–2250.*
Accommodations: *2 double rooms share 1½ baths, 1 suite.*
Amenities: *Deck; air-conditioning; TV/VCR.*
Rates: *$55; full breakfast. MC, V.*
Restrictions: *Smoking outside only, no pets.*

MacMaster House

Don't mind the curiosity of MacMaster House's outgoing innkeeper, Cecilia Murphy— engrossed in her duties, she says she travels vicariously through her guests. Her 1875 Colonial Revival mansion rises high in the West Hills, the 5,000-acre expanse of Washington and Forest parks beginning only two blocks from here.

The downstairs public areas are furnished in a mishmash of kinetic-sculpture modern, fertility-symbol African, bamboo-pattern Asian, and a few carved mock-Tudor chairs for variety.

One of the charms of this vast house is its fireplaces—seven in all. Four guest rooms have one. There are thick down comforters on all the beds, and there's cable TV in every room. The best of the lot is the MacMaster Suite, with its rattan four-poster, a 7-foot glass-fronted wardrobe filled with books, and skyline view from the balcony. The third-floor suite is almost as spacious. Skylights fill the space with light even on inclement days; a pretty wicker chaise and deep couch add to the relaxing ambience.

Address: *1041 S.W. Vista Ave., Portland, OR 97205, tel. 503/223–7362.*
Accommodations: *4 double rooms share 2 baths, 2 suites.*
Amenities: *Air-conditioning; fireplace in 4 rooms.*
Rates: *$70–$95; full breakfast. D, MC, V.*
Restrictions: *Smoking outside only, no pets.*

Mumford Manor

When Courtland Mumford and his wife, Janis—an airline pilot and a flight attendant, respectively—went into the B&B business in 1988, they were determined to create an inn with everything the sterile commercial hotels they once had to stay in didn't have.

The result is Mumford Manor, a lovely European-style inn in a century-old Queen Anne mansion high on King's Hill.

The fine old library with walls of dark green and burgundy, a marble fireplace, mellow Siberian oak floors, and high shelves crammed with books is in the old part of the house; the "new" part of the house, a 1911 addition designed by the great Portland architect A. E. Doyle, blends flawlessly with the old.

Each of the guest rooms is different, but all are furnished in Victorian splendor. In the Master Suite, a striking rose motif covers the walls, bed, and the matching chaises in front of the fireplace. The Oak Room, with its Eastlake bedroom suite of quarter-sawn oak, has a hunting-lodge ambience.

Address: *1130 S.W. King Ave., Portland, OR 97205, tel. 503/243-2443, fax 503/223-9353.*
Accommodations: *1 double room with bath, 2 double rooms share a bath, 1 suite.*
Amenities: *Air-conditioning.*
Rates: *$85–$135; full breakfast. AE, MC, V.*
Restrictions: *No smoking, no pets.*

North Coast

If the rest of the world had heeded the warnings of early explorers along the Oregon's north coast, the area would still be a lonely, windswept wilderness of towering headlands, untracked beaches, and rivers teeming with fish. As it happens, virtually all of these descriptions still apply—except for the "lonely" part.

Four hundred years after Spanish and English adventurers wrote the area off as too stormy to be settled, the 150-mile-long north coast, stretching from Newport in the south to Astoria in the north, is sprinkled with small towns and villages. Fishing fleets leave from Newport, Garibaldi, Depoe Bay, Astoria, and, most quixotically, from tiny Pacific City. Small wineries, galleries, and antiques shops abound. U.S. Highway 101 plays tag with the rugged coastland all the way, providing easy access to an otherwise sparsely populated area.

Sir Francis Drake and Bruno Heceta, two 16th-century explorers who found the area uninhabitable, went a little overboard in their pessimism. But this is a stormy place— more than 80 inches of rain a year is the norm. The good news is that all the rain keeps the thick forests a deep, damp green. The bad news is that swimming in the North Pacific is recommended only for seals, salmon, and the odd overly ambitious surfer. Since the temperature rarely climbs above 75° F, beach walking has always been more popular than taking a dip.

Happily, long, uninterrupted public beaches are a staple of the area. In fact, Oregon has virtually no private beaches; an early 20th-century conservation law declared all land seaward from where the beach grass stops to be public. True, access is sometimes blocked, but seldom for long stretches. And more than 70 state parks—about one every other mile—ensure good access.

Places to Go, Sights to See

Antiques. Small antiques shops are as much a part of the north coast as sand and spray. The broadest selection is to be found in the 30-mile stretch between Newport and Lincoln City. A strong association of merchants produces an up-to-date directory available at virtually every antiques shop in the area. Specialties include nautical items, Asian wood carvings, and furniture from the Civil War period.

Columbia River Maritime Museum (1792 Marine Dr., tel. 503/325–2323). Astoria's history as a seaport dates back to 1811, when it was the only American settlement west of the Rockies. This informative museum features a retired Columbia River lightship and nautical artifacts. A major exhibition commemorating the bicentennial of Captain Robert Gray's exploration of the Columbia River, part of a series of observances in Oregon, Washington, and British Columbia, will be held from May 2, 1992, through November, with artifacts including Gray's sea chest and 17th- and 18th-century British and Spanish charts of the Northwest coast on display.

Depoe Bay. This is the world's smallest harbor, barely 40 feet across as it meets the pounding Pacific between basalt cliffs. A fishing village lies about 100 feet above the sea, but still in reach of the Spouting Horn, a hole in the cliff that allows the ocean to spray completely over Highway 101 during storms.

Ecola State Park (tel. 503/436–2623). This park lies between artsy Cannon Beach and touristy Seaside. A trail to the top of 800-foot-high Tillamook Head affords views of Tillamook Light, a 19th-century lighthouse abandoned to the storms in 1957.

Fort Clatsop National Memorial (Rte. 3, tel. 503/861–2471). In 1805, the Lewis and Clark expedition spent a miserable, stormy winter at this site in Astoria. A reproduction of the fort, with all its discomforts, has center stage. During the summer, park rangers don buckskins and demonstrate frontier skills such as making dugout canoes, smoking salmon, and fashioning clothes out of animal skins.

Fort Stevens (tel. 503/861–2000). Originally built to defend the Oregon country against Confederate attack during the Civil War, this former military reservation in Hammond is the only place in the continental United States attacked during World War II: A Japanese submarine lobbed a shell that landed harmlessly on the beach. A museum lodges a display exploring the fort's history. On the beach lies the remains of the *Peter Iredale*, an Irish bark that ran aground in 1906.

Galleries. Virtually every town in the area has a worthwhile gallery. One of the most interesting is *Artspace* in Bay City (9120 5th St., tel. 503/377-2782), a restaurant that features works both large and small—mostly modern, all eclectic, and all for sale. More mainstream works by Northwest artists are displayed at *Maveety Gallery* in Gleneden Beach (Market Place at Salishan, tel. 503/764-2318).

Three Capes Scenic Loop. Running about 30 miles from Cape Meares in the north to Pacific City in the south, this drive embraces some of the state's most impressive coastline. The small community of Oceanside clings to a steep, forested slope overlooking offshore rocks that loom 200 feet high. *Cape Lookout State Park* includes a 1,000-foot headland, miles of trails, and 15 miles of undisturbed beaches. In the lee of *Cape Kiwanda* is a bright orange sandstone headland jutting out into the sea just north of Pacific City; here brave (some say crazy) dory fishermen run their small craft straight into the waves to reach fertile fishing areas offshore.

Tillamook Cheese Factory (4175 Hwy. 101, tel. 503/842-4481). The world's largest cheese factory, 2 miles north of town, specializes in cheddar, with tours, gift shops, and, of course, dairy delis.

Restaurants

Cafe de la Mer (tel. 503/436-1179) in Cannon Beach offers fresh local seafood with a French twist. **Chez Jeanette** (tel. 503/764-3434) in Gleneden Beach is unpretentious, but its food is the match of any big-city classic French restaurant. **The Dining Room at Salishan** (tel. 503/764-2371) is often rated as the state's finest. Salishan has a remarkable Continental menu plus a full retinue of Northwest specialties, such as grilled salmon, crab, and oysters.

Tourist Information

Astoria Area Chamber of Commerce (111 W. Marine Dr., Box 176, Astoria, OR 97103, tel. 503/325-6311); **Cannon Beach Chamber of Commerce** (207 N. Spruce St., Box 64, Cannon Beach, OR 97110, tel. 503/436-2623); **Greater Newport Chamber of Commerce** (555 S.W. Coast Hwy., Newport, OR 97365, tel. 503/265-8801); **Lincoln City Visitor Center** (3939 N.W. Hwy. 101, Box 109, Lincoln City, OR 97367, tel. 503/994-8378); **Seaside Chamber of Commerce** (7 N. Roosevelt, Box 7, Seaside, OR 97138, tel. 503/738-6391); **Tillamook Chamber of Commerce** (3705 Hwy. 101 N, Tillamook, OR 97141, tel. 503/842-7525).

Reservation Services

Bed & Breakfast—Oregon (2321 N.E. 28th Ave., Portland, OR 97212, tel. 503/287-4704); **Northwest Bed and Breakfast** (610 S.W. Broadway, Portland, OR 97205, tel. 503/243-7616).

Channel House

The town of Depoe Bay is perched above the sea on high black lava cliffs and wrapped around the wooded slopes of the tiny harbor. Depoe Bay's fishing fleet shoots through a 40-foot-wide aperture at full speed, heading straight into the turbulent Pacific.

Right above this meeting of waves and man is the Channel House. Here the views are everything. Whale-watching is a favorite pastime, as is watching the U.S. Coast Guard practice rescues in the rough waters just offshore. The house has some Cape Cod touches, but this is no ordinary saltbox. Indeed, the desire to have all the rooms face the sea has made for some odd interiors. Baths, often cramped, are manageable only because of the judicious use of sliding doors. In some cases, sinks are located in the sleeping area. Aside from a few brass beds, furnishings are sturdy and comfortable but undistinguished. Views are best from the top-floor rooms, and the privacy is optimal. While most of the rooms have hot tubs on decks facing the ocean, on the lower floors you can't help feeling that the fishing and tour boats coming and going have as good a look at you as you do at them.

The dining area has the most distinctive look, decked out as it is with a brass wheel from an old fishing boat, rough-hewn tables, and a huge antique McCray icebox from an old restaurant. In the library you can peruse the collection of books on whales or keep a weather watch at the mini weather station, which gives continual readings of wind-speed velocity and direction as well as barometric pressure.

Depoe Bay is, after all, a fishing community—and Channel House takes full advantage. So you might awake to a robust breakfast of scrambled eggs, bagels and cream cheese, hash browns, and a fine piece of cod baked in a light mushroom sauce.

Managers Rachel and Charles Smith make you feel at home. Charles keeps busy maintaining the storm-tossed building, but he finds time to study whales and go deep-sea fishing once a week to supply the house specialties.

Address: *35 Ellingson St., Box 56, Depoe Bay, OR 97341, tel. 503/765-2140.*
Accommodations: *6 double rooms with baths, 1 suite, 2 housekeeping suites.*
Amenities: *Cable TV, radio, and binoculars in rooms, complimentary newspaper, fireplace and whirlpool bath in many rooms, refrigerator in 6 rooms, kitchen in 3 rooms; deck hot tub in 6 rooms.*
Rates: *$85–$150, small room $52; full breakfast. MC, V.*
Restriction: *2-night minimum on weekends.*

Grandview Bed & Breakfast

Seen from the quiet residential street in Astoria that it faces, the Grandview Bed & Breakfast doesn't stand out, but once you're inside the nearly 100-year-old Shingle Style house, you'll know what's special about it.

Because the Grandview rises so precipitously from a hill that falls away steeply, the views from the inn are spectacular and the feeling of floating is frequent. Innkeeper Charlene Maxwell quickly brings you back to earth, however. She has steeped herself in local lore and shares it with guests in an easygoing but authoritative manner.

The guest rooms upstairs are eccentrically decorated with a mixture of period furnishings and odd modern touches. In one room, fluffy clouds scud across sky blue walls. In brightly painted bookcases, tiny artificial birds perch on bookends. Indeed, with unobstructed vistas of the Columbia River and the coastal range of southern Washington and of the dozens of church steeples of Old Astoria, you'll feel as if you're in an aerie. As if this weren't enough, the Refuge Room features birdcall recordings (the real thing is right outside the window), bird-flocked wallpaper, and a bookcase filled with books on bird-watching.

For those who prefer to be earthbound, there is a very plain two-bedroom suite in the basement with a separate entrance that's perfect for families. Here the wallpaper is patterned with zoo animals, and some of the modern furniture is upholstered in a leopard print.

The arrangement of some of the guest rooms is flexible: Seven double rooms on the second and third floors can be divided into two suites or rented separately. Prices depend on whether you end up with a private bath.

The entrance hall is a bit cluttered with Charlene's work desk, which is located only a few feet from the main door. The dining area, however, is very inviting, positioned in a light-filled turret that offers views of the river and town. For more privacy, some guests opt to dine in a smaller bullet turret on the other side of the kitchen, ideal for two. Muffins, fresh fruit, and juice round out what Charlene calls a "Continental plus" breakfast.

Address: *1574 Grand Ave., Astoria, OR, 97103, tel. 503/325–0000 or 800/488–3250.*
Accommodations: *3 double rooms with baths, 6 double rooms share 3 baths, 1 suite.*
Amenities: *Phones available for 2 rooms, fireplace in 1 room, afternoon refreshments.*
Rates: *$38–$75, suite $75–$98; Continental breakfast. D, MC, V.*
Restrictions: *No smoking, no pets, no alcohol on premises.*

Sandlake Country Inn

Sandlake Country Inn is a peaceful place, located on an old cranberry farm on the road to Sandlake Park. On Christmas morning in 1890, the Norwegian schooner *Struan* was wrecked off Cape Lookout, leaving tons of heavy bridge timbers strewn on the beach. Storm-weary homesteaders with few building materials hauled the timbers off and made sturdy homes. Only a few of these are still standing, the most notable of which is the weathered-shingle Sandlake Country Inn, where innkeepers Margo and Charles Underwood preside.

Besides restoring the natural woodwork, the Underwoods removed the ceiling of the dining room to reveal the old bridge timbers. The sitting room is a fine creation, with firm Victorian settees covered in velvet, travel chests as coffee tables, a stone fireplace, and views of old rosebushes outside.

From the sitting room, French doors open onto a small pink-and-white striped guest room furnished in white wicker, set off by ecru netting that sweeps from the ceiling to the corners of the bed and a log-cabin quilt. The room overlooks another rose garden. Upstairs is the honeymoon suite, taking up the entire upper story. The plum paisley wallpaper with matching duvet and curtains and plum-colored paneling make the room a bit dark, but you can always stroll out onto the deck to survey the 2½-acre property and look out for deer and elk.

Guests often take breakfast at the parlor's gaming table, dating from the 1880s and found in a Portland tavern. Homemade apple oatmeal is a breakfast staple, as are fruit smoothies and green chili soufflés. Breakfast for guests staying in the creekside cottage, about 100 feet from the main house, is delivered to the door in a basket. Here the feeling is plush, with thick carpeting and huge throw pillows on the floor before a black marble fireplace. A large hot tub is strategically located between the bed and the deck, and a modern kitchen allows complete independence and privacy. As in the suite, Arts and Crafts oak period pieces and reproductions predominate.

Address: *8505 Galloway Rd., Cloverdale, OR 97112, tel. 503/965–6745.*
Accommodations: *1 double room with bath, 1 suite, 1 housekeeping cottage.*
Amenities: *Radio/cassette players in rooms, picnic baskets available, TV and VCR in suite and cottage, refrigerator in suite, whirlpool tub and fireplace in cottage; outside hot tub, bicycles.*
Rates: *$60–$100; full breakfast. MC, V.*
Restrictions: *No smoking, no pets; 2-night minimum on weekends in July and Aug., closed Dec. 15– Jan. 15.*

Sylvia Beach Hotel

For years, what is now the Sylvia Beach Hotel was known as a flophouse with a view. Located in Newport, once the state's honeymoon capital, the 1911 hotel overlooking the sea was for decades a low-rent residential hotel before Portland restaurateur Goody Cable and Roseburg partner Sally Ford decided to make it a kind of literary lodging—or a library that sleeps 40.

The plain green clapboard hotel takes its name not from the beach (actually, it's on a bluff on Nye Beach) but from the renowned patron Sylvia Beach, who in the 1920s and '30s ran the Shakespeare & Co. bookstore in Paris, a haven for American literati. Each room is dedicated to a famous writer, with appropriate books and decorating scheme. The Hemingway room, for example, is all the manly Papa could have hoped for: a bed made out of tree limbs beneath a mounted antelope head, and an old Royal typewriter in the corner. The Agatha Christie Suite is all green, with clues from her books lurking everywhere (the three bullets embedded in the wall are particularly menacing).

Down the hall is the Oscar Wilde Room, a smallish place resembling a Victorian gentleman's lodgings. The view, which faces a roof from the other side of the hotel, is far from awe-inspiring. But the managers are way ahead of you. Right next to the window is a framed Wilde quote: "It's altogether immaterial, a view, except to the innkeeper who, of course, charges it in the bill. A gentleman never looks out the window."

The most popular rooms are the Poe Room, a scary place in black and red, complete with raven and pendulum suspended over the bed, and the Colette Room, a sexy French suite with lace canopies, velvet window seat, and peach-colored headboard.

The upper reaches of the hotel are turned over to a large library (some 1,000 books), with plenty of nooks and crannies and comfortable armchairs for book lovers.

The food at the hotel's restaurant—Tables of Content—is excellent. Breakfast is selected from a wide range of offerings on the menu, including frittatas and German-style pancakes served in the pan. But the best meal is dinner, an eight-course gourmet feast served family style.

Address: *267 N.W. Cliff St., Newport, OR 97365, tel. 503/265-5428.*
Accommodations: *20 double rooms with baths.*
Amenities: *Restaurant, evening refreshments, fireplace in 3 rooms.*
Rates: *$55–$115; full breakfast. AE, MC, V.*
Restrictions: *No smoking, no pets; 2-night minimum on weekends. Closed first week in Dec.*

Whiskey Creek Bed & Breakfast

L ocated on Three Capes Scenic Drive about 10 miles west of Tillamook, Whiskey Creek Bed & Breakfast offers quietude in rustic surroundings.

Built in 1900 by the operator of a custom sawmill, the cedar-shingled Whiskey Creek is paneled inside with rough-hewn spruce. The mill operator made spruce oars and used the odd pieces of leftover wood for the main floor. For years, the home and the mill were powered by a small hydroelectric turbine on Whiskey Creek, about 100 feet away and the southern boundary of the property.

Innkeeper Allison Asbjornsen, an artist whose oil paintings, watercolors, collages and sculptures adorn the downstairs suite (no spruce paneling here—just drywall), spends hours in her studio across the driveway. When she does emerge, most likely barefoot, she likes to swap stories with her guests. She talks about the house as it was in the old days, of how on some evenings the lights would suddenly go dim. Realizing what was up, the men of the family would grab a lantern and a gun and head for the creek. Usually they found a bear splashing around, trying to catch a salmon and reducing the water flow, thereby cutting the power to the house.

Bear, elk, and deer still roam this area, and salmon make their way up Whiskey Creek to a state fish hatchery just across the creek from the inn. Here you are always close to nature. (One window in the dining area overlooks Netarts Bay, Oregon's premier bay for oysters and crabs, the other, the 1,000-foot-high bulk of fir-carpeted Cape Lookout.)

Although you'll see husband Forrest Dickerson puttering around, Allison is the one who is most involved in running the B&B, and she did all the decorating. All the rooms have queen-size futon beds and overstuffed chairs, and the two-bedroom suite, complete with kitchen, has a fabulous old wood-burning stove with elaborate wrought-iron ornamentation.

Breakfasts are light, with bran muffins and fresh eggs from the inn's brood of handsome black hens. You might be lucky enough to get Swedish pancakes, a folded crêpe served with powdered sugar or jam. Throughout the cathedral-ceilinged dining area is Allison's rabbit collection.

Address: *7500 Whiskey Creek Rd., Tillamook, OR 97141, tel. 503/842–2408.*
Accommodations: *2 double rooms share bath, 1 double housekeeping suite.*
Amenities: *Cable TV and VCR in suite; barbecue pit.*
Rates: *$60–$80; full breakfast. MC, V.*
Restrictions: *No smoking.*

Astoria Inn

On any given night at the Astoria Inn, you might have as a fellow guest a Bulgarian folk musician or a budding rock star—or both. Here, high above the Columbia River, the views are inspiring and the musical presence constant.

John and Nola Westling have created a unique, relaxing place out of their old house on the east end of historic Astoria. John left the electronics firm he operated in San Diego in 1988 to work full-time on his hobby: harpmaking. All around are the tools and fruits of his craft.

The inn, a Queen Anne farmhouse with gingerbread ornament, sits atop a hill in a sedate residential area. Every effort has been made to return the look of the interior to the last century. Chair rails, imaginative use of wallpapers, decorative touches such as old fan quilts, feather boas, and wooden carousel horses, and, of course, antiques all contribute to this effect. Perhaps the inn's best feature is an airy second-floor library with wing-back recliners, oak moldings, and books on everything from harp-making to bicycling.

Address: *3391 Irving Ave., Astoria, OR 97103, tel. 503/325-8153.*
Accommodations: *3 double rooms with baths.*
Amenities: *Evening snacks and snacks in room, cable TV and VCR in living room.*
Rates: *$67–$80; full breakfast. MC, V.*
Restrictions: *No smoking, no pets.*

The Boarding House

Seaside is a small town with a bad case of schizophrenia. Downtown is dominated by a mile-long loop that turns back at the edge of the sea. Arcades, restaurants, candy stores, and gift shops crowd the narrow street, yet just a few blocks away from the clamor is Old Seaside, an area of well-preserved Victorian homes now finding second life as bed-and-breakfasts. The Boarding House, dating from 1898, when Seaside was a mere village, was the town's first B&B.

Inside you'll find tongue and groove walls, beamed ceilings, and a Victrola that innkeepers Dick and Barb Edwards crank up for guests. The favored colors throughout are blue and white with rose accents. The rooms feature beds of brass and white iron, balloon curtains in floral prints, and claw-foot tubs. A restored Victorian cottage along the river that sleeps five and has its own deck is the inn's gem. Here are only scant reminders of the 20th century, and a sleeping loft allows a good look at the Necanicum River; in season, you can see the salmon moving upstream.

Address: *208 N. Holladay Dr., Seaside, OR 97138, tel. 503/738-9055.*
Accommodations: *5 double rooms with baths, 1 housekeeping cottage.*
Amenities: *Cable TV in rooms, vintage radio in 3 rooms.*
Rates: *$55–$100; full breakfast (guests in main house only). MC, V.*
Restrictions: *No pets; 2-night minimum on weekends.*

Brey House

Lincoln City is best known for its huge resorts, but Brey House is helping the town develop a reputation for clean, quiet, and unpretentious bed-and-breakfasting. Finding the modern wooden beach house from the main drag takes a little time, but the route is well marked.

From the moment you enter Brey House, you know you're in someone's home, but innkeepers Milt and Shirley Brey make that a warm rather than off-putting experience. Ocean views abound from three floors, including a large basement suite, set against the hill, with a kitchen, pool table, and private entrance. The beach is a short walk away. The decorating theme throughout is nautical, with a concentration of old ship bells and deep-sea diver miniatures.

Breakfasts are served in a dramatic room jutting out toward the sea. Milt makes a hearty eggs Benedict, and his crab and ham soufflés never fall flat.

Address: *3725 N.W. Keel Ave., Lincoln City, OR 97367, tel. 503/994-7123.*
Accommodations: *1 double with bath, 1 double shares bath with owners, 1 suite.*
Amenities: *Cable TV in rooms, refrigerator available, game room; outdoor hot tub.*
Rates: *$55–$75; full breakfast. MC, V.*
Restrictions: *Smoking on second floor only, no pets.*

Franklin House

Even if you get this Astoria bed-and-breakfast confused with Franklin St. Station (*see* below) just five blocks away, don't worry: Both are excellent, and they're all in the family; Franklin House is run by the mother of the Franklin St. Station's innkeeper.

Karen Nelson became an innkeeper in 1987 at the age of 71. Undaunted, she took on the renovation of the house, built in 1870, with loads of energy. The result is a luxurious bed-and-breakfast presided over by an archetypal grandma.

Fluted columns inside the living room are topped by cornices painted gold, with leaded-glass bay windows affording views of the town and the Columbia River. The rooms are large and quiet, furnished with simple brass beds and armchairs. Karen adds her personal touch in every room with cross-stitched scenes of local lighthouses and roses made of ribbon that guests may take home. (She sells her crafts in a gift shop on the premises.) Breakfast ranges from rich quiches to eggs over easy with bacon.

Address: *1681 Franklin Ave., Astoria, OR 97103, tel. 503/325-5044.*
Accommodations: *5 double rooms with baths.*
Amenities: *Clock radio in rooms, fireplace in 1 room.*
Rates: *$63–$75; full breakfast. MC, V.*
Restrictions: *No smoking, no pets; 2-night minimum on holiday weekends.*

Franklin St. Station

Located at the edge of downtown Astoria, the 91-year-old Franklin St. Station looks plain enough from the outside, but inside it is a beautifully restored home with spacious guest rooms.

The main floor is sumptuous, with high-back Victorian-style mahogany love seats covered in turquoise velvet in the living room, delicate spindlework spandrels in the archways, and a fine old greenstone fireplace with oak mantel in the dining area.

The main-floor Lewis & Clark Room, once part of the dining room, uses a large china cupboard as a dresser. Upstairs, the Astor Suite is most impressive, with iron and brass beds, original light fixtures, large arched windows covered by hand-stitched balloon shades, and a deck. In the basement is a modern, functional suite with rattan furniture.

Innkeeper Renee Caldwell prepares a simple, filling breakfast of muffins, eggs, and homemade sausage. The dining area has a parquet table and a small niche displaying family china dating back to the early 1800s, one of four such displays in the house.

Address: *1140 Franklin Ave., Astoria, OR 97103, tel. 503/325-4314.*
Accommodations: *3 double rooms with baths, 2 suites.*
Amenities: *Cable TV in 1 suite, wet bar in 1 suite.*
Rates: *$50–$85; full breakfast. MC, V.*
Restrictions: *No smoking, no pets.*

Gilbert Inn

Natural fir tongue and groove walls and ceilings dominate the Gilbert Inn, a block from Seaside's busy downtown and the beach. The 1892 home reminds you why anyone bothered to settle this area in the first place: lumber.

The Gilbert is a large Queen Anne inn with eight spacious double rooms and two suites. Popularity almost swamped the Gilbert a few years ago, but innkeepers Dick and Carol Rees managed to add five rooms without disturbing the integrity of the existing house. The best part of the inn is still the original core, where the aforementioned fir creates a warm, rough-hewn atmosphere. The decor is country French, with wallpaper, down comforters, and bathrooms in matching prints and ruffled valances and balloon shades at the windows. Some of the bedrooms have brass and ceramic bedsteads; in the Turret Room, you'll dream away on a four-poster rice bed. The newer guest rooms are attractively furnished with natural wicker, reproduction black iron and brass beds, and old wardrobes of oak and pine.

Address: *341 Beach Dr., Seaside, OR 97138, tel. 503/738-9770.*
Accommodations: *8 double rooms with baths, 2 suites.*
Amenities: *TV in rooms, large downstairs parlor available for meetings.*
Rates: *$65–$80; full breakfast. D, MC, V.*
Restrictions: *No smoking, no pets; 2-night minimum on weekends.*

Hudson House

At Hudson House, in Cloverdale, the photo album tells the story. Clyde Hudson, a son of the house's builder, was a pioneer photographer on the north Oregon coast. He was among the first to show the world the area's raw beauty through his postcards. The house in which he lived from the early 1900s on has been restored to its former Victorian splendor, thanks to innkeepers Anne and Steve Kuljic.

The two downstairs guest rooms, one with a simple dressing room, have been carved out of an old mud room. Upstairs, the most popular room occupies the house's turret and features views of the Nestucca Valley, a major fishing and dairy region. Here, the fir ceiling complements the Empire oak dresser and the bed frame with pine-cone finials at the foot. Lisa's Room is a bit frilly, with pink floral wallpaper, a cherry hope chest, and a modern chair under a reading lamp.

Address: *37700 Hwy. 101 S, Cloverdale, OR 97112, tel. 503/392–3533.*
Accommodations: *2 double rooms with baths, 4 double rooms share 2 baths.*
Amenities: *Bathrobes, evening refreshments, light dinner fare and picnic meals available; croquet, badminton, horseshoes, complimentary greens fees at nearby golf course for 2-night guests.*
Rates: *$45–$65; full breakfast. MC, V; 5% surcharge with credit cards.*
Restrictions: *No smoking, no pets; 2-night minimum on holiday weekends.*

Inn at Manzanita

Manzanita is a small, quiet town of summer homes clinging to the shoulders of Neah-Kah-Nie Mountain, a 1,700-foot cliff that towers over the Pacific between Tillamook and Cannon Beach.

Built in 1987, the Inn at Manzanita makes the most of its location in what amounts to the center of Manzanita. The feel is Scandinavian modern, with high-beamed ceilings and blond wood everywhere.

Some of the views are dramatic—Manzanita is best known for its 7-mile-long white beach—but many of the decks are closer to neighbors' rooftop picnic areas than to anything else. A Continental breakfast is served in your room, featuring a variety of fresh fruits and juices and a mammoth croissant. While the in-room breakfast may discourage mingling with the others, innkeepers Larry and Linda Martin know that more than half of their guests are either on their honeymoons or are celebrating anniversaries and appreciate the privacy.

Address: *67 Laneda St., Box 243, Manzanita, OR 97130, tel. 503/368–6754.*
Accommodations: *8 double rooms with baths.*
Amenities: *TV, VCR, hot tub, and wet bar in rooms, 2 small meeting rooms, massage available.*
Rates: *$80–$120; Continental breakfast. MC, V.*
Restrictions: *No smoking, no pets; 2-night minimum on weekends and in July and Aug.*

K.C.'s Mansion By-The-Sea

The Pacific is a good 10 miles away, so K.C.'s Mansion By-The-Sea, in Astoria, may be a bit of a misnomer, but that's the only way in which this handsomely restored Queen Anne paradigm falls short.

The only word to describe K.C.'s is ornate. Plates that co-owner Gus Karas collected in his world travels adorn every wall. The living room has a 6-foot-high stone fireplace, baby grand piano, large velvet Victorian couches and the original, elaborate light fixtures hanging from the 12-foot ceiling. Guests might start the day with seafood omelets or salmon, accompanied by muffins filled with local berries.

The ambience of luxury continues in the four guest rooms. All have wall-to-wall carpeting, couches, and brass reproduction Victorian bedsteads. The most spectacular is Monet's Suite, a purple extravaganza with Victorian velvet chairs and a settee in the large sitting area in the turret.

Address: *3652 Duane St., Astoria, OR 97103, tel. 503/325-6172.*
Accommodations: *2 double rooms with baths, 2 suites.*
Amenities: *Sherry available, champagne or sparkling cider for guests in suites, rooms available for meetings and parties.*
Rates: *$75–$100; full breakfast. MC, V.*
Restrictions: *No smoking in rooms, no pets; 2-night minimum Apr.– Sept.*

Columbia River Gorge and Mt. Hood

The gorge, the mountain—to Portlanders, no other names are necessary. The Columbia River gorge, stretching some 70 miles east from the city, supplies the good and the bad: Dozens of waterfalls, high cliffs, mountain trails, and sweeping vistas provide an array of recreational activities.

The bad comes largely in the form of weather. The Columbia River gorge is one of the few places in the world where a river cuts through a major mountain range. That makes for unique scenery, but since the 4,000-foot-deep gash in the Cascade Range connects the high, arid Columbia Plateau with the low, moist western valleys, the collision of weather systems can spell trouble. Most frequently, the product created by this accident of nature is wind, which, in the finest Oregon tradition, the locals have latched on to. These days Hood River, a small town wedged in between Mt. Hood and the Columbia, bills itself as the windsurfing capital of the world.

Overlooking the gorge is snowcapped Mt. Hood, which at 11,235 feet above sea level is the highest point in Oregon. Its five ski areas and hundreds of miles of hiking trails are all within a 90-minute drive of downtown Portland. Sprinkled around the mountain are dozens of clear blue lakes— among them Lost Lake, Timothy Lake, and Badger Lake— each with its particular angle on the ever-changing profile of Mt. Hood. And the rivers spiral out from the glaciers of the mountain: Hood River, White River, Warm Springs River, Salmon River, Zig Zag River, Sandy River, and the Bull Run River.

Despite the area's wild appeal, it is easily reached by good roads. I-84 zips through the gorge to Hood River. Highway 35 climbs through the colorful orchard country of the Hood River valley to the icy slopes of Mt. Hood; and Highway 26 swoops down the south side of Mt. Hood back to Portland.

Each season has its pleasures. Fall brings the apple trees to full color in the Hood River valley, and the reds and golds of the deciduous trees blend into the deep green of the fir and pine forests. Winters can be a skier's paradise, with most ski areas receiving at least eight feet of snow. But ice storms and blizzards fueled by 100-mile-an-hour winds sometimes close the gorge freeway for a few days each winter, leaving motorists stranded. The spring thaw brings snowmelt to the rivers and, once the streams clear, runs of salmon. Summer is the time for hiking, camping, and exploring the alpine country before the fall snows return—sometimes as early as September.

Places to Go, Sights to See

Bonneville Dam (Cascade Locks, tel. 503/374–8820). This mammoth structure, the first dam ever to span the river, stalls the Columbia long enough to generate a million kilowatts of electricity (enough to supply 40,000 single-family homes). Although the dam, opened in 1937, wiped out the most spectacular rapids on the river, it has many wonders of its own. You can view its great turbines from special walkways during self-guided powerhouse tours, and, at the visitor center on Bradford Island, watch migrating salmon and steelhead as they struggle up the fish ladders. The adjoining *Bonneville Fish Hatchery* (tel. 503/374–8393) has ponds teeming with large salmon, rainbow trout, and sturgeon that are used to repopulate the river.

Cascade Locks. During pioneer days boats needing to pass the rapids had to portage around them. In 1896, the locks that gave the town its name were completed, allowing waterborne passage for the first time. Today the locks are used by Native Americans for their traditional dip-net fishing, and Cascade Locks is notable mainly as the home port of the 600-passenger stern-wheeler *Columbia Gorge* (Marine Park, tel. 503/223–3928 or 503/374–8427). From June to September, the ship churns its way upriver, then back again, on daily two-hour excursions through some of the gorge's most awesome scenery.

Columbia River Gorge Scenic Highway (Rte. 30). Built in the early 1900s by lumber magnate Simon Benson expressly for sightseeing, this narrow, curving 22-mile road strings along the upper reaches of the gorge from Troutdale to The Dalles. While the journey affords some awe-inspiring views—there are a dozen waterfalls in a single 10-mile stretch—the road itself is quite an attraction: Graceful arched bridges span moss-covered gorges, and hand-cut stone walls act as guardrails. The route is especially lovely during the fall, but it is often impassable during the winter.

Crown Point/Vista House (tel. 503/695–2240). Here, atop a 733-foot-high bluff, visitors get their first full glimpse of the grandeur of the gorge. Built a few years after the scenic highway on which it is located, Vista House provides a 30-mile view of the gorge and of the lights of Portland.

The Dalles. This historic town at the eastern end of the Columbia River gorge has a fine Old Town district of brick storefronts that date from the 1840s. It was here that Oregon Trail pioneers took a breather to decide whether the final leg of their 2,000-mile journey would be down the wild Columbia River or over the treacherous passes of Mt. Hood. The 130-year-old *Wasco County Courthouse* (404 W. 2nd St., tel. 503/296–2231) and the 1857-vintage *Ft. Dalles Surgeon's Quarters* (15th and Garrison Sts., tel. 503/296–2231) have been converted into museums; both contain outstanding displays and collections illustrating the incredible ordeal of the pioneers' journey. Today the Dalles boasts windsurfing second only to that done on Hood River.

Hood River Valley. Orchards abound in this hanging valley draped down the eastern shoulder of Mt. Hood. At its foot is the town of Hood River, which features some of the best windsurfing in the world, and its own small brewery, the *White Cap Brew Pub* (tel. 503/386–2247). There are even two wineries: *Hood River Vineyards* (4693 Westwood Dr., tel. 503/386–3772) and *Three Rivers Winery* (275 Country Club Rd., tel. 503/386–5453).

Mt. Hood National Forest (tel. 503/666–0700). Mt. Hood, reached by Highway 35 south from Hood River, is believed to be an active volcano, quiet now but capable of the same violence that decapitated nearby Mt. St. Helens in 1980. The mountain is just one feature of the 1.1 million–acre forest. You'll find 95 campgrounds and 150 lakes stocked with brown, rainbow, cutthroat, kohanee, brook, and steelhead trout. The Sandy, Salmon, and other rivers are known for their fishing, rafting, canoeing, and swimming. Both forest and mountain are crossed by an extensive trail system for hikers, cyclists, and horseback riders. The *Pacific Crest Trail*, which begins in British Columbia and ends in Mexico, crosses here at the 4,157-foot-high Barlow Pass, the highest point on the highway.

Multnomah Falls (tel. 503/695–2376). At 620 feet, Multnomah Falls is the highest in the gorge, a breathtaking plunge over the lip of a high basalt cliff. A steep paved trail switchbacks to the top, but the less hearty can retire to the comfort of the Lakecliff Estate, an old stone lodge at the foot of the falls that houses a restaurant, bar, and an inn.

Oneonta Gorge. This narrow cleft hundreds of feet high is right off the scenic highway a few miles east of Multnomah Falls. The walls drip moisture year-round; hundreds of plant species—some of which are found nowhere else—flourish under these conditions. In late summer the intrepid can walk up the shallow creek, the gorge being so narrow that you can touch both sides.

Timberline Lodge (tel. 503/231–7979). Located at the 6,000-foot level of Mt. Hood's southern slope, Timberline is the mountain's oldest ski area. The lodge (*see* Restaurants, below), 6 miles from the intersection of Highway 26 and Timberline Road, was handmade out of mammoth timbers and stone by local craftsmen as part of a 1930s Works Progress Administration project; it's been used as a setting in many films, including *The Shining*, with Jack Nicholson. The Palmer Chair Lift take skiers to the 8,400-foot level for year-round skiing.

Wasson Winery (41901 Hwy. 26, Sandy, tel. 503/668–3124). Best known for its fruit-and-berry wine, this small winery in the rolling hills outside Sandy is gaining a growing reputation for its grapes.

Restaurants

The **Cascade Dining Room** at the Timberline Lodge (tel. 503/272–3311) in Timberlane features Continental cuisine with a Northwest alpine twist. **Stonehedge Inn** (tel. 503/386–3940) in Hood River offers excellent European fare in a restored country house. Also in Hood River, **The Mesquitery** (tel. 503/386–2002) grills lean beef, chicken, and pork over aromatic mesquite, with the emphasis on fresh herbs and tangy marinades. **Ole's Supper Club** (tel. 503/296–6708) is a hidden place in The Dalles, but the prime rib is front and center.

Tourist Information

Cascade Locks Chamber of Commerce (Box 307, Cascade Locks, OR 97014, tel. 503/374–8619); **The Dalles Area Chamber of Commerce** (901 E. 2nd St., The Dalles, OR 97058, tel. 503/296–3385); **Hood River County Chamber of Commerce** (Port Marina Park, Hood River, OR 97031, tel. 503/386–2000); **Mt. Hood Area Chamber of Commerce** (Box 819, Welches, OR 97067, tel. 503/622–3017).

Reservation Services

Bed and Breakfast—Oregon (2321 N.E. 28th Ave., Portland, OR 97212, tel. 503/287–4704); **Northwest Bed and Breakfast** (610 S.W. Broadway, Portland, OR 97205, tel. 503/243–7616).

Hood River Hotel

Although Hood River now bills itself as a kind of rustic Riviera for windsurfers, the newly restored Hood River Hotel is a reminder of the town's older character. True, Hood River's fresh identity as a recreational center is the reason the hotel was worth fixing up, but the hotel existed as a simple railroad stopover as early as 1910.

The 38-room brick-face hotel sits just off Main Street. The rooms are furnished with Georgian reproductions; the beds add a much-needed touch of individuality, be they brass, four-poster, or canopy. The main appeal of the hotel is the two-story-high lobby, bar, and restaurant, which flow into one another.

You may enter past a string duo performing classical riffs before a giant hearth, the flames crackling away. To the left of the lobby, divided into several sitting areas of Chippendale and Queen Anne reproductions, is an imposing wooden bar serving local beers and wines in a classy yet laid-back atmosphere. (Remember, windsurfers are often big spenders, but they hang around in wet suits or Lycra shorts.)

At the front desk is Pasquale Barone, a veteran of the European hospitality industry, who came to the United States to bring a little Continental flair to Hood River. The bar and the dining room, which extends up to the mezzanine over the lobby, are immense, featuring the building's original pine woodwork.

The food continues the hotel's theme of being at once traditional and trendy. Dinners can get pricey, but the perfectly done seafood is worth it. Overnight guests get a $2.50 credit toward breakfast—a down payment on something special, such as a chili relleno with spiced hash browns.

The hotel is close to Hood River's antiques shops, for daytime excursions, and to its nightlife for after dark. A few blocks away is the White Cap Brew Pub (tel. 503/386–2247), home of the Hood River Brewery. Besides serving up its Full Sail Ale ale, one of the Northwest's most popular local ales, the pub has a constant supply of regional and national musical acts. Closer to the hotel is the Brass Rail, a hopping dance club that features bands from the Portland and Seattle club scene.

Address: *102 Oak St., Hood River, OR 97031, tel. 503/386–1900, fax 503/386–6090.*
Accommodations: *32 double rooms with baths, 6 housekeeping suites.*
Amenities: *Cable TV, phone, and ceiling fan in rooms, 2 doubles have kitchens, elevator, 24-hour room service, restaurant with sidewalk café.*
Rates: *$69–$125; $2.50 credit toward breakfast. AE, MC, V.*
Restrictions: *No smoking, no pets.*

Mountain Shadows Bed & Breakfast

It takes some time and effort to get to Mountain Shadows Bed & Breakfast—about 25 miles from Sandy—but the journey up the steep mountain road is well worth it. As you climb the last pitch of the driveway, Mt. Hood looms above the huge log home tucked in among the trees.

Here, it's just you and the mountain. A wraparound deck places you within 10 miles of the summit. With binoculars, you can watch avalanches sweep down the mountain's western profile or see climbing parties traversing the spiny ridges—hopefully, not at the same time. Innkeepers Cathy and Paul Townsend, who left southern California in 1990, have found some peace and quiet on their 38 acres of woodland—and they don't mind sharing it with you.

The home is built entirely of pine logs and sits neatly on a slight incline that rolls down to the property's two creeks. Inside, the high-beamed ceilings evoke the images of both a pioneer log cabin and a grand private ski lodge. A wood-burning stove pumps heat into the public area, which is dominated by large, overstuffed modern couches and an eight-foot-high wardrobe of white pine. The dining area offers more close-enough-to-touch mountain views. During the summer, breakfast is served on the spacious deck, where early risers often see deer traipsing along the creek.

Breakfast is prepared tag-team style, and the results are tasty: rich German pancakes, thick local bacon, and fresh muffins.

The guest rooms are on the main floor down a long hall from the common area. The best room verges on being a suite, with its own wood-burning stove, small sitting area, and private bath. It's not particularly roomy, although the view out to the mountain lends a feeling of space. There is one cautionary note: Paul generally leaves a fire ready to go in the stove, because, even during the summer, at this elevation a solid chill is possible. The room heats up quickly, though.

The other two rooms are less distinguished, but they do have heavy handmade quilts, exposed timbers, and that rustic quality found throughout the house.

Address: *End of Angelsea Rd., Box 147, Welches, OR 97067, tel. 503/622-4746.*
Accommodations: *1 double room with bath, 2 double rooms share bath.*
Amenities: *Stereo in 1 room, wood-burning stove in 1 room, evening refreshments, wine tastings.*
Rates: *$55–$65; full breakfast. No credit cards.*
Restrictions: *No smoking; 2-night minimum on holiday weekends.*

Old Welches Inn

During the days of the Oregon Trail, wagons frequently stopped at Welches on the Salmon River, well below the glaciers of Mt. Hood and its steep passes. Below spread the fertile Willamette Valley, the goal of the weary pioneers. By 1890 the valley had become civilized, and Welches Hotel lured the carriage trade from Portland with the promise of hiking, fishing, and relaxation.

A simple, white clapboard house is all that remains of the hotel, whose dining room once seated 120. The inn combines the atmosphere of a laidback ski lodge and an old country estate. Bleached woodwork accentuates the sunny, airy feel of the place.

Much of that feeling comes from Judi Mondun, who operates the inn with her husband, Ted. The couple, both of whom were involved in finance in Miami, happened upon the Mt. Hood area during the late 1980s when their customary slopes in Colorado lacked snow. While Ted maintains his accounting practice in the Sunshine State, Judi tends to the Old Welches Inn.

A large wood-burning stove set on a base of rounded river rocks lends a rustic look to the living room, which overlooks the river through French doors. The covered patio, with a floor of hand-fitted river stones and lattice walls, boasts an eight-foot-high stone fireplace that was originally part of the old hotel.

The three upstairs rooms share two baths. The largest, which overlooks Resort at the Mountain's 27-hole golf course and has views of Hunchback Mountain, has a sleigh bed, Georgian hunting scenes on the raw silk–covered walls, and a floral upholstered rocking chair. A second room lacks a dramatic view, but the rich cedar paneling and ornate iron bedstand more than compensate. The remaining room on that level has a cannonball-style headboard and is festooned with duck decoys.

An outlying cabin is even closer to the river and the golf course—it overlooks the first hole. The 1901 structure has its own kitchen, two bedrooms, and a river-rock fireplace.

Address: *26401 East Welches Rd., Welches, OR 97067, tel. 503/622–3754.*
Accommodations: *3 double rooms share 2 baths, 1 double housekeeping suite.*
Amenities: *Fireplace in suite.*
Rates: *$55–$65, suite $140; full breakfast (except for suite). AE, MC, V.*
Restrictions: *No smoking; 2-night minimum on holiday weekends.*

Williams House

The family of innkeeper Don Williams can be traced to The Dalles area as far back as 1862. The bed-and-breakfast he runs with his wife, Barbara, is a link to that past, when The Dalles was just a few years removed from being a simple trading post frequented by French and English trappers.

Williams House sits halfway up a steep slope above the town's business district. Directly below is a small creek that meanders through the estate's arboretum. Built in 1899, the house is textbook Queen Anne, with spindlework porch supports and friezes, a round tower, gables aplenty, decorated verge boards, and enough gingerbread for a decade of Christmases.

The grand style continues inside with a broad, open staircase of Nicaraguan mahogany. Two sitting rooms provide ample space for lounging on Victorian settees—one with Roman heads carved on the back—and chairs while you thumb through the Williams's eclectic book collection. Throughout the main floor is the Williams's collection of Chinese plates, bowls, and artifacts, which lend an imperial touch to the house.

A suite on the main floor features a four-poster bed and a private sitting room that face the creek. The bathroom has the original Italian marble and a six-foot-long claw-foot tub. An unusual feature of the suite is the Victorian intercom system.

Upstairs are two guest rooms that share one modern bath. The larger room has an English canopied four-poster bed from the 1750s, a late-18th-century English Adamesque leather-top desk, an American Queen Anne maple highboy, and a private deck with views to the Klickatat Hills across the Columbia River. The other room is furnished largely with Victorian pieces from New England, but the hand-carved headboard with central walnut burl panel dates from 1775.

Breakfast—coddled eggs, cherry-tinted honey, and jam from the fruits of the Williams's orchard—is served on Spode china. In good weather, which occurs often in this, the driest part of the gorge, breakfast is served in a gazebo on the back patio.

A noted local historian who has been active in preserving several old buildings in The Dalles, Don is a font of information on the region.

Address: *608 W. 6th St., The Dalles, OR 97058, tel. 503/296-2889.*
Accommodations: *2 double rooms share bath, 1 suite.*
Amenities: *Air-conditioning; cable TV in rooms, phone available.*
Rates: *$55–$75; full breakfast. AE, D, MC, V.*
Restrictions: *Smoking in common areas only, no pets.*

Chamberlin House

Although it is only 30 minutes from downtown Portland, Corbett is country through and through. The old town clings to the western edge of the Columbia River gorge about 1,000 feet up the steep slopes. In the middle of Corbett is Chamberlin House, a plain brown Craftsman farmhouse that has been weathering gorge winds since 1912 and has always been in owner Nancy Wilson's family.

The house retains its hardwood interior. The rooms are small, and you are always very much aware that you're in a family home; the only public area is essentially the family living room. But those creaking stairs and upright iron beds have an undeniable appeal that harks back to the early part of the century. (Histo-ry is Nancy's hobby, and she serves as research historian at Vista House.)

Breakfast is filling and seemingly endless. Orange-baked French toast and chocolate waffles complement baked-egg dishes and plates of muffins and homemade preserves.

Address: *36817 E. Crown Point Hwy., Corbett, OR 97019, tel. 503/695-2200.*
Accommodations: *2 double rooms share bath.*
Amenities: *Champagne splits in evening.*
Rates: *$50; full breakfast. No credit cards.*
Restrictions: *No smoking, no pets.*

Columbia Gorge Hotel

Staying at the Columbia Gorge Hotel is one of those irresistible, classic experiences. Just west of Hood River, the stuccoed hotel sits atop a 200-foot waterfall that drops into the Columbia River.

Despite the hotel's size—the public rooms are huge, with plaster beams to match—the feeling is intimate—if at times intimidating. Louis XV–style armchairs surround a huge fireplace in the lounge, while such Victorian touches as round tufted velvet seats and domed lamps with hanging crystals enliven other rooms. Guest accommodations range from grand top-floor rooms that feature fireplaces and spectacular views over the falls to more pedestrian offerings on the lower floors.

As good as the dinners are, breakfast is the big production here: baked apples, apple fritters, smoked pork chops, pancakes—it goes on. And when they ceremoniously pour the honey over the biscuits from on high, it's pure theater.

Address: *4000 W. Cliff Dr., Hood River, OR 97031, tel. 503/386-5566 or 800/345-1921.*
Accommodations: *46 double rooms with baths.*
Amenities: *TV and phone in rooms, fireplace in 2 rooms, restaurant, lounge, meeting rooms, catering available.*
Rates: *$175-$225; full breakfast. AE, MC, V.*
Restrictions: *No smoking in restaurant.*

Hackett House

Before 1989, innkeeper Sherry Pobo had never heard of Hood River. But when she decided to leave a stressful job in California's Silicon Valley, she and partner Shirley Johnson soon found the small, windy town. They also found Hackett House, a large Dutch Colonial Revival house just a few doors down from the State Street Bed & Breakfast (*see* below).

The common areas and guest rooms of the house offer plenty of space, although the decor seems to lack inspiration. Overall, Hackett House looks like a regular-issue middle-class home—albeit a squeaky-clean one. Still, there is charm in the family snapshots on the walls. And the house's largely Victorian Anjou Pear Room features original diamond-pane leaded windows, a cherrywood Rococo Revival settee and chairs, and a sitting room.

Breakfast here is excellent, with Shirley serving up everything from eggs Lorraine to pecan waffles with homemade blueberry sauce. If the weather is favorable, you'll dine out on the deck, with Mt. Adams looking over your shoulder.

Address: *922 State St., Hood River, OR 97031, tel. 503/386-1014.*
Accommodations: *3 double rooms and 1 suite share 2½ baths.*
Amenities: *Evening refreshments, dinner available, meeting room.*
Rates: *$35–$55; full breakfast. D, MC, V.*
Restrictions: *Smoking on deck only, no pets.*

State Street Bed & Breakfast

Located in a residential area of Hood River just west of downtown, the State Street Bed & Breakfast is a plain cedar-shake house built in 1932.

Innkeepers Amy Goodbar and Mac Lee moved from the San Diego area to Hood River in 1987 and quickly built a reputation for excellent breakfasts and advice on where to catch the wind or hike. The Massachusetts Room has Colonial reproductions; the California Room features lots of color—three shades of peach—with director's chairs and potted ferns; the Colorado Room has a Southwest look, with Old West knickknacks; and the Maryland Room conveys the graciousness of the antebellum days, with a white iron bedstead and day bed, wicker chairs, and maroon tie-back curtains with white lace. The main common area affords views of the Columbia River through leaded glass windows.

Breakfast is geared to the hearty—and athletic—with such entrées as strawberry crêpes and oatmeal-walnut pancakes supplemented by muffins, homemade granola, and a huge fruit bowl.

Address: *1005 State St., Hood River, OR 97031, tel. 503/386-1899.*
Accommodations: *4 double rooms share 2 baths.*
Amenities: *Game room, storage area for sports equipment.*
Rates: *$55–$70; full breakfast. MC, V.*
Restrictions: *No smoking.*

Central and Eastern Oregon
Including Bend

*Drop unsuspecting travelers into the part of Oregon that's
east of the snowcapped Cascade Mountain range and they'll
swear they're someplace else—Utah, Arizona, Texas,
Switzerland.*

*While the western third of the state is lush and green, the
eastern two-thirds is high, dry, and wild—sparsely
populated, too. The 17 counties of eastern Oregon make up
an area of pine forests, rangeland, and mountains the size
of Missouri, but the population is less than 350,000. There
is only one town with more than 20,000 people, just two
commercial TV stations, and one congressional
representative, whom the vast area shares with southern
Oregon.*

*Central and eastern Oregon begin very visibly in the west
as soon as you reach the summit of the Cascade
Mountains. There the forests turn from fir to pine and the
ground underfoot from soggy to crunchy. The difference
rests simply in the presence of the Cascades, which drain
most of the precipitation out of the Pacific storms,
dumping it on the western slopes of the mountains.
Whereas western Oregon averages 45 inches of rain a year,
the mean to the east is less than 15 inches.*

*Once you're out of the mountains, the land settles down to
a broad plateau that gradually slopes down toward the
Columbia River to the north. On this high plain, much of
it more than 3,500 feet in elevation, are large mountain
ranges: the lumpy Ochocos, the stately Strawberry Range,
the majestic Wallowas, the immense, complex Blue
Mountains. And in the southern deserts, gargantuan fault-
block mountains—Steens Mountain, Hart Mountain, Abert
Rim—thrust straight out of the sagebrush.*

Deer, elk, antelope, cougars, and even wild horses roam these plains. Ranches, some running more than 10,000 head of cattle, are sprinkled throughout the big country. Although there are few developed tourist areas outside the Bend area, the adventuresome are seldom idle in central and eastern Oregon.

The Deschutes River, a cold green stream that heads near Mt. Bachelor, shoots along the eastern edge of the Cascades, providing better than 100 miles of fishing and rafting opportunities. The John Day River winds through thousands of square miles of fossil beds in north-central Oregon. Farther east, the Snake River, bordering Oregon and Idaho, dominates the terrain with Hells Canyon— apologies to the Grand Canyon—the deepest gash on the continent.

Northeastern Oregon's Wallowa Mountains, often called the American Alps because of their combination of granite peaks and hanging glacier valleys, lie just to the west of Hells Canyon, with hundreds of miles of hiking and pack trails.

Only in the southeastern corner of the state, an area about the size of South Carolina, does Oregon have a true desert environment. Here, in an area of more than 30,000 square miles, rivers from the mountains flow into the plain and evaporate in marshes and alkali flats, and birds gather from all along the western flyway.

This is lonely, self-sufficient country, so people are friendly and are likely to wave at you as you drive down the long, lonesome highways. But passersby are few and far between. Sudden snowstorms or flash floods can come out of nowhere virtually anytime of the year. It is advisable to be prepared to fend for yourself at all times.

Places to Go, Sights to See

Baker City. Located on the old Oregon Trail, this former mining town quickly takes you back to the Gold Rush days of northeastern Oregon. At the center of town stands a core of 135 buildings dating from more than a century ago, all listed on the National Register of Historic Places.

Bend. The largest town east of the Cascades and sitting very nearly in the center of Oregon, Bend is a good fueling-up spot for the recreational activities nearby: A half hour to the east, skiers bop down the slopes of Mt. Bachelor, and the fishing and rafting of the wild Deschutes River are within easy reach. Bend is filled with decent restaurants, dance bars, pro shops, and rental places, as well as a surprising number of good hostelries. At the *High Desert Museum* (59800 S. Hwy. 97, 6 mi south of Bend, tel. 503/382–4754), you can walk through a Stone Age Indian campsite, a pioneer wagon camp, an old mine, an Old West boardwalk, and other detailed dioramas, with authentic relics, sounds, even odors. A 150-acre outdoor section features porcupines, birds of prey, and river otters at play.

Century Drive. For 100 miles this forest-highway loop beginning and ending in Bend meanders among dozens of high mountain lakes offering fishing, hiking, waterskiing, and camping. Take Rte. 46 for the first two-thirds of the trip and switch to U.S. 97 at LePine to return to Bend.

John Day Fossil Beds National Monument (2 mi north of the junction of U.S. 26 and Hwy. 19, tel. 503/987–2333). Millions of years ago, the arid canyons of east-central Oregon were tropical forests inhabited by sloths and the prehistoric ancestors of horses. Their remains in the form of well-preserved fossils, many in lake beds of volcanic ash, are found in the valley of the John Day River.

Kah-Nee-Ta (11 mi from Warm Springs on Hwy. 3, tel. 800/831–0100). In the heart of the 600,000-acre Warm Springs Indian Reservation sits this posh resort. The hot mineral springs feeding the Warm Springs River form the focal point of Kah-Nee-Ta, which is operated by the Confederated Tribes of Warm Springs. A double Olympic-size mineral-water pool is open to nonguests for a nominal fee; golf, tennis, hiking, and fishing are also available. Located in a remote canyon, the resort has sunshine 300 days a year—unheard of even in central Oregon.

Owyhee River Country. The far southeastern corner of Oregon is named for the wild, thrashing river that shoots through the canyons. White-water rafting is popular here, as are fishing, hiking, and studying Indian petroglyphs. The town of Vale, at the junction of highways 20 and 26, is the best base for exploring the area.

Pendleton. Famous for its annual mid-September rodeo, this cattle town, reached by I–84, is situated on a plain between the scenic Blue Mountains and the brown Columbia Plateau. An important staging area for shipping cattle, Pendleton seems almost Texan in atmosphere.

Smith Rocks State Park (tel. 503/548–7501). The muddy Crooked River winds through these high precipices north of Redmond. A favorite with rock climbers, 300- to 500-foot-deep canyons form high salt spires, the most famous of which is called Monkey Face. The park, which also encompasses dense pine forest, offers excellent hiking.

Steens Mountain. Currently under consideration as a national park, Steens Mountain is one of the most unusual desert environments in the West. The mountain, a 60-mile-long ridge, has 5,000-foot glacial gorges carved into its sides. The summit, 9,700 feet above sea level, is reached by a passable but rugged road, and overlooks the sandy Alvord Desert. To the north, 6 miles off Rte. 205, lies the mammoth *Malheur National Wildlife Refuge* (tel. 503/493–2612), home to hundreds of species of migratory birds, among them sandhill cranes, snowy white egrets, and white-faced ibis.

Wallowa Mountains. Oregon's northeastern corner is a surprise to most visitors. The mountains form a giant U-shaped fortress between Hells Canyon to the east and the Blue Mountains to the west. Hundreds of high alpine lakes, many more than 7,000 feet high, dot the remote hanging valleys that fall between ridges of 9,000-foot-plus peaks. The most scenic route through the area is Highway 82; take it for 80 miles, starting and finishing at either LaGrande or Joseph.

Restaurants

Pine Tavern (tel. 503/382–5581) in Bend takes its name from the two pine trees growing through the roof. But the place's reputation comes from its flawlessly prepared seafood and fresh trout served up in typically hearty Western helpings. Ask any cowpoke in the Baker Valley who serves the best steak and potatoes, and there's only one answer: **Haines Steak House** (tel. 503/856–3639). One caveat: If you order it rare, that's how you'll get it.

Tourist Information

Central Oregon Visitors Information Center (63085 N. Hwy. 97, Bend, OR 97701, tel. 503/382–3221); **Grant County Chamber of Commerce** (281 W. Main St., John Day, OR 97485, tel. 503/575–0547); **Harney County Chamber of Commerce** (18 West D St., Burns, OR 97720, tel. 503/573–2636); **North Central Oregon Tourism Council** (25 E. Dorion, Pendleton, OR 97801, tel. 800/547–8911); **Ontario Chamber of Commerce** (173 S.W. 1st St., Ontario, OR 97914, tel. 503/889–8012).

Reservation Services

Bed and Breakfast—Oregon (2321 N.E. 28th Ave., Portland, OR 97212, tel. 503/287–4704); **Northwest Bed and Breakfast** (610 S.W. Broadway, Portland, OR, 97205, tel. 503/243–7616).

Elliott House

I n 1908, when Elliott House was built, Prineville was a booming cattle center on the edge of the frontier. Ranching is still big in Crook County, but Prineville is now best known for rock-hounding (within a few miles are huge agate beds where the curious can easily pick up "thunder eggs" and petrified wood). Despite its rough-hewn reputation, Prineville has always been the most genteel town in central Oregon. Elliott House, a Queen Anne Victorian, keeps that tradition of class in the outback alive.

To say that the innkeepers, Tuck and Carol Dunlap, have taken great pains to re-create the past is an understatement: Carol wears a Victorian costume as she welcomes guests into the sitting room for afternoon tea. When they bought Elliott House, the Dunlaps found that in their zeal to modernize, the previous owners had stripped the main floor of all its original woodwork. Luckily, some of the upstairs moldings remained, and when Tuck discovered that he couldn't find similar ones from the same period, he reproduced them himself, adding wainscoting, chair rails, and crown molding.

Tuck isn't the only craftsperson in the family—Carol has created several stained-glass hangings for the living room, sitting room, and downstairs guest room. The sitting room has an opulent look, with bright gold-frame mirrors and a curvaceous Victorian fainting couch in red velvet.

The Dunlaps are working hard to replace any reproduction furniture in the house with antiques. The conversion has not yet been made in the ground-floor room, located next to the kitchen, but a bay window dressed with ecru lace adds some charm. The most romantic guest room is the Sweetheart Room, with a white iron and porcelain bedstead and a turn-of-the-century camelback settee, its top rail and arms of carved wood. The same floral print that covers the settee is used in the window swags.

The most whimsical room is the large bathroom shared by the two upstairs rooms. The velvety-looking Victorian rose-and-black wallpaper fairly jumps out at you, as does a painting of a large, sensual female nude. The sink has a marble top; the claw-foot tub's feet are painted gold. Carol unabashedly calls this her brothel bath.

Address: *305 W. 1st St., Prineville, OR 97754, tel. 503/447-7442.*
Accommodations: *1 double room with bath, 2 double rooms share bath.*
Amenities: *Afternoon refreshments; cable TV and phones available.*
Rates: *$40–$60; full breakfast. No credit cards.*
Restrictions: *No smoking in rooms, no pets.*

Frenchglen Hotel

I t's almost impossible to miss the Frenchglen Hotel—that is, once you *find* Frenchglen, a tiny spot on the map deep in the eastern Oregon desert. The town consists of a school (most of the families live on ranches sprinkled across a 1,000-square-mile area), a store, and the hotel.

Built in 1920, still pioneer days in this remote region, the state-owned hotel resembles a simple prairie church, with a gabled roof that's visible from miles away as you approach from the north. Managers John Ross and Karla Litzenberg spent years as cooks on Alaskan fishing boats, so remoteness is nothing new to them. At least here at the foot of the Steens Mountain, they get a fresh supply of faces every few days.

Inside, the hotel is simple and rustic. A huge camp-type coffee pot is always on the hob in the combination lobby/dining room. Visitors can absorb local history and whet their appetites for touring with a collection of picture books in the lobby. The dining room, really two long pine tables, serves as a gathering place for ranchers and visitors.

The food here has long been a standout. Every evening a large, hearty family-style dinner is served for overnight guests and the general public. A typical group might include a ranching couple who've driven 60

miles to celebrate their anniversary, a pair of bird-watchers, and a local mechanic. John and Karla whip up huge salads, rich casseroles, home-baked rolls, and a main meat dish. Breakfast is also bountiful, although it's served individually from a menu and isn't included in the room rate.

All the rooms are upstairs off a single hallway. The five rooms in the original part of the hotel have plain white walls and wooden bed frames handmade by John. The three rooms at the back of the hotel, added during the 1930s, have knotty pine walls. Views sweep eastward across the broad Blitzen Valley up the gradually sloping shoulders of Steens Mountain. All eight rooms share two bathrooms located midway down the long hall.

Most of the people who stay at the hotel are devoted bird-watchers who are attracted by the nearby Malheur National Wildlife Refuge. In the fall, however, Steens teems with hunters. The mix of hunters, ranchers, and conservationists can make for some lively conversations over breakfast.

Address: *Frenchglen, OR 97736, tel. 503/493-2825.*
Accommodations: *8 double rooms share 2 baths.*
Amenities: *Restaurant.*
Rates: *$40–$48; breakfast not included. MC, V.*
Restrictions: *No smoking in rooms, no pets; closed Nov. 16–Mar. 1.*

Lara House

Staying at Lara House, a cross-gabled Craftsman house built in 1910, gives visitors a glimpse of what life was like in Bend when it was a four-day trip to Portland instead of the present-day three-hour drive. Located beside peaceful Drake Park on the Deschutes River just out of downtown, Lara House stands out, on a huge lot with sloping lawn atop a retaining wall of native lava rocks.

The house's original woodwork can be seen in the trim and door frames all over, and in the alderwood coffered ceiling of the living room. There a large brick fireplace dominates, to be enjoyed from two cream and blue patterned camelback love seats or from the ladderback chairs about the gaming table. The walls here are heavily stuccoed. Walk through the double French doors, and the atmosphere changes radically. Here the huge sun room, which overlooks the 11-acre riverside park, takes its cue from nature. All is soft and subtle green, including the tapestry-covered mahogany sofa and matching easy chair.

Visitors who enjoy the sharply pitched ceilings and nooks and crannies of an attic will enjoy the fourth-floor Summit Room, a two-bedroom suite with the best views in the house. The main bedroom has a king-size bed, country-maple furniture from the 1940s, and stenciled flowers painted on the wall moldings.

One floor down are the other guest rooms, each carpeted, with seating areas and private bathrooms. The L-shaped Drake Room, furnished with dark oak furniture, has a duck theme: wallpaper borders swimming with them, framed prints of them, a wall unit displaying knickknacks of these fine-feathered friends. The black claw-foot tub, original to the house, is big enough for a whole flock of rubber duckies.

Guests have their choice of venues for breakfast: the formal living room, sun room, or terraced redwood deck overlooking a sunken herb garden. Innkeepers Doug and Bobbye Boger will not only arrange rafting tours on the Deschutes, but Doug, a part-time ski instructor, will also lead ski tours to nearby Mt. Bachelor that include lessons.

Address: *640 N.W. Congress St., Bend, OR 97701, tel. 503/388-4064.*
Accommodations: *4 double rooms with baths, 1 double suite.*
Amenities: *Afternoon and evening refreshments, dinner and baby-sitting available, catering, rafting and skiing tours arranged.*
Rates: *$75-$85; full breakfast. MC, V.*
Restrictions: *Smoking outside only, no pets; 2-night minimum on weekends Nov. 15-Apr. 15 and on holiday weekends.*

Shaniko Hotel

Bed and breakfasting in a ghost town may not strike everyone as a good bet. But here on the high dusty plains south of The Dalles, the Old West feeling of the recently restored Shaniko Hotel is palpable.

Guest rooms at the hotel, which first opened in 1901, are spare and perhaps a bit too antiseptic with their period reproduction furniture. (The mock old-fashioned wooden iceboxes acting as night tables *are* clever, however.) The only special room is the pink and white Bridal Suite, which features a small sitting room and a two-person whirlpool tub. Still, there's plenty of atmosphere just outside; guests need only peek out of the window to see a town that's falling down around them as the wind wails through the old buildings and shutters flap eerily.

Shaniko has been a ghost town since the 1940s, when the last rail line leading to town washed out. Yet in 1900, the town's population numbered in the thousands and it was the world's biggest shipper of wool. Stagecoach lines spoked into the frontier of eastern Oregon and Shaniko was the rail head for the only line that then penetrated the high plains.

Despite the slightly sterile feel, owner Jean Farrell, a retired plumbing contractor, does give a personal warmth to the hotel, taking a special interest in the guests. Of course, that's easy to do in this town of 19, where all except 2 work either in the hotel or at its adjoining restaurant. Jean is also the mayor of Shaniko, a delicate job that involves keeping the town looking rundown without allowing it to collapse completely.

Breakfasts are copious, geared to a day of shearing sheep or baling hay, and dinners are mammoth, with huge wads of sweet homemade bread complementing mashed potatoes and gravy with hunks of meat.

All those calories can easily be walked off with a stroll through Shaniko. Some of the buildings, such as the old wooden firehouse, have been kept up to house ancient horse-drawn fire rigs. The blacksmith shop, still operating, is run by a small company that makes reproduction carriages. For real culture shock, guests can tour the tiny, false-fronted Shaniko Post Office. Across the lonesome highway is the old, creaking water tower, the tallest building in town.

Address: *Shaniko, OR, 97057, tel. 503/489-3441.*
Accommodations: *16 double rooms with baths, 1 suite.*
Amenities: *Restaurant, whirlpool tub in suite.*
Rates: *$45–$55, bridal suite $85; breakfast not included. MC, V.*
Restrictions: *No smoking in rooms, no pets.*

Stange Manor

When Bernadine Curry was growing up during the late 1930s in La Grande, the Stange mansion, just three blocks away, seemed a place of unattainable glamour. Owned by lumber baron August Stange, the richest man in the county, the manse on the western edge of this small college and ranching town was an obligatory stop for any political figure and celebrity passing through.

Bernadine remembers slogging through the snow as a child to get the autographs of such house guests as Guy Kibbe and Bing Crosby. Now she still gets autographs from the guests at the old Stange place—these days, however, the signatures are added to the guest book of the stately B&B she runs there with her husband, Gene, and her daughter and son-in-law.

Built in 1924, the imposing Georgian Revival home sits on huge grounds in an otherwise unspectacular residential neighborhood. Stange Manor's interior is full of 1920s-style class. Guests can enjoy the large carved stone fireplace in the living room from an art deco–style semicircular sectional couch upholstered in a rose-print tapestry fabric.

Throw open the French doors of the Fountain Room, complete with a working wall fountain of teal-colored Italian tiles, and the years quickly melt away. Built-in benches line the perimeter of the window-filled room, affording views of the property. White rattan furniture and an old crank-up Victrola add to the Jay Gatsby aura of the room.

As you ascend the grand staircase to the upstairs guest rooms, you'll pass a large Georgian hunting tapestry purchased by Stange and a plaster bust of Aphrodite at the top. The master suite boasts a turn-of-the-century mahogany turned four-poster bed and matching dresser with tilting mirror. The bathroom features the original "foot washer," fed with running water.

Breakfast is a lavish affair served in the dining room beneath a pewter and crystal chandelier that is original to the house. Built-in floor-to-ceiling china display cabinets, flocked wallpaper, and full-length balloon curtains contribute to the formal ambience of the room. Usually Gene joins the guests for breakfast, which might be considered an intrusion if he weren't so cordial, informative, and easygoing.

Address: *1612 Walnut St., La Grande, OR 97850, tel. 503/963–2400.*
Accommodations: *2 double rooms with baths, 2 double suites.*
Amenities: *Cable TV and fireplace in 1 suite.*
Rates: *$55–$85; full breakfast. AE, MC, V.*
Restrictions: *No pets.*

Bed and Breakfast by the River

The Emmel Bros. Ranch sits at the foot of the stunning Strawberry Mountains near Prairie City on more than 3,000 acres of rangeland and forest, with the John Day River winding through it.

The bed-and-breakfast Helen Emmel operates here is far from fancy. The guest quarters look like the teenagers' rooms they are—or were, now that the Emmel brood is away at college. There are some interesting touches: The family room has a hand-carved oak mantel from the 1813 Georgia plantation house where the family lived until they came out west in 1969. The pie safe came from the plantation's slave quarters.

What Bed and Breakfast by the River lacks in interior design, however, is more than made up for in atmosphere. This a working cattle ranch, where the morning begins with biscuits, waffles, homemade bread and preserves, and meat—beef, pork, venison, or elk—all from the ranch or the family's hunting trips. The house is right by the riverbank, and guests get a great view from the breakfast table of the salmon spawning.

Address: *Rte. 2, Box 790, Prairie City, OR 97869, tel. 503/820–4470.*
Accommodations: *3 double rooms with baths.*
Amenities: *Cable TV and pool table in game room.*
Rates: *$50; full breakfast. No credit cards.*
Restrictions: *No smoking, no pets, no alcohol.*

Farewell Bend Bed & Breakfast

Farewell Bend Bed & Breakfast is just at the edge of downtown Bend. From the street, the Dutch Colonial house is common enough, but inside, innkeeper Lorene Bateman has made good use of Bend's many days of sunshine to create an airy, California-style atmosphere.

All guest rooms come with handmade quilts designed by Lorene. The largest room, predominantly mauve, has a king-size bed with modern teak headboard, white wrought-iron day bed, and an alcove sitting area. One lavender-hued room has twin beds and a large English turn-of-the-century mahogany wardrobe. The old-fashioned washstand has a real sink with running water. The third room has a bathroom with a claw-foot tub and a private deck.

Downstairs, the living room is furnished with comfortable contemporary floral-print love seats and wing chairs; it also has a cable TV, VCR, and large library. Breakfast—from Dutch babies to spinach-egg dishes—is served in the modern dining room. More often, guests prefer to dine on the lower backyard deck, especially when the weather is glorious, as it often is in Bend.

Address: *29 N.W. Greeley St., Bend, OR 97701, tel. 503/382–4374.*
Accommodations: *3 double rooms with baths.*
Amenities: *Afternoon refreshments.*
Rates: *$55–$75; full breakfast. MC, V.*
Restrictions: *No smoking, no pets.*

The House at Water's Edge

The only reason this Bend bed-and-breakfast exists is because of an old doctor's vegetable garden. Located on a prime piece of waterfront property on the Deschutes River just across from downtown, the house sits on a plot once marked by rows of tomatoes and corn. Eventually the doctor gave up his garden and Sam Playt, himself a retired pediatrician, and Sally Anderson built a modern, luxurious home—right at the water's edge.

Dramatic as the setting is, the interior is where this cedar-shake house shines: blond wood and exposed beams and an entire wall made of river stones. Furnishings throughout are largely country-French, in light woods. Both upstairs rooms overlook the river and have high, beamed ceilings. Guests can enjoy the river view from their bay-window seats, which have shawls to curl up in, thoughtfully placed at arm's reach. Downstairs, a deck goes right to the riverbank and has a barbecue for guests' use. A hot tub is tucked into one side of the deck, out of public view.

Address: *36 N.W. Pinecrest Court, Bend, OR 97701, tel. 503/382–1266.*
Accommodations: *2 double rooms with baths.*
Amenities: *Afternoon refreshments, washer and dryer available, storage area; outdoor hot tub, canoe.*
Rates: *$60; full breakfast. No credit cards.*
Restrictions: *Smoking outside only, no pets; 2-night minimum on weekends.*

Mirror Pond House

Mirror Pond makes downtown Bend a special place, where mink, beavers, otters, and ducks frolic in the dammed-up Deschutes River. And Mirror Pond House, situated at the south end of the pond, is perhaps the best place from which to experience this magic.

At her handsome Cape Code–style house, innkeeper Beryl Kellum has kept things unpretentious. The high-ceilinged living room is painted off-white, except for the dark mahogany trim around the fireplace. Seating includes a semicircular davenport and floral chintz chairs. The downstairs guest room is done in apricot, with mostly reproduction Colonial furniture, big rose-print wallpaper, and polished brass lamps. Upstairs is a suite featuring a pair of swivel rockers strategically placed before the picture window for guests to enjoy the pond view.

On request, Beryl will cook up any fish guests catch off the deck or from the house canoe. Breakfast might include sticky pecan buns, roast-beef hash and popovers, sweet cheese-filled crêpes with fruit sauce, and fresh-baked corn bread and spoon bread.

Address: *1054 N.W. Harmon Blvd., Bend, OR 97701, tel. 503/389–1680.*
Accommodations: *1 double room with bath, 1 suite.*
Amenities: *Evening refreshments; canoe available.*
Rates: *$60–$80; full breakfast. No credit cards.*
Restrictions: *No pets.*

Sonshine Bed and Breakfast

Dr. Kam Wah Chung was a leader of the Chinese workers who were brought to the gold fields of northeast Oregon during the 1860s. The Kam Wah Chung Museum in John Day explores the Gold Rush from the perspective of the overworked, underpaid Chinese laborers.

Across the street from this fascinating museum is Sonshine Bed and Breakfast, operating out of the doctor's old surgery. To be sure, most of Wah's artifacts are in the museum, but the small lodging has a character all its own, supplied by owners Carl and Carolyn Stout. Carl's hunting trophies, elk and deer, adorn the walls. The two guest rooms are small and plain except for some nicely turned curtains and hand-tied quilts in one and bright Southwest colors in the other.

Breakfasts range from stuffed French toast and ham and cheese croissants to that northeastern Oregon special—elk steak. Evening meals are available.

Address: *210 N.W. Canton St., John Day, OR 97485, tel. 503/575-1827.*
Accommodations: *2 double rooms share bath.*
Amenities: *Cable TV in common area.*
Rates: *$40; full breakfast. V.*
Restrictions: *No smoking, no pets, no alcohol.*

Washington

Washington

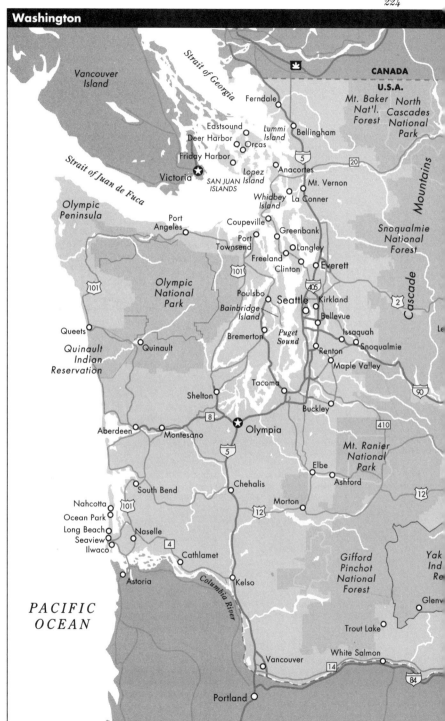

Vancouver Island

Strait of Georgia

CANADA
U.S.A.

Ferndale

Mt. Baker Nat'l. Forest

North Cascades National Park

Eastsound

Lummi Island

Bellingham

Deer Harbor

Orcas

Friday Harbor

5

20

Mountains

Victoria

Lopez Island

SAN JUAN ISLANDS

Anacortes

Mt. Vernon

Strait of Juan de Fuca

Whidbey Island

La Conner

Snoqualmie National Forest

Olympic Peninsula

Port Angeles

Coupeville

Greenbank

Port Townsend

Langley

Freeland

Everett

Clinton

101

Cascade

Olympic National Park

Poulsbo

Seattle

Kirkland

405

Bainbridge Island

Bellevue

2

101

Queets

Bremerton

Puget Sound

Issaquah

Snoqualmie

Le

Quinault Indian Reservation

Quinault

Renton

Maple Valley

90

Tacoma

Shelton

Buckley

410

Aberdeen

Montesano

8

Olympia

Mt. Ranier National Park

5

Elbe

12

Ashford

South Bend

Chehalis

Nahcotta

101

Morton

Ocean Park

12

Long Beach

Naselle

Seaview

4

Ilwaco

Cathlamet

Gifford Pinchot National Forest

Yak Ind Re

Astoria

Columbia River

Kelso

Glenv

PACIFIC OCEAN

Trout Lake

White Salmon

Vancouver

14

84

Portland

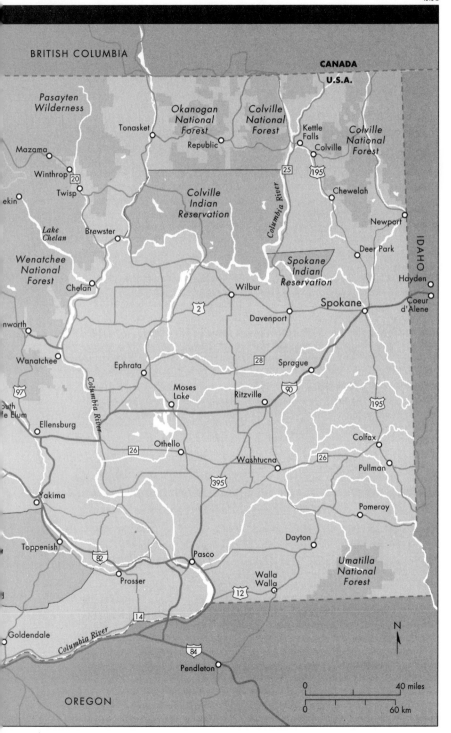

Columbia River and Long Beach Peninsula

The Columbia River Valley and Long Beach Peninsula offer a variety of outdoor experiences. Scenery in the valley is striking, with a deep gorge cutting through forested hills and rugged cliffs. Further west, visitors flock to the peninsula for its sandy beaches, ocean swells, and migrating birds. The peninsula's reputation for fine cuisine is another big drawing card. Both areas offer many opportunities for hiking and nature walks.

The mighty Columbia River, which forms much of the Washington–Oregon border, has a rich geological, cultural, and natural history. Its bounty of salmon once fed many native tribes and later supported a thriving fishing industry. Today, in addition to providing electrical power to much of the Northwest and the West Coast, the river provides water-sports enthusiasts with one of the world's prime boardsailing sites—with winds reaching 30 miles an hour or more, the 70 miles of coast from Bingen to Roosevelt draws more than 200,000 Windsurfers annually.

An 80-mile stretch of Highway 14 traces the wild and scenic river where it slices through a canyon between walls of basalt, designated as the Columbia River Gorge National Scenic Area. The only sea-level cut through the Cascade Mountains, the gorge divides areas of very diverse climates: The wetter western portions get up to 80 inches of rain each year, while the high-desert area on the east may get as little as 20 inches.

Just north of the mouth of the Columbia, in the southwest corner of the state, is the Long Beach Peninsula, with a chain of small fishing villages and the longest uninterrupted stretch (28 miles) of sandy ocean beach in North America. The area offers good hiking and beachcombing, but because of tremendous undertows and shifting sands, this is not a very safe place for swimming, and there are several drownings each year. Driving on the beach is still a hotly disputed issue among residents, but in 1990 the state legislature closed about 40% of it to motor vehicles from April through Labor Day. A new half-mile-long wooden boardwalk in Long Beach features disabled-access ramps, benches, telescopes, and great views, but no vendors. The entire peninsula is a perfect place to enjoy a winter storm, with howling winds and huge breakers crashing on the beach.

A favorite pastime in the area is bird-watching. Migrating white trumpeter swans frequent marshes a mile or two inland, and on Long Island—an islet on the bay side of the peninsula that is home to an old-growth red cedar grove—are found the highly controversial spotted owl and the marbled murrelet.

Places to Go, Sights to See

Columbia River Area

Bingen. Named for Bingen-on-the-Rhine, the town preserves three historic homes, including that of its founder: the *Theodore Suksdorf House* (412 W. Jefferson St.), built in 1905. The area's first white settler, Erastus Joslyn, arrived in 1852 and built his home and farm close to the Columbia River, just west of the present town of Bingen. The home was destroyed in a conflict with Native Americans, but Joslyn eventually built another one, Steuben Street's Joslyn House, renamed the *Grand Old House* for its Victorian architecture. On Lincoln Street is the *Wilhelm Suksdorf House*, built in 1905 for a renowned botanist who named many native plant species. Tours are offered at the *Mont Elise Winery* (315 W. Steuben St., tel. 509/493–3001), one of the oldest family-owned wineries in Washington. The 1911 Methodist Church, at the corner of Steuben and Maple streets, is now the *Gorge Heritage Museum* (tel. 509/493–3228).

Cascade Locks. Before the dams were built on the Columbia River, locks were needed to allow river traffic to bypass the Columbia's dangerous rapids. At the *Cascade Locks Historical Museum* (tel. 503/374–8535), visitors can view the now obsolete locks, a steam locomotive, and other historical artifacts. At Cascade Locks, visitors can board the sternwheeler *Columbia Gorge* (tel. 503/223–3928 or 503/374–8427), where a spirited narrator relates tales of the past to the rhythm of the giant paddle wheel. Day trips, dining cruises, and special excursions are offered.

Cathlamet. The name of this river town—about an hour west of I–5, and the seat of Wahkiakum ("wa-KI-a-kum") County—comes from a Chinook word meaning "stone," so named because the tribe lived here along a stretch of rocky riverbed. Today visitors will find a pleasant marina, some 19th-century houses perched on the hill overlooking the river, and the *Wahkiakum County Historical Museum* (65 River St., no phone). From Cathlamet, one can take a bridge or a ferry—*The Wahkiakum* is the only ferry remaining on the lower Columbia—to *Puget Island.* Settled in 1884 by Scandinavians who brought herds of dairy cattle and built large barns and dikes on the low-lying island, it is popular with bicyclists for its pleasing views of boat moorages, gill-netting boats, dairy farms, and historic churches. About a mile and a half west of Cathlamet on Route 1 is the *Julia Butler Hansen National Wildlife Refuge* (tel. 206/795–3915), named for a woman who served in the U.S. House of Representatives from 1960 to 1975. In addition to protecting the endangered Columbian white-tailed deer, a small deer of the Northwest, the refuge is a wintering area for waterfowl on the Pacific flyway, and home to bald eagles, great blue herons, swans, and herds of elk.

Goldendale. The *Presby Mansion* (127 W. Broadway, tel. 509/773–4303 or 509/773–5443) was built in 1902 for Winthrop Bartlett Presby, a lawyer who migrated from New Hampshire in 1888 and eventually served four years as a Washington state senator. His 20-room mansion is now a museum that illustrates pioneer life in Klickitat County and displays Native American artifacts and a collection of coffee grinders. On the northern edge of the town, the *Goldendale Observatory* (1602 Observatory Dr., tel. 509/773–3141) offers interpretive presentations concerning stars and telescopes, as well as tours and other programs; visitors are welcome to use its 24.5-inch Cassergrain reflecting telescope.

Maryhill Museum of Art (35 Maryhill Museum Dr., Goldendale, tel. 509/773–3733). Built as a "ranch house" in 1914 and resembling a European château, the museum—opened in 1940—was a collaboration among Sam Hill, an important figure with the Great Northern Railway, his friend Loie Fuller, a pioneer of modern dance who found fame in Paris during the 1890s, and Queen Marie of Romania (Sam did war relief work in Romania after WWI; indebted, the Queen came to Washington for the dedication). It includes one of the country's largest collections of Rodin sculpture; a large collection of Native American baskets, clothing, and photographs; and royal costumes and furniture from the late queen. Nearby is Sam Hill's memorial to soldiers who died in World War I, a replica of Britain's Stonehenge.

Mt. Adams (ranger station, Trout Lake, tel. 509/395–2501). At 12,276 feet, Mt. Adams is the second-highest mountain in Washington, but in sheer bulk it is larger than Mt. Rainier. In the vicinity are ice caves, a self-guided-tour area formed by molten lava, and *Big Lava Bed*—12,500 acres of sculptural shapes and caves to be viewed from its edge.

Mt. Hood Scenic Railroad (110 Railroad Ave., Hood River, tel. 503/386–3556). Built in 1906, the train links the Columbia River Gorge with the foothills of snowcapped Mt. Hood, at 11,235 feet the highest peak in Oregon. The route offers views of the Cascades, including Mt. Hood and Mt. Adams.

Along the way, the train may pick up a carload of lumber or pears—it's still a working freight train.

Mt. St. Helens National Monument (Rte. 1, Amboy, tel. 206/247–5473). Devastated by a great volcanic eruption in 1980, Mt. St. Helens is today a national monument. Hiking trails lead up through regenerated evergreen forest to the mile-high crater, its lava dome, and Ape Cave, an extremely long lava tube (12,810 ft). Sporadic eruptions continue to spew steam and gases, giving lucky hikers a free show. There's a visitor center in *Castle Rock* (3029 Spirit Lake Hwy., tel. 206/274–6644).

Long Beach Peninsula

Cape Disappointment. This cape at the start of the peninsula got its name from English fur trader Captain John Meares because of his unsuccessful attempt in 1788 to find the Northwest Passage here. On the bluff is one of the oldest lighthouses on the West Coast, first used in 1856. Below the bluff is the *U.S. Coast Guard Station Cape Disappointment* (tel. 206/642–2384), the largest search-and-rescue station on the Northwest coast. The rough conditions of the Columbia River Bar provide intensive training for its *National Motor Lifeboat School,* the only school of its kind. Here, rescue crews from all over the world learn advanced skills in navigation, mechanics, fire fighting, and lifesaving. The observation platform on the north jetty at *Ft. Canby State Park* (tel. 206/642–3078)—site of an active military post until 1957—is a good viewing spot for watching the motor lifeboats during regular surf drills.

Ft. Columbia State Park and Interpretive Center (Hwy. 101, tel. 206/777–8221). Built in 1903, this fort was one of 27 coastal defense units of the U.S. Army. Many of its 30 structures have been restored to show military life. The park is just 2 miles east of Chinook, a town named for the Native Americans who assisted Lewis and Clark—credited with "discovering" the peninsula—during their stay here in the early 1800s.

Ilwaco. This community of about 600 has a colorful past linked to the fishing industry: From 1884 to 1910, gill-net and trap fishermen were so sensitive about rights to the fishing grounds that they fought each other with knives, rifles, and threats of lynchings. Since then fishermen have developed more amicable relationships, and today charters are available for salmon, crab, tuna, and sturgeon fishing. The *Ilwaco Heritage Museum* (115 S.E. Lake St., tel. 206/642–3446) presents the history of southwestern Washington through such exhibits as dioramas on Native Americans, traders, missionaries, and pioneers. It also contains a model of the "clamshell railroad," a narrow-gauge train that ran on a bed of ground clam and oyster shells to transport passengers and mail up and down the peninsula.

Leadbetter State Park (call Ft. Canby State Park for information; *see* above). At the northern end of the peninsula, this wildlife refuge is a good spot for bird-watching. The dune area at the point is closed from April to August to protect nesting snowy plovers. Biologists have identified some 100 species here, including black brants, yellowlegs, turnstones, and sanderlings.

Long Beach. Go-cart and bumper-car concessions, an amusement park, and beach activities attract tourists to this town of 1,200, which each year hosts the Washington State International Kite Festival the third weekend in August. Other peninsula festivals include the Garlic Festival, a tasty tribute to that pungent bulb, held in mid-June; and the Water Music Festival, featuring chamber music at various locations the third weekend in October.

Oysterville. This tiny community once thrived on the oyster industry but nearly turned into a ghost town when the native shellfish were fished to extinction. Tides have washed away homes and businesses, but a handful of late-19th-century structures still exist. Free maps inside the restored Oysterville Church direct you through the one-street village, now on the National Register of Historic Places.

Restaurants

Mio Amore Pensione (Trout Lake, tel. 509/395-2264) serves Northern Italian dinners nightly by reservation only. **The Ark Restaurant & Bakery** (on Willapa Bay, Nahcotta, tel. 206/665-4133) was praised by the late James Beard for its fresh local seafood. The **Shoalwater Restaurant** at the Shelburne Inn (Seaview, tel. 206/642-4142) serves nationally acclaimed Northwest cuisine—lots of seafood and local produce like edible ferns— vegetarian options, and a children's menu. The **Sanctuary** (Chinook, tel. 206/777-8380), set in a former church, serves a varied menu, including decadent desserts.

Tourist Information

Klickitat County Tourism Committee (Box 1220, Goldendale, WA 98620, tel. 509/773-4395); **Long Beach Peninsula Visitors Bureau** (Box 562, Long Beach, WA 98631, tel. 206/642-2400 or 800/451-2542).

Reservation Services

Pacific Bed & Breakfast Agency (701 N.W. 60th St., Seattle, WA 98107, tel. 206/784-0539). **Travelers Bed & Breakfast** (Box 492, Mercer Island, WA 98040, tel. 206/232-2345). **Washington State Bed & Breakfast Guild** (2442 N.W. Market St., Seattle, WA 98107, tel. 509/548-7171).

Mio Amore
Pensione

About 20 miles north of the Columbia River in the Mt. Adams wilderness, just outside the logger/cowboy town of Trout Lake, is Mio Amore Pensione, known to locals as "that fancy place." It is owned since 1986 by Tom and Jill Westbrook, both retail executives. A vacation to the Trout Lake area convinced them to chuck their life in southern California and become innkeepers.

The 1904 Victorian-style farmhouse —the second house built on the 6-acre property, which was homesteaded in 1883—faces the creek, with expansive decks and creeping phlox–covered terraces stretching down to the river, the hot tub, and an old icehouse. Tom and Jill have renovated the inside of the house, exposing the ceiling beams and decorating it with a combination of contemporary and antique furniture and what will seem to some a heavy dose of memorabilia (including a beer stein collection) from their travels and Tom's service years. The living room is elegant, with Rococo Revival sofa and chairs and a fireplace of Mt. Adams volcanic rock. The dining room has a large sideboard where the evening's dessert usually sits late in the afternoon to tempt you, and a mirrored wall that prompts guests to dive for a spot where they won't have to stare into the mirror during dinner.

The main house has three guest rooms, all with pastoral views. The Venus Room is really a suite, with lilac carpeting, a brass and white-painted-iron queen bed with a white quilt and eyelet flounce, and white-painted armoire. Its sitting room, furnished in white wicker, offers views of the deck, gardens, and creek, and the large bath features a claw-foot tub. Outside is the 1890s icehouse, called the Vesta, a cozy and more rustic room with a wood-burning stove and a loft.

The Westbrooks go out of their way to make your stay memorable. Almost every night Tom cooks a four-course, Northern Italian gourmet dinner, open to guests and the public by reservation only. (While in the service, Tom was "adopted" into a restaurant family in Pisa, Italy.)

Breakfast includes an entrée—such as quiche, soufflé, or veal sausage with potatoes—and up to eight kinds of fresh-baked breads and pastries. Tom will even pack you a goodie bag of leftover cakes and breads.

Address: *53 Little Mountain Rd., Box 208, Trout Lake, WA 98650, tel. 509/395-2264.*
Accommodations: *2 double rooms share bath, 1 suite, 1 cottage.*
Amenities: *Restaurant, gift shop, hot tub.*
Rates: *$60–$135; full breakfast. MC, V.*
Restrictions: *Smoking outside only, pets only with prior permission.*

Shelburne Inn

Sitting along the peninsula's main thoroughfare, behind a white picket fence enclosing rose and other gardens, is a green wood-frame building that is the oldest continuously run hotel in the state. Opened in 1896, the Craftsman-style inn joined to a late Victorian building is owned by Laurie Anderson and David Campiche. David was a professional potter and antiques dealer. He met Laurie—who had worked for a cruise line and traveled widely before settling here—when he helped pull her vehicle out of the sand.

The inn has a homey, country atmosphere. The lobby is somewhat cramped, with a seating area around a fireplace, a church altar as a check-in desk, a large oak breakfast table, and more. The original beaded-fir paneling, as well as large panels of Art Nouveau stained glass rescued from an old church in England, are found throughout the inn. A new section, built in 1983, is quieter than the older sections, though the latter have been soundproofed and carpeted.

Fresh flowers, original artwork, and fine art prints adorn the guest rooms, most of which have decks or balconies. Some rooms feature country pine furnishings, others mahogany or oak. Beds have either handmade quilts or hand-crocheted spreads. Some rooms are rather small, but the suites are spacious.

Suite No. 13, in rose and cream, features large stained-glass panels between the bedroom, highlighted by a brass bed and a richly carved oak armoire, and the sitting room, furnished with natural wicker and an Arts and Crafts secretary. The large bathroom includes a roomy tub with gold-plated ball-and-claw feet.

The Shelburne's breakfast is one of the top three, if not *the* best, in the state. David makes use of regional produce from wild mushrooms to local seafood, and Laurie does all the baking. Guests choose from among five or six entrées, which may include an asparagus omelet or grilled oysters with salsa.

The highly regarded Shoalwater Restaurant, housed in the enclosed front porch, is owned by Tony and Ann Kirshner and offers such elegant entrées as quail with a rosemary, port, and walnut cream sauce. The Heron and Beaver Pub serves light meals, along with the best of Washington's microbreweries.

Address: *4415 Pacific Way, Box 250, Seaview, WA 98644, tel. 206/642–2442, fax 206/642–8904.*
Accommodations: *13 double rooms with baths, 2 suites.*
Amenities: *Restaurant, pub.*
Rates: *$85–$155; full breakfast. AE, MC, V.*
Restrictions: *Smoking outside only, no pets; 2-night minimum on weekends and holidays.*

Sou'wester Lodge

J ust behind the sand dunes on the peninsula is this red-shingled, three-story inn. Make no mistake about it: The Sou'wester is not for everyone. Perhaps more than any other B&B in the state, it is an experience weighted as much by the unique character of the inn-keepers as it is by the setting, a big old lodge built in 1892 as the country estate of Senator Henry Winslow Corbett of Oregon.

Len and Miriam Atkins left their native South Africa in the early 1950s to work in Israel, then moved to Chicago to work with the late child psychologist Bruno Bettelheim. With the idea of establishing a treatment program on the West Coast for emotionally disturbed children, in 1981 they launched a six-month exploration in their camper scouting sites. Instead, they opted to help adults unwind from the stresses of daily life. Most guests are artists, writers, poets, musicians, professionals, and academics, a natural audience for the inn-hosted chamber music concerts, plays, presentations by poets and artists, and other special events.

The lodge is strewn with the acquisitions of a lifetime of world travels, including a hand-carved parlor set inlaid with mother-of-pearl from the Middle East. This is one of several sitting areas in the living room, which features a large fireplace, tongue-in-groove fir paneling, massive-beam ceiling, and Persian rugs.

An unusual aspect of the Sou'wester is that it bills itself not as a B&B but as a B&MYODB (make your own darn breakfast), with kitchen access provided (but not food). Second- and third-story accommodations are suites with full kitchens and views of the Pacific. Guest rooms are furnished with the occasional antique but more often Salvation Army furniture, with marbleized linoleum floors; nicer touches are the handmade quilts or chenille bedspreads and artwork done by various artists while staying in that room.

Another slightly offbeat note that adds to the Sou'wester's charm is the collection of guest cabins and trailers scattered among the firs. The cabins are a bit more rustic than guest rooms. Trailers feature handsome blond-wood interiors with lots of 1950s rounded corners. The Disoriented Express features an exterior mural of a train full of animal passengers.

Address: *Beach Access Rd., Box 102, Seaview, WA 98644, tel. 206/642–2542.*
Accommodations: *3 double rooms share bath; 6 suites, 4 cabins, 9 trailers, all with kitchens.*
Amenities: *Cable/TV available upon request in some units.*
Rates: *$33–$96; no breakfast. MC, V.*
Restrictions: *Smoking outside only, pets in outdoor units only.*

Coast Watch Bed & Breakfast

When Karen Johnston came to the peninsula for a weekend one spring, she saw this contemporary style oceanfront house for sale. Partway home to Bellingham, she turned around, returned to the peninsula, signed an agreement to buy the weathered-shingle house, then rushed back home just in time for work.

Each of the two airy guest suites has a private entry and living room. Both are decorated with contemporary furnishings in earth tones and have views of the Pacific Ocean, the dunes, and the beach. One suite includes a rattan dining room set and rocker and a print by local artist Eric Wiegardt; a fishing net hangs on the wall over the bed.

Karen provides a full fruit basket in each suite and a minifridge to chill guests' wine bottles. Breakfast includes *latte* (café au lait), deadly-to-your-waistline cinnamon rolls served under glass domes, and individual platters of up to eight kinds of fresh fruit. "I start in Ocean Park and I may end up driving as far as Astoria, which is 40 miles from here, to get the fruit I want," says Karen.

Address: *Box 841, Ocean Park, WA 98640, tel. 206/665-6774.*
Accommodations: *2 suites.*
Amenities: *Phones upon request, kites.*
Rates: *$85; Continental breakfast. MC, V.*
Restrictions: *Smoking outside only, no pets.*

Country Keeper Bed & Breakfast Inn

Perched on a hill in Cathlamet overlooking the Columbia River is this Eastlake-style house built in 1907. Real estate appraiser Tony West and his wife, Barbara, a teacher, bought the place in 1991 after seeking a change from their San Francisco Bay Area jobs.

Never remodeled, it retains the original oak floors inlaid with mahogany, and the Douglas fir staircase off the foyer. The living room features built-in bookcases, an overstuffed pink velvet sofa and chair, a pink Oriental rug from the 1930s, and the same Morris chair shown in a 1910 photo of the room.

Each guest room features comfortable, grandma's-attic-type furniture. The Monet Room is decorated in pink and white, with white-painted furniture. The Rose Room features a king-size bed with floral canopy and spread, an Oriental rug, and a large bay window. These two front guest rooms overlook the river and the marina; the back rooms look down on gardens of rhododendrons and roses. A full breakfast includes muffins and a hot dish such as apple pancakes, soufflés, or French toast.

Address: *61 Main St., Cathlamet, WA 98612, tel. 206/795-3030 or 800/551-1691.*
Accommodations: *2 double rooms with baths, 2 double rooms share bath.*
Amenities: *Afternoon refreshments.*
Rates: *$60-$70; full breakfast. V,MC.*
Restrictions: *Smoking outside only, no pets. Closed Christmas Day.*

Flying L Ranch

About 30 miles north of the Columbia, nestled in the ponderosa pines and meadows of the Glenwood Valley, is the Flying L Ranch, with spectacular views of Mt. Adams, 115 miles away. Twins Darvel (a former college instructor/administrator) and Darryl (still a ship's captain) run the 160-acre ranch where they grew up.

The look of the interior is Western ranch–style rustic, with well-worn and mismatched but comfortable furniture. The large common area has wood paneling, a beamed ceiling, Navajo rugs, a stone fireplace whose log mantel is emblazoned with the Flying L brand, and Western art. The simply furnished, almost austere guest rooms feature firm beds with comforters.

Guests can rent bikes to explore the area, or they can stroll the ranch's more than 2 miles of marked trails, pond, and picnic areas where lupine, Indian paintbrush, and other wildflowers grow. Three-night summer packages include escorted day hikes on Mt. Adams, naturalist programs, and dinners at local restaurants.

Address: *25 Flying L La., Glenwood, WA 98619, tel. 509/364–3488.*
Accommodations: *9 double rooms with baths, 4 doubles share bath, 2 housekeeping cabins.*
Amenities: *Bikes, hot tub.*
Rates: *$45–$70; full breakfast. AE, DC, MC, V.*
Restrictions: *Smoking outside only, no pets in lodge.*

Gallery Bed & Breakfast at Little Cape Horn

Along a winding country road in Cathlamet, overlooking a sandy walking beach on the Columbia River, is this contemporary Northwest-style building. Owner Carolyn Feasey opened an art and crafts gallery in 1973 in town, later moving it to the home she shares with her husband, Eric, a forestry engineer.

The interior is open and spacious, with lots of redwood, cedar, and glass. It is decorated in contemporary style with the occasional antique. Large windows in the living room and dining room overlook a multilevel redwood deck and the river.

Guest rooms are small but attractive, with comfortable beds, cozy down comforters, and terry robes. One room has a telescope and deck, where feeders attract hummingbirds. The elegant whirlpool in this room's bath is shared with occupants of an adjoining room and bath, so it's not always private. Another room features pieces of Carolyn's mother's English china and a 1783 survey map.

Address: *4 Little Cape Horn, Cathlamet, WA 98612, tel. 206/425–7395.*
Accommodations: *4 double rooms with baths.*
Amenities: *Outdoor hot tub.*
Rates: *$60–$70; Continental or full breakfast. No credit cards.*
Restrictions: *Smoking outside only.*

Gumm's Bed & Breakfast

Six blocks from the ocean, on an immaculately kept lawn off the peninsula's main highway between Ilwaco and Long Beach, sits Gumm's, a yellow Craftsman house built in 1911. Owner Esther Slack ("Gumm" to her first grandson) welcomes children and has a lot of toys to amuse them, such as a collection of teddy bears and a train "for dads to play with." Still, she manages to keep the nicely decorated house neat and spotless.

The common areas include a spacious living room with beamed ceilings, a river-rock fireplace, an upright piano, two child-size rockers, and a blue-gray sofa and loveseat set against raspberry carpeting. Each guest room is individually decorated: Barb's Room, for example, features

a high four-poster tobacco-and-rice bed with step stool, an Eastlake chest, and a mirrored armoire.

Esther enjoys telling stories about the house, especially of when it was a hospital, during the 1930s; the formal dining room is the old operating room.

Address: *3310 Highway 101, Box 447, Seaview, WA 98644, tel. 206/642-8887.*
Accommodations: *2 double rooms with baths; 2 double rooms share bath.*
Amenities: *Cable TV, hot tub, phones available on request.*
Rates: *$65–$75; full breakfast. MC, V.*
Restrictions: *Smoking outside only, no pets.*

Inn at Ilwaco

Perched on a knoll in the fishing village of Ilwaco, at the mouth of the Columbia River, is this inn, built in 1928 as a Presbyterian church. The Georgian-style building is faced in weathered shingles with white millwork trim. Innkeepers Judy and Dave Clements were last stationed in Guam setting up photography labs—Dave is a professional photographer.

The peach-and-white common area is spacious, with 10-foot ceilings, large windows, Oriental rugs, a pellet-burning stove, and eclectic furnishings, including a French Provincial sofa and chair upholstered in soft green. Guest rooms, occupying the former Sunday school on the second floor, are cozy, with country furnishings and fir floors with throw rugs.

Some—like room 6, with a whitewashed pine armoire and Ralph Lauren fabrics accented by lace curtains—feature dormer windows with window seats, and some have the original board-and-bead wood paneling. The sanctuary remains in use as a wedding chapel, as well as a playhouse for regional productions. Breakfast includes such entrées as quiche or French toast with cream cheese and nuts, and topped with raspberry sauce.

Address: *120 Williams St., Ilwaco, WA 98, tel. 206/642-8686, fax 206/454-3481.*
Accommodations: *7 double rooms with bath, 2 doubles share bath.*
Rates: *$55–$75; full breakfast. MC, V.*
Restrictions: *No smoking, no pets.*

Inn at White Salmon

After 30 years, Roger Holen had had enough of the computer business, so in 1990 he and his wife, Janet, a nurse, became innkeepers. From the outside, their place is short on appeal: a plain brick hotel built in 1937 and set on the main street of the small river town of White Salmon. But don't let appearances deceive you: The interior has a lot more charm.

Highlights of the lobby include beveled glass and a large brass cash register on a marble-topped mahogany desk. The parlor features an 8-foot-tall oak sideboard from the 1890s and hand-painted lithographs. An off-note is struck by the dark hallways and '60s-style carpeting.

Each guest room features a few antiques, such as brass or ornate wood headboards. The bridal suite has a sitting area with a mahogany Eastlake settee upholstered in rose.

Breakfast is an extravaganza: some 20 pastries and breads, including a chocolate raspberry cheesecake, and six egg dishes.

Address: *172 W. Jewett St., White Salmon, WA 98672, tel. 509/493-2335.*
Accommodations: *18 double rooms with bath.*
Amenities: *Air-conditioning, TV, and phone in room; outdoor hot tub.*
Rates: *$79–$89; full breakfast. AE, D, DC, MC, V.*
Restrictions: *No smoking in common rooms, no pets in most rooms.*

Land's End

Isolated amid the sand dunes of the peninsula and facing the Pacific Ocean, Land's End is a large, contemporary, Northwest-style home of former teacher Jackie Faas. The living room is spacious, with a marble fireplace, a grand piano, Eastlake furnishings, Oriental carpets, and 6-foot-high windows framing panoramic ocean views.

On the ground floor are the two guest rooms, done up in country style. The larger room has an ornamental Dutch enamel cookstove; its bath features a large soaking tub with a dark wood surround. A framed antique quilt that may have been made in the 1850s during the ride west in an Oregon Trail wagon train is the focal point of the smaller bedroom.

Jackie prides herself on pampering her guests, stocking each room with fresh fruit, flowers, and candy. She even provides starter kits for beach fires. Breakfast—typically featuring baked apples in sherry, poached eggs over smoked salmon with a white wine sauce, and homemade muffins and jams—is served on silver and china.

Address: *Box 1199, Long Beach, WA 98361, tel. 206/642-8268.*
Accommodations: *2 double rooms with baths.*
Amenities: *Cable TV in room, phone on request.*
Rates: *$75–$85; full breakfast. MC, V.*
Restrictions: *Smoking outside only, no pets.*

Moby Dick Hotel and Oyster Farm

Set on 7 acres of forest on the bay side of the peninsula is this rather plain, boxy stucco structure built in 1930 by a railroad conductor who had struck it rich mining gold in Alaska. The interior, which is fun and campy, is more interesting. The spacious dining room is done in Southwest colors, with several tables for four. Two large living rooms offer guests a fireplace, a telescope, and an upright piano; a skylit upstairs common area features Andy Warhol's *Endangered Species* prints.

Guest rooms are simply furnished; each is provided with a copy of *Moby-Dick* or another Herman Melville classic, along with an artwork or a bedspread that reflects the room's theme, such as a mended heart, birds, or the sea.

The inn's owners, Fritzi and Edward Cohen, also own the Tabbard, a well-known "literary" hotel in Washington, D.C. Breakfasts may include fruit cobbler, homemade shortbread and whipped cream, biscuits, and zucchini bread; and such entrées as scrambled eggs with hot-pepper cheese or fried smelts.

Address: *Sandridge R., Box 82, Nahcotta, WA 98637, tel. 206/665–4543, fax 206/665–6887.*
Accommodations: *10 double rooms share 5 baths.*
Amenities: *Hot tub and sauna under construction.*
Rates: *$60; full breakfast. MC, V.*
Restrictions: *Smoking outside only, pets outdoors only, 2-night minimum on weekends June–Aug.*

Orchard Hill Inn

About 10 miles north of White Salmon, this 1974 Dutch Colonial sits amid fields, vineyards, apple and pear orchards, and a forest, with paths leading down to the White Salmon River.

James and Pamela Tindall opened their B&B in 1985 after three years in Germany. Now Jim teaches high school English and history and Pam runs drug and alcohol programs while caring for their 6-year-old son, Zachary. Without their own private apartment, the Tindalls share the common rooms with guests. The style is casual and comfortable. The three guest rooms are furnished eclectically. The Caldwell Room has a double bed with spindle headboard and a twin four-poster and dresser that once belonged to Jim's grand-

mother. Both beds have hand-stitched quilts.

A German-style breakfast, served in the country-style dining room, includes a variety of cheeses and yogurts, local fresh fruit, bagels, gingerbread or huckleberry-bran muffins, and Pam's homemade jams.

Address: *199 Oak Ridge Rd., White Salmon, WA 98672, tel. 509/493–3024.*
Accommodations: *3 double rooms share 2 baths, 1 bunkhouse for groups.*
Amenities: *Phones on request.*
Rates: *$43–$53; Continental breakfast. MC, V.*
Restrictions: *Smoking outside only, no pets.*

Olympic Peninsula

*Rugged, remote, and densely forested, the Olympic
Peninsula, at the northwest corner of the state, is
dominated by the mountains that rise up out of it and the
water that surrounds it. To the west, the Pacific Ocean
rages wild. The Strait of Juan de Fuca lies to the north,
and the Hood Canal, an 80-mile-long natural inlet to Puget
Sound, borders the peninsula on the east. Just a bit inland,
and visible from more than a hundred miles away, are the
snowcapped Olympic Mountains.*

*These mountains trap incoming clouds, creating the rain
forests of the Olympic National Park to the west and a dry
"rain shadow" to the east. As a result, the peninsula has
both the wettest and the driest climates on the Pacific
Northwest coast.*

*Most of the peninsula is accessible only to backpackers, but
Highway 101, in a 300-mile loop, offers glimpses of some of
the best features. Along the ocean side of the peninsula,
visitors can hike, clam, beachcomb, collect driftwood, watch
tide-pools, and fly kites. Olympic National Park preserves
nearly a million acres of mountains, old-growth forest, and
wilderness coast in their natural states. Mountain hikes
are popular, especially around Hurricane Ridge, just south
of Port Angeles. Fishing is a major activity throughout the
peninsula. Anglers pull in trout and salmon from the
rivers; charter boats out of Neah Bay take halibut and
salmon, while others ply the Aberdeen and Hoquiam area
for bottomfish and salmon.*

*A good perch for launching Olympic Peninsula excursions
is Port Townsend, on Puget Sound. Here, in this little town
of 6,800, a number of exquisite Victorian homes built by
sea captains, bankers, and business people have been
turned into inviting bed-and-breakfasts.*

Places to Go, Sights to See

Hurricane Ridge. South of Port Angeles on Route 101 and nearly a mile above sea level is Hurricane Ridge, with spectacular views of the Olympic Mountains, the Strait of Juan de Fuca, and Vancouver Island. Despite the steep grade, the road is easily traveled. A small visitor center offers interpretive talks, ranger-led walks, and a museum, and leading off from the center are nature trails and miles of cross-country skiing trails.

Neah Bay. The waters of Neah Bay offer fishermen and -women an abundance of king and silver salmon, while its beaches yield treasures of driftwood, fossils, and agate. Trails lead along the shore and through surrounding deep forests to Capa Alava, an important archeological discovery. More than 55,000 artifacts were taken from this unearthed ancient Makah village (now covered back up, leaving nothing to see). Many are on display at the *Makah Museum* (Hwy. 112, Neah Bay 98357, tel. 206/645–2711), where the life of the tribe is documented through relics, dioramas, and reproductions.

Olympic National Park. An information center operated by the U.S. Forest Service is located along Quinault Lake on the South Shore Road. At the road's end is the trailhead to the Enchanted Valley, whose many waterfalls make it one of the peninsula's most popular hiking areas. The Hoh Rain Forest, with an average annual rainfall of 145 inches and a salmon-rich river, is a complex ecosystem of conifers, hardwoods, grasses, mosses, and other flora that shelter such wildlife as elk, otter, beaver, and flying squirrels. Nature trails lead off from the Hoh Visitor Center, at the campground and ranger center, which houses a museum and offers information. There are eight other ranger stations, each with its own visitor center, scattered throughout the park; check at the stations about periodic road washouts. Port Angeles Visitors Center, located just outside the park, is the main one (600 E. Park Ave., tel. 206/452–0330).

Port Gamble. This New England–style waterfront town circa 1853 has been designated a National Historic Site as one of the few company-owned towns left in the U.S. Along with the oldest continuously operating lumber mill in North America, visitors to this town south of Port Townsend will find an 1870 church; the *Of Sea and Shore Museum* (Rainier Ave., tel. 206/297–2426), with fishing and natural history artifacts; and a town historical museum in the General Store.

Port Townsend. This waterfront town with carefully restored Victorian brick buildings was first settled in 1851, becoming a major lumber port in the late 19th century. Several of the grand Victorian Gingerbread homes built on the bluff during these prosperous years overlook downtown and Puget Sound. Today Port Townsend is home to a flourishing community of artists, writers, and musicians. The restored buildings of *Fort Worden* (tel. 206/385–4730), a former Navy base that is a National Historic Landmark, include officers' homes, barracks, a theater, and parade grounds. The *Centrum Foundation* (tel. 206/385–3102), an arts organization based at the fort, presents workshops and performances throughout the summer. A jazz festival is held each July.

Poulsbo. Technically on Puget Sound's Kitsap Peninsula, but considered part of the larger Olympic Peninsula, Poulsbo was once a small Nordic fishing village. Although tourists now outnumber fisher folk, there are many reminders of its heritage, including murals on sides of buildings depicting Scandinavian life; flower-filled window boxes; rosemaling on shutters and signs; and the *Sluys Bakery* (18924 Front St., tel. 206/779–2798), known for its Scandinavian delicacies and nationally distributed whole-grain Poulsbo Bread.

Quilcene. Famous for its Canterbury oysters and the largest oyster hatchery in the world, Quilcene is about 15 miles south of Port Townsend on Highway 101. It's also the site of a fish hatchery and a ranger station for the Olympic National Park.

Sequim and Dungeness. A wide variety of animal life can be found in Sequim (pronounced "skwim") and the fertile plain at the mouth of the Dungeness (pronounced "dun-ja-*ness"*) River. *Dungeness Spit*, part of the *Dungeness National Wildlife Refuge* (tel. 206/457–8451) and one of the longest natural spits in the world, is home to abundant migratory waterfowl as well as to clams, oysters, and seals. The small *Sequim–Dungeness Museum* (175 W. Cedar St., tel. 206/683–8110) displays mastodon remains discovered nearby in 1977 as well as exhibits on Captain George Vancouver, a late-18th-century English explorer of the Pacific coast, and the early Klallam Indians. *Sequim Natural History Museum* (503 N. Sequim Ave., tel. 206/683–8364) features exhibits on more than 80 varieties of birds and wildlife on the Olympic Peninsula. Dioramas show stuffed creatures in their natural habitats—saltwater beaches, marshes, and forest.

Restaurants

Port Townsend offers a number of good eating places. The **Fountain Cafe** (tel. 206/385–1364) specializes in seafood and pasta. **Lanza's Ristorante & Pizzeria** (tel. 206/385–6221) features tantalizing pasta and Continental dishes and live entertainment in a restored 19th-century brick building. The **Restaurant at Manresa Castle** (tel. 206/385–5750) offers elegant regional cuisine and fabulous Sunday brunches.

Tourist Information

Olympic Peninsula Tourism Council (Box 303, Port Angeles 98368, tel. 206/479–3594).

Reservation Services

Pacific Bed & Breakfast Agency (701 N.W. 60th St., Seattle 98107, tel. 206/784–0539); **Travelers Bed & Breakfast** (Box 492, Mercer Island 98040, tel. 206/232–2345); **Washington State Bed & Breakfast Guild** (2442 N.W. Market St., Seattle 98107, tel. 509/548–7171).

James House

High atop a bluff, with sweeping views of Port Townsend's waterfront, the Cascade and Olympic mountains, and Puget Sound, is the 1889 James House.

The gray woodframe Queen Anne house, with gables, dormers, porches, and five redbrick chimneys, is the grandest of all Port Townsend's Victorian accommodations—save for shared baths—and is in immaculate condition. In an era when a large house could be built for $4,000, this one, with 8,000 square feet of living space, cost $10,000.

An atmosphere of elegance and contemplation pervades. The entrance hallway, dominated by a hand-carved cherry staircase made from logs that came around Cape Horn, is a monument to fine woodworking. Like the two front parlors—the perfect setting for reading or listening to music on the vintage gramophone or the Regina music box—the hall features original parquet floors in elaborate patterns of oak, walnut, and cherry. Breakfast is served in the large dining room or in the homey kitchen by the Great Majestic cook stove.

Years of restoration work preceded the house's 1973 opening as one of the first Northwest bed-and-breakfasts. It is furnished with period antiques (some original to the house), Oriental rugs, an antique player piano, and many beveled- and stained-glass windows. Four of the

house's nine original fireplaces remain, with carved mantels and Minton tile framing.

Guest rooms are on three floors of the house and in the cottage out back. The house's master or bridal suite offers unsurpassed views, its own balcony, a sitting parlor, a fireplace, a private bath, and the original late Victorian bed, armoire, and fainting couch. The cottage, which sleeps four, has lots of windows and a more contemporary feel.

Innkeepers Carol McGough and Anne Tiernan, both health care professionals, moved here from Boston in 1990. They enjoy tending the roses, daisies, geraniums, herbs, and other plants that spill out of the James House's gardens, as well as making potpourris for their guests from the blooms. Breakfast includes fruit, scones or muffins, and soufflés or quiches, all made from fresh ingredients.

Address: *1238 Washington St., Port Townsend, WA, tel. 206/385–1238.*
Accommodations: *8 double rooms share 4 baths, 3 suites, 1 cottage.*
Amenities: *Fireplace in 2 rooms; parlor stove in 1 room; TV in rooms.*
Rates: *$60–$90, suites and cottage $80–$120; full breakfast. MC, V.*
Restrictions: *No smoking, no pets; 2-night minimum on holiday and festival weekends.*

Manor Farm Inn

On a country lane on the Kitsap Peninsula, surrounded by roses and a white picket fence, is an 1886 white clapboard house that is the centerpiece of a "gentleman's farm" where guests can experience country life—including sheep, pigs, roosters, chickens, guinea hens, and a pond full of trout—along with all the creature comforts.

When they bought the farm in 1975, British-born Robin Hughes, a one-time veterinarian in the Australian outback, and his wife, Jill, a special education teacher, planned to make it into a children's environmental camp, but they found the bureaucratic obstacles insurmountable. In 1984, after adding two wings to the house, they opened their farm to guests as a bed-and-breakfast inn.

The feeling they have created is one of comfort and casual elegance, highlighted by bounteous displays of fresh flowers. Guest rooms (most in the new wings) are spacious and airy, with white walls and ceilings setting off exposed beams. They are decorated with French and English pine armoires, chests, writing desks or tables, king beds with eiderdown comforters, carpeting in muted colors, and some tall white stucco fireplaces or wood-burning stoves. Amenities include welcoming homemade chocolates and fruit breads.

Dinner here is an experience, not just a meal. Guests gather for pre-dinner sherry and canapés in the drawing room, a pretty room with raspberry-colored sofas and wing chairs and a fireplace. Parties are then escorted to dinner in the two dining rooms, which feature high ceilings with rough-cut beams, pine cabinets, and Appalachian ladder-back chairs drawn up to elegantly set tables. Between courses, guests are encouraged to walk outside or to watch Robin prepares such sophisticated entrées as pheasant with leek and pecan stuffing or sea bass grilled over fennel branches. Jill's desserts range from crème caramel to wild huckleberry pie.

A crowing rooster often rouses guests in the morning. By 8 AM, a tray with scones, jam, and hand-squeezed orange juice is delivered to each guest's door. At 9, a country breakfast is served in the dining rooms, including fresh fruits, juices, eggs, bacon, sausage, kippers, Scotch porridge, maybe even a trout.

Address: *26069 Big Valley Rd. NE, Poulsbo, WA 98370, tel. 206/779–4628.*
Accommodations: *6 double rooms with bath, 2 double rooms share bath.*
Amenities: *Air-conditioning; restaurant; 24-hr room service; pool, outdoor hot tub; tennis; fly-fishing.*
Rates: *$100–$190, full breakfast; beach house $250. MC, V.*
Restrictions: *No smoking, no pets.*

Old Consulate Inn

Another of Port Townsend's Queen Anne Victorians—like the James House, situated on the bluff overlooking the water—this brick red beauty comes complete with conical turret, dormers, white wraparound porch with a touch of gingerbread trim, well-tended gardens, and lots of white Adirondack chairs for lounging. Also known as the F. W. Hastings House, the inn was built as a private home in 1889 by the son of the town's founder, and was the German consulate from 1908 to 1911.

It was a quirk of fate that brought the inn's present owners to innkeeping. Rob and Joanna Jackson had planned to celebrate their 25th anniversary with a large reception in their California home and a trip to Tahiti. Preparation for the event included refinishing their hardwood floors, but in the process, workmen set the house afire. The Jacksons changed their plans: They had a quiet dinner for 10, chucked the Tahiti trip, took a drive up Highway 101, and fell in love with Port Townsend and the Hastings House. Later that year, when they learned that the house was for sale, Rob gave up his contracting job and Joanna her post as corporate controller, and they became innkeepers.

The oak-paneled front parlor features its original chandelier, with large bunches of green glass grapes, and a fireplace framed in Italian tile.

A large sitting room is comfortable for reading and conversation, with a fireplace, Queen Anne sofas and chairs, a baby grand piano, a pump organ once owned by England's royal family, and a chinoiserie chest original to the house and inlaid with mother-of-pearl. A smaller anteroom off the dining room offers cable TV, a VCR, and lots of books. The doll, beer stein, and other collections displayed throughout the house can get a bit overwhelming.

Guest rooms on the second and third floors have a Victorian ambience, with floral wallpapers, custom-made comforters, dolls placed on bureaus, and a picture hat here and there on the walls. From the Tower Room there is a sweeping view of the bay. All suites have claw-foot tubs.

Joanna is one of the friendliest innkeepers and best cooks around. She presides over a sumptuous breakfast, made with only natural ingredients.

Address: *313 Walker St., Port Townsend, WA 98368, tel. 206/385–6753.*
Accommodations: *5 double rooms with bath, 3 suites.*
Amenities: *Air conditioning; afternoon refreshments, billiards.*
Rates: *$69–$155; full breakfast. MC, V.*
Restrictions: *Smoking outside only, no pets.*

Starrett House Inn

T his imposing Queen Anne in Port Townsend, painted in cream, teal, and two shades of green, was built by George Starrett, a contractor, mortician, and sawmill owner, in 1889 at a cost of $6,000 as a wedding present for his wife, Ann. It is now on the National Register of Historic Places.

Some guests may find the almost museum quality of the Starrett House off-putting, but hosts Bob and Edel Sokol are low-key and friendly. Bob is a retired Air Force pilot and was navigator on *Air Force One* for President Jimmy Carter. Edel, a native of Germany, is an avid collector and baker.

The foyer—with a front desk handcrafted in Port Townsend when Washington was a territory—opens to a dramatic free-hung, three-tiered spiral staircase of Honduran and African mahogany, English walnut, oak, and cherry. At the top is the eight-sided tower dome, frescoed by George Chapman with allegorical figures of the four seasons and the four virtues. The dome was designed as a solar calendar: Sunlight coming through small dormer windows on the first days of each new season shines onto a ruby glass, causing a red beam to point toward the appropriate seasonal panel.

Other ceiling frescoes are found in the adjacent dining room and parlor, whose decor is a paean to the period.

Elaborate moldings throughout the house feature carved lions, doves, and ferns. An absence of fireplaces told the Starretts' observant visitors that such antiquated heating devices had been eliminated by modern central heating.

The Master Suite looks like a museum period room. Once the Starretts' master bedroom, it features Persian rugs, a Brussels tapestry tablecloth, an 1880 mahogany Eastlake bedroom suite, and a floral tapestry canopy that extends from the floor to the 12-foot ceiling. The Drawing Room has a little antique tin tub painted with cherubs, and an 1860 Renaissance Revival mahogany bed. The contemporary Gable Suite has a breathtaking third-floor view of Puget Sound and the Cascades, as well as a two-person hot tub.

Breakfast includes champagne, stuffed French toast, homemade muffins, and juice, and is served in the elegant dining room.

Address: *744 Clay St., Port Townsend, WA 98368, tel. 206/385-3205 or 800/321-0644.*
Accommodations: *8 double rooms with bath, 2 double rooms share bath, cottage.*
Amenities: *Hot tub in 1 room.*
Rates: *$68-$135; full breakfast. MC, V.*
Restrictions: *No smoking, no pets; 2-night minimum on holiday and festival weekends.*

Heritage House

This white-trimmed yellow Italianate mansion is another of Port Townsend's Victorian bed-and-breakfast inns now on the National Register of Historic Places. Owners Jim and Pat Broughton and Bob and Carolyn Ellis bought the house, once owned by a retired sea captain, in 1984 and restored it. Jim has made furniture refinishing into an art. In restoring the 1890 Kimball pump organ in the parlor—set with a five-piece Eastlake grouping—he handmade all 66 springs needed to set the 11 stops.

The Morning Glory Room features Victorian cottage furniture and a washstand hand-painted with floral bouquets and geometric designs. Highlights of the Lily Suite are a Dresden china floor lamp and a mahogany Empire-style bed.

Some guests may find the house's museum quality a bit stuffy, but certainly not the innkeepers' style. Guests are called to breakfast on an old firemen's horn. The meal might consist of quiche or pancakes and home-baked pastries.

Address: *305 Pierce St., Port Townsend, WA 98368, tel. 206/385–6800.*
Accommodations: *4 double rooms with bath, 2 double rooms share bath, 1 suite.*
Rates: *$55–$125; full breakfast. AE, MC, V.*
Restrictions: *Smoking outside only, no pets; 2-night minimum on holiday and festival weekends.*

Lake Crescent Lodge

When he inspected Olympic Peninsula, a candidate for a national park, Franklin Roosevelt stayed at this 1920 lodge on the shores of Lake Crescent, 20 miles west of Port Angeles. The building is today a part of the Olympic National Park.

In the lobby, originally known as the Singers Tavern, guests can relax in Arts and Crafts–style chairs and sofa before a huge stone fireplace. Accommodations include five guest rooms in the lodge with a shared hall bath, private-bath motel units, and 17 individual cottages (best bets are the four cottages with fireplaces, overlooking the lake). Not much attention has been paid to the room decor, which has a rather impersonal, motel feel. Guest rooms are paneled in red cedar and filled with nondescript contemporary pine and maple furniture. Most, however, have fine mountain and lake views.

The lakeside dining room features a selection of Northwest seafood and wines, and the gift shop offers Native American crafts.

Address: *HC 62, Box 11, Port Angeles, WA 98362, tel. 206/928–3211.*
Accommodations: *47 double rooms with bath, 5 double rooms in lodge share bath.*
Amenities: *Restaurant, lounge, gift shop; box lunches available; row-boat rentals.*
Rates: *$52–$89; breakfast extra. AE, D, DC, MC, V.*
Restrictions: *No pets without leash. Closed Oct. 29–Apr. 27.*

Lake Quinault Lodge

When this old-fashioned country resort in Olympic National Park was built, men hauled the lumber, brick, glass, and plumbing fixtures over 50 miles of dirt road. They completed the large cedar-shake structure above Lake Quinault at a cost of $90,000 —a very hefty sum in 1926.

The heart of the lodge is the large lobby, with Douglas fir beams, a massive brick fireplace, original wicker settees and chairs, large-burl coffee tables, Northwest art, Native American crafts, and cozy corners. Guest rooms here are small, simple, and rustic, with country furnishings, some antique.

The 36 spacious rooms in the Lakeside Wing—completed in 1990—are decorated with contemporary white wicker, a sofa, and a private balcony. The Fireplace Wing features large rooms with gas fireplaces. The eight-unit annex is quite rustic, used most often by fishermen and guests traveling with pets.

Address: *South Shore Rd., Box 7, Quinault, WA 98575, tel. 206/288–2571 or 800/562–6672, fax 800/288–2415.*
Accommodations: *89 double rooms with bath, 3 suites.*
Amenities: *Nonsmoking rooms; restaurant, gift shop; indoor pool and hot tub, sauna; pool tables; fishing, hiking, boat rentals.*
Rates: *$85–$105, suites $205; breakfast extra. AE, MC, V.*
Restrictions: *No smoking in dining rooms, pets in annex only.*

Lizzie's Victorian Bed & Breakfast

This Italianate Victorian in Port Townsend, built in 1887 by a tugboat captain and his wife, Lizzie, is owned by Bill Wickline, an optometrist, and his wife, Patti, a former interior designer. A woodworking hobbyist, Bill has built a replica of the inn in the backyard for their dog.

Lizzie's is furnished in Victorian style, with antiques in exotic woods and light Victorian-patterned wallpapers. Three cast-iron fireplaces handpainted to look like marble, *faux* wood graining on door panels, and the Parisian wallpaper in the front parlor are all original to the house. Guests are encouraged to use the two 19th-century grand pianos in the parlors. Upstairs, Lizzie's Room has a half-canopied queen mahogany bed, a bay window with sitting area, a fireplace, and a claw-foot tub.

Guests gather in the country kitchen, paneled in oak and knotty pine, for breakfast. A back porch with Adirondack chairs affords views of the pear, apple, cherry, and plum trees in the orchard.

Address: *731 Pierce St., Port Townsend, WA 98368, tel. 206/385–4168.*
Accommodations: *5 double rooms with bath, 3 double rooms share 2 baths.*
Amenities: *Access to health club.*
Rates: *$55–$98; full breakfast. D, MC, V.*
Restrictions: *No smoking, no pets; 2-night minimum on holiday and festival weekends.*

Ravenscroft Inn

A newcomer in Port Townsend accommodations, this dark red clapboard Charleston-style "single house"—with porches across the first and second floors and dormers on the third—was built in 1987.

Williamsburg blue, brick red, and ivory are the predominant colors at Ravenscroft Inn. The foyer leads to a comfortable library on one side and, on the other, to a "great room" with a fireplace, a grand piano, and small tables that face the open kitchen. Guest rooms feature a mix of country antiques and contemporary furnishings, including wicker; French doors that open onto balconies; fluffy comforters; and the occasional teddy bear.

The inn is owned by Leah Hammer, who for years was a manufacturer's rep for fine crystal and china; her father, Sam Turk; and John Ranney, a professional musician for 40 years. Breakfast includes homemade breads and jams, French toast or crêpes, fresh fruit, and juice, served on Leah's collection of china and crystal.

Address: *533 Quincy St., Port Townsend, WA 98368, tel. 206/385–2784, fax 206/385–6724.*
Accommodations: *8 double rooms with bath, 1 suite.*
Amenities: *Fireplace in 2 rooms.*
Rates: *$65–$100, suite $150; full breakfast. MC, V.*
Restrictions: *Smoking outside only, no pets; 2-night minimum on holiday and festival weekends.*

Tudor Inn

Set on a knoll on a quiet residential street of Port Angeles— near Hurricane Ridge and an hour from Olympic National Park— Tudor Inn is a half-timbered home surrounded by gardens of lilies, iris, lupine, columbine, and fuchsia. Built in 1910 by an English dentist, it was bought in 1983 by Texans Jane and Jerry Glass.

Guests can nestle in the sitting room on an antique Victorian Chesterfield sofa. Stained-glass windows from England, fireplaces, and hardwood floors with Oriental rugs adorn the common rooms. All guest rooms— including one with an antique brass bed and a Beaconsfield 1900 bureau—have been soundproofed and feature Roman shades that match the comforters. Several rooms

have views of the water and the mountains.

Breakfast specialties include stuffed sourdough French toast and pancakes, served with homemade fruit syrup, and smoked salmon made from Jerry's catches, accompanied by an egg dish.

Address: *1108 S. Oak St., Port Angeles, WA 98362, tel. 206/452–3138.*
Accommodations: *1 double room with bath, 4 double rooms share 2 baths.*
Amenities: *Cable TV and phone upon request.*
Rates: *$50–$85; full breakfast. MC, V.*
Restrictions: *Smoking outside only, no pets; 2-night minimum on summer weekends and holidays.*

Seattle and Environs

Wedged between Lake Washington on the east and Elliott Bay on the west, Seattle is a city of water, parks, and heady views of the Cascade and Olympic mountains. The city's damp reputation is well deserved. The winter drizzle (which also appears during the spring, summer, and fall) makes the city's extensive park system (designed by Frederick Law Olmsted, creator of New York City's Central Park) lush and green. The rain doesn't hamper people's enjoyment of the city's walking and bicycling paths, especially those at waterfront locations such as Lincoln Park in West Seattle, Myrtle Edwards Park in downtown, Greenlake, north of downtown, Discovery Park in Magnolia, and the Burke-Gilman Trail, along the shores of Lake Washington. Clouds, fog, and long winter nights have also helped to make the city a haven for moviegoers and book readers.

Although its economy was once devoted exclusively to aerospace, lumber, and fishing, Seattle is now a major seaport and a vital link in Pacific Rim trade; the evidence of internationalism is everywhere. This former cultural wasteland now has all the trappings of a full-blown big city, with ad agencies and artists' co-ops, symphonies and ballet companies. There's an innovative new convention center, a covered dome for professional sports, a world-renowned theater scene, an excellent opera company, and a strong music world.

Ever since a number of national publications "discovered" Seattle's sophisticated but comfortable lifestyle, housing prices have climbed, the population has grown (some half million within the city proper, another 2 million in the surrounding Puget Sound region), and jammed freeways are no longer strictly a rush-hour phenomenon. As the city grows, so do crime, drug abuse, homelessness, and poverty. Suburban growth is rampant. But Seattleites—a

diverse bunch, including Asians, Asian Americans,
Scandinavians, African Americans, Native Americans,
Hispanics, and other ethnic groups—are a strong political
group with a great love for their city and a commitment to
maintaining its reputation as one of the most livable cities
in the country.

Places to Go, Sights to See

Brew Pubs. Seattle has become a hotbed of microbrews (high-quality beers made for local distribution). Brew pubs are drinking establishments that are attached to actual breweries and serve a variety of food and nonalcoholic beverages. Some notable establishments include: the *Pacific Northwest Brewing Co.* (322 Occidental Ave. S, tel. 206/621–7002), *Trolleyman* (3400 Phinney Ave. N, tel. 206/548–8000), *Big Time Brewery* (4133 University Way NE, tel. 206/545–4509), *Noggins* (Westlake Mall, 400 Pine St., tel. 206/682–BREW; Brooklyn Sq., 4142 Brooklyn Ave. NE, tel. 206/632–ALES), and *Cooper's Northwest Alehouse* (8065 Lake City Way NE, tel. 206/522–2923). Perhaps the best way to tour the pubs without worrying about who's driving is to take a four-hour tour offered by *Northwest Brewery and Pub Tours* (4224 1st Ave. NE, tel. 206/547–1186), which includes free tastings and van transportation.

Festivals. The *Folklife Festival* is an annual Memorial Day weekend event, showcasing some of the region's best folk singers, bands, jugglers, and other entertainers at the Seattle Center. In late July and early August, there's *Seafair*, saluting Seattle's marine heritage with a parade in downtown and hydroplane races on Lake Washington near Seward Park. Labor Day weekend means *Bumbershoot*, four days of music that includes classical, blues, reggae, zydeco, and pop, at Seattle Center.

International District. Originally a haven for Chinese workers after they finished the Transcontinental Railroad, the "ID" is a 40-block area inhabited by Chinese, Filipinos, and other Asians. The district, which includes many Chinese, Japanese, and Korean restaurants, also houses herbalists, massage parlors, acupuncturists, and social clubs. *Uwajimaya* (519 6th Ave. S, tel. 206/624–6248), one of the largest Japanese stores on the West Coast, stocks china, gifts, fabrics, housewares, and a complete supermarket with an array of Asian foods. Also in this area is the *Nippon Kan Theater* (628 S. Washington St., tel. 206/467–6807), the site of many Asian and Asian-American performances. The *Wing Luke Museum* (4076 7th Ave. S, tel. 206/623–5124) emphasizes Oriental history and culture.

Museum of Flight (9404 E. Marginal Way S, tel. 206/764–5720). The Red Barn, the original Boeing airplane factory, houses an exhibit on the history of aviation, while the Great Gallery, a dramatic structure designed by Seattle architect Ibsen Nelson, contains 38 airplanes—suspended from the ceiling and on the ground—dating from 1916 to the present.

Pike Place Market (1st Ave. at Pike St., tel. 206/682–7453). A Seattle institution, the market began in 1907 when the city issued permits to farmers allowing them to sell produce from their wagons parked at Pike Place. Later stalls were allotted to the farmers on a daily basis. You can buy fresh seafood, which can be packed in dry ice for your flight home, produce, cheese, Northwest wines, bulk spices, tea, coffee, and even arts and crafts.

Pioneer Square. This old section of the city boasts cobblestone streets and restored brick buildings dating from the late 19th century. Start at *Pioneer Park* (Yesler Way and 1st Ave. S), the site of Seattle's original business district, where an ornate iron-and-glass pergola now stands. In 1889, a fire destroyed many of the wood-frame buildings in the area, but residents reclaimed them with fire-resistant brick and mortar. With the Klondike Gold Rush, this area became populated with saloons and brothels; businesses gradually moved north, and the old pioneering area deteriorated. Today Pioneer Square encompasses 18 blocks, the city's largest concentration of art galleries, restaurants, bars, and shops. *The Elliott Bay Book Company* (101 S. Main St., tel. 206/624–6600) hosts lectures and readings by authors of local and international acclaim. Close by is the *Kingdome* (201 S. King St., tel. 206/296–3111), a 660-foot-diameter covered stadium that is the home of the Seattle Seahawks NFL team and the Seattle Mariners baseball team. Built in 1976, it has the world's largest self-supporting roof, which soars 250 feet above the ground. Tours are available. The *Klondike Gold Rush National Historical Park* (117 S. Main St., tel. 206/442–7220) and interpretive center explores Seattle's role in the 1897–98 Gold Rush through film presentations, exhibits, and gold-panning demonstrations.

Seattle Art Museum (1320 2nd Ave., tel. 206/625–8969). The museum, which specializes in Asian, Native American, African, Oceanic, and Pre-Columbian art, has a new five-story building designed by Robert Venturi. A work of art itself, the building features a limestone exterior with large-scale vertical fluting, accented by terra-cotta, cut granite, and marble.

Seattle Center. This 74-acre complex built for the 1961 Seattle World's Fair includes an amusement park; the futuristic-looking *Space Needle*, with observation deck, lounge, and restaurant (tel. 206/443–2100); theaters; the Coliseum; exhibition halls; museums; and shops.

Waterfront. Once the center of activity in Seattle, this area stretches some 19 blocks, from Pier 70 and Myrtle Edwards Park in the north down to Pier 51 in Pioneer Square. At the base of the Pike Street Hillclimb is the *Seattle Aquarium* (Pier 59, tel. 206/386–4320), where visitors can see otters and seals swim and dive in their pools. The "State of the Sound" exhibit explores the aquatic life and ecology of Puget Sound. Just next door is the *Omnidome Film Experience* (Pier 59, tel. 206/622–1868), which showcases 70mm films on a huge, curved screen on such subjects as the eruption of Mt. St. Helens and a study of sharks and whales.

Several guided tours of Seattle's waterfront and nearby areas are available. From Pier 55, *Seattle Harbor Tours* (Pier 55 tel. 206/623–1445) offers one-hour tours exploring Elliott Bay and the Port of Seattle. *Gray Line* (buses to the ships depart from the downtown Sheraton Hotel, 1400 6th Ave., tel. 206/626–5208) runs similar cruises. *Tillicum Village Tours* (Pier 56, tel. 206/443–1244) sails visitors from Pier 56 across Puget Sound to Blake Island for a four-hour experience of traditional Northwest Indian life, including dinner and a traditional dance performance.

Westlake Center (1601 5th Ave., tel. 206/467–1600). Controversial from the time of its inception—some residents wanted the land to be used for a park—this 27-story office tower and three-story shopping structure with enclosed walkways is the major terminus for buses and the Monorail, which goes north to Seattle Center.

Woodland Park Zoo (N. 59th St. and Fremont Ave., tel. 206/684–4800). Many of the animals are free to roam their section of the 92-acre zoo. The African savanna and new elephant house are popular features.

University of Washington. Some 33,500 students attend the U-Dub, as locals call the university, which was founded in 1861. On the northwestern corner of the beautifully landscaped campus is the *Thomas Burke Memorial Washington State Museum* (17th Ave. NE and N.E. 45th St., tel. 206/543–5590). Washington's natural history and anthropological museum, it features exhibits on cultures of the Pacific region and the state's 35 Native American tribes. Nearby, the *Henry Art Gallery* (15th Ave. NE and N.E. 41st St., tel. 206/543–2280) displays paintings from the 19th and 20th centuries, textiles, and traveling exhibitions. At the museum, pick up a brochure of self-guided walking tours of the *Washington Park Arboretum* (2300 Arboretum Dr. E, tel. 206/325–4510), adjacent to the museum. Rhododendron Glen and Azalea Way are in bloom from March through June; during the rest of the year, other plants and wildlife flourish. A new visitor center at the north end of the park will brief you on the species of flora and fauna you'll see here.

Tourist Information

The **Seattle/King County Convention and Visitors Bureau** (800 Convention Pl., tel. 206/461–5840).

Reservation Services

Pacific Bed & Breakfast Agency (701 N.W. 60th St., Seattle, WA 98107, tel. 206/784–0539); **Travelers Bed & Breakfast** (Box 492, Mercer Island, WA 98040, tel. 206/232–2345); **Washington State Bed & Breakfast Guild** (2442 N.W. Market St., Seattle, WA 98107, tel. 509/548–7171).

Bombay House

Located in a quiet, rural setting just a 30-minute ferry ride from Seattle, Bombay House is a three-story Victorian mansion owned by Bunny Cameron, a former caterer, and her husband, Roger Kanchuk, who ran a business that served legal papers. The couple pulled up stakes in Anchorage, Alaska, looking for a better climate. One might question whether Puget Sound is an improvement, but in 1986, after scouring various western locations, Bunny and Roger landed on Bainbridge Island and bought the Bombay House.

The house, which has a widow's walk and wraparound porch, was built in 1907 by a master shipbuilder from Port Blakely (famous for its four-masted schooners built in the heyday of the tall ships). Today it houses comfortable country antiques with a few contemporary pieces. The entrance opens to a spacious, sunny living room with 10-foot-high ceilings, stained-glass windows from Europe, and contemporary off-white sofa and easy chairs facing the massive brick fireplace. A century-old rock maple loom from Maine stands against one wall; a 1912 upright piano stands against another. One guest room, which has a functioning old tin bathtub in the center, is located on the main floor, and an open staircase leads up to the others. The Captain's Suite is a large, airy room decorated in forest green and white, with a wood-burning parlor stove, large bird's-eye maple bed, sofa bed, and claw-foot soaking tub.

From the glass-enclosed dining area, guests can munch on Bunny's special fruit-bran muffins, quick breads, cakes, pastries, and homemade cereals while they watch the large white ferries plying the waters of Rich Passage between Bainbridge Island and the Kitsap Peninsula.

The half-acre yard contains a rough cedar gazebo and informal gardens of roses, daisies, peonies, and lilies exploding with color.

A favorite activity on the 15-mile-long island is berry picking. If you haven't immediately consumed everything you've picked, you'll have an appetite for the fresh seafood and pasta at the Pleasant Beach Grill (4738 Lynwood Center Rd., tel. 206/842–4347), an old home turned restaurant that can be very romantic.

Address: *8490 Beck Rd. NE, Bainbridge Island, WA 98110, tel. 206/842–3926.*
Accommodations: *2 double rooms with bath, 2 double rooms share bath, 1 suite.*
Amenities: *Complimentary beverages.*
Rates: $55–$95; *Continental breakfast. AE, MC, V.*
Restrictions: Smoking outside only, no pets.

Gaslight Inn

The three-story teal-colored Gaslight Inn atop historic Capitol Hill was always a showplace. A developer built the Arts and Crafts foursquare-style home in 1906 to show prospective customers the kind of home they could build after they had bought their lot from him.

Owners Stephen Bennett and Trevor Logan bought the dilapidated building in 1980, and after four years of painstaking restoration, opened it as a bed-and-breakfast. Those who reject the excesses of Victoriana will love the more austere aesthetic here, but no matter what your taste, you'll have to contend with the traffic noise from busy 15th Street.

The inn, named for its original gaslight fixtures, also retains the original beveled and stained-glass windows on all three floors, oak millwork, and oak-paneled wainscoting with egg and dart detailing. All the oak and the muted color schemes lend a cozy feel to the inn, while large windows and unfussy furnishings—authentic Arts and Crafts, Mission, and Eastlake—give it a bright, clean look. The charcoal-gray living room to the south features a glossy green-tiled fireplace with an oak mantel, Stickley rocker, rare oak and green-glass Mission library lamps, wing chairs, an Arts and Crafts sofa, and a large console radio. The parlor contains three Arts and Crafts rocking chairs, sofa, and circa 1900 Victrola with a wooden horn within its hunter-green walls and oak wainscoting. Mounted heads of gazelles and elks hang in the three downstairs sitting rooms.

Each guest room is different, but all are equipped with remote-control TV and a small refrigerator. Some rooms have views of downtown, only a short bus ride away. No. 1 has a crisp, "masculine" appeal, with its ivory-and-blue mattress-ticking wallpaper and lots of wood. It features two Eastlake walnut chests and table, a walnut headboard, a hand-pieced quilt, and a bathroom with dark-stained wainscoting and a small Eastlake mirror. Despite dark taupe walls, room no. 2 is warm and sunny, with white millwork, an elaborately carved golden oak bed and dresser, and an Arts and Crafts armoire. One room is rustic, with a log bed made in the San Juan Islands and pine furniture.

Address: *1727 15th Ave., Seattle, WA 98122, tel. 206/325-3654.*
Accommodations: *5 double rooms with bath, 4 double rooms share 2 baths.*
Amenities: *Fireplace in 1 room, cable TV and refrigerator in rooms; swimming pool.*
Rates: *$58–$88; Continental breakfast. AE, MC, V.*
Restrictions: *No pets; 2-night minimum in summer (Memorial Day–Labor Day) and on weekends.*

M.V. Challenger

In a city that's defined by water, what could be more appropriate than a stay on a tugboat? Doing the improbable, owner Jerry Brown, a real-estate appraiser from the Midwest, bought the 96-foot working tug, built in 1944 for the U.S. Army, in Victoria, British Columbia, renovated it, and opened the *M.V. Challenger* as a bed-and-breakfast. It's certainly not hyperbole to call it unique.

Moored on the south end of Lake Union, a small lake 10 blocks from the heart of Seattle and filled with sailboats, cruisers, and charter boats, the *Challenger* is not for the claustrophobic. Common areas inside the vessel are open and fairly spacious, but some cabins are very snug.

Guests are asked to remove their shoes as they enter the main salon, built over the former cargo hatch, now decorated in ivory, blue, and beige with wood trim, brass candlesticks, and nautical gauges. The check-in area at the bar includes a TV, VCR, stereo, and small aquarium. Walls are covered with nautical maps, and two contemporary couches flank the granite fireplace in an adjoining carpeted conversation pit. The aft-deck solarium, which affords panoramic views of the waterfront, can be opened to the sky on sunny days and, more typically, enclosed with canvas and vinyl for Seattle's fog and drizzle.

Staterooms, some no bigger than a walk-in closet, are papered with nautical maps. Two cabins have bunks, the others double or queen-size beds. All come equipped with radios and phones. The red-striped comforter and matching pillowcases and curtains, towels, and a small painted radiator, also in red, make the Captain's Cabin cozy and bright. If you've been assigned to the Master's Cabin, you might be tempted to take to your bed, from which you can observe the busy comings and goings on the lake. A tub conveniently sits behind the bed.

Jerry, who keeps his tug especially shipshape—notice the gleaming brass—is happy to show guests around the engine room, with its 14,000-pound, 765-horsepower engine. (The tug, by the way, is still fully functional.)

Address: *809 Fairview Pl. N, Seattle, WA 98109, tel. 206/340–1201, fax 206/621–9208.*
Accommodations: *3 double rooms with bath, 3 double rooms share bath, 1 suite.*
Amenities: *Phone, radio, and sink in rooms, TV and VCR in 4 rooms, stereo and refrigerator in some rooms; solarium.*
Rates: *$50–$125; full breakfast. AE, MC, V.*
Restrictions: *No smoking, no pets, no shoes inside.*

Shumway Mansion

ast of Seattle, across Lake
Washington in Kirkland, is the
Shumway Mansion, a gray Shingle Style mansion with two-story bay
windows, dating from 1909–10. Built
by the progressive Shumways,
whose daughter Carrie Holland
Shumway was the first woman in
the state to sit on a city council, the
10,000-square-foot house was saved
from demolition by Richard and Salli
Harris and their oldest daughter,
Julie Blakemore. Backed by investors, the Harrises rescued the 24-
room mansion, moved it 2½ miles to
its present location, and renovated it
to the tune of some $500,000.

A formality pervades the house,
which is decorated largely with 18th-
and 19th-century European pieces,
Oriental rugs, lace curtains, and silk
floral arrangements. The living room
features the original fireplace, with
two parlor sets, one a blue upholstered walnut spindle-style suite
from Austria, the other French Victorian, covered in burgundy mohair.
The sun room is particularly charming, tiled in black and white with
white wicker furniture, pink-and-
white striped wallpaper, and pink
hanging lamps.

Guests can enjoy the grounds from
two rear verandas linked by a long
deck. Downstairs is a ballroom with
four sets of French doors leading to
a patio and gazebo. A recently
opened guest room on the same level
has a private garden, fireplace,

and—an oddity in the bed-and-
breakfast industry—a Murphy bed.

Guest rooms on the second floor
share a tiny reading alcove on the
same floor. Richard, a retired stockbroker, can't abide froufrou (although he does admit tolerating the
odd straw hat with dried flowers
here and there) and is proud of the
soft easy chairs with ottomans,
soundproofing, extra pillows, and
good reading lights in every room.
Each room mixes late-19th-century
European and American furnishings
with traditional-style modern pieces,
old prints on the walls, Laura
Ashley–style print wallpaper and bed
linens, and resident stuffed animals—five or six per room.

Julie's candlelight breakfasts, served
on crystal and china, include a variety of egg dishes or blueberry pancakes, as well as homemade muffins,
scones, and coffee cake.

Address: *11410 99th Pl. NE, Kirkland, WA 98033, tel. 206/823-2303.*
Accommodations: *7 double rooms
with baths, 1 suite.*
Amenities: *Soundproofing, individual heat control, and clock in
rooms, fireplace in 1 room, TV and
phone available, afternoon refreshments; free use of nearby health
club.*
Rates: *$65–$95; full breakfast. AE,
MC, V.*
Restrictions: *Smoking outside only,
no pets.*

The Chambered Nautilus

You can't miss the bright red door of this three-story Georgian Colonial Revival home near the University of Washington's campus. Called the Chambered Nautilus by owners Bunny and Bill Hagemeyer after a seashell found in the Pacific Northwest, the house was built in 1915.

The spacious living room features wood floors, Oriental rugs, large windows, and a fireplace. In one corner is a Hardman-Peck baby grand piano that was made by Bill's grandfather's company. Other interesting pieces in the room include an early English oak fire bench and a collection of rare Peruvian grave artifacts, some 2,000 years old. A 6-foot-tall carved oak headboard from the 1890s is the focal point of the Rose Room, dressed with a rose-and-ivory striped down comforter and floral pillowcases. The Scallop Room takes advantage of the hilltop setting, with windows on three sides. Furnishings include a white iron daybed, carved chestnut armoire, and an early 19th-century commode.

Address: *5005 22nd Ave. NE, Seattle, WA 98105, tel. 206/522-2536.*
Accommodations: *4 double rooms with bath, 2 double rooms share bath.*
Rates: *$65–$92.50; full breakfast. AE, DC, MC, V.*
Restrictions: *No smoking, no pets; 2-night minimum Apr. 15–Oct. 15 and 3-night minimum on holiday weekends.*

Chelsea Station

A Federal-style home built in 1920, Chelsea Station is located in a wooded setting near the Woodland Park Zoo and municipal rose gardens. In 1982, Dick and Marylou Jones merged families—six grown daughters and seven grandchildren—and in 1984 they opened the bed-and-breakfast. The sunny, comfortable house has many of its original features, such as leaded-glass windows, oak floors, cove ceilings, and archways. The inn is sprinkled with family heirlooms and mementos, such as Dick's grandmother's Victrola and stereopticon, and a desk his grandfather used when he worked for the IRS.

The double rooms are on the small side, with good bedside reading lamps, cove ceilings, picture rails, and the original decorative plasterwork on the walls. The Lilac Suite features a green, peach, and lilac color scheme, with lace curtains, a ruffled, floral bedspread, four-poster rice-bed, and an electric fireplace from the 1920s. Since the building was converted into a multifamily dwelling, each suite has its own kitchen.

Address: *4915 Linden Ave. N, Seattle, WA 98103, tel. 206/547-6077.*
Accommodations: *5 double rooms with bath.*
Amenities: *Fireplace in 1 room, kitchens in 2 rooms, kitchen available; hot tub in separate building.*
Rates: *$69–$94; full breakfast. AE, D, DC, MC, V.*
Restrictions: *Smoking outside only, no pets.*

Roberta's

I was sick and tired of working in the 'real world,'" says Roberta Barry of her decision to convert her home into a B&B. After being widowed at an early age, raising children, and teaching for years, she has never looked back. Roberta's Classic Box-style house built in 1903 is located near beautiful Volunteer Park on Capitol Hill. The house has comfortable furniture with the occasional antique, but the real draw here is the inn's vivacious hostess. And since Roberta loves to read, there are loads of books. The dining room contains an ornate cast iron and nickel wood-burning stove that was a wedding present to Roberta's grandmother in 1904.

A dark oak secretary Roberta's grandmother bought in 1910 is the treasure of the Peach Room. The Hideaway Suite on the third floor has a pale green and ivory color scheme, with plenty of angles and skylights over the bed to make it both cozy and airy. Window seats in one alcove offer a view of the Cascade Mountains, or you can retire to the easy chair or brass bed.

Address: *1147 16th Ave. E, Seattle, WA 98112, tel. 206/329-3326.*
Accommodations: *4 double rooms with bath, 1 suite.*
Amenities: *Wood-burning stove in dining room.*
Rates: *$75–$94; full breakfast. AE, DC, MC, V.*
Restrictions: *No smoking, no pets; 3-night minimum on holiday weekends.*

Salisbury House

On a wide, tree-lined avenue in an old residential neighborhood on Seattle's Capitol Hill sits Salisbury House. The Craftsman-style house, built in 1904, is owned by Mary Wiese, a former real-estate broker in California, and her daughter Cathryn.

The house is light and airy, with maple floors, high coffered ceilings, and large leaded-glass windows. The furniture is eclectic, with few noteworthy antiques but lots of comfort. You might prefer to take a volume from the library up to the second-floor sun porch. There you can settle into the wicker chairs and make use of a refrigerator and hot pot.

Guest rooms are individually decorated and have down comforters.

The Rose Room, a large corner room with a canopy bed in rose chintz, is especially pretty. Mary's favorite room is the Lavender Room, where a country-French suite painted pale yellow combines with white wicker chairs and headboard, the lavender walls and purple floral duvet providing the chief color notes.

Address: *750 16th Ave. E, Seattle, WA 98112, tel. 206/328-8682.*
Accommodations: *4 double rooms with bath.*
Amenities: *Claw-foot tub in 1 room; afternoon refreshments available.*
Rates: *$65–$90; full breakfast. AE, DC, MC, V.*
Restrictions: *Smoking outside only, no pets; 2-night minimum holiday and summer weekends.*

Villa Heidelberg

Just two blocks from the shops and restaurants in downtown West Seattle, known to locals as "The Junction," is Villa Heidelberg, owned by John and Barbara Thompson. The Craftsman-style house, clad in clinker brick and old-growth fir, was built in 1909 by a German immigrant from Heidelberg.

Lots of somewhat worn, comfortable furniture and a few antiques make for a homey hodgepodge. The house features the original leaded glass windows, beamed ceilings, gas lighting fixtures, and embossed wall coverings.

The Briar Rose, the most romantic guest room, is decorated in pastel florals, with a brass bed, crystal chandelier, brick fireplace, oak dresser, TV, phone, and a view of Vashon Island and Puget Sound. The bathroom has a large claw-foot tub with shower. A smaller, look-alike room adjoins the Briar Rose and can be rented with it as a suite.

Alki Beach is a five-minute drive away; there you can rent Roller blades and pedal cabs, or picnic, stroll, and dine at the good seafood restaurants.

Address: *4845 45th Ave. SW, Seattle, WA 98116, tel. 206/938-3658.*
Accommodations: *4 double rooms share 2 baths.*
Amenities: *Fireplace, TV, and phone in 1 room.*
Rates: $55–$75; *full breakfast. AE.*
Restrictions: *Smoking outside only, no pets.*

Whidbey Island

Over the years Whidbey Island has been settled by farmers, retirees, executives who don't mind the commute, and families who want to get away from the hubbub of city life. They all grow attached to the rolling terrain of forests and meadows, to the high cliffs and sandy beaches, and to the dramatic views. Here you can tread the bluffs of Fort Ebey, marvel at the sunsets at Fort Casey or Deception Pass, bike along the many miles of wooded country roads and shoreline, or boat and fish off the same long shore.

The first white settlers included Colonel Walter Crockett and Colonel Isaac Ebey, who arrived during the early 1850s and gave their names to Crockett Lake and Ebey's Landing National Historic Reserve. Wildlife is plentiful: eagles, great blue herons, oystercatchers in the air; orcas and gray whales, dolphins, and otters in the water.

Lying 30 miles northwest of Seattle, the island ranks as the second-longest (60 miles; its width is only 8 miles) in the contiguous United States. It's easily accessible from Seattle via a ferry from Mukilteo (muck-il-TEE-oh) or a drive across Deception Pass on Highway 20.

Places to Go, Sights to See

Coupeville. Founded in 1852 by Captain Thomas Coupe, this seaport village (population 1,300) on the island's east coast passed its early years trading in timber, farm produce, and animal pelts. Much of the original town has been restored—it boasts some 54 historic landmarks. The new *Island County Historical Museum* (908 N.W. Alexander St., tel. 206/678–3310) displays artifacts of pioneer families and the town's sea captains. Coupeville hosts an Arts and Crafts Festival in August; a Harvest Festival, with fall foods and a flea market, in October; and the "Greening of Coupeville" when it decorates for the holidays in mid-December.

Deception Pass State Park. (5175 National State Hwy. 20, Oak Harbor, tel. 206/675–2417). Take in the spectacular vista and stroll among the peeling, reddish-brown madrona trees. While walking across the Deception Pass Bridge, you'll have a view of the dramatic gorge below, well known for its tidal currents. The bridge links Whidbey to Fidalgo Island and the mainland; from here, it's just a short distance to Anacortes and ferries to the San Juan Islands.

Ebey's Landing National Historic Reserve (395 N. Fort Ebey Rd., tel. 206/678–4636), west of Coupeville off Highway 20, encompasses more than 1,000 acres—including the areas of Keystone, Coupeville, and Penn Cove. Established by Congress in 1980, the reserve is the first and largest of its kind. It's dotted with some 91 nationally registered historical structures (mainly private homes), as well as farmland, parks, and trails with fine views.

Ft. Casey State Park (1280 S. Fort Casey Rd., tel. 206/678–4519), lies just north of Keystone off Highway 20. The fort, built in 1890, was one of three coastal forts constructed at the entrance of Admiralty Inlet to protect Puget Sound. The park includes the fort, bunkers, and 10-inch disappearing guns, as well as a small interpretive center, campgrounds, picnic sites, fishing areas, and a boat launch.

Greenbank. The tart-sweet loganberry is grown on farms all over the island; now the 125-acre *Whidbey's Loganberry Farm* (657 Wonn Rd., tel. 206/678–7700) in Greenbank also produces Whidbey's Loganberry Liqueur. Free tours are offered daily from 10 to 4. Greenbank is also the site of the 53-acre *Meerkerk Rhododendron Gardens* (3531 S. Meerkerk La., off Resort Rd., tel. 206/321–6682), with 1,500 native and hybrid species of the flowering shrub along numerous trails and ponds. The prime time for viewing blossoms is April and May.

Langley. This quaint town on the island's southeastern shore sits atop a 50-foot-high bluff overlooking Saratoga Passage. A bluff-top sidewalk park offers spectacular views over the passage to Camano Island and the mainland beyond. Sculptor Georgia Gerber's bronze *Boy and Dog* stands sentinel over 1st Street, which is lined with restaurants and shops. The town's small-boat harbor, a 35-slip facility, is protected by a 400-foot timber-pile breakwater and features a 160-foot-long fishing-pier-cum-walkway. The adjacent commercial marina offers fuel and supplies.

Restaurants

The Garibyan Brothers serve up Continental and Greek dishes, including lamb and fresh seafood, in a Mediterranean atmosphere at **Café Langley** (tel. 206/221–3090 in Langley). **Christopher's** (tel. 206/678–5480 in Coupeville) features views of the harbor as well as great stuffed island mussels and other seafood. Also in Coupeville, **Rosi's Garden Restaurant** (tel. 206/678–3989), grandly housed in a restored Victorian, offers a large menu featuring seafood and prime rib. A rustic little place called **Whidbey Fish** (tel. 206/678–3474) in Greenbank serves up great fish chowder, delicious halibut, and fabulous berry pies on picnic tables.

Tourist Information

Central Whidbey Chamber of Commerce (Box 152, Coupeville, WA 98239, tel. 206/678–5434); **Island County Visitors Council** (Box 809, Coupeville, WA 98239, tel. 206/366–5010); **Northwest Regional Tourism Association** (Box 922, Langley, WA 98260, tel. 206/221–8687).

Reservation Services

Pacific Bed & Breakfast Agency (701 N.W. 60th St., Seattle, WA 98107, tel. 206/784–0539); **Travelers Bed & Breakfast** (Box 492, Mercer Island, WA 98040, tel. 206/232–2345); **Washington State Bed & Breakfast Guild** (2442 N.W. Market St., Seattle, WA 98107, tel. 509/548–7171); **Whidbey Island Bed & Breakfast Association** (Box 259, Langley, WA 98260, tel. 206/679–2276).

Cliff House and
Sea Cliff Cottage

High on a cliff above Admiralty Strait, on 400 feet of waterfront, stand the Cliff House and the more secluded Sea Cliff Cottage. Owner Peggy Moore was a divorced mother when she decided to leave suburbia for Whidbey Island. She and her ex-husband had had two houses built during their marriage. "This one I did myself," she says proudly. And rightly so, since the 1981 Cliff House—a contemporary statement in glass, wood, and stone—has brought awards to its architect, Arne Bystrom.

The foyer looks onto a central 30-foot glass atrium that stands open to the elements. On one side there's a large, open kitchen and dining area; on the other, a study and seating area. The sunken living room behind the atrium features a fireplace and a seafoam-green sectional with a perimeter of tiny lights that make it appear to float at night. The floor-to-ceiling windows in the dining and living rooms look out onto Admiralty Strait, Puget Sound, and the Olympic Mountains.

The two large, open bedrooms are upstairs. (Don't worry about privacy—the innkeepers live in the converted garage next door, and they'll rent the two rooms only to guests and their families or friends.) The larger room, decorated in shades of peach and ecru, opens out over the living area. It has a king-size feather bed, and its two upholstered chairs

swivel so that guests can fully appreciate the view.

The second bedroom—decorated mostly in white, with whitewashed pine furniture, Battenberg lace, pink glass lamps, and a pink chintz folding screen—overlooks the kitchen and dining area and offers a view of the forest. There's a skylight in the dark blue tile bathroom.

Sea Cliff Cottage is as romantic and cozy as Cliff House is airy and elegant. The porch has a bit of gingerbread among the driftwood railing, and Adirondack chairs. There's a French-country feel to the living room: whitewashed pine walls, pine armoire, wicker chairs and love seat with pale green and pink cushions, and a brick fireplace. The bedroom is pink, with a wicker headboard and Ralph Lauren linens on the bed, and a cushioned window seat overlooking the trees and the water. There is also a fully equipped kitchenette and a dining area, as well as a bathroom.

Address: *5440 Windmill Rd., Freeland, WA 98249, tel. 206/321-1566.*
Accommodations: *2 double rooms with bath, 1 housekeeping suite.*
Amenities: *Fireplace in suite; outdoor hot tub.*
Rates: *$265, both rooms $365, suite $145; Continental breakfast. No credit cards.*
Restrictions: *Smoking outside only, no pets; 2-night minimum most of the time.*

Colonel Crockett Farm

Colonel Walter Crockett, born in 1786, was a relative of Davy Crockett. He came to Whidbey in 1853 and built a house in about 1855, making five additions (four of them with square nails) later on. Today the house is listed in the National Register of Historic Places, but it was derelict in 1984, when Robert and Beulah Whitlow found it. Robert, a former banker and personnel director, and Beulah, a retired teacher, had become intrigued with the bed-and-breakfast notion during a three-year stint in England. It took 18 months and $235,000 to transform the old farmhouse into an inn.

The Victorian cross-gabled structure has Doric pilasters on pedestals, which lend an incongruous formal grandeur to an otherwise modest house. The entry hall and small solarium feature stained- and leaded-glass windows and white wicker furniture. The main public room is a comfortable and well-stocked library with red oak paneling and a slate fireplace. It's decorated with an English brass rubbing and a collection of bulldogs in an antique glass case. The furniture includes a mirror-back English settee and matching chairs, an upholstered Eastlake chair and matching rocker, and another rocker, this one hand-carved.

The five guest rooms have been individually decorated. The Crockett Room, the inn's bridal suite, is furnished with a draped and canopied queen-size four-poster, a marble-top washstand, and a Belgian field desk. The Edwardian fainting couch is a particularly rare piece. The tub in the bathroom has lion's-head feet. The Alexander Room, with its tiger maple queen-length double bed and dresser, overlooks meadows, Crockett Lake, and Admiralty Bay.

The dining room has another fireplace, as well as a telescope for guests. The small tables are dressed up with pink and white linens, surrounded by the Whitlows' collections of antique porcelain plates, Royal Copenhagen, Wedgwood, and Belleek pieces, and gleaming English silver. From here guests have a view out to the iris gardens (the house stands amid three acres of lawn and flower gardens) and Crockett Lake. Breakfast specialties include eggs Californian and homemade seasonal muffins.

Address: *1012 S. Fort Casey Rd., Coupeville, WA 98239, tel. 206/678–3711.*
Accommodations: *5 double rooms with bath.*
Amenities: *Water views, gardens, fish pond.*
Rates: *$65–$95; full breakfast. MC, V.*
Restrictions: *Smoking outside only, no pets; 2-night minimum on holiday weekends.*

Inn at Langley

The contemporary concrete and wood structure at the edge of the Langley business district is a contemplative melding of earth, sky, water, wood, and concrete. The two cedar-shake, Mission-style buildings—inspired by Frank Lloyd Wright—are surrounded by quiet gardens of herbs, berries, flowers, and fruit trees.

An archway leads to a long, rectangular reflecting pond, which connects with the Country Kitchen, a restaurant that serves Continental breakfast to guests and opens to the public for dinner on Friday and Saturday. Behind the dining room lies a longer building with the same lines and a lot of glass and wood. This structure includes the office, 22 guest rooms, and two suites trailing down the bluff to the beach.

Lawyer/developer Paul Schell discovered Langley when he and his wife, Pam, moved from New York to Seattle during the early 1970s. After doing several redevelopments in Seattle, Paul opened the 13,000-square-foot, $1 million Inn at Langley in June 1989. He plans to add six more rooms by the summer of 1992.

The rooms, with an almost Asian sense of space and understatement, were designed to be restorative. Neutral colors—black, taupe, gray, beige—form a quiet background. The waterside wall is nearly all glass, and beyond the deck lies a staggeringly beautiful view of Saratoga Passage, Camano Island, and the Cascade Mountains. The wicker, maple, cherry, and pine furnishings and the wood-burning fireplace seem to meld with the outdoors. A whirlpool tub with a sliding window looks out to the room and to the view beyond it.

The Country Kitchen might be a wealthy friend's dining room. You'll find no maître d' standing at an official podium, no coat check, and no cash register. The room is a gallery of local crafts. A huge river-rock fireplace rises before you; tables for two line the walls unobtrusively. On the other side of the fireplace stands a locally made Wright-inspired "great table" for 10.

Steve Nogal, the inn's manager, has seen it happen again and again: "People arrive here all aggressive," he said. "They're keyed up after having to wait for a ferry. Slowly, they unwind and blossom."

Address: *400 1st St., Box 835, Langley, WA 98260, tel. and fax 206/221–3033.*
Accommodations: *22 double rooms with bath, 2 suites.*
Amenities: *Fireplace, whirlpool tub, cable TV, and phone in rooms.*
Rates: *$155–$175, suites $225; Continental breakfast. AE, MC, V.*
Restrictions: *Smoking outdoors only, no pets; 2-night minimum on weekends.*

Inn at Penn Cove

I n the middle of historic Coupeville, two historic homes rest side
by side on a wide street leading
down to the waterfront. The Kineth
House—a large peach-colored Victorian Italianate—was built in 1887 for
John Kineth, a farmer and saddle-
maker, and his wife, Jane. The completely restored Kineth house is
listed in the National Register of
Historic Places and is now part of
the Ebey's Landing National Historical Reserve.

Next door stands the 1891 Coupe-
Gillespie House, homestead of James
and Keturah Coupe-Gillespie. Keturah, the first white female to be
born in Coupeville, was the daughter
of Thomas Coupe, the town's sea-
captain founder. The Coupe-Gillespie
House is in the final stages of restoration—it's 90% done.

Owners Jim and Barbara Cinney left
a fast-paced corporate life in the insurance business to become innkeepers. They have done their best to
preserve the homes' original materials. "We wanted to combine the elements of a living museum with
today's comforts," Jim explained.

The foyer of the Kineth house opens
onto the parlor; a dark-green-car-
peted staircase leads to the guest
rooms, while a parquet hallway
takes you to the library/TV room,
the dining room, and the sun porch
beyond. The parlor has fir floors and
dusty pink–and-cream reproduction

Victorian wallpaper; a pink
frosted-glass chandelier hangs over
a cream upholstered sofa, which
faces a fireplace of slate hand-
painted to look like marble. The
room also contains an antique pump
organ, and two 1890s armchairs face
the bay window.

Guest rooms are elegant without
being stuffy. Elizabeth's Room features pale pink walls, lavender carpet, a turn-of-the-century bed, an 8-
foot double-mirrored armoire, and
a carousel horse. A small photo
album of Jim's daughter Elizabeth
rests on one of the tables.

Next door, the main floor of the
Coupe-Gillespie House includes several parlors and meeting rooms. Upstairs are three finished guest
rooms. Plans call for a deluxe suite
downstairs and a gazebo between
the two houses.

Address: *702 N. Main St., Box 85,
Coupeville, WA 98239, tel. 206/678–
8000 or 800/688–COVE, fax
206/678–4747.*
Accommodations: *3 double rooms
with bath, 2 double rooms share
bath, 1 suite.*
Amenities: *Fireplace in rooms,
whirlpool tub in suite, air-
conditioning in Kineth House; complimentary beverages; meeting facilities; exercise facilities.*
Rates: *$70–$125; full breakfast. AE,
D, MC, V.*
Restrictions: *No smoking, no pets.*

Anchorage Inn

Sarah and Bob Shinn considered buying and restoring a Victorian home, but instead they opted to build a reproduction one, with a private wing for themselves. The Anchorage Inn opened during the summer of 1991. The white-walled, red-roofed house rises three stories—to the consternation of some of the neighbors whose view has been obstructed—with such fanciful Victorian touches as gables, dormer windows, and a tower. If newness is something you find off-putting—and everything, from the hardwood floors to the reproduction furniture, is new—you may prefer one of the genuinely historic inns on the island. But if gleaming reproductions are your thing, the Anchorage is for you.

The foyer has a fireplace and a large, open staircase. In room No. 2, you'll find an Eastlake-style bedstead (with a fluffy white comforter) and dresser and a view of the harbor.

The Shinns retired to Coupeville from Alaska, where Bob had worked as a commercial pilot for 32 years. "We wanted to escape the cold," said Sarah.

Address: *807 N. Main St., Coupeville, WA 98239, tel. 206/678-5581.*
Accommodations: *5 double rooms with bath.*
Amenities: *Air-conditioning, cable TV in rooms.*
Rates: *$65–$85; full breakfast. AE, MC, V.*
Restrictions: *No smoking, no pets.*

Captain Whidbey Inn

The Captain Whidbey nestles along the shore of Penn Cove near Coupeville. Built in 1907 from local madrona logs, it is warm and inviting. The sitting room has smooth log walls and a double-sided beach rock and brick fireplace whose other side faces the dining room.

Guest rooms open off the hallway. They all have sinks; the two baths are down the hall. The rooms on one side have a water view, while those on the other side have a forest view. One of the suites has a four-poster bed, blue woven curtains, and a reading chair with matching upholstery. Seven waterfront cottages have fireplaces and, in some cases, kitchens. Another building contains the spacious Lagoon Rooms, all with verandas and private baths.

Dinner is served by candlelight in the dining room, which looks onto Penn Cove. After dinner, guests can relax in the Chart Room, a rustic bar.

Address: *2072 W. Captain Whidbey Inn Rd., Coupeville, WA 98239, tel. 206/678-4097 or 800/366-4097, fax 206/678-4110.*
Accommodations: *12 double rooms with bath, 10 double rooms and 2 suites share 2 baths, 5 suites, 1 housekeeping suite, 2 double housekeeping suites.*
Amenities: *Phone in some rooms, fireplace in cottages.*
Rates: *$65–$150; Continental breakfast. AE, D, DC, MC, V.*
Restrictions: *No pets; 2-night minimum on weekends, 3-night minimum on holiday weekends.*

Country Cottage of Langley

The Country Cottage stands two blocks from downtown Langley on three acres that were part of a farm until 1984. The two-story cottage, with dormer windows and a gabled entrance, went up in 1927. Green, in various shades, is the predominant color, and whitewashed wainscoting is used throughout. The large living room has a stone fireplace, and the seafoam-green dining room is done in a Laura Ashley print. In the TV room there's rattan furniture. Outside there's a large deck with umbrella tables and a boardwalk leading to a gazebo; through the gazebo there's a more recent building housing two large guest rooms. The onetime farmhouse creamery has been converted into a small cottage; it has its own shower, a small refrigerator, and a brass single bed with a trundle that can be pulled out for a second sleeper.

The upstairs guest rooms in the main house feature angled ceilings, brass bedsteads, oak chests, bentwood rockers, and pilgrim-style trunks. One drawback is that only a screen separates the baths from the bedrooms.

Address: *215 6th St., Langley, WA 98260, tel. 206/221-8709.*
Accommodations: *5 double rooms with bath.*
Amenities: *Cable TV.*
Rates: *$80–$90; full breakfast. MC, V.*
Restrictions: *No smoking, no pets; 2-night minimum on summer weekends and holidays.*

Eagles Nest Inn

When Dale and Nancy Bowman retired, they moved from California to Whidbey Island and designed and built their own B&B. The location is serenely rural, with views of the water and the mountains, and their octagonal house is contemporary in design.

The ambience of Eagles Nest Inn is one of comfortable elegance. The foyer opens onto a two-story living room with a 17-foot brick fireplace flanked with elongated octagonal windows in clear and peach-colored glass. Its peach carpet is spread with Chinese rugs on which sit dark-cherry upholstered chairs and a sofa that's mainly black with a peach and white floral design.

Every guest room has a private bath and a view of the woods or Saratoga Passage and the Cascade Mountains. Honeymooners love the fourth-floor peach-and-white penthouse room, which has windows on all eight walls and a white wicker queen-size bed. French doors lead to a deck; from the porch swing you look out to the water and the mountains.

Address: *3236 E. Saratoga Rd., Langley, WA 98260, tel. 206/321-5331.*
Accommodations: *4 double rooms with bath.*
Amenities: *Cable TV and VCR in rooms; complimentary beverages; outdoor hot tub.*
Rates: *$85–$105; full breakfast. MC, V.*
Restrictions: *No smoking, no pets; 2-night minimum holiday weekends.*

Fort Casey Inn

The Fort Casey Inn is the former officers' quarters of the old coastal defense fort, built in 1909. Gordon and Victoria Hoenig have been the owners since 1956; Gina Martin is the vivacious manager.

Victoria has renovated, one at a time, four two-story Georgian Revival duplexes. Each one has a kitchen and a living room on the lower floor and two bedrooms and a bath upstairs. The houses have been individually decorated, with painted floors and braided rag rugs; the high ceilings in the living rooms have the original tin, and you will also come across tin chandeliers, lace curtains, folk art, hand-painted furniture, and claw-foot bathtubs.

Garrison Hall, built in 1991 and decorated, again, in Georgian Revival, can be used for weddings or seminars; it also offers a bed-sitter as smaller, less expensive lodgings.

The Hoenigs leave fresh muffins and cereal in the kitchens so that guests can make their own breakfasts.

Address: *1124 S. Engle Rd., Coupeville, WA 98239, tel. 206/678-8792.*
Accommodations: *1 double room with bath, 1 housekeeping suite, 4 double housekeeping suites.*
Amenities: *Wood-burning fireplaces; bicycles.*
Rates: *$95–$110, bed-sitting-room $75; Continental breakfast. AE, MC, V.*
Restrictions: *No smoking, no pets.*

Guest House Cottages

The Guest House Cottages sit at the edge of a pond on 25 acres in a rural area between Langley and Coupeville. Mary Jane and Don Creeger first started renting their log-cabin guest house as a couples' retreat. Over the years they have added more cabins and cottages. There are no common areas for guests to mingle in, but the pool and small exercise room have earned the Creegers high marks.

At the Emma Jane Cottage old scythes, a runner sled, and a lantern rest on the front porch. The living room has pine floors spread with braided rugs, knotty pine walls, a stone fireplace, a blue mohair overstuffed sofa, rocking chairs, and pilgrim-style trunks. Throughout the cabins there are potpourris and white chocolates. The kitchen tables come set for breakfast, and the refrigerators are stocked with breakfast fixings.

Address: *835 E. Christenson Rd., Greenbank, WA 98253, tel. 206/678-3115.*
Accommodations: *4 housekeeping suites, 3 housekeeping double rooms.*
Amenities: *Air-conditioning in lodge, whirlpool tub in rooms, exercise room; outdoor swimming pool and hot tub.*
Rates: *$125–$175, luxury lodge $225; Continental breakfast. AE, MC, V.*
Restrictions: *No smoking, no pets; 2-night minimum on weekends, 3-night minimum on holiday weekends.*

Home by the Sea
Bed & Breakfast and Cottages

T he two-story modern beach house sitting on the edge of Useless Bay is the Home by the Sea Bed & Breakfast. Sharon Drew, who owns the establishment with her mother, Helen Fritts, decorated with international treasures, such as a hand-carved screen from India and Russian samovars. The main public area in the house has 8-foot windows overlooking the beach.

Upstairs there's a double room and a suite, and attached to the house is the Sandpiper Suite. Each guest room has Ralph Lauren floral spreads, and one of the sitting rooms features a small brass bed from Afghanistan. Home by the Sea also offers visitors four cottage options, all with full kitchens.

Address: *2388 E. Sunlight Beach Rd., Clinton, WA 98236, tel. 206/221-2964.*
Accommodations: *1 double room with bath, 1 suite, 4 housekeeping suites, 1 triple housekeeping suite.*
Amenities: *Air-conditioning and hot tub in B&B; wood-burning stove, phone, and TV in most cottages.*
Rates: *B&B $95–$105; full breakfast. Cottages $135–$145; breakfast basket delivered first morning only. D, DC, MC, V.*
Restrictions: *No smoking, pets in Cape Cod cottage only; 2-night minimum on weekends in cottages.*

Log Castle Bed & Breakfast

T he rustic, Northwest-style Log Castle Bed & Breakfast, owned by Norma and Jack Metcalf, sits on a secluded beach outside Langley.

Norma designed the house and Jack built it, beginning in 1974, from local stone, driftwood, and lumber. The place has a '60s feel: plants hanging in macramé holders, stained-glass lamps, tree-root door handles and drawer pulls, and wormwood for the stairway, doors, and kitchen cupboards. The large living/dining room has the aura of a grand old lodge: massive timbers, cathedral ceiling, large leaded-glass windows, and a table made from an ancient log slab. The red and green carpet sticks out, though.

The four guest rooms are named for the couple's four daughters. Ann's Room, in the third-story tower, is decorated in white and mauve and features a 1912 wood stove, white furniture (including a metal bed), and a flowered quilt made by Norma's grandmother; it has a peaked roof and a widow's walk around the outside.

Address: *3273 E. Saratoga Rd., Langley, WA 98260, tel. 206/321-5483, fax 206/221-3822.*
Accommodations: *4 double rooms with bath.*
Amenities: *Wood stove in 1 room.*
Rates: *$80–$100; full breakfast. D, MC, V.*
Restrictions: *No smoking, no pets; 2-night minimum holiday weekends. Closed 5 days during Christmas.*

Lone Lake Cottage and Breakfast

Dolores Meeks was a restaurant manager who wanted an active retirement, and she got it: She owns and runs the Lone Lake Cottage and Breakfast, which lies along Lone Lake. Her hobby is raising birds: She keeps an aviary of over 200 rare varieties.

At Lone Lake you can stay in one of two cottages or on a houseboat—a tiny stern-wheeler that's permanently moored on the lake at the bottom of the property. Dolores's late husband restored the antique engine and built the boat (at one time it toured the lake). The interior is decorated in shades of blue, with a queen-size loft bed and a tiny galley. The two cottages have Asian furnishings: rattan and wicker and inlaid furniture, screens, and extra-firm queen-size beds; both have covered decks with gas barbecues and views of the lake.

Guests also have use of a minitennis court. Dolores delivers breakfast for the first two days of your stay, but after that you're on your own.

Address: *5206 S. Bayview Rd., Langley, WA 98260, tel. 206/321–5325.*
Accommodations: *1 double room with bath, 1 double suite with bath, 1 housekeeping suite.*
Amenities: *Fireplace, whirlpool tub, CD player, cable TV, and VCR in rooms; bicycles, canoes, rowboat.*
Rates: *$110; Continental breakfast for first 2 days. No credit cards.*
Restrictions: *No smoking, no pets; 2-night minimum on weekends.*

Whidbey Inn

Viewed from Langley's 1st Street, the white wood-frame Craftsman-style building looks like a collection of shops, but that's only half the story: The two floors on the water side hold the Whidbey Inn. The owner, Dick Francisco, also owns Francisco's, a local Italian restaurant.

The only thing between guests at the inn and the water is a pane of glass (and not even that when you're sitting on the deck). Some amenities are lacking: There are no public rooms, for example. On the lower floor there are three doubles, which open onto a deck; upstairs are three (deckless) suites. The Wicker Suite, with a light green and white color scheme, has a small vestibule with a mirrored armoire, a working fire-place, and a wicker love seat, chairs, and a coffee table in a pleasant corner with windows.

Guests are greeted with cheese and crackers and a bottle of sherry in their rooms. The hearty breakfast delivered to the rooms includes enough goodies for guests to pack up a few for a picnic lunch.

Address: *106 1st St., Box 156, Langley, WA 98260, tel. 206/221–7115.*
Accommodations: *3 double rooms with bath, 3 suites.*
Amenities: *Fireplace in suite, complimentary sherry and appetizers.*
Rates: *$95–$145; full breakfast. AE, MC, V.*
Restrictions: *No smoking, no pets.*

San Juan Islands

The San Juan Islands offer the traveler a relaxed pace in a setting that ranges from tranquil to wildly rain- and windswept. There are no thoroughfares, just meandering roads; fierce storms bring power outages; fresh water is a precious commodity.

The San Juan archipelago contains 743 islands at low tide, a number that drops to 428 at high tide. Of this total, 172 are named, 60 are populated, and 10 are state marine parks. The islands are home to seals, porpoises, otters, some 80 orca whales, and more than 60 actively breeding pairs of bald eagles. They offer an unbeatable array of outdoor activities: bicycling, sailing, kayaking, canoeing, golfing, horseback riding, boating, fishing, and on and on.

Nonnative residents have moved here to escape the breakneck pace of life elsewhere, and they become as fierce as the natives about protecting what they find: the natural beauty, the wildlife, the privacy. Visitors who respect the island's values are welcome. Ferries stop at Lopez, Shaw, Orcas, and San Juan (schedules can vary); you'll need a private plane or boat to get to the others.

The first ferry stop, Lopez Island, abounds with orchards, weathered barns, and pastures of grazing sheep and cows. The relatively flat terrain makes it a favorite spot for bicyclists. The Franciscan nuns who run the ferry dock at Shaw Island wear their traditional habits; few tourists disembark here, though, because the island is mostly residential. Orcas, the next in line, is a mountainous, horseshoe-shaped island of 56 square miles, with 125 miles of coastline. The last stop, on San Juan Island, is Friday Harbor, with its colorful and active waterfront. The San Juans lie in the so-called Banana Belt, with an annual average of 247 sunny days; compare that with Seattle's gray weather and you'll begin to understand Friday Harbor's holiday atmosphere.

Places to Go, Sights to See

Moran State Park (Star Rte., tel. 206/376–2326 or 800/562–0990) lies just 10 miles from the Orcas Island ferry landing. It offers 4,600 acres of forest and hiking trails, as well as panoramic views from a lookout tower (at the end of a 6-mile drive on paved roadway) on top of 2,400-foot Mt. Constitution. The park also has 148 campsites.

Roche Harbor (tel. 206/378–2155), at the northern end of San Juan Island, is an elegant site with rose gardens, manicured lawns, a cobblestone waterfront, and hanging flower baskets on the docks. It was constructed during the 1880s as a limestone mining village. The white clapboard restaurant and lounge offer great views of Roche Harbor, though the food is just average. The romantic-looking old Hotel de Haro has seen better days— the guest rooms are very worn at the heel. In addition to the harbor, the resort has a private airport.

Rosario Spa & Resort (Horseshoe Hwy., tel. 206/376–2222), on Orcas Island, was built in 1905 by shipbuilding magnate Robert Moran, who had been told that he had only six months to live and wanted to do it lavishly. Moran put $1.5 million into this Mediterranean-style mansion (there are six tons of copper in the roof); the investment turned out to be a good one, since he lasted another 30 years. In 1960 Rosario became a resort; villas and hotel units were added (since fire codes prohibited rental of the mansion's rooms), but they're a far cry from the exquisite teaks and mahoganies of the original structure. The mansion itself, now listed on the National Register of Historic Places, contains the dining room and spa, with the original swimming pool.

San Juan Goodtime Jazz Festival (Box 98, Friday Harbor 98250, tel. 206/378–5240) attracts musicians from across the country who perform at four sites in Friday Harbor for three days at the end of July.

San Juan Island National Historic Park. For a number of years, both the Americans and the British occupied San Juan Island. In 1859 a Yank killed a Brit's pig, igniting long-simmering tempers. Both nations sent armed forces to the island, but no further gunfire was exchanged in the "Pig War" of 1859–72. The remains of this scuffle are the English Camp, with a blockhouse, commissary, and barracks; and the armaments from the American Camp. The visitor center shares offices with the San Juan Island Chamber of Commerce (*see below*).

Whale Museum (62 1st St. N, tel. 206/378–4710). This modest museum in Friday Harbor focuses on the great cetaceans and doesn't attempt to woo you with expensive exhibits, but it does have whale models, whale skeletons, whalebone, whale recordings, and whale videos. Standing on the ferry dock, you can see it at the top of the hill—it has a whale mural painted on the wall.

Whale-watching. For a chance to see whales cavorting, try the first official whale-watching park in the United States, *Lime Kiln Point State Park* (6158 Lighthouse Rd., tel. 206/378–2044), 9 miles west of Friday Harbor on San Juan Island's west side. Whale-spotting season is mid-June through mid-August. For an even better chance, consider a half-day *Western Prince Cruise* (tel. 206/378–5315), which offers whale-watching during the summer and bird-watching and scuba diving during the spring and fall. Cruises depart from the Main Dock at the Friday Harbor Marina.

Restaurants

Lopez Island: The **Bay Café** (tel. 206/468–3700) features innovative dishes, especially fish, in a casual, cottage-style atmosphere. **Gail's** (tel. 206/468–2150) has a natural-wood Cape Cod look and specializes in fresh seafood and local lamb; Gail grows her own herbs and vegetables. The **Wildflower** (tel. 206/468–2114), a small, brightly decorated café, serves up seafood, steaks, and pastas. Or try the **Lopez Island Market** for picnic items, including locally made (and very mild) beef sausage. Orcas Island: **Christina's** (tel. 206/376–4904) provides fresh local seafood in an elegant atmosphere both inside and on the rooftop terrace. **Bilbo's Festivo** (tel. 206/376–4728), in a stucco house with a courtyard decorated with Mexican tiles, features creative renditions of burritos and enchiladas as well as mesquite-grilled specialties. San Juan Island: **Duck Soup Inn** (tel. 206/378–4878) serves the island's Wescott Bay oysters and other fresh seafood prepared in its Mediterranean-inspired kitchen. The **Springtree Eating Establishment and Farm** (tel. 206/378–4848), in the middle of Friday Harbor, boasts its own organically grown produce as well as fresh fish and pasta dishes. The service is slow and often mindless, though, and it hasn't improved over the years.

Tourist Information

San Juan Islands Chamber of Commerce (Box 98, Friday Harbor, WA 98250, tel. 206/378–5240); **San Juan Islands Tourism Cooperative** (Box 65, Lopez, WA 98261, tel. 206/468–3663).

Reservation Services

Pacific Bed & Breakfast Agency (701 N.W. 60th St., Seattle, WA 98107, tel. 206/784–0539); **Travelers B&B Reservation Service** (Box 492, Mercer Island, WA 98040, tel. 206/232–2345); **Washington State Bed & Breakfast Guild** (2442 N.W. Market St., Seattle, WA 98107, tel. 509/548–7171).

Inn at Swifts Bay

There'll always be another boat, but there may never be another property like this," said Robert Herrman when he and Christopher Brandmeir decided to sell the sailboat they had been grooming for a round-the-world adventure and buy the 1975 mock-Tudor building, 2 miles from the Lopez Island ferry landing, that is now the Inn at Swifts Bay. The inn is surrounded by rhododendrons, madronas, and firs amid three acres of woods, with another acre of beach a four-minute walk away.

Robert and Chris give the inn its heart. These two California transplants have woven themselves into the island community. Robert, a former gemologist and singer, now sits on the board of the local library. Chris, who has been a university administrator and a caterer, teaches speech to island students and serves as president of the Chamber of Commerce.

The inn's decor is sophisticated, but the rooms feel lived-in and loved. The sunny living room has large bay windows, a fireplace, a chintz sofa and chairs on an Oriental rug, and shelves of books on design. The raised dining room, pale yellow with hand-stenciled ivy around the ceiling, is the setting for breakfast, which might include hazelnut waffles with fresh island berries and crème fraîche, or eggs with just-caught Dungeness crabs. The den/music room behind the living room features burgundy Laura Ashley wallpaper, a large brick fireplace, two Queen Anne upholstered wingback chairs, a TV/VCR with more than 150 tapes, and French doors that open onto the deck and the woods.

The individually decorated guest rooms are spacious and airy. Room No. 2 has hunter green walls with cream accents, window swags of patterned fabric, an Arts and Crafts headboard on the queen-size bed, a gateleg desk, and a large darkcherry mirror and chest. The new attic suite (actually a large room with a sitting area) has pale peach walls with a navy fleur-de-lis wallpaper border, a queen-size sleigh bed, and an English armoire and chest; three long, narrow skylights have been cut into the sloping ceiling, and there's a private entrance and small deck.

Address: *Port Stanley Rd., Rte. 2, Box 3402, Lopez Island, WA 98261, tel. 206/468-3636.*
Accommodations: *2 double rooms with bath, 2 double rooms share bath.*
Amenities: *Sherry and mineral water; terry-cloth robes and towels, flip-flops, flashlights; outdoor hot tub.*
Rates: *$75–$115; full breakfast. D, MC, V.*
Restrictions: *Smoking outside only, no pets.*

Orcas Hotel

On the hill overlooking the Orcas Island ferry landing sits a three-story red-roofed Victorian with a wraparound porch and a white picket fence. The Orcas Hotel was built as an inn between 1900 and 1904 by Canadian land-owner William Sutherland. Today the hotel is listed on the National Register of Historic Places; even the flower gardens—drifts of daffodils, wisteria vines, irises and roses—have been restored. The hostelry is managed by Craig and Linda Sanders and Cindy Morgan, three active young people who, when they aren't bicycling, hiking, or playing volleyball or softball, are likely to be in the kitchen cooking gourmet meals.

The hotel has a colorful past. A bullet hole through a veranda post recalls the Prohibition-era escape of a bootlegger who foiled his pursuers by leaping to freedom over the porch railing. Some islanders claim that liquor was smuggled in by small boats and stored in the woodpile and the attic. During the hotel's restoration in 1985, loose planks were discovered in the attic, with enough space underneath to store dozens of bottles of booze. The ghost of Octavia, one of the original managers, was seen as recently as 1985, by two of the workmen who were doing the restoration. (Don't worry—the building has been exorcised.)

The main floor features a lounge, a dining room, and a private parlor for overnight guests; all three rooms have harbor views. The parlor is furnished with Queen Anne settees, marble-top tables, Oriental rugs, and a leather-covered office desk. The dining room (open to the public) overlooks the ferry landing as well as part of the garden. Works by Orcas artists, such as a stained-glass mermaid in the cocktail lounge, grace the building.

Two romantic rooms at the front of the inn each have French doors opening onto a white wicker–furnished sun deck with views of the ferry landing. Both rooms feature feather beds and duvets and marble-top tables, and the Blue Heron Room has an Eastlake parlor set. Each has a large bathroom with a double whirlpool bath. The innkeepers readily admit that temperatures in the building are idiosyncratic, so they've supplied each room with a fan and a space heater.

Address: *Box 155, Orcas, WA 98280, tel. 206/376-4300, fax 206/376-4399.*
Accommodations: *2 double rooms with bath, 2 doubles and 1 triple with half-bath share 2 full baths, 5 doubles and 1 triple share 4 baths.*
Amenities: *Restaurant, cocktail lounge.*
Rates: *$65–$170; full breakfast. AE, D, MC, V.*
Restrictions: *Smoking outside only, no pets; 2-night minimum on holiday weekends.*

Turtleback Farm Inn

Bill and Susan Fletcher abandoned suburban life in the San Francisco Bay Area (he was a real-estate broker, she a homemaker) for 80 acres of meadow, forest, and farmland on Orcas Island, where they now herd French geese and occasionally deliver a baby lamb by flashlight. The farmhouse was derelict when they bought it in 1984. Renovated and expanded the following year, the building preserves the original Folk National style. Forest green with white trim, it stands in the shadow of Turtleback Mountain, with Mt. Constitution to the east, a 10-minute drive from the Orcas Island ferry landing.

Don't expect to spend a lot of time chatting with the innkeepers; the Fletchers appear for breakfast but generally spend the evenings in their own home down the hill. A framed Seattle newspaper clipping by the front door—a 1933 ad for *Tarzan the Fearless*—pays homage to the movie's star and Susan's father, Buster Crabbe.

The inn itself is spacious and airy but spare. The cream-colored sitting room, with a beamed ceiling and peach-and-green accents, includes a Rumford fireplace, a pilgrim-style trunk, a cabbage-rose upholstered sofa, and a corner game table. The salmon dining room has fir wainscoting and five small oak tables.

The guest rooms are decorated with Cape May Collection wallpaper. All have reading lamps, comfortable seating, cream-colored muslin curtains, and meadow and forest views. The Meadow Room has a private deck overlooking the pasture. The light fixtures and crystal doorknobs in most rooms and the claw-foot tubs and bathroom mirrors were rescued from Seattle's old Savoy Hotel before it was razed, and the sinks and beveled-glass bathroom shelves above them come from Victoria's grand old Empress Hotel. The comforters on the beds are stuffed with wool batting from the Fletchers' own sheep.

Breakfast is served in the dining room or, in fine weather, on the deck overlooking the valley, on tables set with bone china, silver, and linen. If you want the recipes, you can buy Susan's cookbook. Full meal service is available by reservation for groups.

Address: *Crow Valley Rd., Rte. 1, Box 650, Eastsound, WA 98245, tel. 206/376-4914.*
Accommodations: *7 double rooms with bath.*
Amenities: *Sherry, fresh fruit, guest refrigerator.*
Rates: *$65–$145; full breakfast. MC, V.*
Restrictions: *Smoking outside only, no pets; 2-night minimum on weekends and May 1–Oct. 31, 3-night minimum on holiday weekends.*

Blair House

Just four blocks up the hill from the Friday Harbor ferry landing stands a farmhouse with a wide wraparound porch furnished in wicker. The Blair House was built in 1909 and has since been enlarged several times. Jane Benson left a career as director of a hospital chemical-dependency program to become the innkeeper.

The large, comfortable living room has rust carpeting, floor-to-ceiling bookshelves at one end, a wood-burning stove, cable TV, tape player, and plenty of books and tapes. The large dining room is decorated with cream wainscoting with rust-and-cream wallpaper in an elaborate stripe-and-poppy pattern that matches the upholstery of the livingroom sofa. Guest rooms follow animal themes, with stenciled animals on room doors and stuffed ones inside. They feature country-print wallpapers with color-coordinated linens and comforters on the beds. A detached three-room cottage with full kitchen can sleep up to five. Breakfast is served in the dining room or, in nice weather, beside the pool.

Address: *345 Blair Ave., Friday Harbor, WA 98250, tel. 206/378–5907, fax 206/378–6940.*
Accommodations: *2 double rooms with half-bath share full bath, 4 double rooms share 2 baths, 1 housekeeping suite.*
Amenities: *Outdoor pool, hot tub.*
Rates: *$70–$80, suite $95; full breakfast. AE, D, MC, V.*
Restrictions: *Smoking outside only, no pets in main building.*

Deer Harbor Inn

Fifteen minutes west of the Orcas Island ferry landing, the Deer Harbor Inn has two parts. The Old Norton Inn—now the restaurant—overlooks Deer Harbor; this was the original hotel. Up a hill is a two-story log cabin that went up in 1988, and this is the inn proper. Hosts Craig and Pam Carpenter live in a house on the property, but their three children and Craig's post as restaurant chef keep them too busy to spend much time chatting with guests.

The new log cabin has high ceilings and light, simple country-style furnishings. Both levels have decks with views of the water off the common sitting rooms, which feature peeled-log sofas, chairs, and tables, and windows swathed in white muslin tieback curtains. The eight guest rooms are furnished with peeled-log beds with white down comforters, and peeled-log chairs and tables. A Continental breakfast is delivered to the rooms in picnic baskets. The restaurant, with lace-covered tables, specializes in fresh seafood and pasta dishes; during the summer it offers deck dining at umbrella tables with splendid views of the harbor.

Address: *Deer Harbor Rd., Box 142, Deer Harbor, WA 98243, tel. 206/376–4110.*
Accommodations: *8 double rooms with bath.*
Amenities: *Restaurant.*
Rates: *$85; Continental breakfast. AE, MC, V.*
Restrictions: *Smoking outside only, no pets.*

The Duffy House

The Duffy House sits above Griffin Bay on the southeast side of San Juan Island, 2 miles south of Friday Harbor, in an isolated spot surrounded by 116 acres of woods, orchards, gardens, groomed lawn, and secluded beach, with unobstructed views of the Olympic Mountains. Innkeeper Jeffrey Beeston, who grew up in the house, is also a professional pilot, and his aerial tasks include towing banners and spotting fish for commercial fishermen in Alaska.

The Tudor-style house has a solid, elegant feel; it has the original leaded-glass windows, coved ceilings, hardwood floors, Oriental carpets, and mahogany woodwork. The Panorama Room upstairs is very romantic, with lace curtains and a floral chintz spread and pillows on the four-poster queen-size bed, and an exceptional view of Griffin Bay and the mountains beyond. Not far from the main house there's a cabin that can sleep up to four; it has an upstairs sleeping loft and a full kitchen.

Address: *760 Pear Point Rd., Friday Harbor, WA 98250, tel. 206/378-5604.*
Accommodations: *5 double rooms share 2 baths, housekeeping suite.*
Amenities: *Hot tub in cabin; private beach.*
Rates: *$70–$80; full breakfast. Cabin $125; no breakfast. MC, V.*
Restrictions: *Smoking outside only, no pets; 3-night minimum last weekend of July, 2-night minimum in cabin.*

Edenwild Inn

The imposing gray Victorian-style farmhouse surrounded by rose gardens in tiny Lopez Village is the Edenwild Inn. Although it looks restored, it's new (1990). Owner Sue Aran is an architectural designer—she designed the inn—and manager Heidi Borenstein is a master gardener.

The entrance opens onto a long hallway with oak floors, handwoven rugs, and framed oils and watercolors by Northwest artists. The muted palette—whitewashed floors, walls of grayed rose and lilac, white woodwork—lends the common areas sophistication. Each of the guest rooms has a different color scheme and individualized furnishings, with custom-made bed frames and wainscoting, botanical prints, large sprays of dried flowers and grapes (and, in season, fresh flowers), Scottish lace curtains, and leaded-glass windows. Four rooms have views of Fisherman's Bay and the San Juan Channel. The blue-gray Honeymoon Suite, overlooking the water, has a fireplace flanked by antique fireplace chairs.

Address: *Box 271, Lopez Island, WA 98261, tel. 206/468-3238.*
Accommodations: *7 double rooms with bath.*
Amenities: *Afternoon hot chocolate and fruit; bicycle rentals, kennel in garage for pets; ferry, seaplane, and airport pickup.*
Rates: *$100–$140; full breakfast. MC, V.*
Restrictions: *Smoking outside only, no pets inside.*

Hillside House

When Dick and Cathy Robinson left San Luis Obispo, California, they spent three years traveling in their 46-foot boat before purchasing Hillside House, which stands—yes—on a hillside a half mile from downtown Friday Harbor. Cathy loves island life, but she jokes that the population of retired professionals—attorneys, doctors, architects—are "just as competitive about the zucchini they grow for the county fair as they used to be about their careers."

The open living and dining room areas give onto a spacious and spectacularly scenic deck above the garden. The living room has a large brick fireplace, an Arts and Crafts coffee table, and overstuffed chairs. The seven sophisticated, comfortable guest rooms are furnished with king- and queen-size beds (except for one room with twins), oak chests, and window seats. In the Charlotte's Web Room there's a quilted chintz bedspread with pink cabbage roses on an ivory background, sea green carpet, and sweet peas blooming on the fence outside.

Address: *365 Carter Ave., Friday Harbor, WA 98250, tel. 206/378–4730, fax 206/378–3830.*
Accommodations: *5 double rooms with bath, 2 double rooms share 2 baths.*
Amenities: *Evening hors d'oeuvres; free use of health club.*
Rates: *$75–$90; full breakfast. MC, V.*
Restrictions: *Smoking outside only, no pets.*

Kangaroo House

Nestled on two acres of lawn and gardens less than a mile from the village of Eastsound is the 1907 Craftsman-style home known as Kangaroo House. The innkeepers are Mike and Jan Russillo; Mike was a career army officer and Jan has been an executive, a teacher, and the director of a crisis line—a combination that equips them to handle just about anything.

There's a solid, old feel to the dark hardwood floors and the Oriental rugs, but there's no need to be anxious about knocking over precious antiques. The living room is spacious, with a sitting area in front of a large stone fireplace, and beamed ceilings, lace curtains, settees, and wing chairs. The Louisa Room—red, teal, and tan—has an old brass double bed and a small twin bed with a painted iron headboard, handmade quilts, and angled ceilings.

The Russillos serve a full breakfast on tables set with china, silver, and linen; they'll also pack coffee and muffins for guests who have to meet an early morning ferry.

Address: *5 N. Beach Rd., Box 334, Eastsound, WA 98245, tel. 206/376–2175.*
Accommodations: *1 double room with bath, 3 double rooms share 1½ baths, 1 suite.*
Amenities: *Guest refrigerator.*
Rates: *$65–$100; full breakfast. MC, V.*
Restrictions: *Smoking outside only, no pets.*

MacKaye Harbor Inn

In 1978 Mike Bergstrom retired from professional golfing so that he could be with his wife, Robin, and their young children. Family and friends enjoyed visiting the Bergstroms so much that they came up with the idea of opening a B&B. In 1985 the Bergstroms bought a 1920s wood-frame Victorian-style sea captain's house along a half mile of beach at the south end of Lopez Island, across the road from MacKaye Harbor.

The sitting room has white wicker furnishings as well as a light blue sofa and love seat in front of a brass-and-glass-door fireplace, and a stained-glass window with roses designed by Robin. This room looks west out to the harbor, as do three of the guest rooms. One large room boasts a fireplace, a private deck, and a golden oak bedroom set from Italy. Robin serves fresh-baked pastries in the afternoon, and in the evening she hangs small baskets of chocolates on the doorknobs of guest rooms; she also cooks a hearty breakfast.

Address: *Rte. 1, Box 1940, Lopez Island, WA 98261, tel. 206/468-2253.*
Accommodations: *1 double room with bath, 4 double rooms share 2½ baths.*
Amenities: *Afternoon refreshments; kayak tours and rental, mountain bikes, rowboat.*
Rates: *$69–$105; full breakfast. MC, V.*
Restrictions: *Smoking outside only, no pets; 2-night minimum July–Sept.*

The Moon and Sixpence

This B&B named after the Somerset Maugham novel was built as a dairy farmer's home in 1900. The restored Victorian farmhouse has an open, airy, arty feel, with stained-glass windows, white woodwork, glossy floors of local fir, a cozy parlor with a wood-burning stove, a pair of original Hepplewhite chairs, and a Pembroke table; and there's a library that contains an old upright piano. The restored water tower has been turned into a suite with a reading loft at the top. Decorated in Early American blue-gray with red accents, it has a stenciled floor, a bed with a hand-stitched wedding-ring quilt, and a copy of *The Moon and Sixpence* on a bedside table.

Today the serenely rural 15-acre farm, 3 miles outside Friday Harbor, belongs to Charles and Evelyn Tuller. Ev's Pennsylvania Dutch background comes to the fore in such touches as bright handwoven blankets, her mother's needlepoint upholstery and rugs and fabrics that she weaves herself.

Address: *3021 Beaverton Valley Rd., Friday Harbor, WA 98250, tel. 206/378-4138.*
Accommodations: *4 double rooms share 2 baths, 1 suite.*
Amenities: *Guest refrigerator; weaving studio.*
Rates: *$65–$95; full breakfast. No credit cards.*
Restrictions: *Smoking outside only, no pets; 2-night minimum July–Aug. and on holiday weekends.*

Olympic Lights

In 1985 Lea and Christian Andrade took a vacation from the San Francisco Bay Area and fell in love with San Juan Island—so much so that they returned a month later and discovered this 1895 farmhouse, 5½ miles south of the Friday Harbor ferry landing.

While many inns are hideaways, Olympic Lights stands out in the open with nary a tree around it to block the view of Puget Sound and the Olympic Mountains. The entire house is available for guests to use—the hosts live nearby in a converted milk shed. Decorated almost exclusively in white (save for a few pale pastels), with no curtains except for white valances, the house feels expansive and open to both sunlight and starlight. The parlor has white wicker furniture with pale peach cushions; breakfast is served (on Lea's aunt's ivory, green, and pink rose-patterned china) either there or in the kitchen. Guest rooms feature brass reading lamps, wicker chairs and tables, and fluffy duvets and pillows.

Address: *4531-A Cattle Point Rd., Friday Harbor, WA 98250, tel. 206/378-3186.*
Accommodations: *1 double room with bath, 1 triple room and 3 doubles share 2 baths.*
Amenities: *Croquet, boccie, horseshoes.*
Rates: *$65–$90; full breakfast. No credit cards.*
Restrictions: *No smoking on property, no pets; 2-night minimum on holiday weekends.*

San Juan Inn

Annette and Skip Metzger began looking for an inn of their own in 1989; after a nationwide search for the right place at the right price, they settled on the San Juan Inn. Facing Friday Harbor's main street, the 1873 Victorian that once housed the town's wireless station stands just a block from the ferry landing.

A rose garden behind the building offers a secluded spot for a picnic or a glass of wine. Inside, the inn is clean and comfortable but not luxurious. The tiny lobby and stairway have stained-wood paneling. An upstairs sitting room features a rose Queen Anne parlor group, a wood-burning stove, a Mission oak rocker, and a harbor view.

The 10 guest rooms, all upstairs, are fitted with brass, wicker, or painted iron bedsteads. The San Juan Room has soft pink walls, wicker headboards and chairs, a pink, white, and blue-green flowered comforter, a washstand, and framed needlework samplers on the walls. The Metzgers serve a Continental breakfast on bone china dishes in the second-floor parlor.

Address: *50 Spring St., Box 776, Friday Harbor, WA 98250, tel. 206/378-2070.*
Accommodations: *10 double rooms share 3 baths.*
Rates: *$70–$90; Continental breakfast. MC, V.*
Restrictions: *Smoking outside only, no large pets. Closed Dec. 25–29.*

Wharfside

Board the *Jacquelyn*, a 60-foot motor-sailer anchored near the Friday Harbor ferry landing, and you'll find yourself on the town's only floating bed-and-breakfast. Clyde Rice and his wife, Bette, decided to combine their love of boating and their flair for hospitality in 1984, when they opened the *Jacquelyn* as a B&B.

The main salon has two sofas and a skylight, a fireplace, and lots of polished wood and brass. The head has a Japanese-style tile soaking tub as well as a shower. The two guest rooms stand at opposite ends of the boat: the aft stateroom, a romantic low-beamed captain's cabin with a queen-size bed, a small settee, and a half-bath; and the forward stateroom, furnished with a double bed and two bunks.

Bette serves a four-course, all-you-can-eat breakfast. She also provides children with nets and cans for gathering shrimp (and jellyfish and other treasures) from the harbor.

Address: *K-Dock, Slip 13, Port of Friday Harbor Marina, Box 1212, Friday Harbor, WA 98250, tel. 206/378-5661.*
Accommodations: *2 double rooms share bath.*
Amenities: *Robes; rowboat, sportfishing and cruise charters available.*
Rates: *$75–$80; full breakfast. MC, V.*
Restrictions: *2-night minimum in summer. Closed Dec. and Jan.*

Whatcom and Skagit Counties
Including Anacortes,
Bellingham, and La Conner

About 90 minutes north of Seattle on the way to
Vancouver, British Columbia, I-95 passes through Skagit
and Whatcom counties, where gently rolling dairy
farmland is juxtaposed with flat rectangles of brilliant
color—fields of commercially grown daffodils and tulips
that are a major attraction for gardeners, photographers,
and city dwellers in search of a pleasant weekend drive. To
the east in these two northernmost counties in coastal
Washington, low foothills often wrapped in mist nestle
against the snowcapped mountains of the Cascade range.

Far from being exclusively agrarian, however, the three
major communities in Whatcom and Skagit counties are
very much associated with the sea. La Conner, at the
mouth of the Skagit River, is a fishing village with
a decidedly artsy accent, a legacy of the 1940s, when
modernist painters Morris Graves and Mark Tobey settled
there. Ferries ply the waters of Anacortes, a fishing and
logging town on Fidalgo Island that serves as the gateway
to the San Juan Islands, while Bellingham, a center of
fishing and lumber activity and the southern terminus of
the Alaska Marine Highway System, is the site of Western
Washington University, a campus that offers splendid views
of Puget Sound. Nowhere are these views more dramatic
than from Chuckanut Drive (Highway 11), a dramatic 20-
mile stretch between Bellingham and Bow along
Chuckanut Bay.

Today in this pastoral area, artists and college professors
coexist with farmers and fishermen. A number of the
residents are descendants of the native tribes that have
existed here for the past 12,000 years or offspring of
relative newcomers: the Spanish, who arrived in 1774, and
the English, who followed four years later.

Bellingham Waterfront. Several spots make for good dock walking, fishing, lounging, and picnicking. *Squalicum Harbor Marina* (Roeder Ave. and Coho Way, tel. 206/676–2542), the second-largest marina on Puget Sound, is home to more than 1,700 commercial and pleasure boats. An aquarium in the adjacent Harbor Center shopping mall contains examples of many of the local sea creatures; children will especially enjoy the "touch tank." *Boulevard Park* (S. State St. and Bayview Dr., tel. 206/676–6985), located midway between downtown and Old Fairhaven, is a 14-acre waterfront park with a half mile of shoreline. With views of both the San Juan Islands and the Cascades, it's a logical choice for picnickers. *Marine Park* (at the foot of Harris St. in Old Fairhaven) is small, but it is popular for crabbing and watching sunsets.

Birch Bay State Park (5105 Helwig Rd., Blaine, tel. 206/371–2800). Most of this 200-acre park, 10 miles from the Canadian border, is heavily wooded, but impressive views of the San Juan Islands can be had from the shore and from a few of the 167 campsites. The clamming and crabbing here are excellent, and opportunities for fishing, swimming, and hiking along interpretive trails are plentiful. Campsites are open year-round but can be reserved only from Memorial Day to Labor Day.

Chuckanut Drive (Highway 11). You're advised to take this 23-mile drive along Chuckanut Bay heading south out of Bellingham; that way you'll have the steep and densely wooded Chuckanut Mountain on your left, with stunning views of Puget Sound and the San Juan Islands relatively unobstructed. The drive begins along Fairhaven Park in Old Fairhaven and joins I-5 in the flat farmlands near Bow in Skagit County. The full loop can be made within a few hours. Several good restaurants are located toward the southern end of the drive, so you may want to plan your jaunt around lunch or dinner (*see* Restaurants, below). In addition to a number of lookout points, there are several other worthwhile stops along the way: *Larrabee State Park* (245 Chuckanut Dr., tel. 206/676–2093), with nearly 1,900 acres of forest and park and 3,600 feet of shoreline; the 6-mile-long *Interurban Trail*, a former train track along the water used for cycling, walking, jogging, and horseback riding; and the *Taylor Oyster Company* (188 Chuckanut Dr., Bow, tel. 206/766–6002), where visitors, by appointment, can watch oysters being harvested, sorted, shucked, and packed. A store on the premises sells oysters, scallops, crabs, and mussels in season. The trailhead begins in the north near 24th Street and Old Fairhaven Parkway and in the south near Larrabee State Park.

Ferndale Parks. *Hovander Homestead Park* (5299 Nielsen Rd., Ferndale, tel. 206/384–3444) is a "farm park" complete with a Victorian-Era farmhouse, farm animals, vegetable gardens, old farm equipment, a blacksmith's shop, and walking trails. *Pioneer Park* (1st and Cherry Sts., Ferndale, tel. 206/384–5113) features a handful of restored log buildings from the 1870s, including a granary, Whatcom County's first church, a hotel, and several houses. *Lake Terrell Wildlife Preserve* (5975 Lake Terrell Rd., Ferndale, tel. 206/384–4723) is an 11,000-acre spread that allows visitors to observe a wide variety of waterfowl. Hunting is permitted in season (ducks and pheasants are most prevalent), and fishing on the lake, year-round, yields trout, catfish, bass, and perch. Nearby is *Tennant Lake Natural History Interpretive Center* (5236 Nielsen Rd., Ferndale, tel. 206/384–3444), featuring an early homestead, nature walks around the lake, and an observation tower from which the 200 acres of marshy habitat, bald eagles, muskrats, otters, and other wildlife can be seen. The rich perfumes emanating from the fragrance garden there is intended for the seeing-impaired, but, naturally, sighted visitors enjoy them as well. Special events include crafts fairs and evening walks with a modern-day Henry David Thoreau in 19th-century costume.

Gaches Mansion (2nd and Calhoun Sts., tel. 206/466–4288). Ever since Morris Graves, Mark Tobey, Kenneth Callahan, and other pioneering American modernist painters settled in La Conner during the 1940s, the town has been an artists' haven. Aside from sampling the local talent at one of the village's many galleries, visitors can see the works of area artists at the Valley Museum of Northwest Art, housed on the second floor of this restored Victorian Tudor mansion. The first and third floors are especially popular because visitors are encouraged to touch and sit on the period furniture that is on display. The turret of the house (open Apr.–Sept., Fri.–Sun. 1–5 PM; Oct.–Mar., Fri.–Sun. 1–4 PM) offers an excellent view of La Conner.

Gardens of Art. (2900 Sylvan St., tel. 206/734–4167). Visitors can wander through this 2½-acre garden in Bellingham that features the works of artists from the Northwest. All of the plants and sculptures are for sale.

Maritime Heritage Center (1600 C St., tel. 206/676–6806). This urban park is a tribute to Bellingham's fishing industry and heritage. On self-guided tours, visitors learn about hatcheries and the life cycles of salmon, watch salmon spawn, see how rearing tanks work, watch mature salmon swim up the fish ladders, and actually fish for salmon and trout.

Padilla Bay (1043 Bay View–Edison Rd., Mount Vernon, tel. 206/428–1558). This estuary features an interpretive center that focuses on the area's natural history, with exhibits and saltwater aquariums, a mile-long nature trail, beachwalk, a pair of resident bald eagles, and a variety of waterfowl and sea life.

Skagit Valley Tulip Festival (Box 10007, Mount Vernon, WA 98273, tel. 800/4-TULIPS). Held during the first three weeks of April in Mount Vernon, Burlington, Anacortes, and La Conner, the festival centers around more than 1,500 acres of spring flowers—daffodils, irises, and, of course, tulips—with tours of the blossoming fields and bulb sales. Festivities include foot races, an art show featuring local talent, a community fair, horsedrawn wagon rides, a salmon barbecue, sailboat regatta, concerts, dance performances, an antiques show, a food fair, petting zoo, and sky-diving and kite-flying demonstrations.

Western Washington University (516 High St., tel. 206/676–3000) overlooks downtown Bellingham and Bellingham Bay. As you drive through the campus to take in the panorama, you'll be treated to a fine collection of outdoor sculpture, including works by Mark DiSuvero, Isamu Noguchi, Richard Serra, and George Rickey.

Whatcom County Museum of History and Art (121 Prospect St., Bellingham, tel. 206/676–6981). Housed in a large redbrick Victorian building in downtown Bellingham, the museum concentrates on the early coal and lumber industries, the history and culture of Native American tribes that lived in the area, and the habitat and characteristics of local waterfowl. The museum also hosts traveling exhibitions.

Restaurants

At **Boomers Landing** (tel. 206/293–5108), in Anacortes, you can dine on some of the town's best seafood while watching the sun set over Guemes Channel. The well-regarded French cuisine at **La Petite** (tel. 206/293–4644) is served in a romantic setting. If you enjoy the bustle of a marina, try Anacortes's **Slocum's** (tel. 206/293–0644), which offers fresh salmon, seafood, prime rib, and pasta. Among Bellingham's dining spots, seek out **Il Fiasco** (tel. 206/676–9136) which, despite its name, serves good Italian fare, and **La Belle Rose** (tel. 206/647–0833), a country-French restaurant that specializes in seafood. The **Oyster Creek Inn** (tel. 206/766–6179), in Bow, overlooks a rushing creek on Chuckanut Drive and specializes in—what else?—oysters. The **Black Swan** (tel. 206/466–3040), in La Conner, features Mediterranean cooking. Also in La Conner, **Barkleys** in the **La Conner Country Inn** (tel. 206/446–4261) prepares pasta and seafood in country-French style.

Tourist Information

Anacortes Chamber of Commerce (1319 Commercial Ave., Anacortes, WA 98221, tel. 206/293–3832); **La Conner Chamber of Commerce** (109 South 1st St., Box 644, La Conner, WA 98257, tel. 206/466–4778); **Mount Vernon Chamber of Commerce** (325 E. College Way, Box 1007, Mount Vernon, WA 98273, tel. 206/428–8547); **Whatcom Chamber of Commerce** (1203 Cornwall Ave., Box 958, Bellingham, WA 98227, tel. 206/734–1330).

Reservation Services

Bed & Breakfast Service (Box 5025, Bellingham, WA 98227, tel. 206/733–8642); **Fidalgo Island Bed & Breakfast Guild** (Box 982, Anacortes, WA 98221, tel. 206/293–0535); **Pacific Bed & Breakfast Agency** (701 N.W. 60th St., Seattle, WA 98107, tel. 206/784–0539); **Travelers Bed & Breakfast** (Box 492, Mercer Island, WA 98040, tel. 206/232–2345); **Whatcom County Bed & Breakfast Guild** (tel. 206/676–4560, phone rotates among members).

The Channel House

Midway between downtown Anacortes and the ferry terminal is the Channel House, a shingled Craftsman bungalow with awe-inspiring views of Guemes Channel and the ferry landing that can be seen from most rooms. Owners Dennis and Patricia McIntyre dreamed of acquiring a smaller business when their daughter went off to college, but when she turned 15, they thought, "Why wait?" An ad in the *Los Angeles Times* turned up the Channel House.

The dining room, certainly the most spectacular room in the house, features lush ferns and other potted plants that stand against dark blue and peach floral print wallpaper, white painted wainscoting, and the original glazed terra-cotta tile floor with cobalt-blue borders. A window with the original stained glass depicts lily pads in shades of green and pink. As guests dine on the house specialty—French toast stuffed with cream cheese, pineapple, and pecans—they can watch the ferries plying Rosario Strait.

Ten steps up are the living room, with open beams and a 12-foot-high ceiling, and a cozy study. Both rooms display porcelain dolls made by Dennis's mother from antique molds, complete with hand-painted features and hand-sewn costumes.

Each guest room has its own style, but all are spacious and light, with high ceilings, hardwood floors, Oriental rugs, and a mix of contemporary furniture in traditional styles as well as such antiques as an 1878 Comstock Castle wood-burning stove and several treadle sewing machines. Grandma's Room is furnished with an antique brass bed, a log cabin–style quilt, and a turn-of-the-century Eastlake-type oak dresser; children's boaters hang on the walls. The more formal Canopy Room has a canopy bed covered with the same antique lace that dresses the window, and an early 19th-century fainting couch upholstered in cream-colored damask. The walls are covered with a cream and green striped paper with a floral border. The Victorian Rose Suite seems a perfect spot for reverie; its window seat is crowded with soft throw pillows, and the fireplace has cream tiles with hand-painted pink roses that are echoed in the pale pink walls and ceiling border of roses against a black background.

Address: *2902 Oakes Ave., Anacortes, WA 98221, tel. 206/293–9382.*
Accommodations: *2 double rooms with bath, 2 double rooms share bath, 2 suites.*
Amenities: *Evening coffee, tea, and cookies, morning coffee delivered to rooms, whirlpool baths and fireplaces in suites; outdoor hot tub.*
Rates: *$69–$89; full breakfast. D, MC, V.*
Restrictions: *Smoking outside only, no pets.*

Majestic Hotel

Many of the guests who use the Majestic Hotel merely as a stopover on the way to the nearby San Juan Islands end up wishing they could linger. Dominating the historical district of Anacortes, the Majestic is one of the Northwest's premier small hotels.

Standing in the two-story-high lobby, filled with 19th-century English leather sofas and wing chairs, an elegant brass chandelier, and a white marble mantelpiece flanked by engaged columns, it's difficult to believe that this space was part of a meat market until 1954. Happily, Jeff and Virginia Wetmore, restaurant and inn developers from northern California, recognized this diamond in the rough, which was built in 1889. Stripping away everything except the original framework, they opened the hotel in 1990 after six years of restoration. You're unlikely to meet the Wetmores at the marble-top front desk (from an 1890 Montana hotel); they leave the business of guest relations to the competent staff. However, they do enjoy working behind the scenes, hunting for the unusual Victorian and Edwardian antiques that are combined with contemporary furnishings at the Majestic.

The Wetmores take particular pride in the Rose & Crown Pub, behind the lobby, where guests are served a Continental breakfast and can enjoy light snacks and draft beers from local microbreweries amid 200-year-old English mahogany wainscoting, a backbar from a Victorian ice-cream parlor, and beveled- and stained-glass doors from a London pub. More substantial fare is served at dinner (Thursday to Sunday) and at Sunday brunch in the bistro, which specializes in such seasonal seafood as the local pink scallops, salmon, and Penn Cove mussels.

Each of the hotel's 22 guest rooms is individually decorated. The Scottish Highland Room sports fishing rods, baskets, and old shotguns mounted on the walls, and there is a Scottish military chest from the 1880s. In the Asian Room the walls have been japanned, and Japanese, Korean, and Chinese furniture and art are featured. An oak-paneled cupola affords a 360-degree view of Puget Sound, the marina, the San Juan Islands, and the Cascade and Olympic mountains.

Address: *419 Commercial Ave., Anacortes, WA 98221, tel. 206/293–3355, fax 206/293–5214.*
Accommodations: *22 double rooms with bath.*
Amenities: *Cable TV, phone, and coffeemaker in rooms; wet bar, refrigerator, VCR, and soaking tub in some rooms; restaurant and pub, 2 meeting rooms.*
Rates: *$79–$150; Continental breakfast. AE, D, MC, V.*
Restrictions: *Smoking on second floor only, no pets.*

Willows Inn

You could say that heartbreak made the Willows Inn, on the west shore of Lummi Island, what it is today. When Victoria Flynn stopped by in 1985 to revisit the resort her grandparents had run when she was a girl, she discovered her old haunt had been subdivided into small, dark apartments and the 28 cabins that housed the guest rooms reduced to one. "Overcome by nostalgia," recalls Flynn, "my heart wanted to rescue it." Not long afterward, she and her husband, Gary, a retired submarine officer, found themselves innkeepers. They gutted the main house, cabin, and staff dormitory to restore them to the appearance that had kept families coming back to the remote, 10-mile-long island for decades. Visitors seeking nightlife and a variety of restaurants would be better off in Bellingham or Vancouver, but those drawn to a peaceful and bucolic retreat with views of the water everywhere need look no farther.

The Flynns have a particular weakness for old advertising signs, and in the game room in the basement, which contains the original Willows pool table and a poker table, you'll find old brewery and pub mirrors displayed. Inherited family pieces such as the overstuffed, mohair-covered club chair in the living room—guests love it—mingle with antiques chosen less for their aesthetic appeal than for their quirky origins (for example, an old commercial shoe rack now displays the wines to be served at dinner). Guests in one room sleep in Victoria's childhood bed, which is Eastlake style in walnut, others in her parents' mahogany American Renaissance Revival bed.

Guests who covet their privacy may prefer the honeymoon suite in the cottage, amid the prize-winning English country-style garden, or the Highland Home, in the old dorm, filled with tartans and knickknacks.

Coffee and hot Irish soda bread delivered to the rooms at 8 AM are followed by a three-course country breakfast in the dining room. Guests may also purchase wine and beer by the glass. Dinners are served on Friday and Saturday only.

Address: *2579 West Shore Dr., Lummi Island, WA 98262, tel. 206/758-2620.*
Accommodations: *2 double rooms with bath, 2 double rooms share 1 bath, 1 suite, 1 double housekeeping suite with 2 baths.*
Amenities: *1 suite with 2-person whirlpool bath, phone, TV, and stereo in suites; restaurant, licensed for beer and wine.*
Rates: *$90–$250, double housekeeping suite $250; full breakfast, MAP available. Fifteen percent service charge for dinner. MC, V.*
Restrictions: *Smoking outside only, no pets; 2-night minimum in summer. Closed to lodgers Dec.–Jan.*

Anderson House

A few miles south of the Canadian border, just off I-5 in Ferndale, Anderson House sits atop a hill just west of downtown. In 1986 Dave Anderson, a pilot and former ski salesman, and his wife, Kelly, a medical technician, bought the American Foursquare house, built by the town's first butcher in 1897, and restored it.

The foyer is paneled with the original fir, but the living room, where guests congregate, is nondescript modern. The guest rooms have been decorated more imaginatively, with white-iron reproduction bedsteads featuring porcelain finials, Pilgrim-style trunks that double as luggage racks, crystal reading lamps, and some of the most comfortable mattresses in the Northwest.

Breakfast is served at a large oak table in the dining room overlooking the flower gardens. Kelly designed the crystal chandelier with Bavarian swans that hangs over the table in honor of the graceful trumpeter swans that winter in the area.

Address: *2140 Main St., Box 1547, Ferndale, WA 98248, tel. 206/384-3450.*
Accommodations: *1 double room with bath, 2 doubles share bath, 1 suite.*
Amenities: *Complimentary sherry.*
Rates: *$45–$55, suite $75; full breakfast. AE, MC, V.*
Restrictions: *Smoking outside only, no pets; 2-night minimum on holiday weekends.*

Downey House

It is difficult to believe that Jim and Kaye Frey got their 1904 two-story Victorian-style farmhouse "free for the moving" in 1965 from a farm called Downey Place. They moved the house to a pastoral site less than 4 miles from downtown La Conner; in the dining room there's a photograph of the house mounted on wooden beams to prove it.

The house is filled with objects associated with family and friends. The parlor boasts a pump organ from Jim's home state of Nebraska.

Rooms are wallpapered in small floral patterns and feature photographs and antiques from Kaye's great-grandparents. The McCormick Room features bay windows, an old brass-and-iron bed, a Pilgrim-style family trunk and a mannequin wearing Kaye's grandmother's wedding nightgown. Each night the Freys serve up their pièce de résistance—homemade wild blackberry pie à la mode and coffee.

Address: *1880 Chilberg Rd., La Conner, WA 98257, tel. 206/466-3207.*
Accommodations: *1 double room with bath, 2 double rooms share bath, 2 suites.*
Amenities: *Evening refreshments; outdoor hot tub.*
Rates: *$75–$95, suites $90–$115; full breakfast. MC, V.*
Restrictions: *Smoking outside only; 2-night minimum first 3 weekends in Apr.*

Heather House

Located within easy walking distance of downtown La Conner, with views of farmland, Mt. Baker, and the Cascade Mountains, Heather House is a replica of a turn-of-the-century Cape Cod house. Wayne Everton and his wife, Bev, bought the house in 1982.

The Evertons live next door, an arrangement that gives guests maximum privacy. The kitchen is always stocked with coffee and an array of sodas, juices, cheeses, and cookies. The Continental breakfast, equally generous and served by Wayne, always includes fresh-baked scones and an entrée such as poached apples with sour-cream sauce, peach melba, or strawberry cobbler. Comfort is the watchword at Heather House; you won't find anything out of the pages of *Architectural Digest*, but you'll probably feel very much at home. Thumbing through the short-story collections and magazines, trying your hand at the resident games and puzzles, and taking in the views from the back porch are encouraged; the Evertons take pride in not having a television.

Address: *505 Maple Ave., La Conner, WA 98257, tel. 206/466–4675.*
Accommodations: *3 double rooms share 2 baths.*
Amenities: *Off-street parking, bicycles.*
Rates: *$50–$70; Continental breakfast. MC, V.*
Restrictions: *No smoking inside, no pets.*

Heron Inn

Co-owner Jim Gibbons is heron crazy, and this new Victorian-style inn five blocks from the La Conner waterfront is just brimming with them, from stained-glass windows of herons to the heron watercolors, prints, and etchings on every wall. Even the outside is painted a heron blue-gray.

Large windows with lace curtains and a high cove ceiling contribute to the light, airy feel of the lobby/parlor, where guests can relax on the Queen Anne–style camelback couch or in wingback chairs in front of the fireplace.

Guest rooms, all carpeted and featuring a blue-and-rose color scheme, mix modern reproductions, such as wing chairs and beds with oak, walnut, and brass headboards, with antique armoires. All the suites have gas fireplaces.

When guests tire of antiquing on Morris Street, a half block away, they can sit on the old-fashioned cast-iron and wood park benches on the deck or soak in the outdoor hot tub.

Address: *117 Maple Ave., La Conner, WA 98257, tel. 206/466–4626.*
Accommodations: *9 double rooms with baths, 3 suites.*
Amenities: *TV, clock radio, and phone in rooms, 1 suite with 2-person whirlpool bath; outdoor hot tub.*
Rates: *$65–$78, suites $95–$115; Continental breakfast. AE, MC, V.*
Restrictions: *Smoking outside only; no pets.*

Hotel Planter

Located in downtown La Conner, the Hotel Planter is a masonry building that was constructed in 1907 of solid concrete blocks made on location. The hotel, whose clientele consisted of lumber-mill and fish-cannery workers, merchants, and tourists from Seattle, was modern for its day, with indoor plumbing—one bathroom for 22 rooms—electricity, and a cement sidewalk. Later the writers, artists, and craftspeople responsible for La Conner's reputation as a cultural center moved in. Today guests can enjoy that artistic heritage by stepping right out onto 1st Street, La Conner's charming main street, which is lined with art galleries, bookstores, crafts shops, and restaurants.

Owners Donald and Cynthia Hoskins bought the building in 1986 and opened their street-level Earthenworks Gallery, then renovated the second-story hotel. Now creamy walls, custom-made basswood headboards and armoires, and wicker chairs in natural, green, and peach tones lend a country-French atmosphere. To keep the feeling of the old hotel, the original doors, window moldings, railings, trim, and many of the old light fixtures were restored.

Address: *715 1st St., La Conner, WA 98257, tel. 206/466–4710.*
Accommodations: *12 double rooms with bath.*
Amenities: *Phone, TV, and clock radio in room; hot tub.*
Rates: *$70–$110; no breakfast. AE, MC, V.*
Restrictions: *No smoking, no pets.*

Schnauzer Crossing

On a slope above Lake Whatcom sits this contemporary cedar home that dispels the notion that B&Bs in this area mean Victoriana. The three guest rooms have a Japanese feel to them: A Japanese iris print covers the down comforters and futon furniture, and the cottage suite features Oriental-style furniture.

The unusual name of this B&B derives from innkeeper Donna McAllister's present job: breeding schnauzers. Guests pretty much have the run of the main-floor kitchen and living room, whose windows reach up to a dramatic cathedral ceiling. Breakfast, accompanied by classical music, is a special occasion—with individual quiches, rhubarb crisps, and blueberries and raspberries fresh from the garden (guests may pick their own). The pampering extends to fruit baskets, fresh flowers, terry robes, and "schnauzer" slippers in every room.

Address: *4421 Lakeway Dr., Bellingham, WA 98226, tel. 206/733–0055 or 206/734–2808.*
Accommodations: *1 double room with bath, 2 suites.*
Amenities: *Cable TV, VCR, whirlpool tub, and fireplace in suites; microwave and wetbar in 1 suite; outdoor hot tub, tennis court, canoe and small sailboat available.*
Rates: *$95, suites $145 and $175; full breakfast. AE, MC, V.*
Restrictions: *No smoking indoors; 2-night minimum in cottage, 2-night minimum on weekends and holidays.*

White Swan Guest House

Tucked away along a narrow country road near the Skagit River, between I–5 and La Conner, is the White Swan Guest House. In 1898 a Scandinavian farmer, who ran the ferry across the river, built the Queen Anne clapboard farmhouse with a turret from which he could watch for passengers. A few years ago, New Yorker Peter Goldfarb fell in love with the house and used his training as an interior designer to make each room colorful and airy, yet warm. Public and guest rooms feature bright pastel walls, white trim, lace curtains, handmade quilts, fresh flowers, and a collection of needlework samplers.

Guest rooms in the main house have king- or queen-size beds with brass and iron headboards and hand-hooked rugs. The two-story cottage has more contemporary furnishings, in pine and other light woods, wicker chairs, and Pendleton Indian blankets.

Before breakfast you can fetch a cup of coffee from the kitchen, and if you're lucky enough to snare the Pink Room, take it next door to the little sitting area in the six-sided turret.

Address: *1388 Moore Rd., Mount Vernon, WA 98273, tel. 206/445–6805.*
Accommodations: *3 double rooms share 2 baths; 11 housekeeping suites.*
Rates: *$70–$100; Continental breakfast. MC, V.*
Restriction: *No pets in main house.*

Cascade Mountains

Dominated by Mt. Rainier, the Cascades form the backbone of western Washington state, stretching from the Oregon border to Canada. This massive mountain range—which actually begins in California, a continuation of the Sierra Nevada—offers spectacular scenery, good skiing in winter, and hiking, camping, fishing, river rafting, and wildlife viewing in summer.

Day trips and longer excursions from Seattle, just west of the range, take visitors into the heart of the Cascades to sample the scenery, a sprinkling of mountain villages— some originally gold- or coal-mining towns from the last century, some simple ski resorts—and a variety of inns and lodges nestled in valleys or perched on crests.

A variety of mountain experiences can be had within two hours of the city. Interstate 90, for example, leads east to Snoqualmie Pass, with both downhill and cross-country skiing, and on to the mining towns of Roslyn and Cle Elum. Highway 2 heads northeast across Stevens Pass, another downhill skiing area, to the Bavarian-style village of Leavenworth. Not far from the Canadian border, Highway 20 (closed during the winter months) cuts through North Cascades National Park, a half-million-acre preserve studded with glaciers and mountain lakes. Heading south out of Seattle, highways 12, 706, 165, and 410 take you to various entrances of Mt. Rainier National Park.

Drives through the Cascades take you past mountain valleys, alpine meadows, lakes, and waterfalls, but only by hiking the trails can one really experience the beauty and grandeur of the mountains. Not all the trails are rugged; in fact, some are more like alpine walks. The best time to view mountain wildflowers is from the end of July to early August.

Places to Go, Sights to See

Lake Chelan. Take a scenic excursion up the 55-mile-long lake aboard one of the *Lady of the Lake* boats (tel. 509/682–2224). Leaving from the town of Chelan on the south shore, where the sun shines 300 days a year, the tour boat takes you to the northern terminus town of Stehekin. There passengers can get out for a picnic lunch or a short tour in an open bus before returning to Chelan, where you'll find rentals for waterskiing, sailing, boating, fishing, and cross-country skiing.

Leavenworth. This former mining and railroading town with a population of about 1,500 is located at an elevation of 1,170 feet, surrounded by mountains rising to 8,000 feet. Thirty years ago, Leavenworth was a has-been; when civic leaders turned it into an alpine village, giving every downtown building a Tyrolean-style facade, tourists flocked.

Mt. Rainier National Park (tel. 206/569–2211). Designated in 1899 as the nation's fifth national preserve, the park encompasses all of Mt. Rainier, at 14,410 feet, the state's highest mountain. Among the park's 240,000-plus acres are forests, alpine meadows, and glacier (when the weather is cooperative, hiking trails lead right up to the glaciers' edge). Major visitor centers are at Paradise, Sunrise, and Ohanapecosh; some offer slide shows, summer videos, naturalist-guided hikes, and information on hiking trails and the many breathtaking lookouts.

Mt. Rainier Scenic Railroad (206/569–2588). A vintage steam locomotive takes you on a 14-mile trip across spectacular bridges and through lush, tall forests with views of Mt. Rainier. The train departs from Elbe in season. The trip takes 90 minutes and is accompanied by live banjo and guitar music.

Northwest Trek (near Eatonville, tel. 206/832–6116). This is one of the country's most unusual parks. Through 5½ miles of forest, bog, and pasture, trams take visitors to view North American wildlife—elk, deer, bears, bison, caribou, bighorn sheep, pronghorn antelopes, mountain goats, moose, gray wolves, cougars, lynx, bobcats, birds, waterfowl—in their native habitats.

Puget Sound and Snoqualmie Valley Railroad (tel. 206/746–4025). This steam-locomotive-driven train, operated by volunteers, runs between Snoqualmie and North Bend (just east of Seattle on I-90) from May through September. Tickets can be purchased in the restored 1890 depot in downtown Snoqualmie.The ride takes about 70 minutes and offers views of mountains, forest, and meadowland—views that may already be familiar to fans of the "Twin Peaks" series, which was filmed largely in this area. (Try the cherry pie at North Bend's Mar-T Cafe—the actual setting for Agent Cooper's favorite restaurant.)

Roslyn. This old mining town, off I–90 near Cle Elum, has mostly fallen into disrepair but manages to support a handful of retail shops, two restaurants (*see below*), and a first-run movie theater (in an old mortuary). It has been described as more Alaskan than Alaska by the folks who chose to film the television series "Northern Exposure" here.

Snoqualmie Falls. These 268-foot falls just outside the town of Snoqualmie are a crashing spectacle in the spring, when the mountain snows thaw, and when fall rains come thundering down. At the top is an observation deck and a mile-long marked trail down to the base of the falls.

Winthrop. This historic town on Route 20, the North Cascades Highway, is about a four-hour drive from Seattle. Once a bustling gold-mining town, Winthrop has been returned to its colorful 1890s appearance with barn-board storefronts, hitching posts, and boardwalk-style sidewalks. You can inspect an excellent collection of Old West memorabilia at the *Schafer Historical Museum*, in a 100-year-old log cabin, or rest at *Three-Fingered Jack's* (Hwy. 20 and Bridge St., tel. 509/996–2411), the state's oldest saloon.

Restaurants

Alexander's Country Inn (tel. 206/569–2300) in Ashford serves trout fresh from the pond behind the inn, plus seafood, pasta, and delicious desserts. **The Herbfarm** (tel. 206/784–2222) in Fall City allows guests to tour the farm and watch as six-course gourmet extravaganzas are prepared. **Mama Vallone's Steak House & Inn** (tel. 509/674–5174) in Cle Elum can be counted on for great pasta, steak, and service. The **Roslyn Cafe** (tel. 509/649–2763) offers a jukebox with vintage 78s and good pasta and burgers. The **Old Honey Farm Country Inn** (tel. 206/888–9399) in Snoqualmie serves good country fare at reasonable prices in a room with pasture and mountain views. The **Salish Lodge** (tel. 206/888–2556 or 800/826–6124), also in Snoqualmie, serves gourmet cuisine and a very popular brunch in its dining room, with large windows overlooking Snoqualmie Falls.

Tourist Information

South Puget Sound Tourism Association (Box 1754, Tacoma 98401, tel. 206/627–2836); **North Central Washington Tourism Association** (324 S. Pioneer Way, Moses Lake 98837, tel. 509/765–7888 or 800/992–6234 in WA).

Reservation Services

Leavenworth Area Bed & Breakfast Association (Box 285, Leavenworth 98826, tel. 509/548–6936); **Pacific Bed & Breakfast Agency** (701 N.W. 60th St., Seattle 98107, tel. 206/784–0539); **Travelers Bed & Breakfast** (Box 492, Mercer Island 98040, tel. 206/232–2345); **Seattle Bed & Breakfast Association** (2442 N.W. Market St., Seattle 98107, tel. 206/547–1020).

Mazama County Inn

East of the North Cascades National Park, nestled in a valley laced with cross-country skiing trails, is this serenely rural, rustic mountain lodge. Owned by Cal and Ann Merriman, the Mazama is a sprawling two-story wood-sided building with a front entry of stone and log posts, dormer windows, and a brick-red roof set against a backdrop of pine trees and mountains.

The spacious dining and living room features a massive Russian stone fireplace, vaulted ceiling, peeled-log furniture, and floor-to-ceiling windows that look out at the valley floor and the mountains beyond. Glass doors lead to the deck, furnished with umbrella tables for picnic lunches. Watercolor landscapes by a local artist are displayed throughout.

Guest rooms are comfortable, but certainly not opulent. A section added in 1990 comprises four larger rooms connected by covered walkway to the lodge.

Also available are two cabins and the original, six-bedroom ranch house (for families or groups), which have kitchens, bathrooms, and wood-burning stoves.

The inn attracts guests who want a mountain experience. In summer, the area offers mountain biking, hiking, horseback riding, river rafting, llama trekking, and fishing. In winter, the inn itself offers ski rentals and lessons and arranges for heli-skiing and inn-to-hut ski touring. One of the hedonistic experiences enjoyed by guests after a day of cross-country skiing is slipping into the outdoor hot tub, surrounded by snowbanks, and gazing at the stars.

Winter breakfasts include hearty oatmeal, eggs, biscuits, coffee cake, and fruit. In summer, guests order entrées off the restaurant menu, such as a vegetarian omelet or whole-wheat sesame-seed waffles. Makings for sandwiches are set out after breakfast for guests to fix their own brown-bag lunches. Winter dinners are served family style and include appetizer, entrée, and dessert. In summer, dinners are ordered off the menu and may include Cajun shrimp or chicken fettuccine with broccoli and artichokes; a favorite dessert is chocolate mousse cake.

Address: *Hwy. 20, Box 223, Mazama, WA 98833, tel. 509/996–2681 or in WA, 800/843–7951.*
Accommodations: *14 double rooms with bath, 2 housekeeping cabins, 6 farmhouse rooms share 2 baths.*
Amenities: *Restaurant; sauna; outdoor hot tub.*
Rates: *Summer $50–$90, full breakfast; Winter $145–$185, AP; cabins $95; no breakfast. MC, V.*
Restrictions: *No smoking, no pets, 2-night minimum in cabins and farmhouse.*

Run of the River Inn

On the Icicle River a half mile from Leavenworth, with a bird refuge on two sides, is this bed-and-breakfast in a classic log structure built in 1979 to take advantage of extraordinary views of the river, Tumwater and Icicle canyons, and the towering Cascades.

A second story with cathedral ceilings was added by innkeepers Karen and Monty Turner, who moved here in 1987 from Las Vegas, where they both taught fifth grade. Karen still teaches, while Monty runs the inn and maintains his collection of classic and antique bicycles. Both are sports enthusiasts and work out regularly.

Though the fireplace-warmed dining, living, and kitchen area downstairs is really the Turners' domain, guests do enjoy their breakfasts there. The country breakfast may include yogurt with fruit or a fresh fruit plate, hash browns, cinnamon rolls, and a cheese and sausage strata.

A guest sitting room is at the top of the circular staircase; supported by hand-peeled logs fashioned by a local craftsman, the staircase is one of the inn's many hand-hewn log features custom-made for the Turners. Like the rest of the inn, the sitting room has an upscale country look, with handmade willow furniture and a stenciled pine dry sink. Beverages and fresh gingerbread cookies are set out to make guests feel at home.

Bedrooms have high cathedral ceilings of pine, hand-hewn log furniture, and locally made hand-embroidered quilts on queen-size beds. Each room has a commanding view of the natural surroundings, along with an old fly rod, ski pole, or snowshoe on one wall as a reminder of the diversions the area offers.

The inn overlooks 70 acres of wetlands, including a small island in the river. The Turners' own landscaping includes a small pond with a log bench, a wildflower meadow with a few trails, and recently planted aspen and alpine fir trees.

In the winter, the area offers guests rides in a sleigh drawn by thoroughbred Belgian draft horses, as well as plenty of cross-country skiing and snowmobiling. Summer activities include hiking, white-water rafting, bicycling, horseback riding, fishing, golfing, and harvesting fruit at peach, apple, and plum orchards.

Address: *9308 E. Leavenworth Rd., Box 285, Leavenworth, WA 98826, tel. 509/548-7171.*

Accommodations: *3 double rooms with bath, 1 suite.*

Amenities: *Cable TV in rooms, phones on request; hot tub; rental bikes.*

Rates: *$85, suites $105–$120; full breakfast. AE, MC, V.*

Restrictions: *No smoking, no pets; 2-night minimum on weekends.*

Salish Lodge

At the crest of Snoqualmie Falls is the lodge whose authentic Northwest look and dramatic site made it the choice for exterior shots of the Great Northern Hotel in the TV series "Twin Peaks." The lodge was rebuilt in 1988 following the style of the original roadway inn built here in 1916, with dormers, porches, and balconies.

The entire inn, which has an excellent restaurant, is decorated in a casual but elegant country theme, with warm red-hued woods, rusticated stone, and fabrics and wallpapers in rich shades of rust, blue, and cream. Northwest art and Indian crafts complement the decor.

The library is a warm room, with hardwood floor, hefty maple beams, and rows of maple bookshelves; coffee is always available here, and tea and cookies are set out in the afternoon. A sofa, comfortable armchairs, and a game table are arranged around the large stone fireplace. Although the lodge is used for meetings and the restaurant is open to the public, access to this room, as well as to the open-air rooftop hot tub and the fitness center, is restricted to overnight guests.

Guest rooms have stone fireplaces, plus minibars, natural wicker and Shaker-style furniture, either a balcony or a window seat, and goose-down comforters. All baths feature double whirlpool tubs, with French windows that open for fireplace viewing (candles are provided); each comes with thick, hooded terry robes. Each of the four corner suites offers spectacular views of the waterfalls.

Lighted paths leading to the top of the falls make for romantic evening walks. Walking trails lead to the bottom of the falls, and bike paths connect with extensive country roads. A sports court (for pickleball, volleyball, and badminton) is located across the road.

The dining room serves excellent regional cuisine and a large selection of champagnes and wines, with a particularly strong Northwest collection. The country breakfast is legendary, with course upon course of oatmeal, eggs, bacon, trout, pancakes, hash browns, and fresh fruit.

Address: *37807 S.E. Snoqualmie Falls Rd., Box 1109, Snoqualmie, WA 98065, tel. 206/888–2556 or 800/826–6124, fax 206/888–2533.*
Accommodations: *82 double rooms with baths, 4 suites.*
Amenities: *Air-conditioning; sauna, exercise room; TV; whirlpool tubs, and phones in rooms; VCRs and movie rentals available, restaurant, lounge; outdoor hot tub, 3 lighted sports courts, bikes.*
Rates: *$150–$175, suites $450; breakfast extra. AE, D, DC, MC, V.*
Restrictions: *No pets.*

Sun Mountain Lodge

Perched high on a mountaintop above the former gold-mining town of Winthrop, this recently renovated grand resort offers panoramic vistas of the 2,000 acres of wilderness surrounding the resort, 500,000 acres of national forest, the North Cascades, and the Methow Valley below. The lodge, built in 1968, underwent a multimillion-dollar renovation in 1990.

In keeping with its mountain setting, the lodge is constructed from massive timbers and local stone. In the lobby of the main building—a busy place, with the restaurants, meeting rooms, and many other guest facilities—sitting areas include hand-hewn furniture, stone floors, and large picture windows. A huge wrought-iron chandelier dates back to the days of the Pony Express.

Guest rooms feature hand-hewn birch furniture, hand-painted bedspreads, original regional art, and, of course, fine views. The best views are from the Gardner Wing, actually a separate building adjacent to the lodge. All rooms there are equipped with lava-rock gas fireplaces, private decks, wet bars, and refrigerators. (Some main-lodge rooms also feature fireplaces and wet bars.) Housekeeping cabins, with kitchenettes, brick fireplaces, and walls of natural pine, are available on Patterson Lake, about a mile from the main lodge.

The original dining room and lounge, which feature expansive views, were retained during the renovation. Dinner entrées in the main dining room may include applewood-smoked duckling, autumn-run salmon, or pork with cilantro and red chili butter. A second dining room serves sandwiches and other simple meals.

An interpretive center offers a full program of nature activities, including slide shows as well as guided walks along the resort's hiking trails through wildflower meadows, towering forests, alpine paths, and aspen groves. Trail rides, riding lessons, hay rides, cookouts, and rental rowboats, sailboats, canoes, and mountain bikes are available. In winter, the lodge offers sleigh rides, ice skating, more than 50 miles of cross-country trails, and ski lessons.

Address: *Patterson Lake Rd., Box 1000, Winthrop, WA 98862, tel. 509/996–2211 or 800/332–5523; 800/572–0493 in WA.*
Accommodations: *74 double rooms with bath, 4 suites, 8 housekeeping cabins.*
Amenities: *Phone in lodge rooms, lounge, exercise room, 2 restaurants, gift shop, ski shop, meeting rooms; heated outdoor pool, 2 outdoor hot tubs, 2 tennis courts; horseback riding, ice-skating rink; 2 playgrounds.*
Rates: *$75–$125, suites $150–$200; breakfast extra. AE, MC, V.*
Restrictions: *No smoking in main dining room, no pets.*

Alexander's Country Inn

One mile from an entrance to Mt. Rainier National Park is this Victorian-style inn built in 1912. Today's innkeepers, Jerry Harnish and Bernadette Ronan, bought it in 1980, but the original builders' presence is still felt through the many old photographs of the family on display.

Beyond the front doors, inset with two 1890 Viennese stained-glass panels of Romeo and Juliet, is the inn's public restaurant. Upstairs is a large, open living room with a fireplace.

Many of the guest rooms have wicker headboards and handmade quilts, Art Deco stained glass, and some fine antiques, such as room 10's New England armoire with fruit-basket designs inlaid in wood and mother-of-pearl. For the Tower Suite, you'll need to be fairly agile to climb a carpeted ladder up from the white wicker sitting room to the bedroom, where you'll find a 1920s suite of fan-detailed bird's-eye maple furniture and stained glass in a fleur-de-lis design.

Address: *37515 State Rd. 706 E, Ashford, WA 98304, tel. 206/569–2300 or 800/654–7615.*
Accommodations: *6 double rooms with bath, 5 double rooms share 2 baths, 3 suites.*
Amenities: *Restaurant; outdoor hot tub.*
Rates: *$79–$98; full breakfast. MC, V.*
Restrictions: *No smoking, no pets.*

Cashmere Country Inn

Once the first post office of the fruit-growing town of Cashmere, just 10 minutes from Leavenworth, this 1907 Victorian farmhouse has been thoroughly renovated by owners Dale and Patti Swanson. In the dining room, French windows on three sides overlook well-manicured gardens, an outdoor pool, and an orchard.

With lots of windows and white, the whole house has a light and airy feel. The four guest rooms, on the second story, are furnished with homey pieces, creating a grandma's-attic look.

By prearrangement, Patti serves candlelight dinners in the dining room or at sunset on Battenburg lace–covered tables beside the pool.

The farm was originally on 180 acres, and Patti's dream is to buy it all back. Meanwhile, the Swansons have just acquired an acre of orchard, so in the fall, guests can pick apples and use the inn's cider press.

Address: *5801 Pioneer Dr., Cashmere, WA 98815, tel. 509/782–4212.*
Accommodations: *2 double rooms with bath, 2 double rooms share bath.*
Amenities: *Phone available on request, dinner by prearrangement; outdoor pool, hot tub, ski packages available.*
Rates: *$60–$75; full breakfast. AE, MC, V.*
Restrictions: *Smoking outside only, no pets; 2-night minimum on weekends Sept.–Feb. and on holiday and festival weekends.*

Hous Rohrbach Pensione

On a hillside a mile outside Leavenworth, this alpine chalet with window boxes full of red geraniums has views of the valley, the village, and the Cascades. It has been owned since 1978 by the Harrilds: Robert, a former phone company cable splicer, and Kathryn, who comes from a family of resort-motel owners.

With clean lines and dark pine wainscoting, the house has a somewhat Spartan, impersonal look, softened by white eyelet curtains and the occasional dried-flower arrangement. The comfortable common room, with a large open kitchen, wood-burning stove, sofas, and game tables, looks out to the deck that runs across the front of the house. Guest rooms, some with handcrafted pine bed-steads, are decorated in cream with rose and soft blue accents.

Homemade desserts—pies, sundaes, rhubarb crisp, white chocolate mousse cake—are available for purchase in the evening. Kathryn will pack a picnic for you if you want to explore the countryside.

Address: *12882 Ranger Rd., Leavenworth, WA 98826, tel. 206/548-7024.*
Accommodations: *6 double rooms with bath, 4 double rooms share 2 baths.*
Amenities: *Air-conditioning, hot tub; outdoor pool.*
Rates: *$65–$95; full breakfast. AE, D, MC, V.*
Restrictions: *Smoking outside only, no pets; 2-night minimum on weekends Sept.–mid-Mar.*

Maple Valley Bed & Breakfast

The idea of turning their home into a B&B was, for the Hurlbutts, a natural progression. Jayne, who had worked in the travel industry in the Bay Area, and Clarke, a Northwesterner and retired air traffic controller (now a stone mason), started by taking in Japanese exchange students. Later, the students' families visited. In 1977 they went public.

The house—a contemporary cedar in a wooded area 40 minutes southeast of Seattle—has a rustic look, open-beam ceilings, peeled-pole railings, and cedar walls. A large room downstairs has a huge stone fireplace and couches with sheepskin throws. The upstairs sitting room offers games, books, and a field guide and binoculars for spotting wildlife in the pond it overlooks. One guest room features a four-poster bed of hand-hewn logs, topped with a floral comforter and lacy pillow shams, gracefully accented with lace curtains, crystal lamps, and French doors that open onto a deck.

A fun, thoughtful touch: On cool evenings the Hurlbutts give guests a "hot baby," a bed warmer filled with heated sand.

Address: *20020 S.E. 228th St., Maple Valley, WA 98038, tel. 206/432-1409.*
Accommodations: *2 double rooms share bath.*
Rates: *$50–$60; full breakfast. No credit cards.*
Restrictions: *Smoking outside only, no pets.*

Moore House Bed & Breakfast

In the town of South Cle Elum, by the old tracks of the Chicago, Milwaukee, St. Paul & Pacific Railroad, is a woodframe building that once housed railroad employees. Built in 1909, it's now owned by Eric and Cindy Sherwood.

The inn is crammed with railroad memorabilia, including vintage photographs, model trains, and schedules. The large sitting room has a two-foot-tall train for kids to play on. Guest rooms—decorated with calico prints, coordinating colors, and some antiques—include written descriptions of the railroad workers and their lives.

Outside are two caboose cars that have been converted to suites with oversize decks. In the red caboose, with dark green wallpaper and carpet, bleached pine wainscoting, rolltop desk, and brass reading lamps, you can climb a ladder up to the cupola to sit and read.

Address: *Box 2861, 526 Marie Ave., South Cle Elum, WA 98943, tel. 509/674–5939 or 800/22–TWAIN.*
Accommodations: *3 double rooms with bath, 6 double rooms share 2½ baths, 3 suites.*
Amenities: *Air-conditioning; minifridge, coffeemaker, and TV in suites, full meal service for groups by prior arrangement; outdoor hot tub.*
Rates: *$41–$95; full breakfast. AE, MC, V.*
Restrictions: *No smoking in guest rooms, no pets, 2-night minimum mid-Dec.–Feb.*

Mount Meadows Inn

Pigs and chickens as well as a visiting herd of elk frequent the parklike grounds of this rambling, homey inn 6 miles from the entrance to Mt. Rainier National Park. The Colonial-style woodframe house was built in 1910 for the superintendent of what was then the largest sawmill west of the Mississippi. A large veranda with rocking chairs and hanging baskets of fuchsias overlooks a trout pond and 14 acres of woods with walking trails.

Owner Chad Darrah has collected hundreds of pieces of railroad memorabilia, including model trains, displayed in the dining and living room alongside a 1909 player piano. Guest rooms include queen- and king-size beds with duvets, calico prints, and reproduction Early American furnishings.

In the summer, Chad hosts evening campfires by the pond; in winter, the 90 miles of cross-country ski trails nearby beckon. Guests are welcome in the kitchen while Chad and a helper prepare country breakfasts of home-raised pork, eggs, and fruit on an 1889 wood-fired cookstove.

Address: *28912 State Rte. 706 E, Ashford, WA 98304, tel. 206/569–2788.*
Accommodations: *4 double rooms with bath, 2 single rooms share bath, 1 suite.*
Amenities: *Access to sauna and hot tub.*
Rates: *$55–$80; full breakfast. MC, V.*
Restrictions: *No smoking, no pets.*

Mountain Home Lodge

Three miles up a winding, rutted mountain road outside Leavenworth you emerge into a lush alpine meadow that surrounds the inn. The remote location affords breathtaking views of the Cascades and soothing quiet. (When conditions are bad, the owners—Chris Clark and her husband, Charlie Brooks—will transport guests for a fee.)

The contemporary cedar and redwood inn has broad decks for summer barbecues and dining. A massive stone fireplace at the center of the dining room is flanked by large sofas crafted from burled redwood and covered with shaggy sheepskins. Guest rooms are clean and neat, but lack the personality of the lounge area.

Guests will find miles of hiking and cross-country ski trails, a tennis court, badminton, volleyball, and a 1,700-foot-long toboggan run.

Address: *Mountain Home Rd., Box 687, Leavenworth, WA 98826, tel. 509/548-7077.*
Accommodations: *8 double rooms with bath.*
Amenities: *Air-conditioning; outdoor pool, year-round hot tub, tennis court.*
Rates: *Summer $78–$108 (weekends $88–$118), breakfast extra; winter $148–$188 (weekends $168–$198), AP. AE, MC, V.*
Restrictions: *Smoking outside only, no pets; 2-night minimum Dec.–Mar.*

Old Honey Farm Country Inn

Halfway between Seattle and Snoqualmie Pass is this Colonial-style country inn, set on a 35-acre farm with unobstructed pasture and mountain views. Built in 1989 by Conrad and Mary Jean Potter, and Conrad's sister, Marilyn, all former university professors, the inn has a simple, country flavor. The lobby is furnished with a sofa and comfortable chairs before a fireplace. The open and airy dining room is flanked by windows with views of the pasture and Mt. Si. A large backyard deck is used for outdoor dining in summer.

Most guest rooms are simply decorated, with down comforters on queen-size beds, rocking chairs, pine furnishings, and a calico-print stuffed animal to cuddle with if you

didn't bring your own. The mountain-view suite has a reclining love seat facing the fireplace, a king-size bed, and a whirlpool tub. Terry robes and a bottle of champagne add to the atmosphere of self-indulgence. The full-service dining room, which specializes in fresh seafood and local wines, also serves Saturday and Sunday brunch.

Address: *8910 384th Ave. SE, Snoqualmie Falls, WA 98065, tel. 206/888-9399 or 800/826-9077.*
Accommodations: *9 double rooms with bath, 2 double rooms share bath, 1 suite.*
Amenities: *Restaurant.*
Rates: *$35–$75, suite $125; full breakfast. D, MC, V.*
Restrictions: *No smoking, no pets.*

The Silver Bay Bed and Breakfast and Guest Cabins

Situated on 700 feet of Lake Chelan waterfront, with expansive lawns and panoramic views of 9,000-foot mountain peaks, this inn near the Stehekin terminus of the *Lady of the Lake* tour boat (the only means of access) is nicely situated for hikers, swimmers, and nature observers.

The solar home and two cabins (which sleep six) are owned by Randall and Kathy Dinwiddie. They are furnished with antiques and original art—guest rooms have down comforters and handmade quilts. The suite has two private decks with views; its bathroom has delicate calico-print wallpaper, pine-paneled walls, a Persian carpet, and a soaking tub surrounded by Italian tile.

Breakfast is served in a long sun-room decorated with a collection of fruit-label art, Indian baskets, and stained-glass windows. A large library is also available to guests.

Address: *Box 43, Stehekin, WA 98852, tel. 509/682-2212.*
Accommodations: *1 double room with bath, 1 suite, 2 housekeeping cabins.*
Amenities: *Wood-burning stove in cabins; croquet, lake swimming.*
Rates: *$95–$110, full breakfast, cabins $75–$95, no breakfast. No credit cards.*
Restrictions: *No smoking, no pets; 2-night minimum in suite (closed mid-Oct.–mid-May), 5-night minimum in cabins July–mid-Sept.*

Wildflower Inn

About 30 minutes east of Seattle, this grandmotherly bed-and-breakfast was created by Laureita Caldwell on her retirement 5 years ago as an executive secretary. She designed the log house, set amid 12 acres of lawns and fir woods.

The look is pure country: lots of knotty pine, braided rugs, wicker, and old quilts hand-stitched by Laureita's grandmother. Each bedroom has a high, sloped ceiling and a curtain-framed window seat—a perfect place for curling up with a cup of tea and gazing into the woods or reading a good book.

Guests can enjoy breakfast in the dining room, by the wood-burning stove, or can take it on a tray either to the wicker-filled atrium looking out on the woods, or to the gazebo in the meadow.

Guests can go hiking and horseback riding nearby; less than 15 minutes away is Gilman Village, a collection of restored historic buildings housing 50 shops.

Address: *25237 S.E. Issaquah–Fall City Rd., Issaquah, WA 98027, tel. 206/392–1196.*
Accommodations: *2 double rooms with bath, 2 double rooms share bath.*
Amenities: *Air-conditioning.*
Rates: *$55; full breakfast. No credit cards.*
Restrictions: *Smoking outside only, no pets.*

Spokane and Environs
Including Coeur d'Alene

Because of Seattle's moist climate, many think of
Washington State as being waterlogged from Idaho all the
way to the Pacific Ocean. But poised between the Cascade
and Rocky mountains is Spokane, with weather that's both
dry and sunny most of the year. Three hundred miles east
of Seattle, Spokane is Washington's second-largest city
(population 177,000), and, with a plethora of mountains,
forests, and lakes in the area, a year-round paradise for
outdoors enthusiasts. At the same time, the city's slow pace
and reversals of fortune make it an inviting place for
strollers and history buffs to explore.

The fur trade first drew white men to the Spokane River
valley, and in the early 19th century they coexisted more or
less peacefully with the Spokane Indians and other tribes
of the region. By 1858, however, a fierce battle waged
against the Northwest tribes had forced the Native
Americans onto reservations, and the white settlers began
to develop the area aggressively.

The gold, silver, and lead in the nearby Coeur d'Alene
Mountains and in British Columbia drew many
prospectors who soon began to pour mining money into
Spokane, officially founded in 1871. Millionaires were
created overnight, and the city attracted gamblers,
adventurers, and dance-hall girls. By the turn of the
century, the nouveau riche were building elaborate
mansions in a neighborhood called Browne's Addition,
importing materials and furnishings from Europe at
tremendous cost in their game of one-upmanship.
Spokane's economic upswing continued as the
transcontinental railroad brought more commerce and
more settlers to the city. Spokane's fortunes have since
waxed and waned with those of the mines, the timber
industry, and agriculture.

*When the city entered a period of economic decline during
the 1960s, civic leaders moved to rejuvenate it in a bid for
an international exposition. Expo '74 drew more than 5
million visitors. Riverfront Park, created for the event,
remains a popular tourist spot in the heart of downtown.
Its 100 acres feature a century-old carousel, a movie
theater with a five-story-high screen, carnival rides, and
ducks and swans feeding along a willow-bordered river.*

*Spokane maintains a gentle hustle-bustle. It has the feel of
a small town, with many of its low-rise buildings dating
from the early part of the century. These days, the city's
livelihood is heavily based on service industries and the
wholesale and retail trade, although mining, timber, and
agriculture still play an important role in the region's
economy. During the past decade, many transplants from
California and other parts of the country have added
diversity to the city. And its well-earned reputation for
a hardworking labor force and good public schools has
drawn such corporations as Boeing and Seafirst Bank,
which have recently transferred some of their operations
there from Seattle.*

*One of the biggest advantages of Spokane's compact size is
the fact that the countryside can be reached within
minutes. The Selkirk and Coeur d'Alene mountains, rising
to the north and east, 76 lakes, and four major rivers are
all located within a 50-mile radius of the city, offering
activities ranging from swimming, boating, rafting, hiking,
and fishing to downhill and cross-country skiing and
snowmobiling.*

*Just 35 miles from Spokane is Coeur d'Alene, Idaho, site of
a postcard-perfect lake with 125 miles of shoreline, ringed
by richly forested mountains. Coeur d'Alene is Spokane's
most popular playground, especially during the summer,
when residents and visitors flock to the sandy beach and
boardwalk at the edge of the lake. The Coeur d'Alene
Resort offers a breathtaking view to those who take*

refreshment at its restaurants or lounges. The resort has recently added to its list of amenities a world-class golf course, complete with a floating green in Lake Coeur d'Alene.

Places to Go, Sights to See

Browne's Addition. This was Spokane's first residential community, named for lawyer J. J. Browne, who bought its original 160 acres in 1878, when Spokane was a small settlement with fewer than 50 residents. Planned during the early 1880s, this neighborhood in southwest Spokane went on to become one of the most socially correct addresses in the city. During the 1880s, Queen Anne architecture was predominant. As mining money began to pour into the area during the next decade, mansions became more ostentatious, built in historical revival styles that included Greek, Tudor, and Colonial Revival. Today many of the buildings remain, and Browne's Addition is a mixture of trendy and down-at-the-heels. Some of the old homes are now apartments and halfway houses, while others have been lovingly restored. Architecture buffs can stop at the *Cheney Cowles Museum bookstore* (*see below*) for a booklet offering a self-guided walking tour of the neighborhood. Along the way, be sure to stop for refreshments at the *Elk Drugstore* (1931 W. Pacific St., tel. 509/624–2436). A square brick-and-tile building dating from 1940, Elk's still has its original soda fountain. Now a popular restaurant, it serves breakfast, lunch, and light fare for dinner.

Cheney Cowles Memorial Museum (W. 2316 1st Ave., tel. 509/456–3931). Located in Browne's Addition, the Cheney Cowles Museum has exhibits that trace the history of the Northwest, including the early days of Spokane, and hosts shows featuring nationally known and regional artists. The adjacent Grace Campbell House, built in 1898, features period rooms that show visitors how a mining tycoon and his family lived during Spokane's "Age of Elegance."

Green Bluff Growers (tel. 509/238–6978). This consortium of fruit and vegetable growers can be found 16 miles north of Spokane in the foothills of Spokane between Mead and Colbert. They produce many of the apples for which Washington is famous, plus cherries, strawberries, and other seasonal bounty. Depending on the season, you can pick your own fruit in their orchards. To locate their farms, produce stands, and antiques and gift shops, which feature locally produced crafts, homemade preserves, and honey, request a map and brochure from Green Bluff Growers, East 9423 Green Bluff Road, Colbert, WA 99005.

Manito Park (tel. 509/456–4331). South of downtown Spokane, in the midst of residential neighborhoods, Manito Park was designed in 1912 by landscape architects Frederick Law Olmsted (of New York's Central Park fame) and John Charles Olmsted. Today it is a serene, 91-acre oasis for walkers, joggers, and bicyclists. Garden aficionados will enjoy the formal Japanese garden, rose garden featuring 180 varieties, Duncan Garden, with its annuals arranged in geometric symmetry around the Davenport fountain, and a greenhouse brimming with warm-weather plants.

Mt. Spokane State Park (off Hwy. 2, tel. 509/456–4169; ski information: 509/238–6282). Located 30 miles northeast of downtown, Mt. Spokane State Park is a popular spot for winter recreation, with an alpine ski resort and 35 groomed trails for cross-country skiers. During warm weather it offers hikers scenic trails along mountain ridges and through cool forests.

Riverside State Park (tel. 509/456–3964). Just 3 miles northwest of downtown Spokane, Riverside State Park is minimally developed, offering a wild and natural setting on 3,000 acres. Ponderosa pines tower above the Spokane River, which is enjoyed by fishermen and rafters. Hikers can venture up Deep Creek Canyon to explore the fossil beds of a forest that existed more than 7 million years ago, or view centuries-old Indian rock paintings. You can rent a horse at *Trailtown Stables* (tel. 509/456–8249) and roam the basalt cliffs above the river. At the Spokane House Interpretive Center (closed mid-September–early April), site of an early trading post, visitors can view exhibits that examine the fur trade during the early 19th century.

Silverwood (Hwy. 95, Athol, ID, tel. 208/772–0515). An Old West theme park 15 miles north of Coeur d'Alene, Silverwood is a popular summer attraction. It offers rides on an old-style locomotive, an antique-airplane museum and air show, plus carnival rides and entertainment.

Skiing. Downhill skiers seeking more challenging slopes than those of Mt. Spokane can find three larger resorts within 90 miles of Spokane: *49 Degrees North* (Chewelah, WA, tel. 509/935–6649), with 8 runs, 4 double chair lifts, and condominium rentals; *Schweitzer* (Sandpoint, ID, tel. 208/263–9555), with 48 runs and 6 chair lifts, hotels, a guest lodge, and restaurants; and *Silver Mountain* (Kellogg, ID, tel. 208/783–1111), with 50 runs and 4 chair lifts but no lodgings.

Wineries. Tours are offered at four wineries near downtown Spokane. *Arbor Crest Wine Cellars* invites visitors to tastings at their Cliff House, a national historic site that overlooks the Spokane River (4705 N. Fruithill Rd., Spokane, tel. 509/927–9463). Built in 1924, the Tuscan villa–style house is built in white stucco with a red-tile roof. Most of the house is now reserved for private parties, but its dramatic location, perched on a brink of a cliff, provides visitors with a panoramic view of the Spokane River, Spokane Valley, and Idaho as they enjoy the cool gardens surrounding the house. Visitors can also take part in tours and tastings at *Latah Creek* (E. 13030 Indiana Ave., Spokane, tel. 509/926–0164); *Worden* (off I–90 on Thorpe Rd., Spokane, tel. 509/455–7835); and *Livingstone Winery* (E. 14 Mission Ave., Spokane, tel. 509/328–5069).

Restaurants

Any list of Spokane's finest restaurants should include **Amore's** (tel. 509/838–8640), which serves up such Italian dishes as salmon and Gorgonzola fettuccine in a funky setting where religious kitsch adorns the walls. **Milford's Fish House** (509/326–7251) takes its specialty seriously, offering a daily menu with many fresh regional fish and shellfish dishes. Housed in a century-old building with a tin ceiling, the restaurant, open for dinner only, caters to a young and energetic crowd. Look for spicy Cajun crayfish pie and halibut divan on the menu. **Patsy Clark's Mansion** (tel. 509/838–8300) was the turn-of-the century residence of Patrick Clark, who in 1895 commissioned local architect Kirtland Cutter to design and build the mansion for a reported $1 million. Its ornate rooms now offer intimate dining areas where patrons can enjoy such dishes as duck with amaretto sauce and lamb with cream of shallot sauce. **Spezia** (tel. 509/467–2149) serves up regional Italian cuisine in a spacious and stylishly modern environment. **Beverly's** (tel. 208/765–4000 or 800/688–5253), located on the seventh floor of the Coeur d'Alene Resort, is famous for its beautiful view of Lake Coeur d'Alene and its fine seasonal cuisine, which features traditional Northwest dishes prepared with a French influence. Its wine cellar boasts some 9,000 selections.

Tourist Information

Spokane Regional Convention and Visitors Bureau (W. 924 Sprague, Spokane, WA 99204, tel. 509/624–1341 or 800/248–3230); **The Greater Coeur d'Alene Convention & Visitors Bureau** (Box 1088, Coeur d'Alene, ID 83814, tel. 208/664–0587 or 800/CDA–4YOU).

Reservation Services

Spokane Bed & Breakfast Reservation Service (E. 627 25th Ave., Spokane, WA 99203, tel. 509/624–3776).

Clark House on Hayden Lake

Visit the Clark House on Idaho's Hayden Lake, a 40-minute drive from Spokane, and you will instantly be caught up in the history and mystery surrounding the place. A reclusive mining millionaire, F. Lewis Clark had the home built as a copy of a summer palace of Kaiser Wilhelm II of Germany. With 33 rooms and 10 fireplaces, the building, whose construction began in 1895, wasn't completed until 1910. Clark and his wife, Winifred, lived in the house for four years; then he and all of his money disappeared mysteriously. Winifred waited patiently for her husband's return but was soon forced to sell off the land, furnishings, and eventually the house to pay back taxes.

Innkeeper Monty Danner and his son Mark bought and extensively restored the mansion after it had sat empty for 20 years. The result is a sumptuously comfortable hostelry on a secluded eight-acre estate. Each of the five guest rooms has a bathroom with an immense Roman tiled tub. Beds are equipped with both puffy down comforters and European-style featherbeds atop firm mattresses. Light filters through grand Palladian windows at both ends of the long gallery linking the upstairs bedrooms.

Monty has decorated Clark House in an uncluttered, eclectic way, using furniture with simple lines and the occasional spectacular decorative flourish, such as the cascading French crystal chandelier in the reception room or the intricately carved walnut buffet crafted in Connecticut during the 1870s. Oriental vases, lamps, and screens and bronze sculptures by Erté add to the elegance. Guest rooms are similarly lacking in froufrou, with neutral colors favored, whether in the white- and gold-trimmed Louis XIV–style writing table and high chest in Mrs. Clark's Room or in the Hayden Lake Room, where natural wicker furniture and a ceiling fan give it a summery look. (This room, by the way, has the best view of the lake.) French doors are in every room, some leading outdoors to deck and terrace areas, a lush lawn overlooking Hayden Lake, and a wildflower-filled garden. Guests can swim at a sandy beach 1½ miles away or rent boats at a nearby marina.

Address: *E. 4550 S. Hayden Lake Rd., Hayden Lake, ID 83835, tel. 208/772–3470 or 800/765–4593, fax 208/772–3328.*
Accommodations: *5 double rooms with bath.*
Amenities: *Fireplace in 2 rooms, TV upon request; wine and beer available; meeting facilities.*
Rates: *$100–$175; full breakfast. MC, V.*
Restrictions: *Smoking in kitchen or outside only; no pets; 2-night minimum on holiday weekends.*

ravelers between Spokane and Seattle can pull off the freeway and find respite at The Portico, a beautifully restored historic landmark in an unlikely place—Ritzville, a farming town 60 miles southwest of Spokane. At first glance, there seems to be little to see or do here, but this unassuming little town is home to a 1937 Art Deco movie house, a nine-hole golf course, a bowling alley, and a park, which, coupled with Ritzville's clean, safe streets, evoke a simpler time.

Built in 1902, The Portico was originally the home of Nelson H. Greene, a prominent merchant, financier, and wheat broker. When the town burned down in 1889, Greene financed its reconstruction, encouraging the use of brick, hence The Portico's unusual mating of material—buff-colored brick—and Queen Anne, Classical Revival, and Craftsman styles.

Innkeepers Bill and Mary Anne Phipps are passionate about architecture and period furnishings; their attention to detail is evident, starting with the entrance hall, whose parquet floor bears a pattern of unstained dark and light oak, bordered withserpentine work in bird's-eye maple. In the parlor the wallpaper, inrich reds and golds, is a reproduction of a turn-of-the-century design. A bearskin rug lies at one end, where the fireplace is framed by oak spindle work supported by Ionic col-

umns. The ceiling, which resembles pressed tin, is actually anaglyph, a process favored at the turn of the century for creating a design in relief.

The restoration has so far created two guest rooms, one very large and the other fairly small. The bigger one is decorated with rich paisley wallpaper and mid- to late-19th-century English furniture. A carved walnut bed sports a two-tailed mermaid at its head and an angel protecting a child at its foot, both symbols of good luck. A settee covered in crewelwork is shaped to allow two ladies to sit comfortably without wrinkling their gowns. The other room is bright and cheerful, with a white wrought-iron bed topped with a quilt handmade by Mary Anne.

Breakfast is fresh and generous. Not only does Mary Anne squeeze her own orange juice, she also makes her own butter, which melts deliciously into her yeasty waffles. The meal often includes raspberries and blackberries from the garden.

Address: *502 S. Adams St., Ritzville, WA 99169, tel. 509/659–0800.*
Accommodations: *2 double rooms with baths.*
Amenities: *Air-conditioning; cable TV in rooms.*
Rates: *$56–$68; full breakfast. AE, D, MC, V.*
Restrictions: *Smoking outside only.*

Waverly Place

Waverly Place offers lodgings in a quiet old neighborhood just five minutes from downtown Spokane. The turreted Queen Anne house sits across the street from Corbin Park, whose 11½ acres encompass tennis courts, a jogging track, a baseball diamond, and a playground. Waverly Place, built in 1902, is one of several turn-of-the-century houses bordering the park; the neighborhood is listed on the state's Register of Historic Places.

Innkeepers Marge and Tammy Arndt are a mother and daughter team whose love for rambling Victorian houses led them to buy the building five years ago. With distinctive late-Victorian pieces—many of them from Marge's mother-in-law's attic—they've created an environment in which the furnishings seem truly at home amid the graceful architecture of the house. Guests have exclusive use of two parlors, where the gleaming fir woodwork includes intricate beading around the mantelpiece and Grecian columns that separate the rooms. Most of the original lighting is intact, including the dining room chandelier in brass, cupids perching at its sides. Victorian lamps throughout the house sport fringed shades handmade by Tammy. Both women enjoy researching the house; in painting its exterior they consulted old photographs and the builder's grandson in order to remain faithful to the original look: bright white with green and red trim.

Although they both have outside jobs—Tammy is a pharmaceutical sales rep and Marge is a consultant for a church directory service—one of the women is always on hand. The guest rooms are airy and comfortable, with queen-size reproduction beds—one four-poster, one sleigh bed, and one in white wrought iron—and braided and dhurrie rugs over shiny hardwood floors.

Breakfast is, in Tammy's words, "decadent, delicious, and high in fat and cholesterol," although Waverly Place is quick to accommodate special diets. The usual fare, served in the dining room on Haviland china, reflects the innkeepers' Swedish heritage. Menus feature puffy Swedish pancakes with huckleberry sauce and almond-flavored pastries called *kringla* as well as egg dishes, sausage, and fresh fruit and juice.

Address: *W. 709 Waverly Pl., Spokane, WA 99205, tel. 509/328–1856.*
Accommodations: *1 double room with bath, 2 double rooms share bath.*
Amenities: *Air-conditioning in 1 room, TV available.*
Rates: *$50–$60; full breakfast. AE, D, MC, V.*
Restrictions: *No smoking, no pets; 2-night minimum first weekend in May. Closed Dec. 23–30.*

Blackwell House

Although Blackwell House sits on Coeur d'Alene's main street, the grand proportions of the house and generous garden seem to insulate it from the hustle-bustle of the town.

Owner Kathleen Sims began a two-year remodeling of this Georgian Revival home in 1984. She now promotes the house, built in 1904, not only as a bed-and-breakfast but also as a setting for weddings and dinner parties. Indeed, the house's common areas feel more like hotel banquet facilities than family rooms.

Most of the guest rooms are large, light-filled, and comfortable, and all are furnished with turn-of-the-century pieces or replicas. Three have large sitting areas. Shower lovers, beware: Many of the bathrooms are equipped only with claw-foot tubs. Breakfast is served in the cheerful morning room, where French doors open onto the garden and bright-colored stenciling decorates the doorway, ceiling, and fireplace.

Address: *820 Sherman Ave., Coeur d'Alene, ID 83814, 208/664–0656.*
Accommodations: *6 double rooms with bath, 2 double rooms share bath.*
Amenities: *Fireplace in 1 room; air-conditioning in some rooms; evening refreshments.*
Rates: *$59–$109; full breakfast. AE, D, MC, V.*
Restrictions: *No pets; closed Dec. 20–27 every other year.*

Blakely Estates

Five miles east of Spokane, Blakely Estates enjoys a serene wooded setting on the banks of the Spokane River. In this modern brick ranch-style house, guests have an unusual degree of privacy, staying in the lower level with their own sitting room, which opens onto a lawn overlooking the river and landscaped bank. The bedrooms are decorated with ruffled curtains and furnished with Early American–style turned-wood beds and contemporary club chairs. Porcelain dolls abound; they're handmade by Kathy Smith, who runs the B&B with her husband, John, an optometrist with a love for antique cars and airplanes (he possesses both). Guests who prefer a private bathroom may opt for a higher rate; the second guest room will remain unoccupied.

Kathy rises as early as 5 AM each morning to prepare her quiches, muffins, and other breakfast dishes. In fine weather, guests breakfast outside on a deck overlooking the river. They can work off extra calories on the Centennial Trail, a few steps away, where walkers and joggers join bicyclists on a lush greenbelt along the river.

Address: *E. 7710 Hodin Dr., Spokane, WA 99212, tel. 509/926–9426.*
Accommodations: *2 double rooms share bath.*
Amenities: *Robes; outdoor hot tub.*
Rates: *$45–$55; full breakfast. MC, V.*
Restrictions: *No smoking, no pets, no alcoholic beverages; 2-night minimum on weekends.*

Cricket on the Hearth Bed and Breakfast Inn

Those who are turned on by theme rooms will have their fantasies fueled at the Cricket on the Hearth Bed and Breakfast Inn. Hosts Al and Karen Hutson have made their theme rooms a popular feature of their 1920 stucco Craftsman cottage that's 10 minutes from downtown Coeur d'Alene. Miss Kitty from "Gunsmoke" was the inspiration for one of them, where a large claw-foot tub sits in the middle of the floor, illuminated by a brass lamp with red-fringed shade. A patchwork quilt-covered brass bed completes the "naughty but nice" atmosphere. If your taste is more rustic, there's the Navajo Room, filled with lodgepole pine furniture handmade by Al, as well as Navajo and Zuni pottery and weaving.

Guests can relax in the game room, decorated with a tiger's head, deer antlers, and other trophies and hunting memorabilia (the former owner was a big-game hunter). The room opens onto a deck equipped with a grill for barbecuing; the Hutsons provide charcoal and utensils for those who wish to use it.

Address: *1521 Lakeside Ave., Coeur d'Alene, ID 83814, tel. 208/664–6926.*
Accommodations: *3 double rooms with bath, 2 rooms share bath.*
Amenities: *Guest refrigerator; ski packages available.*
Rates: *$45–$75; full breakfast. No credit cards.*
Restrictions: *Smoking outside and in game room only, no pets.*

Fotheringham House

In the heart of historic Browne's Addition in Spokane, Fotheringham House is a century-old Queen Anne home built by the first mayor of Spokane. Among the many decorative features original to the house are tin ceilings throughout most of the building, ball-and-spindle fretwork separating the entrance hall and living room, and an intricately carved oak fireplace and open staircase. The common rooms have been furnished with period furniture, from claw-foot sofas to lawyers' bookcases and brass standing lamps. Innkeepers Howard and Phyllis Ball are collectors of Native American art, and a large selection of Indian baskets, jewelry, and artifacts is displayed.

The guest rooms have romantic flowered wallpaper, chintz and lace curtains, and oak and mahogany reproduction Victorian beds. Guests breakfast in the dining room, where carved cherubs grace a china cabinet and a gilt mirror hangs above a marble-top buffet. Tennis courts are available in Coeur d'Alene Park just across the street, and architecture aficionados will enjoy strolling through this Victoriana-filled neighborhood.

Address: *2128 W. 2nd Ave., Spokane, WA 99204, tel. 509/838–4363.*
Accommodations: *1 double room with bath, 2 double rooms share bath.*
Amenities: *Air-conditioning.*
Rates: *$45–$55; Continental breakfast. AE, MC, V.*
Restrictions: *No smoking, no pets.*

Gregory's McFarland House

At Gregory's McFarland House in Coeur d'Alene, a spacious 1905 Craftsman house boasting elegant family heirlooms, old meets new, flawlessly, with modern comforts and conveniences.

Innkeepers Winifred, Stephen, and Carol Gregory share with guests a home full of family history; many of their 19th-century antiques came from Winifred's ancestral home in England. The carved claw-foot table in the dining room, which once made a journey around Cape Horn, sits on one of several Chinese rugs scattered throughout the house's gleaming bird's-eye maple floors. Guest rooms are large and bright, with rose and pink accents, hand-crocheted bedspreads, and curtains of German lace. One room features an inlaid-wood bedroom suite from the 1860s, with a marble-top table and low dresser. Several rooms have four-poster beds. Located on a quiet tree-lined street, Gregory's McFarland House provides a soothing atmosphere only six blocks from downtown.

Address: *601 Foster Ave., Coeur d'Alene, ID 83814, tel. 208/667-1232.*
Accommodations: *5 double rooms with bath.*
Amenities: *Air-conditioning; complementary refreshments, high tea upon request.*
Rates: *$75–$95; full breakfast. MC, V.*
Restrictions: *Smoking outside only, no pets; 2-night minimum on summer and holiday weekends.*

Kimbrough House

Eighty miles south of Spokane, Kimbrough House is located only steps away from Washington State University. The 1916 house was once owned by Herbert Kimbrough, who started the music department at the university. Built in the Craftsman style with half-timbering in the second story, the shingled house is now owned by five women, three associated with the university.

The dining room's dark oak woodwork includes a beamed ceiling, built-in buffet and china cabinets, and French doors leading out to a bright sun room. Another sun room, with white-wicker furniture, offers a cheerful environment for reading and relaxing. The bedrooms, though fairly small, are cool and comfortable. Some have brass beds, and many have Tudor-style armoires in a richly patterned oak. Guests may use the university's sports facilities, and high tea is offered at extra cost every Thursday.

Address: *505 Maiden La., Pullman, WA 99163, tel. 509/334-3866.*
Accommodations: *2 double rooms with bath, 1 double room and 2 single rooms share bath.*
Amenities: *High tea and catering available.*
Rates: *$59–$69; full breakfast. MC, V.*
Restrictions: *Smoking outside only; no pets, 2-night minimum during Homecoming Weekend, Graduation Weekend, Dads' Day, Mothers' Weekend.*

Lakeside Manor

It's hard to imagine a more serene setting than Lakeside Manor. One hour north of Spokane in Colville, this contemporary cedar and basalt house is surrounded by cool lakes and dense forest, all visible through the many floor-to-ceiling windows. It offers many temptations for outdoors enthusiasts: hiking and cross-country ski trails maintained by the U.S. Forest Service; snowmobile trails; a scenic bike route; and swimming, waterskiing, canoeing, and fishing.

Guest accommodations are on the lower level of the house, where a sitting room leads outside to Lake Gillette just a few feet beyond; ducks and even bears often come up on the lawn to be fed. Innkeeper Pat Thomas is both friendly and attentive, though her decorating may not be to everyone's taste: An upstairs living room has ornate contemporary furniture upholstered in lime and gold velour, with guest rooms equipped with king-size water beds. Adjacent Beaver Lodge Resort provides boat rentals and take-out food; it can also be a source of noise on holiday weekends.

Address: *2425 Pend Oreille Lake, Colville, WA 99114, tel. 509/684–8741.*
Accommodations: *2 double rooms share bath.*
Amenities: *Air-conditioning; hot tub.*
Rates: *$70; Continental breakfast. No credit cards.*
Restrictions: *Smoking outside only, no pets.*

Love's Victorian Bed and Breakfast

Forty-five minutes from downtown Spokane, Love's Victorian Bed and Breakfast is a salute to Victoriana. Indeed, the exterior is a veritable encyclopedia of gingerbread. Innkeepers Bill and Leslie Love built this reproduction house in 1986. Working from the plans of an 1886 Queen Anne house, Bill incorporated original Victorian decorative elements: In the sitting room, he fashioned a mantelpiece out of the remains of an 1858 piano; grill- and fretwork in the entrance hall and balusters on the stairway and porch were salvaged from turn-of-the-century houses in Spokane.

The largest guest room boasts a fireplace, balcony, and a sitting area occupying the house's turret. Chintz balloon shades, floral wallpaper, Victorian memorabilia, and breakfast by candlelight give the house an unabashedly romantic air. Amid fields, evergreen forests, and rolling hills, this house is a place where you can get away from it all. Evening walks offer encounters with deer and even moose. Guests can swim or fish at nearby lakes, and cross-country ski trails are five minutes away.

Address: *31317 N. Cedar Rd., Deer Park, WA 99006, tel. 509/276–6939.*
Accommodations: *3 double rooms with baths.*
Amenities: *Indoor hot tub, air-conditioning, evening refreshments; bikes and cross-country skis available.*
Rates: *$65–$180; full breakfast. AE.*
Restrictions: *Smoking outside only.*

Marianna Stoltz House

Marianna Stoltz House sits across from Gonzaga University, five minutes from downtown Spokane. Innkeepers Jim and Phyllis Maguire named the classic American Foursquare for Phyllis's mother. The decor is a strange mix: Elegant features that suit the architecture, such as the original dark fir woodwork, leaded-glass china cabinets, and Rococo Revival and Renaissance Revival settees and armchairs in the parlor and sitting room share space with lamps and fake-flower arrangements that you would expect at a Motel Six. Still, the service is both friendly and unobtrusive.

Upstairs, brass and mahogany beds are covered in quilts that have been in Phyllis's family for decades. One private bathroom has a 7-foot-long claw-foot tub. The largest room, boasting a king-size brass bed, is also the noisiest, facing a busy street; the smallest room has twin beds. In the evening, the Maguires offer their guests homemade liqueurs and local wines.

Address: *427 E. Indiana Ave., Spokane, WA 99207, tel. 509/483-4316.*
Accommodations: *2 double rooms with bath, 2 double rooms share bath.*
Amenities: *Air-conditioning; TV available; evening refreshments.*
Rates: *$45–$50; full breakfast. AE, MC, V.*
Restrictions: *Smoking outside only; 2-night minimum on holiday weekends.*

My Parents' Estate

Nestled in the Selkirk Mountains less than two hours from Spokane, in Kettle Falls, My Parents' Estate possesses both a scenic setting and a unique history. Opened as a mission in 1873, its 47 acres were home to the Sisters of Providence and later a convent for Dominican nuns who ran a school on the site. The main house was once the Mother Superior's quarters and office. It also contained a chapel, now the two-story-high living room reserved for guests. Reminders of the property's history abound, including religious statues once used in services and intricate linen handwork done by the nuns.

Owner Bev Parent, a professional artist, has amassed collections of handmade quilts and antique tools and kitchenware, and painted designs on several old pieces in the guest rooms. One room has a rare hand-painted bedroom suite of so-called cottage furniture from the 1890s. All of the rooms feature Laura Ashley–style bed linens and wonderful views of surrounding pastureland and mountains.

Address: *719 Hwy. 395, Kettle Falls, WA 99141, tel. 509/738-6220.*
Accommodations: *3 double rooms with bath.*
Amenities: *Hot tub in winter; air-conditioning; pool table; half basketball court in gymnasium; ice skating.*
Rates: *$65–$75; full breakfast. No credit cards.*
Restrictions: *No smoking, no pets. Closed Dec. 20–Jan. 2.*

Warwick Inn

Travelers who long to check their car keys at the door and explore an area on foot may do so at the Warwick Inn. Located a block from Lake Coeur d'Alene, this bed-and-breakfast is just steps away from the lake's sandy beach and boardwalk.

The 1905 Craftsman house was built as officers' quarters when the property was on the grounds of Fort Sherman. Given the architectural style of the house, innkeepers James and Bonnie Warwick have taken an unorthodox approach to the decorative details, giving its exterior a "painted lady," multicolor scheme, painting the interior woodwork a glowing white, and adding Victorian gingerbread detailing. The final effect is a bright and cheerful environment, with all the ground floor curtains matching the light blue and rose floral-and-ribbon print of the living room sofa. Pierre Deux fabrics and bone china dress the breakfast room table. Guest rooms are large, with lace curtains, antique quilts, and turn-of-the-century oak furniture.

Address: *303 Military Dr., Coeur d'Alene, ID 83814, tel. 208/765-6565.*
Accommodations: *3 double rooms with baths.*
Amenities: *Evening refreshments; guest robes; off-street parking.*
Rates: *$75–$95; full breakfast. AE, D, MC, V.*
Restrictions: *Smoking outside only, no pets; 2-night minimum on holiday weekends.*

Directory 1
Alphabetical

Directory 2
Geographical

California

Amador City
Culbert House Inn *107*
Anaheim
Anaheim Country Inn *27*
Angels Camp
Cooper House *112*
Arroyo Grande
Rose Victorian Inn *41*
Avalon
Inn on Mt. Ada *28*
Ballard
Ballard Inn *38*
Berkeley
Gramma's Inn *75*
Calistoga
Quail Mountain *87*
Cambria
The Blue Whale Inn *34*
J. Patrick House *40*
Capitola by the Sea
Inn at Depot Hill *52*
Carlsbad
Pelican Cove Inn *16*
Carmel
Happy Landing Inn *51*
Sea View Inn *53*
Cazadero
Timberhill Ranch *99*
Clio
White Sulphur Springs *121*
Columbia
Fallon Hotel *113*
Dana Point
Blue Lantern Inn *24*
Dulzura
Brookside Farm *14*
Elk
Harbor House *96*
Eureka
Carter House *100*

"An Elegant Victorian Mansion" *100*
Ferndale
Gingerbread Mansion *95*
Fort Brag
Grey Whale Inn *101*
Geyserville
Hope-Merrill House *86*
Glen Ellen
Beltane Ranch *85*
The Gaige House *86*
Gualala
St. Orres *98*
Half Moon Bay
The Mill Rose Inn *72*
Old Thyme Inn *76*
Healdsburg
Madrona Manor *84*
Homewood
Rockwood Lodge *124*
Hope Valley
Sorensen's *120*
Idyllwild
Strawberry Creek Inn *16*
Inverness
Blackthorne Inn *74*
Ten Inverness Way *77*
Ione
The Heirloom
Julian
Julian Hotel *12*
Kenwood
Kenwood Inn *83*
La Jolla
Bed and Breakfast Inn at La Jolla *11*
Laguna Beach
Eiler's Inn *28*
Lodi
Wine & Roses Country Inn *110*
Los Angeles
Salisbury House *29*

Terrace Manor *30*
Los Alamos
Union Hotel/Victorian Mansion *37*
Mendocino
The Headlands Inn *101*
Joshua Grindle Inn *97*
Rachel's Inn *102*
Monterey
The Jabberwock *48*
Old Monterey Inn *49*
Muir Beach
The Pelican Inn *73*
Napa
Cross Roads Inn *85*
Newport Beach
Little Inn on the Bay *29*
Olemo
Roundstone Farm *76*
Pacific Grove
Gatehouse Inn *50*
Gosby House *51*
Green Gables Inn *47*
Martine Inn *52*
Seven Gables Inn *53*
Palm Springs
Ingleside Inn *15*
Villa Royale *17*
Palo Alto
Cowper Inn *74*
The Parsonage *36*
Simpson House Inn *43*
Pocket Canyon
Applewood: An Estate Inn *94*
Quincy
The Feather Bed *123*
Rancho Cucamonga
Christmas House *27*
Rutherford
Auberge du Soleil *82*
Sacramento
Aunt Abigail's *111*

The West

Please help us evaluate B&Bs and country inns for the next edition of this guide. Mail your response to Fodor's Travel Publications, Inc., 201 E. 50th St., New York, NY 10022.

B&B or Inn

City/State

Comments

B&B or Inn

City/state

Comments

General Comments

Your Name *(Optional)*

Number/Street

City/State/Zip

Fodor's Travel Guides

U.S. Guides

Alaska	Las Vegas, Reno,	Pacific North Coast	Texas
Arizona	Tahoe	Philadelphia & the	USA
Boston	Los Angeles	Pennsylvania	The U. S. & British
California	Maine,Vermont,	Dutch Country	Virgin Islands
Cape Cod, Martha's	New Hampshire	Puerto Rico	The Upper Great
Vineyard, Nantucket	Maui	(Pocket Guide)	Lakes Region
The Carolinas & the	Miami & the	The Rockies	Vacations in
Georgia Coast	Keys	San Diego	New York State
The Chesapeake	National Parks	San Francisco	Vacations on the
Region	of the West	San Francisco	Jersey Shore
Chicago	New England	(Pocket Guide)	Virginia & Maryland
Colorado	New Mexico	The South	Waikiki
Disney World & the	New Orleans	Santa Fe, Taos,	Washington, D.C.
Orlando Area	New York City	Albuquerque	Washington, D.C.
Florida	New York City	Seattle &	(Pocket Guide)
Hawaii	(Pocket Guide)	Vancouver	

Foreign Guides

Acapulco	Cancun, Cozumel,	Italy 's Great Cities	Paris (Pocket Guide)
Amsterdam	Yucatan Peninsula	Jamaica	Portugal
Australia	Caribbean	Japan	Rome
Austria	Central America	Kenya, Tanzania,	Scandinavia
The Bahamas	China	Seychelles	Scandinavian Cities
The Bahamas	Czechoslovakia	Korea	Scotland
(Pocket Guide)	Eastern Europe	London	Singapore
Baja & Mexico's Pacific	Egypt	London	South America
Coast Resorts	Europe	(Pocket Guide)	South Pacific
Barbados	Europe's Great Cities	London Companion	Southeast Asia
Barcelona, Madrid,	France	Mexico	Soviet Union
Seville	Germany	Mexico City	Spain
Belgium &	Great Britain	Montreal &	Sweden
Luxembourg	Greece	Quebec City	Switzerland
Berlin	The Himalayan	Morocco	Sydney
Bermuda	Countries	New Zealand	Thailand
Brazil	Holland	Norway	Tokyo
Budapest	Hong Kong	Nova Scotia,	Toronto
Budget Europe	India	New Brunswick,	Turkey
Canada	Ireland	Prince Edward	Vienna & the Danube
Canada's Atlantic	Israel	Island	Valley
Provinces	Italy	Paris	Yugoslavia

Wall Street Journal Guides to Business Travel

Europe	International Cities	Pacific Rim	USA & Canada

Special-Interest Guides

Bed & Breakfast and	Cruises and Ports	Fodor's Flashmaps	Smart Shopper's
Country Inn Guides:	of Call	Washington, D.C.	Guide to London
Mid-Atlantic Region	Healthy Escapes	Shopping in Europe	Sunday in New York
New England	Fodor's Flashmaps	Skiing in the USA &	Touring Europe
The South	New York	Canada	Touring USA
The West			